KEATS: THE CRITICAL HERITAGE

THE CRITICAL HERITAGE SERIES

GENERAL EDITOR: B. C. SOUTHAM, M.A., B.LITT. (OXON.)
Formerly Department of English, Westfield College, University of London

---

For list of books in the series see back end paper

KEATS

THE CRITICAL HERITAGE

Edited by
G. M. MATTHEWS
Reader in English Literature, University of Reading

LONDON: ROUTLEDGE & KEGAN PAUL

First published 1971
by Routledge & Kegan Paul Limited
Broadway House, 68–74 Carter Lane
London, EC4V 5EL

ISBN 0 7100 7147 7

Printed in Great Britain by
Richard Clay (The Chaucer Press) Ltd
Bungay, Suffolk
Set in Monotype Bembo

General Editor's Preface

The reception given to a writer by his contemporaries and near-contemporaries is evidence of considerable value to the student of literature. On one side we learn a great deal about the state of criticism at large and in particular about the development of critical attitudes towards a single writer; at the same time, through private comments in letters, journals, or marginalia, we gain an insight upon the tastes and literary thought of individual readers of the period. Evidence of this kind helps us to understand the writer's historical situation, the nature of his immediate reading-public, and his response to these pressures.

The separate volumes in the *Critical Heritage Series* present a record of this early criticism. Clearly, for many of the highly productive and lengthily reviewed nineteenth- and twentieth-century writers, there exists an enormous body of material; and in these cases the volume editors have made a selection of the most important views, significant for their intrinsic critical worth or for their representative quality—perhaps even registering incomprehension!

For earlier writers, notably pre-eighteenth century, the materials are much scarcer and the historical period has been extended, sometimes far beyond the writer's lifetime, in order to show the inception and growth of critical views which were initially slow to appear.

In each volume the documents are headed by an Introduction, discussing the material assembled and relating the early stages of the author's reception to what we have come to identify as the critical tradition. The volumes will make available much material which would otherwise be difficult of access and it is hoped that the modern reader will be thereby helped towards an informed understanding of the ways in which literature has been read and judged.

B. C. S.

Contents

Lamia, Isabella, The Eve of St Agnes, and Other Poems (1820)

Obituaries

Posthumous Reputation

Acknowledgments

I am grateful for assistance derived from all the books and articles listed in the Bibliography, and especially from Professor J. R. MacGillivray's *Keats: A Bibliography and Reference Guide with an Essay on Keats' Reputation* (Toronto, 1949), and Professor G. H. Ford's *Keats and the Victorians* (New Haven, 1944). Bibliographies of several of the Romantic poets are very thin for the Victorian period, and in Keats's case these works help to supply a serious lack. I would also like to acknowledge a general debt to the two volumes of Professor H. E. Rollins's *The Keats Circle* (Cambridge, Mass., 1948), and a more selective one to the various writings of Professor Edmund Blunden, which never fail to provide unfamiliar references, as well as to the survey of Keats's reviewers in Miss Dorothy Hewlett's *Adonais* (1937), now revised as *A Life of John Keats* (1970).

The extracts from Bod. MS. Shelley adds. e.7, from *Letters of Matthew Arnold* to *A. H. Clough*, ed. H. F. Lowry (1932), from *The Letters of William and Dorothy Wordsworth*, ed. E. de Selincourt (1935–9), revised by Mary Moorman and A. G. Hill (1970), from Keats's *Poetical Works*, ed. H. W. Garrod (1958), and from *The Letters of Percy Bysshe Shelley*, ed. F. L. Jones (1964), are reprinted by permission of the Clarendon Press, Oxford; those from *The Keats Circle*, volumes I and II (1948), and *The Letters of John Keats*, volume I (1958), ed. Hyder Edward Rollins, by permission of Harvard University Press; and the extracts from *Letters and Journals of Lord Byron*, volumes IV and V, ed. R. E. Prothero (1902), from *Byron: A Self-Portrait*, volume II, ed. P. Quennell (1950), from *Elizabeth Barrett to Miss Mitford*, ed. Betty Miller (1954), and from *Elizabeth Barrett to Mr. Boyd*, ed. B. P. McCarthy (1955), by permission of John Murray (Publishers) Ltd.

Note on the Text

The earliest versions of the texts printed in this volume have almost always been those followed (exceptions are Nos. 53 and 54), and the punctuation is original, except that the form of reference to titles has been regularized. The punctuation of earlier critics is part of their whole manner of thought. Typographical errors have been silently corrected (in square brackets when the change is substantial), but old spellings are unaltered unless merely eccentric. Thus Leigh Hunt's 'Lorrenzo' (No. 27) has been changed, but not his 'ungainness' (No. 42)—an unfamiliar but perfectly good word. 'Keat's' is an eccentricity; but 'Keates' helps, in its small way, to recreate the passions of the time. A writer who has corrected himself in a later reprint of his own work has sometimes been permitted the correction, if this is simply grammatical. Thus Jeffrey's 1844 correction: 'neither of them . . . a voluminous writer' is printed under an earlier date—but not his possibly significant change of 'volume' into 'volumes' (No. 30). Author's footnotes are numbered, original notes designated by asterisks. Long quotations have been omitted unless essential to the context; but full details are always supplied. The two famous reviews in *Blackwood's* and the *Quarterly*, however, are reprinted without abridgment, so that they can be read as nearly as possible as Keats and his contemporaries read them.

Note on the Text

Introduction

KEATS'S REPUTATION: THE PATTERN OF CHANGE

Virtually the whole course of Keats criticism, directly until the 1840s and indirectly until about 1900, was determined by two exceptional circumstances: his supposed death at the hands of the reviewers, and the early age at which he died. His death decided what attitude the reader should take, for or against, and his youth discouraged the critic from doing much more than simply take sides. Except for a brief spell of innocence (Nos. 1–9) before *Blackwood's* began their campaign against the 'Cockneys', it was not possible to discuss Keats's work without prejudice, and for this reason the present volume gives a good deal of space to the controversy. His friends thought he was a genius; his friends' political enemies represented him either as a charlatan or a foolish boy, 'Johnny Keats', whose head had been turned by the company he kept. A review of 1848, looking back over thirty years, sums up the situation:

> It was the misfortune of Keats as a poet, to be either extravagantly praised or unmercifully condemned. The former had its origin in the generous partialities of friendship, somewhat obtrusively displayed; the latter in some degree, to resentment of that friendship, connected as it was with party politics, and peculiar views of society as well as of poetry.[1]

There is therefore less useful *criticism* in the early notices of Keats than in the corresponding notices of Shelley. The principal literary issue was part of the controversy: Keats was seen as introducing a system of versification, and a vocabulary, in conscious opposition to those of Pope. These early reviews show that in some ways Keats's poetry was felt to be even more disturbingly unlike what poetry ought to be than Wordsworth's. Wordsworth, after all, had developed a tradition of simplicity already partly familiar from the poems of Cowper and Goldsmith, whereas in going back to the Elizabethans, in writing run-on couplets like Chapman instead of end-stopped ones like Pope, Keats was throwing away the technical gains of the eighteenth century in favour of uncouthness and affectation. This is not an unusual situation

[1] *New Monthly Magazine*, lxxxiv (September 1848), 105.

in the history of art, but it troubled Keats's early readers. In 1860 David Masson, with the 'Pre-Raphaelite Brotherhood' in recent memory, labelled it 'Pre-Drydenism' (although in fact both Keats and Leigh Hunt admired Dryden). And of course there was a real affinity, for which Hallam's essay (No. 46) had supplied some theoretical basis, between the 'primitivism' of Keats and of Dante Gabriel Rossetti.

Serious criticism could not be written while Keats's verse was mainly an issue in a political dispute. The poet's working lifetime coincided with a period of intense social and political unrest in England, which Lord Liverpool's Tory government, in its defence of privilege, met with ever-fiercer repression. The *Edinburgh Review*, started as a literary quarterly in 1802 by a group of clever young Whigs, quickly became a powerful voice of protest against the corruptions of the old order; and in 1809 the Tories were angered into founding a rival review, the *Quarterly*, which was published by John Murray. In this way, literary and political opinion tended to coalesce and to polarize round the leading organs of criticism, so that it was hardly possible for a creative writer associated with one side to receive fair treatment from a reviewer employed by the other. For about twenty years the anonymous 'great Reviews' virtually dictated upper-class tastes; everyone literate regarded them as obligatory reading, and reputations and sales alike were at their mercy. Then, within a few more years, their inflated influence collapsed, even before the old political order had died with the passing of the first Reform Bill in 1832. 'The abuse of power has destroyed itself,' wrote the *Athenaeum* in 1828, 'and we doubt whether two hundred persons in the kingdom would now attach the slightest importance to the most violent lucubrations of Mr Murray's critics.'[1] This was not yet quite true, as Tennyson soon discovered; nevertheless the prognosis was accurate.

Prejudice now had less and less part in what was said about Keats, but an awkward difficulty remained. It had been agreed by friend and foe alike that Keats had died before his promise had been fulfilled; obviously, therefore, it would not be fair to apply the rigours of criticism to a body of work unfit to be criticized. To the extent that its many faults allowed, Keats's poetry could be enjoyed and wondered at, but not analysed or judged. So for half a century the appreciation of Keats's poems remained an affair of passionate cultivation by small groups of individuals. Public comment was on his life and death; on the iniquity of reviewers; on the rich promise wasted; and on the many beauties to

[1] *Athenaeum* (29 January 1828), 71.

be found among the many faults. This pattern continued into the 1860s. The 'faults' were easy to enumerate: bad rhymes, irregular metre, affected epithets, a habit of imitating Leigh Hunt. But those struck by the 'beauties' in Keats generally contented themselves with saying so, and rarely tried to explain exactly what they consisted in. The elder Patmore admitted this in his discussion of *Endymion* (No. 21). It was difficult, he said,

> if not impossible, to state its peculiar beauties as a whole, in any other than general terms. And, even so, we may exhaust all the common-places of criticism in talking about the writer's active and fertile imagination, his rich and lively fancy, his strong and acute sensibility, and so forth,—without advancing one step towards characterising the work which all these together have produced.

Leigh Hunt made the bravest attempts to discover how Keats's verse actually works; otherwise, with rare and brief exceptions, the *constructive* phase of Keats criticism did not even begin until after 1860.

It has been said that the recognition of Keats as an artist came before his recognition as a 'thinker', but this is misleading except in a very loose sense of the word 'artist'. Most of those who knew Keats had always stressed his tough-mindedness; C. W. Dilke, editor of the *Athenaeum*, was moved to interrupt one of his own contributors in 1832 to protest that 'Keats . . . had a resolution, not only physical but moral, greater than any man we ever knew: it was unshakable by everything but his affections.'[1] But Keats's *artistry* could not be detected until it had been realized that this moral strength had its counterpart in his work, in the controlling, structuring energy of the full powers of the mind. So Keats was seen at first as an untutored genius, getting his effects by the sheer abundance of his gifts. Chambers's *Cyclopedia of English Literature* (1844) gives a good text-book summary:

> In poets like Gray, Rogers, and Campbell, we see the ultimate effects of this taste [classical simplicity]; in Keats we have only the materials, unselected and often shapeless. His imagination was prolific of forms of beauty and grandeur, but the judgment was wanting to symmetrise and arrange them, assigning to each its due proportion and its proper place. His fragments, however, are the fragments of true genius—rich, original, and various. (ii. 404.)

Most of this could easily have been written of Shakespeare during the age of Pope. It had to be established that Keats's actual achievement was not one of 'fragments' merely, but a body of work equal in substance to any other poet's, and this was a slow process.

[1] *Athenaeum* (4 August 1832), 502.

Both Keats and Shelley were held to be supreme 'singers', and as 'singers' both enjoyed a high reputation in the eighties. Swinburne in the *Encyclopedia Britannica* (ninth edition, 1882) found Keats's Odes the 'nearest to absolute perfection, to the triumphant achievement and accomplishment of the very utmost beauty possible to human words.' If anything, Shelley was the more indiscriminately admired of the two, as more 'spiritual'. But neither was valued much for the intellectual substance of his work, Shelley because his thinking was impious, and therefore negligible, Keats because he had repudiated the intellect: for him, Newton had spoilt the rainbow, and sensations were better than thoughts. When, around 1900, a reaction set in against the whole Romantic attitude, Shelley's reputation promptly started to evaporate, while Keats's remained almost constant. One reason is that once the glamour was gone, in the supposed absence of intellectual interest there seemed nothing left in Shelley's verse except intangible lights and shadows, whereas Keats's verse continued to evoke the sensuous substance of the material world.

Of course this is an oversimplification. But on the whole it is true to say that an 'undissociated' Keats, in whose work there was strenuous mental activity as well as brilliant fancy, an *artist*, had hardly entered the critical consciousness before the twentieth century.

THE SCOPE OF THE COLLECTION

The unusual circumstances of Keats's case have made it impracticable to include in this book all the known commentaries on his work printed during his lifetime, but the aim has been to make the collection of contemporary notices and reviews of his published poetry as complete as possible. These make up nearly half the numbered items in the book. The record of Keats's treatment by the reviewers, an essential part of the story, is told at some length in the Introduction. From the many obituary notices, a few have been chosen to represent the differing reactions produced by his death.

During the interregnum between 1821 and the appearance of the first English *Poetical Works* in the 1840s, the critical material is thin and scattered. Most of the important items are reproduced whole or in part, although one or two (such as 'Gaston's' touching poem on Keats) have been omitted with reluctance.

R. M. Milnes's *Life, Letters and Literary Remains of John Keats* (subsequently referred to as 'Milnes's *Life*'), published in 1848 when Keats's fortunes were already rising fast, produced a heavy crop of reviews in almost all the leading journals (*Blackwood's* and the *Quarterly* were conspicuous exceptions), and stringent choice was necessary among these. In the 1850s, writings on Keats are numerous but again fragmentary, and there are few extended pieces of criticism. Those selected, therefore, are representative rather than outstanding. The sixties, on the other hand, open with three long and important documents, two of which are printed in full. Masson's sixteen-page study (No. 69) is the work of an English don discussing an established classic author, and marks the beginning of modern Keats criticism. Cowden Clarke and Severn (Nos. 70, 71), both old men, look back on the roles they played in the career of a poet whose fame is now finally secure. This has seemed the logical and fitting point for the present collection to end.

In each period except the last, the formal printed documents have been supplemented by some of the more desultory opinions on Keats and his work recorded in letters, diaries, and conversations. There are many such records, particularly towards the end; and again the selection has had to be rigorous, and perhaps arbitrary.

One conclusion is worth underlining as a footnote. The evidence of this collection does not support the notion, maliciously started by *Blackwood's* but perpetuated in good faith by some recent scholars, that Leigh Hunt did not really believe in Keats and failed to champion his poetry as he ought. Hunt was the first to publish Keats, and the first to acclaim him in prose (No. 2), and he was still vigorously defending him in the year he died, 1859. Between these dates, forty-three years apart, Hunt worked tirelessly and constructively for Keats's success. He was the first ever to apply methods of 'close analysis' to an individual Keats poem, which he did by reprinting the entire 'Eve of St Agnes' with a line-by-line 'loving commentary', first in a weekly paper and then in a book (No. 49). In 1828 Hunt smuggled a specimen of his work into the first *Keepsake*; and in the same year, long before his reputation was secure, installed him as a major poet, first in an encyclopedia entry, then in *Lord Byron and Some of His Contemporaries* (No. 42). That Hunt did not answer the attacks on *Endymion* is no reproach (though he reproached himself), since the pivot of all the attacks was precisely Keats's willingness to be praised by the despicable Hunt. Keats's irritation at being considered Hunt's '*élève*' only developed after *Blackwood's* had started operations against the 'Cockney School' in October 1817. It is true that soon after the attacks Keats echoed the reviewers in calling Hunt 'vain, egotistical, and disgusting [i.e. insipid] in matters of taste and of morals,' making 'fine things petty and beautiful things hateful'; and true that Hunt was wounded when he learned (via the spiteful Haydon) of similar remarks from the friend he invariably defended, so that in 1837 W. B. Scott sensed 'indifference and reticence' towards Keats on Hunt's part.[1] But this did not stop Hunt, in 1844, from describing *Hyperion* as nearly faultless, the 'Eve of St Agnes' as 'full-grown poetry of the rarest description', and even Keats's earliest poems as containing 'passages of as masculine a beauty as ever were written' (No. 49b); nor did his reservations about *Endymion*, which he never concealed or changed, deter him from defending it angrily against Cardinal Wiseman's strictures (No. 67):

I must own that, desirous as I am to observe conventional proprieties, and to treat with due courtesy a personage who is said to be so distinguished for urbanity of manners in private as this great church dignitary, I find it difficult to express myself as I could wish. . . . For I knew Keats himself as well as his poetry; knew him both in his weakness and his strength; knew . . . with what 'glow' and 'emotion' he has written of the best moral principles, public and private. . . . It is to be regretted perhaps that Keats . . . took Endymion for the hero of his first considerable effort in poetry; and it is not to be denied that the poem, with all its genius, is as sensuous of its kind and as full of external glitter as the Cardinal's favourite descriptions are in their own way. . . . Keats was sorry afterwards that he wrote *Endymion*; but it is only one of his poems, and a most false impression is left upon the minds of his critic's believers by constituting it the representative of all which his poetry contains. Even *Endymion* is not without strong evidences of an affectionate and warm-hearted nature to those who are not unwilling to find them . . .[2]

—after which he wickedly turned the opening lines of Book III, 'There are who lord it o'er their fellow-men With most prevailing tinsel', etc., against the Cardinal himself. The patron, in fact, comes out a good deal better than the protégé from this miserable affair.

PUBLICATION HISTORY

Keats was twenty-one when his first collection of poems—in writing to Shelley later he called them 'my first blights'—appeared. Shelley, no doubt thankful his own youthful 'Esdaile' poems had escaped print, advised Keats not to publish them; but finding him resolved, gave what practical help he could, which probably meant getting his own

[1] *Autobiographical Notes of the Life of William Bell Scott*, ed. W. Minto, 1892, i. 128.

[2] 'English Poetry *versus* Cardinal Wiseman', *Fraser's Magazine*, lx (December 1859), 759–60.

publishers, the Ollier brothers, to undertake the work.[1] There were six reviews of *Poems*, which appeared on 3 March 1817, all of them generally favourable; but half were by personal friends (Nos. 4, 6, 7), and no influential journal noticed the book. As Cowden Clarke recalled, Keats's friends had anticipated a sensation. But 'Alas! the book might have emerged in Timbuctoo with far stronger chance of fame and approbation.' It was so little in demand that most of the edition (probably 500) was eventually remaindered, still unbound, at 1½*d.* a copy to a bookseller who 'paid twopence-halfpenny for boarding, and sold the lot very slowly at eighteenpence.'[2] Perhaps the publisher had been at fault; at any rate Keats switched his business to Taylor and Hessey, and his brother George wrote to break off the earlier connection. That letter is lost, but the Olliers replied as follows on 29 April 1817:

Sir,—We regret that your brother ever requested us to publish his book, or that our opinion of its talent should have led us to acquiesce in undertaking it. We are, however, much obliged to you for relieving us from the unpleasant necessity of declining any further connexion with it, which we must have done, as we think the curiosity is satisfied, and the sale has dropped. By far the greater number of persons who have purchased it from us have found fault with it in such plain terms, that we have in many cases offered to take the book back rather than be annoyed with the ridicule which has, time after time, been showered upon it. In fact, it was only on Saturday last that we were under the mortification of having our own opinion of its merits flatly contradicted by a gentleman, who told us he considered it 'no better than a take in'. These are unpleasant imputations for any one in business to labour under, but we should have borne them and concealed their existence from you had not the style of your note shewn us that such delicacy would be quite thrown away. We shall take means without delay for ascertaining the number of copies on hand, and you shall be informed accordingly.[3]

Keats persevered, and *Endymion* appeared at the end of April 1818, again in a modest edition of probably 500 copies but at a higher price (nine shillings instead of six shillings). This time there were eight reviews (not counting the *Edinburgh*'s, which was apparently held back for over two years). Three of these were by personal friends (Nos. 12, 13, 18), and three were devastatingly hostile (Nos. 14, 15, 16). The

[1] [John Dix], *Pen and Ink Sketches of Poets, Preachers, and Politicians*, 1846, 144.

[2] W. C. Hazlitt, *Four Generations of a Literary Family*, 1897, i. 276. Robert Gittings has pointed out that this reference is really to *Poems*, 1817.

[3] *Athenaeum* (7 June 1873), 725.

mighty *Quarterly*, with its circulation of 12,000 and its readership of 'fifty times ten thousand', contemptuously dismissed the poem, which never paid its expenses.[1] Byron once argued that a hostile review in the *Quarterly* had '*sold* an edition of the *Revolt of Islam*, which, otherwise, nobody would have thought of reading', but although this was Keats's own wishful hope, the *Quarterly* did undoubtedly kill off any chance of serious interest. Six months after publication, Hessey was reporting the sale of single copies, as if even this marked an upturn of trade.

Lamia, Isabella, The Eve of St Agnes, and Other Poems, Keats's third and final volume, was published at the end of June 1820 when the poet was already mortally ill, once more in a small edition of 500 copies but at the lower price of seven and sixpence. It attracted twelve reviews proper (this time including the *Edinburgh*'s delayed article, which was almost wholly on *Endymion*). Two were by friends (Nos. 24, 27), six others were entirely or mainly favourable (Nos. 25, 30, 31, 32, 33, 35), and four were hostile, though only one of these unequivocally so (Nos. 26, 28, 29, 36). This was a great improvement; moreover, a major critic had come down on Keats's side and was already influencing other reviewers. But it was too late to undo the prejudice created. Nearly a third of the edition had been subscribed on publication, yet on 14 August, when half the reviews were out, Taylor told John Clare: 'We have some Trouble to get through 500 Copies of his Work, though it is highly spoken of in the periodical Works';[2] and although *Lamia . . . and Other Poems* did pay its expenses that edition was never sold off, either.[3] Just before 1830, Robert Browning was able to buy original copies of both *Endymion* and *Lamia . . . and Other Poems*, 'just as if they had been purchased a week before, and not years after [,] the death of Keats!'[4]

No one in his own country ventured to reprint Keats's poems until nearly twenty years after his death. Galignani's 'unauthorized' Paris edition of Coleridge, Shelley, and Keats (1829), the first collected edition, whose text of Keats was reproduced over and over again in America, could only be bought abroad, and outside the small band of

[1] Edmund Blunden, *Keats's Publisher*, 1936, 85. Keats was paid £100 for the copyright and at the time of his death his publishers said they were 'still minus £110 by *Endymion*'.

[2] Blunden, op. cit., 111–12.

[3] 'Of Keats's Poems there have never yet been 500 sold' (Taylor to Clare, 18 March 1822, *Life and Letters of George Darley*, C. C. Abbott, 1928, 8).

[4] *Letters of Robert Browning to Various Correspondents*, ed. T. J. Wise, 1895, ii. (1st series), 83.

Keats's friends, already lessening through death, there seemed to be no demand at home. 'Mr Keats's reputation is at present but the shadow of a glory,' wrote the *Athenaeum* in 1828;[1] indeed, long after this date Keats was still earning the sneers of some reviewers. 'I should like to print a complete Edition of Keats's Poems,' Taylor wrote on 9 January 1835, 'but the world cares nothing for him—I fear that even 250 copies would not sell,'[2] and at about the same time Keats's friend Brown gave up his idea of publishing a biography. 'By the experience I had at our Institution [a lecture given in Plymouth], and by what I read in the works of the day, I fear that his fame is not yet high enough.'[3] Thus Fanny Brawne's reluctance in 1829 to see Keats's name again brought before the public (for which she has been criticized) was the only sensible attitude for her to take.

But propaganda continued to be made by his admirers. In 1831 Shelley's friend Trelawny included no less than fifty-four passages from Keats as chapter-headings in his popular *Adventures of a Younger Son*, many of these from unpublished material supplied by Brown; and this novel was soon reprinted, pirated in America, and translated into German. At last, in 1840, *The Poetical Works of John Keats* appeared as a paperback in William Smith's 'Standard Library'. This must have sold moderately well, as it was reissued four years later and was followed in 1841 by a more readable hardback version. It was a transitional phase in Keats's commercial fortunes. Holman Hunt found his copy of Keats 'on a bookseller's stall labelled, "this lot 4." '[4] But by the late 1840s popularity was assured; Moxon, who was already successfully marketing Shelley's works, became responsible also for Keats's, and from 1846 onwards the succession of editions was effectively that of a classic author in steady demand.

Keats's admission into the serious nineteenth-century anthologies followed a similar pattern, but was still slower. Anthologies are notoriously conservative, often borrowing shamelessly from one another, and Keats's work was rumoured to be morally unsound as well as artistically immature. This made it even less attractive than Shelley's to anthologists who catered largely for a young female market and (to a lesser extent at first) for seminaries and schools. For a long time Keats made almost no impression on entrenched prejudices.

[1] 29 January, v, 71.
[2] Blunden, op. cit., 199.
[3] Letter to Leigh Hunt, June 1837, quoted in the *Life of John Keats by Charles Armitage Brown*, ed. D. H. Bodurtha and W. B. Pope, 1937, 19.
[4] W. Holman Hunt, *Pre-Raphaelitism and the Pre-Raphaelite Brotherhood*, 1905, 2nd ed. 1913, 72.

He was not among the moderns admitted to the 1824 edition of *Elegant Extracts*, a standard collection of verse and prose, nor among those similarly admitted to Enfield's *Speaker*[1] as late as 1850–1; and although Shelley and Tennyson both appeared in the thirtieth edition (1852) of Ewing's equally reputable *Principles of Elocution*, Keats did not. *Lyrical Gems* (1824) had Byron, Wordsworth, and Shelley, but not Keats; so too with *The Juvenile Poetic Selector* (1829). *The Boy's Second Help to Reading* (1854), 'for more advanced pupils', contained Shelley, Tennyson, and—ironically—John Wilson, but left out Keats. On the other hand, *The Girl's Second Help to Reading* (1854), which claimed to present 'such passages as referred specifically to the high duties which woman is called upon to perform in life', staggeringly included three stanzas (xxiii–xxv) from 'The Eve of St Agnes'. To summarize: of thirty-three representative anthologies containing nineteenth-century poetry which were published between 1819 and 1859, twenty-six ignored Keats altogether; and the two most generous exceptions (*Select British Poets, or New Elegant Extracts* (1824), and *Imagination and Fancy* (1844)) were compiled by personal friends, Hazlitt and Leigh Hunt respectively. Among the other earlier exceptions, only George Croly's *Beauties of the British Poets* (1828), with *Specimens of the Lyrical, Descriptive, and Narrative Poets of Great Britain* (1828), gave Keats a fair hearing. Charles Mozley's *Poetry Past and Present* (1849) printed two Keats Odes (half as many poems as were allowed to Tennyson and to Milnes), and David Scrymgeour's *The Poetry and Poets of Britain, from Chaucer to Tennyson* (fourth edition Edinburgh 1852) printed 3¼ pages of Keats's verse ('his writings are fervid but untrained')—fewer than were allotted to Lockhart or James Hogg. Fair representation began at last with William Allingham's excellent *Nightingale Alley* (1860), although this still allowed Keats only five poems compared with Tennyson's seventeen; and more especially with *The Golden Treasury* (1861), that most prevailing of all anthologies, compiled by F. T. Palgrave and Tennyson himself. Here eleven poems were included, half the number of Shelley's and a quarter the number of Wordsworth's; but a note (page 320) implied that these three (with Scott and Campbell) were now regarded as the decisive forces in early nineteenth-century poetry.

Volumes of selections from Keats's poems alone were rare before the nineties, and the two earliest (1852 and 1876) were published in New York and Boston respectively. The first English selection, *Endymion and*

[1] 'An established school-book . . . in everybody's hands' (Preface to *Readings in Poetry*, 1816).

other Poems, only appeared (in Cassell's National Library) in 1887. It is not surprising, therefore, that nearly all the translations of Keats into European languages were made after 1900. There was, however, a German volume of selected poems in 1897. The first recorded French translation is dated 1907; but some idea of Keats's work had been given to French readers by the translations of Philarète Chasles (including letters) in a long review of Milnes's *Life* in 1848.[1] Keats's life-story—the Keats myth—was well-known in France at an early date; but comment before the 1860s did not go much beyond lamenting over this, or echoing the remarks of English journals. Amédée Pichot's brief observations of 1825 are among the more pertinent:

> John Keats, a poet more contemplative than Leigh Hunt, more incorrect, and quite as diffuse. . . . It was his aim to imbue the deities of the antient mythology with the metaphysical sentiments of modern passion. His *Endymion* and *Lamia* are replete with vivid strokes of painting.[2]

THE EARLY CRITICISM

It was unlucky for Keats that his earliest works should have been presented as a kind of manifesto against the prevailing rules of literary taste. This was partly accidental. Leigh Hunt had just published a preface with his *Story of Rimini* (1816) to justify his own procedures in that poem. For the most part it is only a re-hash of Wordsworth's critical prefaces, but its new emphases had some influence on Keats and Shelley. Hunt stressed two things. First, that 'Pope and the French school of versification' (by which he meant the eighteenth-century couplet-writers, supposedly followers of Boileau) 'have known the least on the subject, of any poets, perhaps that ever wrote', mistaking mere smoothness for harmony; whereas 'the great masters of modern versification' are Dryden, Spenser, Milton, Ariosto, Shakespeare, and Chaucer. Second, 'with the endeavour to recur to a freer spirit of versification, I have joined one of still greater importance,—that of having a free and idiomatic cast of language.' Here the right models are Chaucer, Pulci, Ariosto, and Homer. Thus the key notion was *freedom* ('freer versification', 'free and idiomatic language'), and its recommended practitioners were the 'Pre-Drydenist' poets and the Italians, especially Ariosto. First Hunt in the *Examiner*, 1816 (No. 2), then Reynolds in the *Champion*, 1817 (No. 4), then Hunt again in the

[1] *Revue des Deux Mondes*, ser. 5, xxiv (1848), 584–607.

[2] *Historical and Literary Tour of a Foreigner in England and Scotland*, 1825, i. 228.

Examiner, 1817 (No. 7), hailed Keats as a hopeful reinforcement to those who would 'overthrow that artificial taste which French criticism has long planted amongst us.' For Reynolds, who always had to abase the mighty in order to exalt the humble, Keats was rising amid the stars of Byron, Moore, Rogers, and Campbell 'with a genius that is likely to eclipse them all', and he quoted the 'rocking-horse Pegasus' passage from 'Sleep and Poetry' with barely-restrained satisfaction.

Hunt's opponents, of course, chose to believe that the 'new school' he was advocating was simply the school of Hunt, the 'Cockney School', and that the true origin of Keats's irregularities and affectations was not so much Spenser or Ariosto as *The Story of Rimini*. 'The first and most serious charge we have to bring against these literary adventurers,' declared Gold's *London Magazine* in 1820, 'is their want of harmony, and total disregard to the established canons of classical versification.'[1] Byron took much the same view (No. 20). It looked like a move to replace the civilized literary principles of the Augustans by a sort of ignorant, 'shabby-genteel' orgy. Some of Keats's friends also objected to the campaign he had got himself involved in. G. F. Mathew in the *European Magazine*, 1817 (No. 6) was angered by Keats's attack on Pope, which seemed to him, too, a plea for structural licence. 'In his enmity to the French school, and to the Augustan age of England, he seems to have a principle, that plan and arrangement are prejudicial to natural poetry.' Mathew also disliked Reynolds's over-praise of Keats at the expense of other living poets. Certainly Reynolds's review was the first to call Keats a genius; but in all fairness it must be said that nearly all the very high claims for Keats were made in the face of exaggerated mockery. Hunt believed steadily in Keats's greatness, but he never made inflated claims for him. It was the unhappy Benjamin Bailey, trying to forestall the critical attack for which he had innocently supplied ammunition, who in the *Oxford Herald*, 1818 (No. 12) appealed to the patriots of England to recognize 'the vernal genius of her sons', claiming to have found in Keats's *Poems* the work of a young Milton, 'the richest promise I ever saw of an etherial imagination maintained by vast intellectual power.' (Keats himself was touched but rueful at this naïve extravagance.) And in his protest after the *Quarterly*'s attack, Reynolds in the *Alfred*, 1818 (No. 18) defiantly called Keats 'a genius of the highest order', again pulling Byron down in order to do so ('Mr Keats has none of this egotism').

Bailey's recognition of 'vast intellectual power' in *Poems*, 1817, was

[1] *London Magazine and Monthly Critical and Dramatic Review*, i (March 1820), 303.

a minority view, to say the least. In an interesting discussion in the *Eclectic Review*, 1817 (No. 8), the lack of intellectual content was just what Josiah Conder complained of most. Even good contemporary poets, he argued (Wordsworth and Scott were in his mind), have wrongly dispensed with rational thought. It was all very well taking the Elizabethans for models as Keats had done, in order to be quaint and original, 'but originality forms by no means a test of intellectual pre-eminence.' Then he proposed what sounds like the earliest formulation of a 'dissociation of sensibility' theory: 'We consider poetry . . . in the present day . . . as having suffered a forcible divorce from thought.' But Conder seems not to have meant this in quite the 'metaphysical' way now familiar to us, but rather that Keats's poetry did not convey 'noble thoughts'. There was promise, fancy, and skill in his *Poems*, but little that was 'positively good', i.e. edifying. Conder later became an almost exclusively religious poet, and this fairly friendly attitude to Keats hardened after reading his next two volumes (No. 36).

The quality universally noticed in *Poems*, 1817, was a freshness and abundance of imaginative life. The *Monthly Magazine*, 1817 (No. 5) found in Keats 'a rapturous glow and intoxication of the fancy—an air of careless and profuse magnificence in his diction—a revelry of the imagination and tenderness of feeling.' Hunt, more restrained, spoke of 'a fancy and imagination at will, and an intense feeling of external beauty', but criticized the 'super-abundance of detail' (No. 7). The *Scots Magazine*, 1817 (No. 9) would likewise have preferred simplicity to 'the giddy wanderings of an untamed imagination', and blamed the meretricious stylistic features of the poetry, the 'leafy luxury' and 'jaunty streams', on Hunt, but ended by wishing there had been more of it: 'we are loth to part with this poet of promise.'

KEATS AND THE REVIEWERS

Two early reviews of *Endymion* were unaffected by the coming storm. The first, in the *Literary Journal*, 1818 (No. 11), carried on almost from where the *Scots Magazine* had left off: baffled at first by an unfamiliar kind of poetry, the writer (like his predecessor in No. 9) was finally 'induced to give our most unqualified approbation of this poem' and (unlike his successor in No. 16) would have preferred it to be longer. The second, in the *Champion*, 1818 (No. 13), contains the first really searching passages of criticism on Keats's work. The unknown writer apologized for having held back his review (it was still only the second to appear) to see what other opinions would be voiced, which implies that he may have been familiar with *Endymion* before publication, and there are internal indications that he may have discussed some of the topics in it with Keats himself. These circumstances, together with the wary tone and thoughtful, groping style, suggest that the author is likely to have been Keats's friend Richard Woodhouse. What interested him in *Endymion* was not primarily the sensuous detail or the diction, but the peculiar dramatic qualities embodied in its characters. This was, in fact, the first hesitant discussion of Keats's 'empathy', his characteristic dramatic power of suppressing his own identity so as to inhabit that of other persons, and even other creatures and things (to Woodhouse he said once that he could 'conceive of a billiard Ball that it may have a sense of delight from its own roundness, smoothness & very volubility').

Endymion, the writer affirmed, was a great original work. Other modern poets were found everywhere in their poems (he was thinking of Byron, and of Wordsworth's 'egotistical sublime'), and what their readers sympathized with was the poet's intense subjective feeling.

But Mr Keats goes out of himself into a world of abstractions:—his passions, feelings, are all as much imaginative as his situations. Neither is it the mere outward signs of passions that are given: there seems ever present some being that was equally conscious of its internal and most secret imaginings.

Like Shakespeare's *Venus and Adonis*, *Endymion* is 'a *representation* and not a *description* of passion'.

To transfer the mind to the situation of another, to feel as he feels, requires an enthusiasm, and an abstraction, beyond the power or the habit of most people. ... When [Keats] writes of passion, it seems to have possessed him. This, however, is what Shakespeare did, and if *Endymion* bears any general resemblance to any other poem in the language, it is to *Venus and Adonis* on this very account.

Similar ideas are mulled over in some of Woodhouse's notes, written after reading *Endymion*.[1] Already Shakespeare was being mentioned in relation to Keats, not just as an influence, but as a poet whose habits of mind in some ways resembled Keats's.

The first full onslaught came from the *British Critic*, 1818 (No. 14), which parodied the poem by retelling the story in a malicious selection

[1] *The Keats Circle: Letters and Papers 1816–1878*, ed. H. E. Rollins, Cambridge, Mass., 1948, i. 57–60. Rollins dates these notes 'about 27 October 1818', but parts of them could well be a little earlier.

of Keats's own 'monstrously droll' phrases. Although this was shameless caricature, a mosaic of 'Cockneyisms', it was adroitly done, and exposed some genuine weaknesses. But nothing was more difficult for the critical purists of the day than to grasp how the same idiom that in Leigh Hunt was coy or prettified, could be Keats's natural language, the expression of a sensuous vitality. For the modern reader, who takes Keats's use of that idiom for granted, it is sometimes hard to see just what an early reviewer thought objectionable about the words he italicized, especially when the very same words were sometimes italicized as strikingly effective by one of Keats's admirers. Thus the description of Hermes as the 'star of Lethe', which Lamb found wonderful (No. 24), was picked out as ludicrous; and so (later) was the prolepsis in 'Isabella' that Leigh Hunt celebrated (No. 42a): 'So the two brothers and their murder'd man Rode past fair Florence'. Keats's idiom seems to have been the obstacle when Henry Crabb Robinson tried in 1821 to interest the vicar of Hatfield and his friends in Keats's poetry: 'I read to the party Keats's "Isabella", which neither Cargill nor Mrs Pattisson enjoyed as much as they ought. Cargill was offended by the mixture of ludicrous phraseology with tender feelings.'[1]

The real target of the *Quarterly*'s and *Blackwood's* attacks was not Keats at all, but Hunt. *Poems*, 1817, had been dedicated to Hunt, and contained a provocative sonnet beginning 'What though, for showing truth to flatter'd state, Kind Hunt was shut in prison'—that is, from the Tory point of view, for being rude to the Prince Regent. The fire of the enemy had been openly drawn; hence the great concern in Keats's camp over the wording of his preface to *Endymion* (No. 10), which was tinkered with until it had lost its disarming spontaneity without any defensive advantage. After *Endymion*'s appearance, there was warning of both the critical blows that impended. 'I have been calling this morning on Mr Gifford,' Taylor reported on 15 May 1818:

> I had heard that he is writing an Article on Leigh Hunt, Shelley and Keats. I wished him to understand that Keats was a young Man of great Promise, whom it would be cruel to sacrifice on the sole account of his Connexion with Hunt, a Connexion which would doubtless soon be Dissolved by the Differences of their Characters. He heard and assented to all I said, but I fear it is too late to be of much Service, for he pointed to an Article in which they are noticed, then lying on his Table, and I fear it will not experience any alteration from my Appeal.[2]

[1] *Diary of Henry Crabb Robinson on Books and their Writers*, ed. E. J. Morley, 1938, i. 263.
[2] *London Mercury*, xii (July 1925), 258.

The real author of the article, J. W. Croker, had been briefed by the *Quarterly*'s publisher, John Murray, who had written:

I send the Volume [*Endymion*] in case you wish to refer to it—or to penetrate farther—& I have added a former Volume [*Poems*, 1817] in order to give you the gentlemans compleat measure—He is thought to possess some talent totally misdirected if not destroyed by the tuition of Leigh Hunt—to whom you will observe that the earlier volume is dedicated.[1]

Taylor's appeal was not too late in a temporal sense, as in 1818 the 'April' issue of the *Quarterly* did not appear until late in September, so that the *Blackwood's* review, published in August, just achieved priority. Here too an attempt was made to forestall trouble—this time calamitously. As early as May, *Blackwood's* had referred ominously to Hunt's room

where, amiable but infatuated bardling, Mister John Keats slept on the night when he composed his famous Cockney Poem in honour of

> Him of the rose, the violet, and the spring,
> The social smile, *the chain for freedom's sake*.[2]

In July, Keats's friend Bailey met Lockhart in Scotland, and tried to wipe out the smear of Keats's association with Hunt by detailing the respectable facts about his family and his medical calling.[3] These confidences were exultingly used in the review, though Lockhart had promised Bailey that *he* would not use them. Bailey had inferred, however, that someone would; and warned Taylor at the end of August: 'I fear *Endymion* will be dreadfully cut up in the *Edinburgh Magazine* (*Blackwood's*)'.[4]

According to the myth—one of the most powerful in literature—Keats died in consequence of one or both of these attacks. Byron's stanza in *Don Juan* (XI.lx), though typically sceptical, fixed the form of the myth:

> John Keats, who was killed off by one critique,
> Just as he really promised something great,
> If not intelligible, without Greek
> Contrived to talk about the gods of late
> Much as they might have been supposed to speak.
> Poor fellow! His was an untoward fate;
> 'Tis strange the mind, that very fiery particle,
> Should let itself be snuffed out by an article.

[1] Undated letter, *Keats-Shelley Journal*, xii (Winter 1963), 8.
[2] *Blackwood's Edinburgh Magazine*, iii (May 1818), 197.
[3] *The Keats Circle*, i. 34; i. 245–7; ii. 298–300.
[4] Ibid. i. 34.

A literal reading of these lines determined Keats's poetic standing for a quarter of a century, and both the legend and the facts have strongly affected the directions of criticism for much longer than that.

The major critical journals of the time exercised a powerful influence on the small reading public, so it is not surprising that a hostile review sent Mrs Hemans to her bed, and Byron to three bottles of claret. Of course Keats was emotionally shocked by *Blackwood's* and dismayed by the *Quarterly*, whose strictures, however flippantly expressed, had critical point. Shelley's account, from Hunt, may not be greatly exaggerated of one who was totally committed to his art and who, according to his brother, had a 'nervous morbid temperament': 'The first effects are described to me to have resembled insanity, & it was by assiduous watching that he was restrained from effecting purposes of suicide.'[1] Haydon said that as a result of the first review (No. 15), 'He became morbid and silent, would call and sit whilst I was painting for hours without speaking a word.'[2] An 1825 account gives a similar picture:

> [Fanny Brawne] and his sister say they have oft found him, on suddenly entering the room, with that review in his hand, reading as if he would devour it—completely absorbed—absent, and drinking it in like mortal poison. The instant he observed anybody near him, however, he would throw it by, and begin to talk of some indifferent matter.[3]

But this third-hand description is certainly unreliable: the writer himself had not then met either of the two women, and at the time required they had not even met each other; nor could the fifteen-year-old Fanny Keats have 'oft found' her brother in any such situation—or even have grasped what the situation was. It is unlikely that Keats was more than momentarily shaken. Outwardly, at any rate, he soon mastered the shock. 'Keats was in good spirits,' Hessey told Taylor as early as 16 September; 'He does not seem to care about *Blackwood*, he thinks it is so poorly done, and as he does not mean to publish anything more at present he says it affects him less.'[4] Keats's claim that his own self-criticism had given him more pain than any review is convincingly characteristic; he knew of *Endymion*'s weaknesses, and knew he could transcend them.

[1] *The Letters of Percy Bysshe Shelley*, ed. F. L. Jones, 1964, ii. 252.
[2] Tom Taylor, *Life of B. R. Haydon*, 1853, i. 349.
[3] *The Life of Gerald Griffin*, by his brother, 2nd edition, Dublin, 1857, 147.
[4] Quoted from Guy Murchie, *The Spirit of Place in Keats*, 1955, 112.

But things began to look different towards the end of 1819, and especially after the haemorrhage he suffered on 3 February 1820. The imminence of death changed everything; it meant that the reviewers had destroyed his chances of happiness (because he was still in debt to his publishers and could not marry), as well as his chance of 'being among the English poets' (because whatever reputation he might already deserve had been withheld). Now there was no time to repair the damage. The *injustice* of being so cheated of life was what embittered his end. 'The last time I saw him,' Haydon recorded in March 1821,

was at Hampstead, lying in a white bed with a book, hectic, weak, & on his back, irritable at his feebleness, and wounded at the way he had been used; he seemed to be going out of the world with a contempt for this and no hopes of the other. I told him to be calm, but he muttered if he did not soon recover he would cut his throat.[1]

Despair led to paranoia. According to Reynolds, 'poor Keats attributed his approaching end to the poisonous pen of Lockhart', and told Taylor before going to Italy, 'If I die you must ruin Lockhart.'[2] In the final months the pugnacious fighter would not fight for his own life; and to this extent at least the myth is true. But the attack on Keats was not simply a matter of two articles; it was a campaign sustained over many years.

Keats's reported words suggest that it was the *Blackwood's* review that stuck in his mind. The *Quarterly*'s critical weight was of course far greater, and with 12,000 copies an issue it had double the sales of *Blackwood's*, whose London circulation was only 1,500;[3] but the liveliness of the new Scottish journal tended to appeal to the young of both political factions. Mary Russell Mitford, for instance, frankly enjoyed it more than the liberal *London Magazine* for which she herself wrote:

I will tell you just what it is—a very libellous, naughty, wicked, scandalous, story-telling, entertaining work . . . abusing the wits and poets and politicians of *our* side and praising all of *yours*; abusing Hazlitt, abusing John Keats, abusing Leigh Hunt . . . and lauding Mr Gifford, Mr Croker, and Mr Canning. But

[1] *Diary of Benjamin Robert Haydon*, ed. W. B. Pope, Cambridge, Mass., 1960, ii. 318.

[2] *Life of John Keats by Charles Armitage Brown*, ed. D. H. Bodurtha and W. B. Pope, 1937, 29.

[3] Samuel Smiles, *A Publisher and his Friends*, 1891, ii. 4; M. Oliphant, *Annals of a Publishing House*, 1897, i. 99; i. 191.

all this, especially the abuse, is very cleverly done; and I think you would be amused by it.[1]

Moreover, the *Quarterly*'s ridicule was largely technical, and could be answered merely by making it obsolescent; whereas Lockhart's ribaldry was directed at Keats's education, social being, and friendships, and was unanswerable. All the same Croker's article made a better myth for Keats's supporters, because here the official literary voice of the Establishment could be said to have jeered a good poet out of existence by pretending, for political reasons, that he was a bad one.

BLACKWOOD'S EDINBURGH MAGAZINE, 1817–44

After the full-scale attacks by 'Z' on the 'Cockney School' in 1817–18, the abuse was kept up almost continuously, though with some inconsistency due to the magazine's curious collective editorship. In 1819 there was an article praising Leigh Hunt's *Literary Pocket Books*, one of which contained some work by Keats:

Two Sonnets, with the signature T., we opine to be the property of the 'Muse's Son of Promise,'—'two feats of Johnny Keates.' We cannot be mistaken of them. Whatever be the name of the supposed father—Tims or Tomkins—Johnny Keates gignated these sonnets. To each of them we may say,

Sleep image of thy Father, sleep my Boy!

As we are anxious to bring this young writer into notice, we quote his sonnets.

['Four seasons fill the measure of the year' and 'To Ailsa Rock' are quoted in full.]

The first of these compositions is very well—a common and hackneyed thought is illustrated in a novel and also natural manner—and we thank Mr Keates for his sonnet. But who but himself could form a collocation of words to produce such portentous folly as in the second? Mister John Keates standing on the sea-shore at Dunbar, without a neckcloth, according to custom of Cockaigne, and cross-questioning the Craig of Ailsa!

Thou answerest not for thou art dead asleep!

. . . There is much smartness in the idea of 'two dead eternities.' An eternity

[1] Letter to Sir William Elford, 9 November 1818, in *The Life of Mary Russell Mitford*, ed. A. G. L'Estrange, 1870, ii. 42–3. Wordsworth banned both the *London Magazine* and *Blackwood's* from Rydal Mount for 'want of principle', but his womenfolk had a 'great curiosity to see' *Blackwood's*, and used to smuggle it in. (*The Letters of Sara Hutchinson from 1800 to 1835*, ed. K. Coburn, 1954, 157, 227.)

especially, past with whales, is enough to make the stoutest reader blubber. Do not let John Keates think we dislike him. He is a young man of some poetry; but at present he has not more than about a dozen admirers,—Mr Leigh Hunt whom he feeds on the oil-cakes of flattery till he becomes flatulent of praise,—Mr Benjamin Haydon, who used to laugh at him till that famous sonnet—three engrossing clerks—and six or seven medical students, who chaunt portions of *Endymion* as they walk the hospitals, because the author was once an apothecary. We alone like him and laugh at him. He is at present a very amiable, silly, lisping, and pragmatical young gentleman—but we hope to cure him of all that—and should have much pleasure in introducing him to our readers in a year or two speaking the language of this country, counting his fingers correctly, and condescending to a neckcloth. . . . It would greatly amuse us, to meet in company together Johnny Keates and Percy Bysshe Shelley. . . . A bird of paradise and a Friezeland fowl would not look more absurdly, on the same perch.[1]

Hazlitt suggested that *Blackwood's* praised Shelley because he was a gentleman and derided Keats and Hunt because they were not. This provoked a long, furious, incoherent denial from Lockhart: Keats was a poet of feeling and power (he had just published *Lamia . . . and Other Poems*) but a wretched writer; *Blackwood's* were sorry if they had done him harm, but it was in order to do him good; they had no personal animus against the Cockneys, except that they were all contemptible vermin:

As for Mr Keats, we are informed that he is in a very bad state of health, and that his friends attribute a great deal of it to the pain he has suffered from the critical castigation his *Endymion* drew down on him in this magazine. If it be so, we are most heartily sorry for it, and have no hesitation in saying, that had we suspected that young author, of being so delicately nerved, we should have administered our reproof in a much more lenient shape and style. The truth is, we from the beginning saw marks of feeling and power in Mr Keats' verses, which made us think it very likely, he might become a real poet of England, provided he could be persuaded to give up all the tricks of Cockneyism, and forswear for ever the thin potations of Mr Leigh Hunt. We, therefore, rated him as roundly as we decently could do, for the flagrant affectations of those early productions of his. In the last volume he has published, we find more beauties than in the former, both of language and thought, but we are sorry to say, we find abundance of the same absurd affectations also, and superficial conceits, which first displeased us in his writings;—and which we are again very sorry to say, must in our opinion, if persisted in, utterly and entirely prevent Mr Keats from ever taking his place among the pure and classical poets of his mother tongue. It is quite ridiculous to see how the vanity of these Cockneys

[1] *Blackwood's*, vi (December 1819), 238–41.

makes them overrate their own importance, even in the eyes of us, that have always expressed such plain unvarnished contempt for them, and who do feel for them all, a contempt too calm and profound, to admit of any admixture of any thing like anger or personal spleen. We should just as soon think of being wroth with vermin, independently of their coming into our apartment, as we should of having any feelings at all about any of these people, other than what are excited by seeing them in the shape of authors. Many of them, considered in any other character than that of authors, are, we have no doubt, entitled to be considered as very worthy people in their own way. Mr Hunt is said to be a very amiable man in his own sphere, and we believe him to be so willingly. Mr Keats we have often heard spoken of in terms of great kindness, and we have no doubt his manners and feelings are calculated to make his friends love him. But what has all this to do with our opinion of their poetry? . . . What is the spell that must seal our lips, from uttering an opinion . . . plain and perspicuous concerning Mr John Keats, viz. that nature possibly meant him to be a much better poet than Mr Leigh Hunt ever could have been, but that, if he persists in imitating the faults of that writer, he must be contented to share his fate, and be like him forgotten? Last of all, what should forbid us to announce our opinion, that Mr Shelley, as a man of genius, is not merely superior, either to Mr Hunt, or to Mr Keats, but altogether out of their sphere, and totally incapable of ever being brought into the most distant comparison with either of them. It is very possible, that Mr Shelley himself might not be inclined to place himself so high above these men as we do, but that is his affair, not ours.[1]

To a modern reader there is something hysterical, and unpleasantly familiar, in the intensity of loathing aroused in some quarters by the 'Cockneys', even as late as 1844:

This is the life into which the slime of the Keateses and Shelleys of former times has fecundated! The result was predicted about a quarter of a century ago in the pages of this Magazine . . . but our efforts at that time were only partially successful; for nothing is so tenacious of life as the spawn of frogs.[2]

The earlier writers of *Blackwood's* were in fact prompt to translate insult into physical violence. When an exposé of the journal was published in October 1818, Lockhart and John Wilson challenged the anonymous author to a duel. He curtly declined, recommending his challengers to beg pardon of God and country for the iniquity of their polluted pens. Two months later, John Scott, editor of Baldwin's *London Magazine* and a moderate champion of Keats (Nos. 17, 33),

[1] *Blackwood's*, vii (September 1820), 686–7.

[2] *Blackwood's*, lvi (September 1844), 342. This review, of Coventry Patmore's first book, *Poems* (1844), was by James Ferrier, then Professor of History in the University of Edinburgh.

'branded' *Blackwood's* in two articles as 'a publication, in which . . . the violation of decency was to render it *piquant*, and the affectation of piety render it persuasive, and servility to power render it profitable'. Lockhart had called Hunt 'King of the Cockneys', so Scott dubbed Lockhart 'Emperor of the Mohocks' (from the upper-class hooligans of Addison's day). As a consequence, Scott eventually fought a duel with Lockhart's friend John Christie in February 1821, was fatally wounded, and died within a few days of Keats himself.

This affair, together with a libel action, kept *Blackwood's* quiet for a while; but the anniversary of these two deaths was not left unmarked:

Poor Keates! I cannot pass his name without saying that I really think he had some genius about him. I do think he had something that might have ripened into fruit, had he not made such a mumbling work of the buds—something that might have been wine, and tasted like wine, if he had not kept dabbling with his fingers in the vat, and pouring it out and calling lustily for quaffers, before the grounds had time to be settled, or the spirit to be concentrated, or the flavour to be formed.[1]

Adonais (referred to by one of *Blackwood's* contributors as 'Shelley's what d'ye call it about Master Clysterpipe the dead poet'[2]) was now becoming well-known in Britain, and the growth of the myth kept *Blackwood's* in two minds: whether to shelter behind the *Quarterly*'s imputed guilt (so that they could claim always to have recognized 'some genius' about Keats), or whether out of pride and distaste to claim precedence in the assassination. Editorial policy lurched meaninglessly from one to the other:

Signor Z, whoever he be, gibbetted everlastingly Hunt, Hazlitt, Keats, Webb, and all the Cockney school. Has any one dared to take them down from that bad eminence? Have they dared to shew their faces in decent society, branded as they are on the countenance with that admirably adapted title? Have not their books been obliged to skulk from the tables of gentlemen, where they might formerly have been seen, into the fitting company of washerwomen, merchants' clerks, ladies of easy virtue, and mythological young gentlemen, who fill the agreeable office of ushers at boarding-schools? What is the reason that they sunk under it? Because they were, are, and ever will be, ignorant pretenders, without talent or information. . . . All the clamour about cruel criticism is absurd—it will do no harm to the mighty,—and as for the pigmies, let them be crushed for daring to tread where none but the mighty should

[1] *Blackwood's*, xi (March 1822), 346.

[2] Letter from William Maginn to William Blackwood, 17 December 1821, quoted from N. I. White, *The Unextinguished Hearth*, 1938, 290.

enter. . . . As for malignity, &c. it is almost all cant. . . . The majority who criticise, do so to raise the wind, not caring whether they are right or wrong,—or they are fellows of fun, who cut up an author with whom they would sit down five minutes after, over a bowl of punch. . . . As to people being killed by it, that is the greatest trash of all . . . lately, Johnny Keats was cut up in the *Quarterly*, for writing about Endymion what no mortal could understand, and this says Mr Shelly doctored the apothecary. . . . Is there any man who believed such stuff? Keats, in publishing his nonsense, knew that he was voluntarily exposing himself to all sort and manner of humbugging; and when he died, if his body was opened, I venture to say that no part of his animal economy displayed any traces of the effects of criticism. God rest him, to speak with our brethren of the Church of Rome;—I am sorry he is dead, for he often made me laugh at his rubbish of verse, when he was alive.[1]

No more shameless admission could be made: 'The majority who criticise, do so to raise the wind, not caring whether they are right or wrong,—or they are fellows of fun.' The fun was kept up, in the same spirit, long after Keats's death:

Round the ring we sat, the stiff stuff tipsily quaffing.
(Thanks be to thee, Jack Keats; our thanks for the dactyl and spondee;
Pestleman Jack, whom, according to Shelley, the Quarterly murdered
With a critique as fell as one of his own patent medicines.)[2]

The account of Shelley's own death, in his *Posthumous Poems* (1824), offered an opening for more facetiousness:

What a rash man Shelley was, to put to sea in a frail boat with Jack's poetry on board! Why, man, it would sink a trireme. In the preface to Mr Shelley's poems we are told that 'his vessel bore out of sight with a favourable wind;' but what is that to the purpose? It had *Endymion* on board, and there was an end.[3]

What could Leigh Hunt, or anyone else, have replied to this kind of thing? Yet when Hunt's *Lord Byron and Some of His Contemporaries* appeared in 1828, Lockhart taunted Hunt with having pretended to ignore the earlier attacks on Keats. 'His intimate friend dying of this Magazine, and Hunt, the physician, unable from the symptoms to conjecture the complaint!' But it was all lies, anyway:

Mr Keats died in the ordinary course of nature. Nothing was ever said in this Magazine about him, that needed to have given him an hour's sickness; and had he lived a few years longer, he would have profited by our advice, and been

[1] *Blackwood's*, xi (July 1822), 59–60.
[2] *Blackwood's*, xiv (July 1823), 67.
[3] *Blackwood's*, xvi (September 1824), 288.

grateful for it, although perhaps conveyed to him in a pill rather too bitter. Hazlitt, Hunt, and other unprincipled infidels, were his ruin. Had he lived a few years longer, we should have driven him in disgust from the gang that were gradually affixing a taint to his name. His genius we saw, and praised; but it was deplorably sunk in the mire of Cockneyism.[1]

'His genius we saw, and praised.' In 1828 it was wise to begin changing the line a little, and Haydon had recently supplied a new one. 'That poor youth' had been ruined, not by his enemies, but by his friends. Next year John Wilson returned to the subject:

But we killed Keates. There again you—lie. Hunt, Hazlitt, and the godless gang, slavered him to death. Bitterly did he confess that, in his last days, in language stronger than we wish to use; and the wretches would now accuse us of the murder of that poor youth, by a few harmless stripes of that rod, which 'whoever spareth injureth the child;' while they strut convicted, even in their Cockney consciences, of having done him to death, by administering to their unsuspecting victim, dose after dose, of that poison to which there is no antidote—their praise.[2]

Outraged by *Lord Byron and Some of His Contemporaries*, Haydon had written a scurrilous sequel, 'Leigh Hunt and Some of His Companions', which he had given to Lockhart to supplement the latter's review of Hunt. When, in remorse, Haydon withdrew the article, he found that Lockhart had thought of amending his pseudonym to read 'by Z'—the signature of the notorious attacks on the Cockney School in 1817–18. Haydon was appalled at Lockhart's duplicity. 'Though he repented of his trick by his red ink scratch, the very conception shews the Nature of his Mind!'[3] So the article was never printed; but the information it contained was used, and had some influence.

THE QUARTERLY REVIEW, 1818–88

The young men of *Blackwood's* admired Shelley and knew perfectly well (or some of them did) that Keats was an important poet, but it suited them to jeer at him. The elderly men of the *Quarterly* did not go in for personal abuse, but had no suspicion whatever of Keats's literary importance. The *Quarterly* was therefore more consistent. It is true that in answer to representations the editor seems to have admitted that Croker's review (No. 16) was less than fair. Miss Mitford (presumably via Haydon) reported Gifford as having 'sent word that if he [Keats]

1 *Blackwood's*, xxiii (March 1828), 403–4.
2 *Blackwood's*, xxvi (September 1829), 525.
3 *Diary of B. R. Haydon*, iii. 258.

wrote again his poem should be properly reviewed, which was admitting the falsity of the first critique, and yet says that he has been Keats's best friend; because somebody sent him twenty-five pounds to console him for the injustice of the *Quarterly*'.[1] But this promise, if made, was not kept. The record is complicated by the fact that Lockhart himself took over the editorship of the *Quarterly* in 1826, and its first comment, after Croker's notorious review, was characteristically his: 'Our readers', he wrote in 1828, 'have probably forgotten all about *Endymion, a poem*, and the other works of this young man, the all but universal roar of laughter with which they were received some ten or twelve years ago, and the ridiculous story (which Mr Hunt denies) of the author's death being caused by the reviewers.'[2] Nothing, however, had affected the calm, settled, imperturbable sarcasm of Croker five years later when he reviewed Tennyson's *Poems* (1832). He realized, as everyone did, that Keats's poetry was what had made Tennyson's possible; but this meant only that Tennyson could be dismissed in the same way. 'I undertake Tennyson and hope to make another Keats of him',[3] he told the *Quarterly*'s publisher. And the review itself (No. 47), in tone as in content, simply reaffirmed his old critical position of 1818. Even in 1833, it was an obtuse line to take. In 1848 the *Quarterly* (still edited by Lockhart) doggedly ignored Milnes's *Life* altogether. But at last Murray was forced to confess to Croker:

I have just refreshed my recollection of your paper on Keats. 'Tis very clever and very just—but this degenerate age is carried away by mawkish notions of liberality and the want of true literary discernment, and I fear reads the rubbish. At any rate he has lately found an editor.[4]

This last was an understatement; Keats had not only found an editor by 1854 but at least ten English editions. However, the *Quarterly* never outgrew Croker's very clever 'paper on Keats'. In 1888 it was vindicated afresh by R. E. Prothero (Lord Ernle), who was reviewing (anonymously) Colvin's *Keats* and Rossetti's *Life of Keats*:

Under the date of April 1818, a criticism of Keats's *Endymion* appeared in these pages, which has proved the nucleus of a widely-accepted literary myth. . . . But it may be said, at the outset, that there is little, or nothing, of the adverse

[1] Letter to Sir William Elford, 5 July 1820, *Life of Mary Russell Mitford*, ii. 105.

[2] *Quarterly Review*, xxxvii (March 1828), 416.

[3] Letter to John Murray, 7 January 1833, quoted in M. F. Brightfield, *John Wilson Croker*, Berkeley, 1940, 350.

[4] Letter of John Murray to Croker, 11 October 1854, ibid., 349.

criticism contained in that famous review, which we desire to withdraw even after the lapse of seventy years.[1]

The five adverse criticisms, still upheld, were:

> that the poem is meaningless and therefore unreadable; that the poet's prosodial notions are crude; that he follows the associations of sounds rather than of ideas, and that the rhyme of the last line is the catchword for the thought of the next; that his diction is newly coined, far-fetched, and barbarous; that his faults are those of the so-called 'Cockney School' of which Leigh Hunt is the hierophant. From first to last there is no personal allusion to Keats or his profession, and not the slightest trace of political animosity.[2]

But the future editor of Byron's letters had to admit, after all, that 'The spirit of the age in which we live is inspired by Wordsworth and by Keats; they, and not their admired contemporaries [Scott and Byron] directed the tendencies of the future.'[3]

THE EDINBURGH REVIEW, 1820–48

The role played by the *Edinburgh Review* was mystifying. Keats's friends naturally expected the leading Whig journal to defend him, at least against personal insult, while Jeffrey's literary approval, once conferred, would have neutralized any assault from the other side. But the *Edinburgh* kept silence throughout 1818, and for two years afterwards. At last in August 1820 Francis Jeffrey published a review (No. 30) ostensibly of both *Endymion* and *Lamia . . . and Other Poems*. It began: 'We had never happened to see either of these volumes till very lately.' Jeffrey could not have seen *Lamia . . . and Other Poems* 'till very lately', as it had only been published at the very end of June; and he had been away on circuit—he was a hard-working barrister—when *Endymion* appeared. Still, it is hard to take his statement literally; Taylor would naturally have made certain that a copy of *Endymion* was available to the editor of the journal he chiefly relied on, and it had been available, a subject of fierce controversy, for two and a half years. 'The *Edinburgh Review* are affraid to touch upon my Poem,' Keats told his brother:

> They do not know what to make of it—they do not like to condemn it and they will not praise it for fear . . . they dare not compromise their Judgments on so puzzling a Question. If on my next Publication they should praise me and so lug

[1] *Quarterly Review*, clxvi (April 1888), 308.
[2] Ibid., 330.
[3] Ibid., 309.

in *Endymion*—I will address [them] in a manner they will not at all relish. The Cowardliness of the *Edinburgh* is worse than the abuse of the *Quarterly*.[1]

When the article appeared, Keats was too ill to care, but his guess had probably been very near the mark. Although *Lamia . . . and Other Poems* was an incomparably better book, almost the whole review was of *Endymion*, the remaining space being given to quotations bridged by hasty and superficial comments. It seems very possible that Jeffrey did write an article defending *Endymion*, but lost his nerve in the face of all the mockery, and withheld it.[2] When *Lamia . . . and Other Poems* appeared, he realized he would have been safe, and a letter from Reynolds on 13 July finally nudged him into action;[3] but instead of writing on the new book he tried to make his original article do for both, improvising modifications that seem to have left traces on the style: for instance, 'this [blossom] which is now before us' (singular), 'his whole works . . . require . . . all the indulgence that can be claimed for a first attempt' (an odd construction and a confused idea: a poet's third volume is scarcely a first attempt). One revealing slip has hitherto escaped notice. Discussing the *general* qualities of Keats's poetry, Jeffrey wrote: 'to this censure a very great part of the volume before us will certainly be exposed.' Reprinting the essay in 1844, he changed *volume* to the plural, 'the volumes before us', and this is the form in which the sentence has generally been reproduced since. Was the singular only a misprint?

If the *Endymion* review was deliberately held back, it is easy to understand Jeffrey's subsequent remorse ('regret that I did not go more largely into the exposition of his merits' (1844); 'never regretted anything more than to have been *too late* with my testimony' (1848)), and the terms of Milnes's dedication to him of Keats's *Life* must have been galling: 'The merits which your generous sagacity perceived under so many disadvantages, are now recognised by every student and lover of poetry in this country.'

CRITICAL REACTIONS (I) UP TO 1848

Milnes's last quoted statement was pretty accurate in 1848, but the recognition had been slow. The champions of neo-classical taste were

[1] Letter of 17–27 September 1819, *The Letters of John Keats*, ed. H. E. Rollins, 1958, ii. 200.

[2] *Endymion*'s controversial status gave it a curious posthumous existence as a review-poem. Besides Jeffrey's belated notice, it was reviewed in the *Dublin University Magazine* (June 1843), and again in the *Edinburgh Review* (July 1885).

[3] *The Times* (30 October 1928), 19.

entrenched in unexpected places. Shelley's friends T. J. Hogg and T. L. Peacock read Keats's sonnet 'This pleasant tale is like a little copse' in the March 1817 *Examiner*, and as Mary Shelley sardonically told the editor: 'Both of the menagerie were very much scandalized by the praise & sonnet of Keats and mean I believe to petition against the publication of any more.'[1] Hogg later responded to Shelley's gift of *Adonais* by observing facetiously: 'surely it is rather glorious than base to slay a bad poet'.[2] The very myth that served to keep Keats's name alive as a reproach to the philistines was for a long time the main obstacle to a serious study of his work. For if Keats had been destroyed 'just as he really promised something great', then it was axiomatic that his poetry had missed greatness.

At least everyone knew Keats's name and story, and his grave in Rome almost at once became a place of international pilgrimage. The American N. P. Willis, visiting it in 1833, could truthfully say: 'Every reader knows his history and the cause of his death. . . . Keats was, no doubt, a poet of very uncommon promise',[3] and from a very early date it was American devotion and generosity that ensured the upkeep of the grave (No. 71). There were many European pilgrims, too. In 1838 the French poet Auguste Barbier found it the most compelling spot in that beautiful cemetery:

> The grave which interested me the most and held me near it the longest was that of the unfortunate *John Keats*, author of *Endymion*, the English poet who, in modern times and after our own André Chénier, had the finest and tenderest feeling for the beauty of antiquity. . . . Poor Keats![4]

Joseph Severn (No. 71) never regretted his harrowing association with the poet. 'Keats' name is rising,' he told his sister as early as 1824, 'and everyone respects my character for it. You would be surprised how often . . . I am pointed out as the friend of the Poet, Keats.'[5] This was in Italy. In England for the next twenty years Keats was read by eager but isolated idolaters, often by way of individual poems reprinted in publications such as Hone's *Table Book*, or sampled in short extracts such as those scattered through *Flora Domestica* (1823, reprinted 1825),

[1] Letter to the Hunts, 18 March 1817, *The Letters of Mary W. Shelley*, ed. F. L. Jones, Norman, 1944, i. 24.

[2] Letter to Shelley, 29 January 1822, *Shelley and Mary*, ed. Lady Jane and Sir Percy F. Shelley, 1882, iii. 738.

[3] *Pencillings By the Way*, 1835, ed. L. S. Jast, 1842, i. 121.

[4] *Souvenirs personnels et Silhouettes contemporaines*, Paris, 1883, 73.

[5] Letter of 4 October 1824, *The London Mercury*, xxx (August 1934), 348.

a gardening book 'with illustrations from the works of the poets', compiled by Leigh Hunt's sister-in-law, Elizabeth Kent. The opening and closing lines of a poem dated November 1826, by someone who evidently knew and hero-worshipped Keats, evokes very well this period in the late twenties, when it seemed as if the only writers who cherished his name were people who had known him:

> Thy name, dear Keats, is not forgotten quite
> E'en in this dreary pause—Fame's dark twilight—
> The space betwixt death's starry-vaulted sky,
> And the bright dawn of immortality.
> That time when tear and elegy lie cold
> Upon the barren tomb, and ere enrolled
> Thy name upon the list of honoured men,
> In the world's volume writ with History's lasting pen. . . .
>
> I laid in wait to catch a glimpse of thee,
> And plann'd where'er thou wert that I might be.
> Mixt admiration fills my heart, nor can
> I tell which most to love—the Poet or the Man.[1]

Three years later, the brilliant group of Cambridge undergraduates calling themselves the Apostles, which included Tennyson, Arthur Hallam, and R. M. Milnes (Lord Houghton, Keats's future biographer), found a publisher ('after some difficulty') to reissue Shelley's *Adonais*, out of enthusiasm for both poets. It is significant that a corresponding group at Harvard, which has since become such a great centre of Keats scholarship, was flourishing at about the same time; but at Harvard, too, enthusiasts had to circulate their own private copies of the poems.[2]

Galignani's edition, with its brief memoir by Cyrus Redding (No. 45), proved invaluable, particularly for American readers. Texts had been scarce even in England, where appeals were made like the Quaker Mary Howitt's, 'Dost thou recollect some months ago, in *The Nottingham Review*, some lines by Keats on Autumn? And canst thou procure a copy of them for Goodman Wender?'[3] There was no initial class-prejudice to overcome in America. 'The American public', James Russell Lowell dryly remarked, quoting Milnes's *Life*, 'will perhaps not

[1] 'Extemporaneous Lines, suggested by some thoughts and recollections of John Keats, the Poet', in William Hone's *Every-Day Book and Table Book*, 1827, iii. Part 2, cols. 371–2. Edmund Blunden has suggested that the author, 'Gaston', may have been W. S. Williams of Taylor's publishing firm, who saw Keats embark for Italy.

[2] H. E. Rollins, *Keats' Reputation in America to 1848*, Cambridge, Mass., 1946, 38–42.

[3] *Mary Howitt: An Autobiography*, ed. M. Howitt, 1889, i. 154.

be disturbed by knowing that the father of Keats . . . was employed in the establishment of Mr Jennings, the proprietor of large livery-stables on the Pavement in Moorfields, nearly opposite the entrance into Finsbury Circus.'[1] Although for some time American journals were content to copy or paraphrase the English ones, Keats's poetry was better known and earlier honoured in America than in his own country.[2]

One powerful stimulus to the underground culture that strengthened Keats's reputation during the 1830s and 1840s was the number of his admirers who were themselves young practising poets, so that Keats's work had imperceptibly been assimilated into the living poetic tradition even before it was itself widely read. As Thomas Hood the younger explained in an encyclopedia article, 'his poetry is rather acceptable to poets than to ordinary readers, whose minds cannot, or do not care to essay, following the flight of his genius.'[3] The Brownings are obvious examples (No. 51); 'Barry Cornwall' (B. W. Procter) is another (Nos. 38, 43); and so are Thomas Hood the elder, Ebenezer Elliott the 'Corn-Law Rhymer', and Alexander Smith. All three of the Apostles already named, including Milnes, were published poets. Verses on Keats, mostly biographical and sentimental, appeared constantly in periodicals.[4] But the major role was Tennyson's. His first volume (*Poems, chiefly Lyrical*, 1830) was recognized to be

> full of precisely the kind of poetry for which Mr Keats was assailed, and for which the world is already beginning to admire him. . . . There is the same fulness of thoughts and fervour of feeling, with much of the same quaintness of expressions,—an equal degree of idolatry of the old writers, mixed with a somewhat more apparent reverence for the moderns,—fewer faults, perhaps, and certainly fewer dazzling and bewildering beauties.[5]

This greater pictorial clarity, with its less complex imaginative challenge, was just what made it easier for the ordinary reader to absorb Tennyson's work, and thus the follower helped to pave the way for the master. It has already been shown how Tennyson tended to gain admission to the anthologies before Keats. Tennyson's second volume (*Poems*, 1832) confirmed his 'Keatsian' qualities—and was duly praised

[1] *The Poetical Works of John Keats*, Boston, 1854, ix.

[2] H. E. Rollins, *Keats' Reputation in America to 1848*, 29.

[3] *The Imperial Dictionary of Universal Biography*, 1857–63, iii. Division XII, 76.

[4] M. B. Forman and E. Blunden, 'Tributes and Allusions in Verse to Keats, During the Years 1816–1920', *Notes and Queries*, June–November 1947, May 1948.

[5] *New Monthly Magazine*, iii, Part I (1 March 1831), 111.

and assailed for them by the appropriate journals. In 1848, a review of Milnes's *Life* in *Fraser's*, significantly entitled 'Keats and his School', still suggested that Keats's 'real place in our literature is hardly yet determined', but conceded that 'he has had a hand in creating the taste of a considerable section of his countrymen', including Tennyson's—which, however, was sounder, because Tennyson lived among Cambridge Apostles instead of London Cockneys. Tennyson was, in fact, a sort of *Reader's Digest* version of Keats:

> Mr Tennyson . . . gives all, or nearly all that Keats gives, only in a more satisfactory way: the display of his treasures is less astonishing, perhaps, at the moment, but more ultimately effective, from the pains which have been spent in avoiding all useless extravagance, any mere commonplace strokes of art, so that the spectator is rarely if ever dazzled by unseasonable magnificence, or drawn off from the enjoyment of some graceful piece of workmanship to attend to the curious quaintness of the details.[1]

By this time it was unusual for anyone interested in literature not to have read Keats. 'He has held his throne now long enough for mere possession to give him undisputed right', asserted the *Westminster Review* in 1849.[2] So Hunt's prediction that the details given in *Lord Byron and Some of His Contemporaries* would prove not to be trivial 'because his readers will not think them so twenty years hence' had been exactly justified.

It is an appropriate convention to take R. M. Milnes's *Life, Letters and Literary Remains* (No. 57) as the dividing-line between Keats's obscurity and his fame. The moment was ideal: a biography could succeed in 1848 because of the interest in Keats that was already quickening, and by its success could give that interest a strong push in the right direction. So far as it was 'composition', the book was rather pedantic and evasive, but Milnes preferred to call it a 'compilation', and his Boswellian method of narrating as much as possible through the writings of the subject himself was a great success. Substantial parts of Keats's letters were now made public for the first time, and these, above all, immediately began to make the poet seem a greater man. Whether from caution or conviction, however, Milnes's own claims were very modest: 'let us never forget, that wonderful as are the poems of Keats, yet, after all, they are rather the records of a poetical education than the accomplished work of the mature artist.' This was to remain orthodoxy

[1] *Fraser's Magazine*, xxxviii (November 1848), 502.

[2] January 1849, i. 349.

for another twenty years or more, and it was an attitude that disarmed constructive as well as destructive criticism.

(II) 1848–1900

A less predictable impetus was now given to Keats's progress by the cult of his poems which developed among the painter-poets associated with Dante Gabriel Rossetti, although these expressed their homage mainly in shapes and colours. The pictorial possibilities of Keats's verse were exciting; and it is noticeable that in the later reviews the passage most frequently quoted was the one describing Madeline preparing for bed in the moonlight—'the Prayer at the Painted Window', as Leigh Hunt called it. The discovery of Keats seems to have been made by several of the Pre-Raphaelites independently. William Bell Scott had admired him since 1832, and Holman Hunt since his (undated) fourpenny bargain on the bookstall. Holman Hunt, in his turn, was unknown to Rossetti before exhibiting his picture 'The Eve of St. Agnes' in 1848, when, in Hunt's words, 'Rossetti came up to me . . . loudly declaring that my picture . . . was the best in the collection.'[1] From this time throughout the sixties scenes from Keats's poems, as well as scenes from Tennyson's, were frequently painted and exhibited. Millais's 'Lorenzo at the House of Isabella' (1849) was followed by his 'Mariana' (1851) and his 'Eve of St. Agnes' (1863); Arthur Hughes also painted an 'Eve of St. Agnes' (1856), and Holman Hunt an 'Isabella and the Pot of Basil' (1868); while in the fifties Rossetti himself made drawings from 'La Belle Dame Sans Merci'. About 1868 William Morris acknowledged to Cowden Clarke his debt to 'Keats, of whom I have such boundless admiration, and whom I venture to call one of my masters'.[2]

What attracted the Pre-Raphaelites and their followers to Keats's verse was not only its sensationalism and its antique colour, but its assumed remoteness from practical life. The relationship in Victorian art between otherworldliness and fact—what Humphry House diagnosed as 'the imposition of feeling as an afterthought upon literalness'[3]—is far from simple, either in Tennyson's poetry or in Rossetti's painting, but there was certainly a tendency to polarize *art* and *industrial civilization*, and therefore some disposition to see Poesy

[1] *Pre-Raphaelitism and the Pre-Raphaelite Brotherhood*, 72.

[2] J. W. Mackail, *Life of William Morris*, 1907, i. 200.

[3] *All in Due Time*, 1955, 141.

as an alternative to Life. The poet who crowned his sage tutor Apollonius with thistle and who drank 'confusion to mathematics' appealed to the aesthetic fastidiousness which reached a climax in the nineties (Oscar Wilde was a great admirer of Keats) and which left its mark on subsequent criticism. Hallam in his manifesto of 1831 (No. 46) had pointed the way:

> [Shelley and Keats] are both poets of sensation rather than reflection. Susceptible of the slightest impulse from external nature, their fine organs trembled into emotion at colours, and sounds, and movements, unperceived or unregarded by duller temperaments. . . . Other poets *seek* for images to illustrate their conceptions; these men had no need to seek; they lived in a world of images.

The life of art was another and a higher life. So in 1926 H. W. Garrod could declare that Keats's 'best work, his purest work, we get from him only when . . . he falls back upon an order of things where nothing cries or strives, nothing asks questions or answers them.'[1]

But if many artists and critics commended Keats's disdain of science and social life, many Victorian critics and moralists deplored it. G. H. Lewes in 1848 had expressed himself almost in Garrod's words, but it was to expose the limitations of Keats's attitude, not to endorse it: 'He will always remain in our literature as a marvellous specimen of what mere sensuous imagery can create in poetry. . . . He questioned nothing. He strove to penetrate no problems. He was content to feel and to sing.'[2] The historian of English poetry, W. J. Courthope, agreed in 1872 that Keats's 'immediate successors have . . . monopolised the field of poetry and silenced opposition', but thought it was due to Keats's 'intellectual opium-eating' that those successors had become alienated from contemporary life:

> As far as we know, there is not in the poems of Keats a single allusion to passing events, there is certainly nothing to show that he was interested in them. . . . Too soft and sensuous by nature to be exhilarated by the conflict of modern opinions, he found at once food for his love of beauty, and an opiate for his despondency, in the remote tales of Greek mythology.[3]

Such a self-indulgent refusal to grapple with the stern problems of life argued weakness of character. There had always been those who seemed to imply that Keats, like the first Mrs Dombey, need not have

[1] *Keats*, 1926, 2nd edition 1939, 133.
[2] *British Quarterly Review*, viii (November 1848), 329.
[3] *Quarterly Review*, cxxxii (January 1872), 61.

died if only he had made an effort;[1] and in the age when self-discipline was so obligatory a virtue, Haydon's tales of Keats's intemperance, and of his epicurean experiments with claret and pepper, encouraged disapproval, not only from Englishmen. Louis Étienne in 1867, with a slight Continental shift of perspective, took a similar view:

He is undeniably a very attractive figure, this twenty-five-year-old Epimenides, this Ionian youth from the days of Homer, who had slept in the cave of the nymphs and now awakens among Britons and Picts; but is it not obvious that he can never acclimatize himself on this dull soil, under a pale grey sky? . . . Keats is perhaps the least English of the poets produced by Great Britain during our century. He lacks that *manliness* [the English word is used] whose first impulse is to emerge from sterile dreams and effeminate lamentation, to accept what cannot be altered and make the best of it.[2]

In the United States, Walt Whitman's attitude to Keats's poetry had a more practical emphasis: 'Of life in the nineteenth century it has none, any more than statues have. It does not come home at all to the direct wants of the bodies and souls of the century.'[3] For Cardinal Wiseman (No. 67) the failure of staying-power was both moral and religious: Keats might have been unrivalled in his depiction of natural beauty 'had his moral faculties been equal to his perceptive organisation.'

But it was some of Keats's exact contemporaries, such as the poet George Darley, and Thomas Carlyle, who most trenchantly maintained the view that Keats's work represented mere sensuality without substance. Darley's own style was indebted to that of Keats, yet his disapproval was strong:

Keats has written many beautiful passages, but the general character of his poetry cannot be too much condemned—beyond all other injurious to a taste not yet formed. It is 'sicklied o'er with the very palest cast of thought,' & at best resembles one of those beauties who fed upon rose-leaves instead of wholesome flesh, fish, & fowl.[4]

[1] e.g. Abraham Hayward on Keats, *Quarterly Review*, lxv (March 1840), 463–4: 'we have no sympathy for your pretended men of genius who die under the lash of a critic. Ambition should be made of sterner stuff.'

[2] 'Le Paganisme poétique en Angleterre', *Revue des Deux Mondes*, lxix, Part 1 (15 May 1867), 297–8.

[3] Quoted from MS. note, *c.* 1846–8, by Iris Origo, *Times Literary Supplement*, 23 April 1970, 458.

[4] Letter to Miss Darley, 9 January 1842, *Life and Letters of George Darley*, ed. C. C. Abbott, 1928, 239.

Carlyle's distaste was stronger still. About 1849 he told Milnes: 'Keats is a miserable creature, hungering after sweets which he can't get; going about saying, "I am so hungry; I should so like something pleasant!" '[1] Twenty years later his opinion had only become more epigrammatic: 'Keats wanted a world of treacle!'[2] His poetry was bound to reflect this lack of moral fibre: 'the whole consists in a weak-eyed maudlin sensibility, and a certain vague random tunefulness of nature.'[3] The underlying sexual resentment showed up more distinctly in Mrs Carlyle's verdict: 'Almost any young gentleman with a sweet tooth might be expected to write such things. "Isabella" might have been written by a seamstress who had eaten something too rich for supper and slept upon her back.'[4] (Did she really mean the 'Eve of St. Agnes'?)

This sort of socio-sexual revulsion is an oddly persistent feature of Keats criticism. One of *Endymion's* earliest reviewers (No. 14) had surprisingly found in the poem 'imaginations better adapted to the stews', and of course the revulsion had been explicit in *Blackwood's* ('he wrote *indecently*, probably in the indulgence of his social propensities';[5] 'He outhunted Hunt in a species of emasculated pruriency, that . . . looks as if it were the product of some imaginative Eunuch's muse within the melancholy inspiration of the Haram'[6]). Its origin seems to lie in the disturbance created by a deep response to Keats's poetic sensuality[7] in conflict with a strong urge towards sexual apartheid. At any rate, Byron's astonishing outbursts (Nos. 20c, d) must have had some such components. That is, it was more or less accepted—since Crabbe and Wordsworth had insisted on it—that the domestic emotions of the lower classes were a fit subject for poetry; but that a poet of the lower classes should play with *erotic* emotions was insufferable, unless these were expressed in a straightforward peasant dialect, as with Burns or Clare.

The publication of Keats's letters to Fanny Brawne in 1878 caused shock and distaste, and temporarily revived the fading image of a self-indulgent man helplessly at the mercy of his sensations. It was probably Matthew Arnold's famous essay of 1880, originally prefacing a selection

[1] Wemyss Reid, *Life, Letters, and Friendships of R. M. Milnes*, 1890, i. 435.

[2] *William Allingham's Diary* (1907), ed. H. Allingham and D. Radford, 1967, 205. The entry is under 1871.

[3] *Edinburgh Review*, xlviii (December 1828), 301.

[4] *William Allingham's Diary* (under 20 March 1881), 310.

[5] *Blackwood's*, x, Part II (December 1821), 697.

[6] *Blackwood's* xviii (January 1826), xxvi.

[7] Bagehot noted of Shelley, Keats, and Tennyson that their poetry was 'written, almost professedly, for young people . . . of rather heated imaginations.' (No. 64c).

of Keats's poems,[1] that did most to preserve critical sanity. Arnold was ambivalent about Keats (No. 59), simultaneously attracted and disapproving, but he firmly discounted the Fanny Brawne revelations. He refused to judge, he said, letters written 'under the throttling and unmanning grasp of mortal disease'. Instead he found 'the elements of high character' in Keats, as well as 'the effort to develop them'; there was 'flint and iron in him', and in his poems 'that stamp of high work which is akin to character, which is character passing into intellectual production'. The passion of his poetry was 'an intellectual and spiritual passion'. Gradually this view passed into orthodoxy. By the turn of the century, Byron's proverbial remark that the poet had been snuffed out 'just as he really promised something great' was being completely reversed; for Francis Thompson, all Keats's promise had been fulfilled, and he had

died in perfect time,
In predecease of his just-sickening song.[2]

(III) SINCE 1900

It is not possible to indicate even in outline the course of twentieth-century criticism of Keats, which has been uninterrupted and many-directional. Although different paths have been followed, however, criticism has not committed itself to opposite and sometimes irreconcilable viewpoints, as in Shelley's case. The single, hard-won achievement of the century following his death was the almost universal acceptance of an 'integrated' Keats, a poet whose extraordinary inventive resources, imaginative and linguistic—which had always been recognized—cannot be separated from a brilliant and versatile intelligence. Study of his letters, above all, has brought this about: those letters which, according to T. S. Eliot, 'are certainly the most notable and the most important ever written by any English poet';[3] and from A. C. Bradley's lecture published in 1909[4] to Lionel Trilling's essay half a century later,[5] and beyond, practically every reader has sought in their qualities and insights a deeper understanding of the work as a

[1] T. H. Ward, *The English Poets*, 1880, iv, 427–64.
[2] 'The Cloud's Swan-Song', *New Poems*, 1897.
[3] *The Use of Poetry and the Use of Criticism*, 1933, 100.
[4] *Oxford Lectures on Poetry*, 1909, 209–44.
[5] 'The Poet as Hero: Keats in his Letters', in *The Opposing Self*, New York, 1955, 3–49.

whole. Perhaps it is broadly true to say that while Keats's contemporaries saw the Titanic *Hyperion* as the summit of his achievement, and the later nineteenth century the pictorial 'Eve of St. Agnes', modern interest has placed the symbolic Odes at the centre, especially the 'Ode on a Grecian Urn', and tends to underestimate the 'social' meaning in his work. But Keats's poetry was too firmly attached to the realities of the world he lived in—to all its realities—for such neglect to continue very long.

FIRST PROMISE

1. A wanderer in the fields of fancy

1816

Poem entitled 'To a Poetical Friend', signed 'G.F.M.', in the *European Magazine, and London Review*, (October 1816), lxx, 365.

George Felton Mathew, a few months older than Keats and author of a review of his *Poems* (No. 6), worked in business and on the Poor Law Commission. He had known Keats for some years in 1816 and had received one of Keats's verse Epistles (November 1815), which is quoted in this poem. Although the poem praises early 'tales of chivalry' in the manner of 'Calidore' and 'Specimen of an Induction to a Poem', it is in the metre of Keats's 'On Receiving a curious Shell', which was addressed to Mathew's cousins Caroline and Ann, and it quotes the last two lines of Keats's sonnet beginning 'O Solitude!'

O thou who delightest in fanciful song,
  And tellest strange tales of the elf and the fay;
Of giants tyrannic, whose talismans strong
  Have power to charm gentle damsels astray;

Of courteous knights-errant, and high-mettled steeds;
  Of forests enchanted, and marvellous streams;—
Of bridges, and castles, and desperate deeds;
  And all the bright fictions of fanciful dreams:—

Of captures, and rescues, and wonderful loves;
  Of blisses abounding in dark leafy bowers;—
Of murmuring music in shadowy groves,
  And beauty reclined on her pillow of flowers:—

O where did thine infancy open its eyes?
And who was the nurse that attended thy spring?—
For sure thou'rt exotic to these frigid skies,
So splendid the song that thou lovest to sing.

Perhaps thou hast traversed the glorious East;
And like the warm breath of its sun, and its gales,
That wander 'mid gardens of flowers to feast,
Are tinctured with every rich sweet that prevails?

O no!—for a Shakspeare—a Milton are ours!
And who e'er sung sweeter, or stronger than they?
As thine is, I ween was the spring of *their* powers;
Like theirs, is the cast of thine earlier lay.

It is not the climate, or scenery round,
It was not the nurse that attended thy youth,
That gave thee those blisses which richly abound
In magical numbers to charm, and to soothe.

O no!—'tis the Queen of those regions of air—
The gay fields of Fancy—thy spirit has blest;
She cherish'd thy childhood with fostering care,
And nurtur'd her boy with the milk of her breast.

She tended thee ere thou couldst wander alone,
And cheer'd thy wild walks amidst terror and dread;—
She sung thee to sleep with a song of her own,
And laid thy young limbs on her flowery bed.

She gave thee those pinions with which thou delightest
Sublime o'er her boundless dominions to rove;
The tongue too she gave thee with which thou invitest
Each ear to thy stories of wonder and love.

And when evening shall free thee from Nature's decays,*
And release thee from Study's severest control,
Oh warm thee in Fancy's enlivening rays,
And wash the dark spots of disease from thy soul.

* Alluding to his medical character.

And let not the spirit of Poesy sleep;
  Of Fairies and Genii continue to tell—
Nor suffer the innocent deer's timid leap
  To fright the wild bee from her flowery bell.

2. Leigh Hunt introduces a new poet

1816

Extract from a notice headed 'Young Poets' in *Examiner*, (1 December 1816), No. 466, 761–2.

James Henry Leigh Hunt (1784–1859), journalist and poet, was Keats's earliest, most generous, and most constant champion, although by an unlucky irony his championship, as editor of a Radical weekly that was at war both with the governing classes and their standards of literary taste, caused most of Keats's troubles and came to put a severe strain on their friendship (see Introduction, pp. 5–6). The reference to 'the departure of the old school' was to a recent review of Swift's *Works* in the *Edinburgh Review* (September 1816), xxvii, 1–58, in which the editor had said: 'We are of opinion . . . that the writers who adorned the beginning of the last century have been eclipsed by those of our own time . . . the present times—in which the revolution in our literature has been accelerated and confirmed by the concurrence of many causes . . . have created an effectual demand for more profound speculation, and more serious emotion than was dealt in by the writers of the former century.'

In sitting down to this subject, we happen to be restricted by time to a much shorter notice than we could wish; but we mean to take it up again shortly. Many of our readers however have perhaps observed for themselves, that there has been a new school of poetry rising of late, which promises to extinguish the French one that has prevailed among us since the time of Charles the 2d. It began with something excessive, like most revolutions, but this gradually wore away; and an evident aspiration after real nature and original fancy remained, which called to mind the finer times of the English Muse. In fact it is wrong to call it a new school, and still more so to represent it as one of innovation, it's only object being to restore the same love of Nature, and of *thinking* instead of mere *talking*, which formerly rendered us real poets, and not merely versifying wits, and bead-rollers of couplets.

We were delighted to see the departure of the old school acknowledged in the number of the *Edinburgh Review* just published,—a candour the more generous and spirited, inasmuch as that work has hitherto been the greatest surviving ornament of the same school in prose and criticism, as it is now destined, we trust, to be still the leader in the new. . . .

The object of the present article is merely to notice three young writers, who appear to us to promise a considerable addition of strength to the new school.

[The first two writers are Shelley, and J. H. Reynolds.]

The last of these young aspirants whom we have met with, and who promise to help the new school to revive Nature and

To put a spirit of youth in every thing,—

is, we believe, the youngest of them all, and just of age. His name is JOHN KEATS. He has not yet published any thing except in a newspaper; but a set of his manuscripts was handed us the other day, and fairly surprised us with the truth of their ambition, and ardent grappling with Nature. In the following Sonnet there is one incorrect rhyme, which might be easily altered, but which shall serve in the mean time as a peace-offering to the rhyming critics. The rest of the composition, with the exception of a little vagueness in calling the regions of poetry 'the realms of gold', we do not hesitate to pronounce excellent, especially the last six lines. The word *swims* is complete; and the whole conclusion is equally powerful and quiet:—

[Quotes 'On First Looking into Chapman's Homer' in full.]

We have spoken with the less scruple of these poetical promises, because we really are not in the habit of lavishing praises and announcements, and because we have no fear of any pettier vanity on the part of young men, who promise to understand human nature so well.

3. Wordsworth on Keats

1817, 1820

William Wordsworth (1770–1850), always thrifty in his praise of others, was nevertheless the first major poet to express admiration of Keats's work. There are several versions of the incident related in Extract (b), which must have occurred in December 1817, but although the locale and the witnesses are disputed, the facts are no doubt substantially as Haydon gives them.

(a) Extract from letter, 20 January 1817, to B. R. Haydon: 'Your account of young Keats interests me not a little; and the sonnet ['Great spirits now on earth are sojourning'] appears to be of good promise, of course neither you nor I being so highly complimented in the composition can be deemed judges altogether impartial—but it is assuredly vigorously conceived and well expressed; Leigh Hunt's compliment is well deserved, and the sonnet is very agreeably concluded.' (*Letters of William and Dorothy Wordsworth*, ed. E. de Selincourt, revised by Mary Moorman and A. G. Hill (1970), ii. Part ii, 360–1.)

(b) Extract from letter of B. R. Haydon, 29 November 1845, probably to Edward Moxon: 'When Wordsworth came to Town, I brought Keats to him, by his Wordsworths desire—Keats expressed to me as we walked to Queen Anne St East where Mr Monkhouse Lodged, the greatest, the purest, the most unalloyed pleasure at the prospect. Wordsworth received him kindly, & after a few minutes, Wordsworth asked him what he had been lately doing, *I* said he has just finished an exquisite ode to Pan—and as he had not a copy I begged Keats to repeat it—which he did in his usual half chant, (most touching) walking up & down the room—when he had done I felt really, as if I had heard a young Apollo—Wordsworth drily said

'a Very pretty piece of Paganism—[']

This was unfeeling, & unworthy of his high Genius to a young Worshipper like Keats—& Keats felt it *deeply*—so that if Keats has said any thing severe about our Friend; it was because he was wounded—and though he dined with Wordsworth after at my table—he never forgave him.

It was nonsense of Wordsworth to take it as a bit of Paganism for the Time, the Poet ought to have been a Pagan for the time—and if Wordsworth's puling Christian feelings were annoyed—it was rather ill-bred to hurt a youth, at such a moment when he actually trembled, like the String of a Lyre, when it has been touched.' (*The Keats Circle: Letters and Papers 1816–1878* (Cambridge, Mass., 1948), ed. H. E. Rollins, ii. 143–4.)

(c) Extract from letter, 16 January 1820, to B. R. Haydon: 'How is Keates, he is a youth of promise too great for the sorry company he keeps.' (*Letters of William and Dorothy Wordsworth*, ii. Part ii, 578.)

POEMS

March 1817

4. Unsigned review by J. H. Reynolds, *Champion*

9 March 1817, 78–81

John Hamilton Reynolds (1794–1852), later an unsuccessful solicitor, was a witty and lively writer when Keats knew him, one of the three 'Young Poets' brought into notice by Leigh Hunt (No. 2), and author of the first parody of Wordsworth's *Peter Bell*—a parody which Keats in turn reviewed in the *Examiner* (25 April 1819).

Here is a little volume filled throughout with very graceful and genuine poetry. The author is a very young man, and one, as we augur from the present work, that is likely to make a great addition to those who would overthrow that artificial taste which French criticism has long planted amongst us. At a time when nothing is talked of but the power and passion of Lord Byron, and the playful and elegant fancy of Moore, and the correctness of Rogers, and the sublimity and pathos of Campbell (these terms we should conceive are kept ready composed in the Edinburgh Review-shop) a young man starts suddenly before us, with a genius that is likely to eclipse them all. He comes fresh from nature,—and the originals of his images are to be found in her keeping. Young writers are in general in their early productions imitators of their favourite poet; like young birds that in their first songs, mock the notes of those warblers, they hear the most, and love the best; but this youthful poet appears to have tuned his voice in solitudes,—to have sung from the pure inspiration of nature. In the simple meadows he has proved that he can

> —See shapes of light aerial lymning
> And catch soft floating from a faint heard hymning.

We find in his poetry the glorious effect of summer days and leafy spots on rich feelings, which are in themselves a summer. He relies directly and wholly on nature. He marries poesy to genuine simplicity. He makes her artless,—yet abstains carefully from giving her an uncomely homeliness:—that is, he shows he can be familiar with nature, yet perfectly strange to the habits of common life. Mr Keats is faced, or 'we have no judgment in an honest face;' to look at natural objects with his mind, as Shakspeare and Chaucer did,—and not merely with his eye as nearly all modern poets do;—to clothe his poetry with a grand intellectual light,—and to lay his name in the lap of immortality. Our readers will think that we are speaking too highly of this young poet,—but luckily we have the power of making good the ground on which we prophesy so hardily. We shall extract largely from his volume:—it will be seen how familiar he is with all that is green, light, and beautiful in nature;—and with what an originality his mind dwells on all great or graceful objects. His imagination is very powerful,—and one thing we have observed with pleasure, that it never attempts to soar on undue occasions. The imagination, like the eagle on the rock, should keep its eye constantly on the sun,—and should never be started heavenward, unless something magnificent marred its solitude. Again, though Mr Keats' poetry is remarkably abstracted it is never out of reach of the mind; there are one or two established writers of this day who think that mystery is the soul of poetry—that artlessness is a vice—and that nothing can be graceful that is not metaphysical;—and even young writers have sunk into this error, and endeavoured to puzzle the world with a confused sensibility. We must however hasten to the consideration of the little volume before us, and not fill up our columns with observations, which extracts will render unnecessary.

The first poem in the book seems to have originated in a ramble in some romantic spot, 'with boughs pavillioned.' The poet describes a delightful time, and a little world of trees,—and refreshing streams,—and hedges of filberts and wild briar, and clumps of woodbine

> —taking the wind
> Upon their summer thrones;

and flowers opening in their early sunlight. He connects the love of poetry with these natural luxuries.

For what has made the sage or poet write,
But the fair paradise of Nature's light?

This leads him to speak of some of our olden tales; and here we must extract the passages describing those of Psyche, and Narcissus. The first is exquisitely written,

So felt he, who first told, how Psyche went
On the smooth wind to realms of wonderment;
What Psyche felt, and Love, when their full lips
First touch'd; what amorous and fondling nips
They gave each other's cheeks; with all their sighs,
And how they kist each other's tremulous eyes;
The silver lamp—the ravishment—the wonder—
The darkness—loneliness—the fearful thunder;
Their woes gone by, and both to heaven upflown,
To bow for gratitude before Jove's throne.

The following passage is not less beautiful,

[Quotes 'I stood tip-toe', lines 163–80, misquoting 'sad Echo's bale' as 'sad Echo's Vale'.]

This poem concludes with a brief but beautiful recital of the tale of Endymion,—to which indeed the whole poem seems to lean. The address to the Moon is extremely fine.

[Quotes 'I stood tip-toe', lines 113–24.]

The 'Specimen of an Induction to a Poem,' is exceedingly spirited,—as is the fragment of a Tale of Romance immediately following it; but we cannot stay to notice them particularly. These four lines from the latter piece are very sweet.

The side-long view of swelling leafiness,
Which the glad setting sun in gold doth dress;
Whence ever and anon the jay outsprings,
And scales upon the beauty of its wings.

The three poems following, addressed to Ladies, and the one to Hope are very inferior to their companions;—but Mr Keats informs us they were written at an earlier period than the rest. The imitation of Spenser is rich. The opening stanza is a fair specimen.

[Quotes 'Imitation of Spenser', lines 1–9.]

The two Epistles to his friends, and one to his brother are written with great ease and power. We shall extract two passages, both equally beautiful.

[Quotes 'Epistle to George Felton Mathew', lines 31–52.]

The next passage is from the opening of the poet's letter to a friend.

[Quotes 'To Charles Cowden Clarke', lines 1–20.]

Except in a little confusion of metaphor towards the end, the above passage is exquisitely imagined and executed.

A few Sonnets follow these epistles, and, with the exception of Milton's and Wordsworth's, we think them the most powerful ones in the whole range of English poetry. We extract the first in the collection, with the assurance that the rest are equally great.

[Quotes the sonnet 'To My Brother George', in full.]

We have been highly pleased with the Sonnet which speaks—

> Of fair hair'd Milton's eloquent distress,
> And all his love for gentle Lycid drown'd;—
> Of lovely Laura in her light green dress,
> And faithful Petrarch gloriously crown'd.

But the last poem in the volume, to which we are now come, is the most powerful and the most perfect. It is entitled 'Sleep and Poetry.' The poet passed a wakeful night at a brother poet's house, and has in this piece embodied the thoughts which passed over his mind. He gives his opinion of the Elizabethan age,—of the Pope's school,—and of the poetry of the present day. We scarcely know what to select,—we are so confused with beauties. In speaking of poetry, we find the following splendid passage:—

[Quotes 'Sleep and Poetry', lines 71–84, from 'Also imaginings' to 'immortality'.]

The following passage relating to the same event, is even greater. It is the very magic of imagination.

[Quotes 'Sleep and Poetry', lines 125–37, from 'For lo!' to 'trees and mountains'.]

We have not room to extract the passages on Pope and his followers, who,

—With a pulling force,
Sway'd them about upon a rocking horse,
And thought it Pegasus.

Nor can we give those on modern poets. We shall conclude our extracts with the following perfect and beautiful lines on the busts and pictures which hung around the room in which he was resting.

[Quotes 'Sleep and Poetry', lines 381–95.]

We conclude with earnestly recommending the work to all our readers. It is not without defects, which may be easily mentioned, and as easily rectified. The author, from his natural freedom of versification, at times passes to an absolute faultiness of measure:—This he should avoid. He should also abstain from the use of compound epithets as much as possible. He has a few of the faults which youth must have;—he is apt occasionally to make his descriptions overwrought,—But on the whole we never saw a book which had so little reason to plead youth as its excuse. The best poets of the day might not blush to own it.

We have had two Sonnets presented to us, which were written by Mr Keats, and which are not printed in the present volume. We have great pleasure in giving them to the public,—as well on account of their own power and beauty, as of the grandeur of the subjects; on which we have ourselves so often made observations.

[Quotes the sonnets 'To Haydon, with a Sonnet written on seeing the Elgin Marbles' ('Haydon! forgive me'), and 'On seeing the Elgin Marbles' ('My spirit is too weak'), in full.]

5. Unsigned notice, *Monthly Magazine*

April 1817, xliii, 248

A small volume of poems, by Mr Keats, has appeared; and it well deserves the notice it has attracted, by the sweetness and beauty of the composition. For the model of his style, the author has had recourse to the age of Elizabeth; and, if he has not wholly avoided the quaintness that characterizes the writings of that period, it must be allowed by every candid reader that the fertile fancy and beautiful diction of our old poets, is not unfrequently rivalled by Mr Keats. There is in his poems a rapturous glow and intoxication of the fancy—an air of careless and profuse magnificence in his diction—a revelry of the imagination and tenderness of feeling, that forcibly impress themselves on the reader.

6. G. F. Mathew on Keats's *Poems*, 1817

1817

Review signed 'G.F.M.' in the *European Magazine* (May 1817), lxxi, 434–7.

There are few writers more frequent or more presumptuous in their intrusions on the public than, we know not what to call them, versifiers, rhymists, metre-ballad mongers, what you will but poets. The productions of some among them rise, like the smoke of an obscure cottage, clog the air with an obtrusive vapour, and then fade away into oblivion and nothingness. The compositions of others equally ephemeral, but possessing, perhaps, a few eccentric features of originality, come upon us with a flash and an explosion, rising into the air like a rocket, pouring forth its short-lived splendour and then falling, like Lucifer, *never to rise again.*

The attention of the public, indeed, has been so frequently arrested and abused by these exhalations of ignorance, perverted genius, and presumption, that 'poems' has become a dull feature upon a title page, and it would be well for the more worthy candidates for regard and honour, particularly at this physiognomical, or, rather craniological period, could the spirit of an author be reflected there with more expressive fidelity. A quotation from, and a wood-engraving of *Spencer,* therefore, on the title page of Mr Keats's volume, is very judiciously and appropriately introduced as the poetical beauties of the volume we are about to review, remind us much of that elegant and romantic writer.

For the grand, elaborate, and abstracted music of nature our author has a fine ear, and now and then catches a few notes from passages of that never-ending harmony which God made to retain in exaltation and purity the spirits of our first parents. In 'places of Nestling green for poets made,' we have this gentle address to Cynthia:

[Quotes 'I stood tip-toe', lines 116–24, 'O Maker of sweet poets' to 'tell delightful stories'.]

And also in his last poem, concerning sleep, the following interrogations and apostrophes are very pleasing:

[Quotes 'Sleep and Poetry', lines 1–11, 'What is more gentle' to 'What, but thee, Sleep?', misprinting line 7 as 'More healthful than the leafings of dales?']

The volume before us indeed is full of imaginations and descriptions equally delicate and elegant with these; but, although we have looked into it with pleasure, and strongly recommend it to the perusal of all lovers of real poetry, we cannot, as another critic has injudiciously attempted, roll the name of Byron, Moore, Campbell and Rogers, into the milky way of literature, because Keats is pouring forth his splendors in the Orient. We do not imagine that the fame of one poet, depends upon the fall of another, or that our morning and our evening stars necessarily eclipse the constellations of the meridian.

Too much praise is more injurious than censure, and forms that magnifying lens, through which, the faults and deformities of its object are augmented and enlarged; while true merit looks more lovely beaming through the clouds of prejudice and envy, because it adds to admiration and esteem the association of superior feelings.

We cannot then advance for our author equal claim to public notice for maturity of thought, propriety of feeling, or felicity of style. But while we blame the slovenly independence of his versification, we must allow that thought, sentiment, and feeling, particularly in the active use and poetical display of them, belong more to the maturity of summer fruits than to the infancy of vernal blossoms; to that knowledge of the human mind and heart which is acquired only by observation and experience, than to the early age, or fervid imagination of our promising author. But if the gay colours and the sweet fragrance of bursting blossoms be the promise of future treasures, then may we prophecy boldly of the future eminence of our young poet, for we have no where found them so early or so beautifully displayed as in the pages of the volume before us.

The youthful architect may be discovered in the petty arguments of his principal pieces. These poetical structures may be compared to no gorgeous palaces, no solemn temples; and in his enmity to the French school, and to the Augustan age of England, he seems to have a principle, that plan and arrangement are prejudicial to natural poetry.

The principal conception of his first poem is the same as that of a contemporary author, Mr Wordsworth, and presumes that the most ancient poets, who are the inventors of the Heathen Mythology, imagined those fables chiefly by the personification of many appearances in nature; just as the astronomers of Egypt gave name and figure to many of our constellations, and as the late Dr Darwin ingeniously illustrated the science of Botany in a poem called 'the Loves of the Plants'.

After having painted a few 'places of nestling green, for poets made' thus Mr Keats:

[Quotes 'I stood tip-toe', lines 163–80, 'What first inspired a bard' to 'sad Echo's bale.']

In the fragment of a Tale of Romance, young Calidore is amusing himself in a little boat in the park, till, hearing the trumpet of the warder, which announces the arrival of his friends at the castle, he hastens home to meet them: in after times we presume he is to become the hero of some marvellous achievements, devoting himself, like

Quixotte, to the service of the ladies, redressing wrongs, dispelling the machinations of evil genii, encountering dragons, traversing regions aerial, terrestrial, and infernal, setting a price upon the heads of all giants, and forwarding them, trunkless, like 'a cargo of famed cestrian cheese,' as a dutiful tribute to the unrivalled beauty of his fair Dulcenea del Toboso. This fragment is as pretty and as innocent as childishness can make it, save that it savours too much,—as indeed do almost all these poems,—of the foppery and affectation of Leigh Hunt!

We shall pass over to the last of some minor pieces printed in the middle of the book, of superior versification, indeed, but of which, therefore, he seems to be partly ashamed, from a declaration that they were written earlier than the rest. These lines are spirited and powerful:

[Quotes the sonnet 'Ah! who can e'er forget so fair a being?' down to line 8, 'A dove-like bosom.']

There are some good sonnets; that on first looking into Chapman's Homer, although absurd in its application, is a fair specimen:

[Quotes the sonnet in full.]

'Till I heard Chapman speak out loud and bold' however is a bad line—not only as it breaks the metaphor—but as it blows out the whole sonnet into an unseemly hyperbole. Consistent with this sonnet is a passage in his 'Sleep and Poetry'.

[Quotes lines 181–206, 'a schism' to 'Boileau!', the last word misprinted 'BOILLARD!']

These lines are indeed satirical and poignant, but levelled at the author of 'Eloise', and of 'Windsor Forest', of the Essays and the Satires, they will form no sun, no centre of a system; but like the moon exploded from the South Sea, the mere satellite will revolve only around the head of its own author, and reflect upon him an unchanging face of ridicule and rebuke. Like Balaam's ass before the angel, offensive only to the power that goads it on.

We might transcribe the whole volume were we to point out every instance of the luxuriance of his imagination, and the puerility of his sentiments. With these distinguishing features, it cannot be but many passages will appear abstracted and obscure. Feeble and false thoughts are easily lost sight of in the redundance of poetical decoration.

To conclude, if the principal is worth encountering, or the passage worth quoting, he says:

[Quotes 'Sleep and Poetry', lines 259–72, 'let there nothing be' to 'hide my foolish face?']

Let not Mr Keats imagine that the sole end of poesy is attained by those

Who strive with the bright golden wing
Of genius, to flap away each sting
Thrown by the pitiless world.

But remember that there is a sublimer height to which the spirit of the muse may soar; and that her arm is able to uphold the adamantine shield of virtue, and guard the soul from those insinuating sentiments, so fatally inculcated by many of the most popular writers of the day, equally repugnant both to reason and religion, which, if they touch us with their poisoned points, will contaminate our purity, innoculate us with degeneracy and corruption, and overthrow among us the dominion of domestic peace and public liberty.

Religion and the love of virtue are not inconsistent with the character of a poet; they should shine like the moon upon his thoughts, direct the course of his enquiries, and illuminate his reflections upon mankind. We consider that the specimens here presented to our readers, will establish our opinion of Mr Keats's poetical imagination; but the mere luxuries of imagination, more especially in the possession of the proud egotist of diseased feelings and perverted principles, may become the ruin of a people—inculcate the falsest and most dangerous ideas of the condition of humanity—and refine us into the degeneracy of butterflies that perish in the deceitful glories of a destructive taper. These observations might be considered impertinent, were they applied to one who had discovered any incapacity for loftier flights—to one who could not appreciate the energies of Milton or of Shakspeare—to one who could not soar to the heights of poesy,—and ultimately hope to bind his brows with the glorious sunbeams of immortality.

7. Leigh Hunt announces a new school of poetry

1817

Unsigned review, *Examiner*, (1 June 1817), No. 492, 345; (6 July 1817), No. 497, 428–9; (13 July 1817), No. 498, 443–4.

This is the production of the young writer, whom we had the pleasure of announcing to the public a short time since, and several of whose Sonnets have appeared meanwhile in the *Examiner* with the signature of J. K. From these and stronger evidences in the book itself, the readers will conclude that the author and his critic are personal friends; and they are so,—made however, in the first instance, by nothing but his poetry, and at no greater distance of time than the announcement above-mentioned. We had published one of his Sonnets in our paper, without knowing more of him than any other anonymous correspondent; but at the period in question, a friend brought us one morning some copies of verses, which he said were from the pen of a youth. We had not been led, generally speaking, by a good deal of experience in these matters, to expect pleasure from introductions of the kind, so much as pain; but we had not read more than a dozen lines, when we recognized 'a young poet indeed.'

It is no longer a new observation, that poetry has of late years undergone a very great change, or rather, to speak properly, poetry has undergone no change, but something which was not poetry has made way for the return of something which is. The school which existed till lately since the restoration of Charles the 2d, was rather a school of wit and ethics in verse, than any thing else; nor was the verse, with the exception of Dryden's, of the best order. The authors, it is true, are to be held in great honour. Great wit there certainly was, excellent satire, excellent sense, pithy sayings; and Pope distilled as much real poetry as could be got from the drawing-room world in which the art then lived,—from the flowers and luxuries of artificial life,—into that exquisite little toilet-bottle of essence, the *Rape of the Lock*. But there was little imagination, of a higher order, no intense feeling of nature, no sentiment, no real music or variety. Even the writers who gave evidences meanwhile of a truer poetical faculty, Gray, Thomson, Akenside, and Collins himself, were content with a great deal of second-hand workmanship, and with false styles made up of other languages and a certain kind of inverted cant. It has been thought that Cowper was the first poet who re-opened the true way to nature and a natural style; but we hold this to be a mistake, arising merely from certain negations on the part of that amiable but by no means powerful writer. Cowper's style is for the most part as inverted and artificial as that of the others; and we look upon him to have been by nature not so great a poet as Pope: but Pope, from certain infirmities on his part, was thrown into the society of the world, and thus had to get what he could out of an artificial sphere:—Cowper, from other and more distressing infirmities, (which by the way the wretched superstition that undertook to heal, only burnt in upon him) was confined to a still smaller though more natural sphere, and in truth did not much with it, though quite as much perhaps as was to be expected from an organization too sore almost to come in contact with any thing.

It was the Lake Poets in our opinion (however grudgingly we say it, on some accounts) that were the first to revive a true taste for nature; and like most Revolutionists, especially of the cast which they have since turned out to be, they went to an extreme, calculated rather at first to make the readers of poetry disgusted with originality and adhere with contempt and resentment to their magazine common-places. This had a bad effect also in the way of re-action; and none of those writers have ever since been able to free themselves from certain stubborn affectations, which having been ignorantly confounded by others with the better part of them, have been retained by their self-love with a still less pardonable want of wisdom. The greater part indeed of the poetry of Mr Southey, a weak man in all respects, is really made up of little else. Mr Coleridge still trifles with his poetical as he has done with his metaphysical talent. Mr Lamb, in our opinion, has a more real tact of humanity, a modester, Shakspearean wisdom, than any of them; and had he written more, might have delivered the school victoriously from all its defects. But it is Mr Wordsworth who has advanced it the most, and who in spite of some morbidities as well as mistaken theories in other respects, has opened upon us a fund of thinking and imagination, that ranks him as the successor of the true and abundant poets of the older time. Poetry, like Plenty, should be represented with a cornucopia, but it should be a real one; not swelled out and insidiously *optimized* at the top, like Mr Southey's stale strawberry baskets, but fine and full to the depth, like a heap from the vintage. Yet from the time of Milton till lately, scarcely a tree had been planted that could be called a poet's own. People got shoots from France, that ended in nothing but a little barren wood, from which they made flutes for young gentlemen and fan-sticks for ladies. The rich and enchanted ground of real poetry, fertile with all that English succulence could produce, bright with all that Italian sunshine could lend, and haunted with exquisite humanities, had become invisible to mortal eyes like the garden of Eden:—

And from that time those Graces were not found.

These Graces, however, are re-appearing; and one of the greatest evidences is the little volume before us; for the work is not one of mere imitation, or a compilation of ingenious and promising things that merely announce better, and that after all might only help to keep up a bad system; but here is a young poet giving himself up to his own impressions, and revelling in real poetry for its own sake. He has had his advantages, because others have cleared the way into those happy bowers; but it shews the strength of his natural tendency, that he has not been turned aside by the lingering enticements of a former system, and by the self-love which interests others in enforcing them. We do not, of course, mean to say, that Mr Keats has as much talent as he will have ten years hence, or that there are no imitations in his book, or that he does not make mistakes common to inexperience;—the reverse is inevitable at his time of life. In proportion to our ideas, or impressions of the images of things, must be our acquaintance with the things themselves. But our author has all the sensitiveness of temperament requisite to receive these impressions; and wherever he has turned hitherto, he has evidently felt them deeply.

The very faults indeed of Mr Keats arise from a passion for beauties, and a young impatience to vindicate them; and as we have mentioned these, we shall refer to them at once. They may be comprised in two;—first, a tendency to notice every thing too indiscriminately and without an eye to natural proportion and effect; and second, a sense of the proper variety of versification without a due consideration of its principles.

The former error is visible in several parts of the book, but chiefly though mixed with great beauties in the Epistles, and more between pages 28 and 47, where are collected the author's earliest pieces, some of which, we think, might have been omitted, especially the string of magistrate-interrogatories about a shell and a copy of verses. See also (p. 61) a comparison of wine poured out in heaven to the appearance of a falling star, and (p. 62) the sight of far-seen fountains in the same region to 'silver streaks across a dolphin's fin.' It was by thus giving way to every idea that came across him, that Marino, a man of real poetical fancy, but no judgment, corrupted the poetry of Italy; a catastrophe, which however we by no means anticipate from our author, who with regard to this point is much more deficient in age than in good taste. We shall presently have to notice passages of a reverse nature, and these are by far the most numerous. But we warn him against a fault, which is the more tempting to a young writer of genius, inasmuch as it involves something so opposite to the contented common-place and vague generalities of the late school of poetry. There is a super-abundance of detail, which, though not so wanting, of course, in power of perception, is as faulty and unseasonable sometimes as common-place. It depends upon circumstances, whether we are to consider ourselves near enough, as it were, to the subject we are describing to grow microscopical upon it. A person basking in a landscape for instance, and a person riding through it, are in two very different situations for the exercise of their eyesight; and even where the license is most allowable, care must be taken not to give to small things and great, to nice detail and to general feeling, the same proportion of effect. Errors of this kind in poetry answer to a want of perspective in painting, and of a due distribution of light and shade. To give an excessive instance in the former art, there was Denner, who copied faces to a nicety amounting to a horrible want of it, like Brobdignagian visages encountered by Gulliver; and who, according to the facetious Peter Pindar,

> Made a bird's beak appear at twenty mile.

And the same kind of specimen is afforded in poetry by Darwin, a writer now almost forgotten and deservedly, but who did good in his time by making unconscious caricatures of all the poetical faults in vogue, and flattering himself that the sum total went to the account of his original genius. Darwin would describe a dragon-fly and a lion in the same terms of proportion. You did not know which he would have scrambled from the sooner. His pictures were like the two-penny sheets which the little boys buy, and in which you see J Jackdaw and K King, both of the same dimensions.

Mr Keats's other fault, the one in his versification, arises from a similar cause,—that of contradicting over-zealously the fault on the opposite side. It is this which provokes him now and then into mere roughnesses and discords for their own sake, not for that of variety and contrasted harmony. We can manage, by substituting a greater feeling for a smaller, a line like the following:—

I shall roll on the grass with two-fold ease;—

but by no contrivance of any sort can we prevent this from jumping out of the heroic measure into mere rhythmicality,—

How many bards gild the lapses of time!

We come now however to the beauties; and the reader will easily perceive that they not only outnumber the faults a hundred fold, but that they are of a nature decidedly opposed to what is false and inharmonious. Their characteristics indeed are a fine ear, a fancy and imagination at will, and an intense feeling of external beauty in it's most natural and least expressible simplicity.

We shall give some specimens of the least beauty first, and conclude with a noble extract or two that will shew the second, as well as the powers of our young poet in general. The harmony of his verses will appear throughout.

The first poem consists of a piece of luxury in a rural spot, ending with an allusion to the story of Endymion and to the origin of other lovely tales of mythology, on the ground suggested by Mr Wordsworth in a beautiful passage of his *Excursion*. Here, and in the other largest poem, which closes the book, Mr Keats is seen to his best advantage, and displays all that fertile power of association and imagery which constitutes the abstract poetical faculty as distinguished from every other. He wants age for a greater knowledge of humanity, but evidences of this also bud forth here and there.—To come however to our specimens:—

The first page of the book presents us with a fancy, founded, as all beautiful fancies are, on a strong sense of what really exists or occurs. He is speaking of

A gentle Air in Solitude

There crept
A little noiseless noise among the leaves,
Born of the very sigh that silence heaves.

Young Trees

There too should be
The frequent chequer of a youngling tree,
That with a score of light green brethren shoots
From the quaint mossiness of aged roots:
Round which is heard a spring-head of clear waters.

Any body who has seen a throng of young beeches, furnishing those natural clumpy seats at the root, must recognize the truth and grace of this description. The remainder of this part of the poem, especially from—

Open afresh your round of starry folds,
Ye ardent marigolds!—

down to the bottom of page 5, affords an exquisite proof of close observation of nature as well as the most luxuriant fancy.

The Moon

Lifting her silver rim
Above a cloud, and with a gradual swim
Coming into the blue with all her light.

Fir Trees

Fir trees grow around,
Aye dropping their hard fruit upon the ground.

This last line is in the taste of the Greek simplicity.

A starry Sky

The dark silent blue
With all it's diamonds trembling through and through.

Sound of a Pipe

And some are hearing eagerly the wild
Thrilling liquidity of dewy piping.

The 'Specimen of an Induction to a Poem', and the fragment of the Poem itself entitled 'Calidore', contain some very natural touches on the human side of things; as when speaking of a lady who is anxiously looking out on the top of a tower for her defender, he describes her as one

Who cannot feel for cold her tender feet;

and when Calidore has fallen into a fit of amorous abstraction, he says that

—The kind voice of good Sir Clerimond
Came to his ear, as something from beyond
His present being.

The Epistles, the Sonnets, and indeed the whole of the book, contain strong evidences of warm and social feelings, but particularly the 'Epistle to Charles Cowden Clarke', and the Sonnet to his own Brothers, in which the 'faint cracklings' of the coal-fire are said to be

Like whispers of the household gods that keep
A gentle empire o'er fraternal souls.

The Epistle to Mr Clarke is very amiable as well as poetical, and equally honourable to both parties,—to the young writer who can be so grateful towards his teacher, and to the teacher who had the sense to perceive his genius, and the qualities to call forth his affection. It consists chiefly of recollections of what his friend had pointed out to him in poetry and in general taste; and the lover of Spenser will readily judge of his preceptor's qualifications, even from a single triplet, in which he is described, with a deep feeling of simplicity, as one

Who had beheld Belphoebe in a brook,
And lovely Una in a leafy nook,
And Archimago leaning o'er his book.

The Epistle thus concludes:—

Picture of Companionship

[Quotes 'Epistle to Charles Cowden Clarke', lines 109, 115–30, which end:—]

'Life's very toys
With him,' said I, 'will take a pleasant charm;
It cannot be that ought will work him harm.'

And we can only add, without any disrespect to the graver warmth of our young poet, that if Ought attempted it, Ought would find he had stout work to do with more than one person.

The following passage in one of the Sonnets passes, with great happiness, from the mention of physical associations to mental; and concludes with a feeling which must have struck many a contemplative mind, that has found the sea-shore like a border, as it were, of existence.

He is speaking of

The Ocean

The Ocean with it's vastness, it's blue green,
It's ships, it's rocks, it's caves,—it's hopes, it's fears,—
It's voice mysterious, which whoso hears
Must think on what will be, and what has been.

We have read somewhere the remark of a traveller, who said that when he was walking alone at night-time on the sea-shore, he felt conscious of the earth, not as the common every day sphere it seems, but as one of the planets, rolling round him in the mightiness of space. The same feeling is common to imaginations that are not in need of similar local excitements.

The best poem is certainly the last and longest, entitled 'Sleep and Poetry'. It originated in sleeping in a room adorned with busts and pictures, and is a striking specimen of the restlessness of the young poetical appetite, obtaining its food by the very desire of it, and glancing for fit subjects of creation 'from earth to heaven.' Nor do we like it the less for an impatient, and as it may be thought by some, irreverend assault upon the late French school of criticism and monotony, which has held poetry chained long enough to render it somewhat indignant when it has got free.

The following ardent passage is highly imaginative:—

An Aspiration after Poetry

[Quotes 'Sleep and Poetry', lines 47–9, 'O Poesy!' to 'wide heaven', and lines 55–84, 'yet, to my ardent prayer' to 'immortality'.]

Mr Keats takes an opportunity, though with very different feelings towards the school than he has exhibited towards the one above-mentioned, to object to the morbidity that taints the productions of the Lake Poets. They might answer perhaps, generally, that they chuse to grapple with what is unavoidable, rather than pretend to be blind to it; but the more smiling Muse may reply, that half of the evils alluded to are produced by brooding over them; and that it is much better to strike at as many *causes* of the rest as possible, than to pretend to be satisfied with them in the midst of the most evident dissatisfaction.

Happy Poetry Preferred

[Quotes 'Sleep and Poetry', lines 230–47, 'These things are doubtless' to 'lift the thoughts of man'.]

We conclude with the beginning of the paragraph which follows this passage, and which contains an idea of as lovely and powerful a nature in embodying an abstraction, as we ever remember to have seen put into words:—

> Yet I rejoice: a myrtle fairer than
> E'er grew in Paphos, from the bitter weeds
> Lifts it's sweet head into the air, *and feeds*
> *A silent space with ever sprouting green.*

Upon the whole, Mr Keats's book cannot be better described than in a couplet written by Milton when he too was young, and in which he evidently alludes to himself. It is a little luxuriant heap of

> Such sights as youthful poets dream
> On summer eves by haunted stream.

8. A very facetious rhymer

1817

Unsigned review, *Eclectic Review*, (September 1817), n.s. viii, 267–75.

Josiah Conder (1789–1855), London proprietor of the *Eclectic Review*, was a journalist and nonconformist preacher with strong religious views. His article is the first to censure Keats's poetry for its 'forcible divorce from thought', while praising its taste and originality. (See also No. 36.)

There is perhaps no description of publication that comes before us, in which there is for the most part discovered less of what is emphatically denominated *thought*, than in a volume of miscellaneous poems. We do not speak of works which obviously bear the traits of incapacity in the Author. Productions of this kind abound in more than one department of literature; yet in some of those which rank at the very lowest degree of mediocrity, there is occasionally displayed a struggling effort of mind to do its best, which gives an interest and a character to what possesses no claims to originality of genius, or to intrinsic value. But poetry is that one class of written compositions, in which the business of expression seems often so completely to engross the Author's attention, as to suspend altogether that exercise of the rational faculties which we term *thinking*; as if in the same limited sense as that in which we speak of the arts of music and painting, poetry also might be termed an art; and in that case indeed the easiest of arts, as requiring less previous training of faculty, and no happy peculiarity either in the conformation of the organs, or in the acquired delicacy of the perceptions. So accustomed however are we to find poetry thus characterized, as consisting in the mysteries of versification and expression, so learnedly treated of in all the 'Arts of Poetry' extant, from Horace down to Mr Bysshe, that it is not surprising that the generality of those who sit down to write verses, should aim at no higher intellectual exertion, than the melodious arrangement of 'the cross readings of memory.' Poetry is an art, and it is an elegant art: and so is the writing of prose, properly speaking, an art likewise; and they are no otherwise distinguishable from each other, than as being different styles of composition suited to different modes of thought. Poetry is the more ornate, but not, perhaps, in its simpler forms, the more artificial style of the two: the purpose, however, to which it is directed, requires a more minute elaboration of expression, than prose. But what should we think of a person's professedly sitting down to write prose, or to read prose composition, without reference to any subject, or to the quality of the thoughts, without any definite object but the amusement afforded by the euphonous collocation of sentences? As a school exercise, the employment, no doubt, would be beneficial; but were the writer to proceed still further, and publish his prose, not for any important or interesting sentiment conveyed in his work, but as presenting polished specimens of the beautiful art of prose-writing, it would certainly be placed to the account of mental aberration.

On what ground, then, does the notion rest, that poetry is a something so sublime, or that so inherent a charm resides in words and syllables arranged in the form of verse, that the value of the composition is in any degree independent of the meaning which links together the sentences? We admit that rhythm and cadence, and rhymed couplets, have a pleasurable effect upon the ear, and more than this, that words have in themselves a power of awakening trains of association, when the ideas which they convey are very indistinct, and do not constitute or account for the whole impression. It may be added, that the perception of skill or successful art, is also attended with pleasurable emotions; and this circumstance forms, in addition to what we have already mentioned, a powerful ingredient in the whole combination of effect produced by genuine poetry: but that the mere art of setting words to the music of measure, should come to be regarded as the chief business of poetry, and the ultimate object of the writer, is so whimsical a prejudice, that after a brief exposition of the fact, it may be worth while to inquire a little into its cause.

As to the fact, it would be travelling too far out of the record, to make this notice of a small volume of poems, a pretence for instituting an examination of all the popular poets of the day. Suffice it to refer to the distinct schools into which they and their imitators, as incurable mannerists, are divided, as some evidence that mode of expression has come to form too much the distinguishing characteristic of modern poetry. Upon an impartial estimate of the intellectual quality of some of those poems which rank the highest in the public favour, it will be found to be really of a very humble description. As works of genius, they may deservedly rank high, because there is as much scope for genius in the achievements of art as in the energies of thought; but as productions of mind, in which respect their real value must after all be estimated, they lay the reader under small obligations. Wordsworth is by far the deepest thinker of our modern poets, yet he has been sometimes misled by a false theory, to adopt a puerile style of composition; and it is remarkable, that the palpable failure should be charged on his diction, which is attributable rather to the character of the thoughts themselves; they were not adapted to any form of poetical expression, inasmuch as they are not worth being expressed at all. Scott, of all our leading poets, though the most exquisite artist, occupies the lowest rank in respect to the intellectual quality of his productions. Scarcely an observation or a sentiment escapes him, in the whole compass of his poetry, that even the beauty of expression can render striking or worth being treasured up by the reader for after reference. The only passages recurred to with interest, or cited with effect, are those admirable specimens of scenic painting in which he succeeds beyond almost every poet, in making one see and hear whatever he describes. But when we descend from such writers as confessedly occupy the first rank, to the *οι πολλοι* of their imitators, respectable as many of them are, and far above mediocrity considered as artists, the characters of sterling thought, of intellect in action, become very faint and rare. It is evident that, in their estimation, to write poetry is an achievement which costs no laborious exercise of faculty; is an innocent recreation rather, to which the consideration of any moral purpose would be altogether foreign.

Now, on turning from the polished versification of the elegant *artists* of the present day, to the rugged numbers of our early poets, the most obvious feature in the refreshing contrast is, the life and the vividness of thought diffused over their poetry. We term this originality, and ascribe the effect either to their pre-eminent genius, or to the early age in which they flourished, which forced upon them the toil of invention. But originality forms by no means a test of intellectual pre-eminence; and we have proof sufficient, that originality does not necessarily depend on priority of time. Provided the person be capable of the requisite effort of abstraction, nothing more is necessary in order to his attaining a certain degree of originality, than that his thoughts should bear the stamp of individuality, which is impressed by self-reflective study. In the earlier stages of the arts, we behold mind acting from itself, through the medium of outward forms, consulting its own purpose as the rule of its working, and referring to nature as its only model. But when the same arts have reached the period of more refined cultivation, they cease to be considered as means through which to convey to other minds the energies of thought and feeling: the productions of art become themselves the ultimate objects of imitation, and the mind is acted upon by them instead of acting through them from itself. Mind cannot be imitated; art can be: and when imitative skill has brought an art the nearest to perfection, it is then that its cultivation is the least allied to mind: its original purpose, as a mode of expression, becomes wholly lost in the artificial object,—the display of skill.

We consider poetry as being in the present day in this very predicament; as being reduced by the increased facilities of imitation, to an elegant art, and as having suffered a forcible divorce from thought. Some of our young poets have been making violent efforts to attain originality, and in order to accomplish this, they have been seeking with some success for new models of imitation in the earlier poets, presenting to us as the result, something of the quaintness, as well as the freedom and boldness of expression characteristic of those writers, in the form and with the effect of novelties. But after all, this specious sort of originality lies wholly in the turn of expression; it is only the last effort of the cleverness of skill to turn eccentric, when the perfection of correctness is no longer new. We know of no path to legitimate originality, but one, and that is, by restoring poetry to its true dignity as a vehicle for noble thoughts and generous feelings, instead of rendering meaning the mere accident of verse. Let the comparative insignificance of art be duly appreciated, and let the purpose and the meaning be considered as giving the expression all its value; and then, so long as men think and feel for themselves, we shall have poets truly and simply original.

We have no hesitation in pronouncing the Author of these Poems, to be capable of writing good poetry, for he has the requisite fancy and skill which constitute the talent. We cannot, however, accept this volume as any thing more than an immature promise of possible excellence. There is, indeed, little in it that is positively good, as to the quality of either the thoughts or the expressions. Unless Mr Keats has designedly kept back the best part of his mind, we must take the narrow range of ideas and feelings in these Poems, as an indication of his not having yet entered in earnest on the business of intellectual acquirement, or attained the full development of his moral faculties. To this account we are disposed to place the deficiencies in point of sentiment sometimes bordering upon childishness, and the nebulous character of the meaning in many passages which occur in the present volume. Mr Keats dedicates his volume to Mr Leigh Hunt, in a sonnet which, as possibly originating in the warmth of gratitude, may be pardoned its extravagance; and he has obviously been seduced by the same partiality, to take him as his model in the subsequent poem, to which is affixed a motto from the *Story of Rimini*. To Mr Hunt's poetical genius we have repeatedly borne testimony, but the affectation which vitiates his style must needs be aggravated to a ridiculous excess in the copyist. Mr Hunt is sometimes a successful imitator of the manner of our elder poets, but this imitation will not do at second hand, for ceasing then to remind us of those originals, it becomes simply unpleasing.

Our first specimen of Mr Keats's powers, shall be taken from the opening of the poem alluded to.

[Quotes 'I stood tip-toe', lines 1–60.]

There is certainly considerable taste and sprightliness in some parts of this description, and the whole poem has a sort of summer's day glow diffused over it, but it shuts up in mist and obscurity.

After a 'Specimen of an Induction to a Poem,' we have next a fragment, entitled 'Calidore', which, in the same indistinct and dreamy style, describes the romantic adventure of a Sir Somebody, who is introduced 'paddling o'er a lake,' edged with easy slopes and 'swelling leafiness,' and who comes to a castle gloomy and grand, with halls and corridor, where he finds 'sweet-lipped ladies,' and so forth; and all this is told with an air of mystery that holds out continually to the reader the promise of something interesting just about to be told, when, on turning the leaf, the Will o' the Wisp vanishes, and leaves him in darkness. However ingenious such a trick of skill may be, when the writer is too indolent, or feels incompetent to pursue his story, the production cannot claim to be read a second time; and it may therefore be questioned, without captiousness, whether it was worth printing for the sake of a few good lines which ambitiously aspired to overleap the portfolio.

The 'epistles' are much in the same style, *all about* poetry, and seem to be the first efflorescence of the unpruned fancy, which must pass away before anything like genuine excellence can be produced. The sonnets are perhaps the best things in the volume. We subjoin one addressed 'To my brother George.'

[Quotes the sonnet 'Many the wonders I this day have seen' in full.]

The 'strange assay' entitled 'Sleep and Poetry', if its forming the closing poem indicates that it is to be taken as the result of the Author's latest efforts, would seem to shew that he is indeed far gone, beyond the reach of the efficacy either of praise or censure, in affectation and absurdity. We must indulge the reader with a specimen.

[Quotes 'Sleep and Poetry', lines 270–93, 'Will not some say' to 'The end and aim of Poesy'.]

We must be allowed, however, to express a doubt whether its nature has been as clearly perceived by the Author, or he surely would never have been able to impose even upon himself as poetry the precious nonsense which he has here decked out in rhyme. Mr Keats speaks of

> The silence when some rhymes are coming out,
> And when they're come, *the very pleasant rout*;

and to the dangerous fascination of this employment we must attribute this half-awake rhapsody. Our Author is a very facetious rhymer. We have *Wallace* and *solace*, *tenderness* and *slenderness*, *burrs* and *sepulchres*, *favours* and *behaviours*, *livers* and *rivers*;—and again,

Where we may soft humanity put on,
And sit and rhyme, and think on *Chatterton.*

Mr Keats has satirized certain *pseudo* poets, who,

With a puling infant's force,
Sway'd about upon a rocking horse,
And thought it Pegasus.

Satire is a two-edged weapon: the lines brought irresistibly to our imagination the Author of these poems in the very attitude he describes. Seriously, however, we regret that a young man of vivid imagination and fine talents, should have fallen into so bad hands, as to have been flattered into the resolution to publish verses, of which a few years hence he will be glad to escape from the remembrance. The lash of a critic is the thing the least to be dreaded, as the penalty of premature publication. To have committed one's self in the character of a versifier, is often a formidable obstacle to be surmounted in after-life, when other aims require that we should obtain credit for different, and what a vulgar prejudice deems opposite qualifications. No species of authorship is attended by equal inconvenience in this respect. When a man has established his character in any useful sphere of exertion, the fame of the poet may be safely sought as a finish to his reputation. When he has shewn that he can do something else besides writing poetry, then, and not till then, may he safely trust the public with his secret. But the sound of a violin from a barrister's chamber, is not a more fatal augury than the poet's lyre strummed by a youth whose odes are as yet all addressed to Hope and Fortune.

But perhaps the chief danger respects the individual character, a danger which equally attends the alternative of success or failure. Should a young man of fine genius, but of half-furnished mind, succeed in conciliating applause by his first productions, it is a fearful chance that his energies are not dwarfed by the intoxication of vanity, or that he does not give himself up to the indolent day-dream of some splendid achievement never to be realized. Poetical fame, when conceded to early productions, is, if deserved, seldom the fruit of that patient self-cultivation and pains-taking, which in every department of worthy exertion are the only means of excellence; and it is but the natural consequence of this easy acquisition of gratification, that it induces a distaste for severer mental labour. Should, however, this fatal success be denied, the tetchy aspirant after fame is sometimes driven to seek compensation to his mortified vanity, in the plaudits of some worthless coterie, whose friendship consists in mutual flattery, or in community in crime, or, it may be, to vent his rancour in the satire of envy, or in the malignity of *patriotism*.

Exceptions, brilliant exceptions, are to be found in the annals of literature, and these make the critic's task one of peculiar delicacy. The case has occurred, when a phlegmatic Reviewer, in a fit of morning spleen, or of after-dinner dulness, has had it in his power to dash to the ground, by his pen, the innocent hopes of a youth struggling for honourable distinction amid all the disadvantages of poverty, or to break the bruised reed of a tender and melancholy spirit; but such an opportunity of doing mischief must of necessity be happily rare. Instances have also been, in which the performances of maturer life have fully redeemed the splendid pledge afforded by the young Author, in his first crude and unequal efforts, with which he has had to thank the stern critic that he did not rest self-satisfied. Upon the latter kind of exceptions, we would wish to fix Mr Keats's attention, feeling perfectly confident, as we do, that the patronage of the friend he is content to please, places him wholly out of the danger of adding to the number of those who are lost to the public for want of the smile of praise.

Mr Keats has, however, a claim to leave upon our readers the full impression of his poetry; and we shall therefore give insertion to another of his sonnets, which we have selected as simple and pleasing.

[Quotes the sonnet 'Happy is England! I could be content' in full.]

9. Unsigned review, *Edinburgh Magazine, and Literary Miscellany (Scots Magazine)*

October 1817, i, 254–7

Of the author of this small volume we know nothing more than that he is said to be a very young man, and a particular friend of the Messrs Hunt, the editors of the *Examiner*, and of Mr Hazlitt. His youth accounts well enough for some injudicious luxuriancies and other faults in his poems; and his intimacy with two of the wittiest writers of their day, sufficiently vouches both for his intellect and his taste. Going altogether out of the road of high raised passion and romantic enterprise, into which many ordinary versifiers have been drawn after the example of the famous poets of our time, he has attached himself to a model more pure than some of these, we imagine; and, at the same time, as poetical as the best of them. 'Sage, serious' *Spencer*, the most melodious and mildly fanciful of our old English poets, is Mr Keats's favourite. He takes his motto from him,—puts his head on his title-page,—and writes one of his most luxurious descriptions of nature in his measure. We find, indeed, *Spencerianisms* scattered through all his other verses, of whatsoever measure or character. But, though these things sufficiently point out where Mr K. has caught his inspiration, they by no means determine the general character of his manner, which partakes a great deal of that *picturesqueness* of fancy and licentious brilliancy of epithet which distinguish the early Italian novelists and amorous poets. For instance, those who know the careless, sketchy, capricious, and yet archly-thoughtful manner of *Pulci* and *Ariosto*, will understand what we mean from the following specimens, better than from any laboured or specific assertion of ours.

[Quotes 'I stood tip-toe', lines 61–106, 'Linger awhile' to 'her locks auburne'; and 'Epistle to my brother George', line 110, 'Could I, at once, my mad ambition smother', to the end.]

This is so easy, and so like the ardent fancies of an aspiring and poetical spirit, that we have a real pleasure in quoting, for the benefit of our readers, another fragment of one of Mr Keats's *epistles:*

[Quotes 'Epistle to Charles Cowden Clarke', lines 1–14, 'Oft have you seen' to 'like hours into eternity'.]

All this is just, and brilliant too,—though rather ambitious to be kept up for any length of time in a proper and fitting strain. What follows appears to us the very pink of the smart and flowing conversational style. It is truly such elegant *badinage* as should pass between scholars and gentlemen who can feel as well as judge.

[Quotes line 109, 'But many days have past', to the end.]

These specimens will be enough to shew that Mr K. has ventured on ground very dangerous for a young poet;—calculated, we think, to fatigue his ingenuity, and try his resources of fancy, without producing any permanent effect adequate to the expenditure of either. He seems to have formed his poetical predilections in exactly the same direction as Mr Hunt; and to write, from personal choice, as well as emulation, at all times, in that strain which can be most recommended to the favour of the general readers of poetry, only by the critical ingenuity and peculiar refinements of Mr Hazlitt. That style is vivacious, smart, witty, changeful, sparkling, and learned—full of bright points and flashy expressions that strike and even seem to please by a sudden boldness of novelty,—rather abounding in familiarities of conception and oddnesses of manner which shew ingenuity, even though they be perverse, or common, or contemptuous. The writers themselves seem to be persons of considerable taste, and of comfortable pretensions, who really appear as much alive to the socialities and sensual enjoyments of life, as to the contemplative beauties of nature. In addition to their familiarity, though,—they appear to be too full of conceits and sparkling points, ever to excite any thing more than a cold approbation at the long-run—and too fond, even in their favourite descriptions of nature, of a reference to the factitious resemblances of society, ever to touch the heart. Their verse is straggling and uneven, without the lengthened flow of blank verse, or the pointed connection of couplets. They aim laudably enough at force and freshness, but are not so careful of the inlets of vulgarity, nor so self-denying to the temptations of indolence, as to make their force a merit. In their admiration of some of our elder writers, they have forgot the fate of Withers and Ben Jonson, and May: And, without forgetting that Petrarch and Cowley are hardly read, though it be decent to profess admiration of them,—they seem not to bear in mind the appalling doom which awaits the faults of mannerism or the ambition of a sickly refinement. To justify the conclusions of their poetical philosophy, they are brave enough to sacrifice the sympathetic enthusiasm of their art, and that common fame which recurs to the mind with the ready freshness of remembered verse,—to a system of which the fruits come, at last, to make us exclaim with Lycidas,

Numeros memini, si verba tenerem.[1]

If Mr Keats does not forthwith cast off the uncleannesses of this school, he will never make his way to the truest strain of poetry in which, taking him by himself, it appears he might succeed. We are not afraid to say before the good among our readers, that we think this true strain dwells on features of manly singleness of heart, or feminine simplicity and constancy of affection,—mixed up with feelings of rational devotion, and impressions of independence spread over pictures of domestic happiness and social kindness,—more than on the fiery and resolute, the proud and repulsive aspects of misnamed humanity. It is something which bears, in fact, the direct impress of natural passion,—which depends for its effect on the shadowings of unsophisticated emotion, and takes no merit from the refinements of a metaphysical wit, or the giddy wanderings of an untamed imagination,—but is content with the glory of stimulating, rather than of oppressing, the sluggishness of ordinary conceptions.

It would be cold and contemptible not to hope well of one who has expressed his love of nature so touchingly as Mr K. has done in the following sonnets:

[Quotes 'O Solitude! if I must with thee dwell', and 'To one who has been long in city pent', in full.]

Another sonnet, addressed to Mr Haydon the painter, appears to us very felicitous. *The thought*, indeed, of the first eight lines is altogether admirable; and the whole has a veritable air of Milton about it which has not been given, in the same extent, to any other poet except Wordsworth.

[Quotes 'High-mindedness, a jealousy for good' in full.]

We are sorry that we can quote no more of these sweet verses which have in them so deep a tone of moral energy, and such a zest of the pathos of genius. We are loth to part with this poet of promise, and are

[1] 'I remember the *tune*, if only I could recall the words' (Virgil, *Eclogue* IX, 45).

vexed that critical justice requires us to mention some passages of considerable affectation, and marks of offensive haste, which he has permitted to go forth into his volume. 'Leafy luxury,' 'jaunty streams,' 'lawny slope,' 'the moon-beamy air,' 'a sun-beamy tale;' these, if not namby-pamby, are, at least, the 'holiday and lady terms' of those poor affected creatures who write verses 'in spite of nature and their stars.'—

A little noiseless noise among the leaves,
Born of the very sigh that silence heaves.

This is worthy only of the Rosa Matildas whom the strong-handed Gifford put down.

To possess but a span of the hour of leisure.
No sooner had I stepped into these pleasures.

These are two of the most unpoetical of Mr K.'s lines,—but they are not single. We cannot part, however, on bad terms with the author of such a glorious and Virgilian conception as this:

The moon lifting her silver rim
Above a cloud, and with a gradual swim
Coming into the blue with all her light.

A striking natural vicissitude has hardly been expressed better by Virgil himself,—though the severe simpleness of his age, and the compact structure of its language, do so much for him in every instance:

Ipse Pater, mediâ nimborum in nocte, *coruscâ*
Fulmina molitur dextra.[1]

[1] 'The Father himself, in the midnight of storm-clouds, wields his thunderbolts with his flashing right hand' (Virgil, *Georgics* I, 328–9).

ENDYMION: A POETIC ROMANCE

April 1818

10. Letters and prefaces

1818

Nothing better reveals Keats's defiant self-sufficiency and readiness for literary combat than his attitude before the publication of *Endymion*. Extract (a) shows that Leigh Hunt disliked *Endymion* ('But who's afraid?'). The preface Keats intended to print, Extract (b), is 'an undersong of disrespect to the Public', which is 'a thing I cannot help looking upon as an Enemy'; nevertheless, he is prepared to accept criticism, for 'there must be conversation of some sort.' By 'a London drizzle or a scotch Mist' he means 'a damping reaction from the *Quarterly* or the *Edinburgh Review*.' His modified preface 'in a supple or subdued style', Extract (d), forced on him by the alarm of his publishers and friends, is an awkward compromise between ingenuousness and deference which left him more vulnerable than the original one would have done. Taylor had a hand in the wording of it. Even in this approved form, Reynolds afterwards called it 'a strange and rash preface'.

(a) Extract from letter, 23 January 1818, to George and Thomas Keats: 'Leigh Hunt I showed my 1st Book to, he allows it not much merit as a whole; says it is unnatural and made ten objections to it in the mere skimming over. He says the conversation is unnatural and too high-flown for Brother and Sister—says it should be simple, forgetting do ye mind that they are both overshadowed by a Supernatural Power, and of force could not speak like Franchesca in the *Rimini*. He must first prove that Caliban's poetry is unnatural,—This with me completely overturns his objections. The fact is he and Shelley are hurt, and perhaps justly, at my not having showed them the affair officiously—and from several hints I have had they appear much disposed to dissect and anatomize, any trip or slip I may have made.—But who's afraid?' (*Letters of John Keats*, ed. H. E. Rollins, 1958, i. 213–14.)

(b) Keats's draft preface to *Endymion*: 'In a great nation, the work of an individual is of so little importance; his pleadings and excuses are so uninteresting; his "way of life" such a nothing; that a preface seems a sort of impertinent bow to strangers who care nothing about it.

A preface however should be down in so many words; and such a one that, by an eye glance over the type, the Reader may catch an idea of an Author's modesty, and non opinion of himself—which I sincerely hope may be seen in the few lines I have to write, notwithstanding certain proverbs of many ages' old which men find a great pleasure in receiving for gospel.

About a twelve month since, I published a little book of verses; it was read by some dozen of my friends who lik'd it; and some dozen who I was unacquainted with, who did not. Now when a dozen human beings, are at words with another dozen, it becomes a matter of anxiety to side with one's friends;—more especially when excited thereto by a great love of Poetry.

I fought under disadvantages. Before I began I had no inward feel of being able to finish; and as I proceeded my steps were all uncertain. So this Poem must rather be considered as an endeavour than a thing accomplish'd: a poor prologue to what, if I live, I humbly hope to do. In duty to the Public I should have kept it back for a year or two, knowing it to be so faulty: but I really cannot do so:—by repetition my favorite Passages sound vapid in my ears, and I would rather redeem myself with a new Poem—should this one be found of any interest.

I have to apologise to the lovers of simplicity for touching the spell of loveliness that hung about Endymion: if any of my lines plead for me with such people I shall be proud.

It has been too much the fashion of late to consider men biggotted and adicted to every word that may chance to escape their lips: now I here declare that I have not any particular affection for any particular phrase, word or letter in the whole affair. I have written to please myself and in hopes to please others, and for a love of fame; if I neither please myself, nor others nor get fame, of what consequence is Phraseology?

I would fain escape the bickerings that all works, not exactly in chime, bring upon their begetters:—but this is not fair to expect, there must be conversation of some sort and to object shows a Man's consequence. In case of a London drizzle or a scotch Mist, the following quotation from Marston may perhaps 'stead me as an umbrella for an hour or so: "let it be the Curtesy of my peruser rather to pity my self hindering labours than to malice me"

One word more:—for we cannot help seeing our own affairs in every point of view—Should anyone call my dedication to Chatterton affected I answer as followeth:

"Were I dead Sir I should like a Book dedicated to me"—

Teignmouth March 19th 1818—(text from *The Poetical Works of John Keats*, ed. H. W. Garrod (2nd edition, 1958), xciii–iv.)

(c) Extract from letter, 9 April 1818, to J. H. Reynolds: 'Since you all agree that the thing is bad, it must be so—though I am not aware there is any thing like Hunt in it, (and if there is, it is my natural way, and I have something in common with Hunt) look it over again and examine into the motives, the seeds from which any one sentence sprung—I have not the slightest feel of humility towards the Public—or to anything in existence,—but the eternal Being, the Principle of Beauty,—and the Memory of great Men—When I am writing for myself for the mere sake of the Moment's enjoyment, perhaps nature has its course with me—but a Preface is written to the Public; a thing I cannot help looking upon as an Enemy, and which I cannot address without feelings of Hostility—If I write a Preface in a supple or subdued style, it will not be in character with me as a public speaker—I wo[d] be subdued before my friends, and thank them for subduing me—but among Multitudes of Men—I have no feel of stooping, I hate the idea of humility to them—

I never wrote one single Line of Poetry with the least Shadow of public thought.

Forgive me for vexing you and making a Trojan Horse of such a Trifle, both with respect to the matter in Question, and myself—but it eases me to tell you—I could not live without the love of my friends—I would jump down Ætna for any great Public good—but I hate a Mawkish Popularity.—I cannot be subdued before them—My glory would be to daunt and dazzle the thousand jabberers about Pictures and Books—I see swarms of Porcupines with their Quills erect "like lime-twigs set to catch my Winged Book" and I would fright 'em away with a torch—You will say my preface is not much of a Torch. It would have been too insulting "to begin from Jove" and I could not

[set] a golden head upon a thing of clay—if there is any fault in the preface it is not affectation: but an undersong of disrespect to the Public.—if I write another preface, it must be done without a thought of those people—I will think about it. If it should not reach you in four—or five days—tell Taylor to publish it without a preface, and let the dedication simply stand "inscribed to the Memory of Thomas Chatterton".' (*The Letters*, i. 266–7.)

(d) Preface to *Endymion*: 'Knowing within myself the manner in which this Poem has been produced, it is not without a feeling of regret that I make it public.

What manner I mean, will be quite clear to the reader, who must soon perceive great inexperience, immaturity, and every error denoting a feverish attempt, rather than a deed accomplished. The two first books, and indeed the two last, I feel sensible are not of such completion as to warrant their passing the press; nor should they if I thought a year's castigation would do them any good;—it will not: the foundations are too sandy. It is just that this youngster should die away: a sad thought for me, if I had not some hope that while it is dwindling I may be plotting, and fitting myself for verses fit to live.

This may be speaking too presumptuously, and may deserve a punishment: but no feeling man will be forward to inflict it: he will leave me alone, with the conviction that there is not a fiercer hell than the failure in a great object. This is not written with the least atom of purpose to forestall criticisms of course, but from the desire to conciliate men who are competent to look, and who do look with a zealous eye, to the honour of English literature.

The imagination of a boy is healthy, and the mature imagination of a man is healthy; but there is a space of life between, in which the soul is in a ferment, the character undecided, the way of life uncertain, the ambition thick-sighted: thence proceeds mawkishness, and all the thousand bitters which those men I speak of must necessarily taste in going over the following pages.

I hope I have not in too late a day touched the beautiful mythology of Greece, and dulled its brightness: for I wish to try once more, before I bid it farewel.

Teignmouth, April 10, 1818' (text from *The Poetical Works*, 64.)

11. Unsigned review, *Literary Journal and General Miscellany of Science, Arts*, etc.

1818

In two parts: 17 May 1818, i, 114–15; 24 May 1818, i, 131. Fadladeen, the Great Chamberlain in Thomas Moore's poem *Lalla Rookh* (1817), was a censorious critic.

In this *poetizing age* we are led to look with an eye of suspicion on every work savouring of rhyme; especially if (as in this case,) its author is but little known in the literary world. It was with this feeling that we took up the present volume, and we regret to add, that it remained undiminished for the first thirty lines; when, like the Great Chamberlain in the exquisite poem of *Lalla Rookh*, we began to elevate our critical eye-brows, and exclaim, 'And this is poetry!' A few seconds, however, taught us, that this severity of criticism, like that of Fadladeen's, was premature; and the admiration we felt at the beautiful simplicity of the following lines, amply compensated for any previous defects in the versification:—

[Quotes *Endymion*, Book 1, lines 34–62.]

The plot of the poem, to which the preceding passage is an introduction, is founded on a most beautiful portion of the Greek mythology. Endymion, Prince of Caria, reposing on Mount Latmos, is discovered by Diana, who causes a deep sleep to fall upon him: his dream, as related to his sister Peona, who seeks to discover the cause of his melancholy, evidently bespeaks its author to possess a vivid imagination and refined mind, though the verse is frequently irregular, and sometimes unmetrical:—

[Quotes *Endymion*, Book 1, lines 578–671, 'Methought I lay' to 'an Oread as I guess'd'.]

The following lines bear a strong analogy to a beautiful passage in the *Arabian Tales*, in which Prince Ahmed is led, in search of an arrow, to the residence of the fairy Banou:—

[Quotes *Endymion*, Book I, lines 929–71, 'hurling my lance' to 'Whither are they fled?']

After having been led by a Naiad, in search of the 'fair unknown,' to a most beautiful cavern, he invokes the assistance of Venus, who directs him onward, and he is shortly wafted by an eagle from the regions of 'middle air' to a delightful garden: his description of this spot, and subsequent meeting with Diana, is written with a warmth of feeling, and a tenderness of expression, we seldom find exceeded even in some of our most popular poets:—

[Quotes *Endymion*, Book II, lines 670–853, 'It was a jasmine bower' to 'tradition of the gusty deep.']

After awaking from the slumber into which he had fallen on the departure of Diana, Endymion commences a pilgrimage through the 'vasty deep:' in the course of his wanderings he meets with a solitary man, who afterwards relates his adventures, which consist chiefly of his transformation from youth to age, by Circe, as the consequence of having freely indulged in her enchanting luxuries. In this state of premature debility he is doomed to remain, until released by the appearance of a young stranger. The meeting with Endymion convinces the old man that his hour of freedom is at hand. The anxious desire of liberty, and almost maddening anticipation of its possession, expressed by Glaucus, after having been spell bound for a thousand years, is described with considerable spirit. Indeed the whole passage will strongly remind the reader of the rapturous exclamations of Ariel, when promised his freedom by Prospero.

[Quotes *Endymion*, Book III, lines 234–55, ' "Thou art the man! Now" ' to ' "pine. Thou art the man!" ']

The fourth book opens with the following invocations to the muse of Britain:—

[Quotes *Endymion*, Book IV, lines 1–29.]

The following passage, descriptive of the aërial passage of Endymion, accompanied by Diana, contains some beautiful lines:—

[Quotes *Endymion*, Book IV, lines 484–512, 'The good-night blush of eve' to 'hawkwise to the earth'.]

The measure of this poem, which is nearly allied to that of Chaucer, frequently reminds us of Mr Hunt's *Rimini*, though many of the faults so justly attributed to that author, have been avoided in the present work. Indeed, with the exception of two passages, we are induced to give our most unqualified approbation of this poem: and, first,

The sleeping kine,
Couch'd in thy brightness, dream of fields divine.

This may be a very happy thought, and extremely poetical; but in our finite judgment, the giving to the brute creation one of the greatest and most glorious attributes of a rational being, is not only very ridiculous, but excessively impious. And from the following passage we dissent most decidedly, as we feel persuaded, that genius, like that possessed by Mr K., may with safety venture in the highest walk of poetry:—

——O 'tis a very sin
For one so weak to venture his poor verse
In such a place as this. O do not curse,
High Muses! let him hurry to the ending.

12. Bailey advertises *Endymion*

1818

Two letters, signed 'N.Y.', addressed to the Editor of the *Oxford University and City Herald, and Midland County Chronicle.* The first was published 30 May 1818, the second 6 June 1818.

Benjamin Bailey (1791–1853), who was ordained in 1817, had been an Oxford undergraduate when Keats stayed with him at Magdalen College to write Book III of *Endymion.* Bailey had the misfortune to be partly responsible for *Blackwood's* attack on the poem (see Introduction, p. 16), and tried to make amends by publishing these letters in its defence. Keats called his efforts 'honorable Simplicity'.

Let me recommend to the perusal of your readers the poem of *Endymion*, which is the most original production I ever read. Some account of its author may not be uninteresting.

John Keats the author of *Endymion*, is a very young man, about 22 years of age. About a year ago he published a small volume of Poems, in which was the richest promise I ever saw of an etherial imagination maintained by vast intellectual power. One passage from the largest poem in the volume may give the reader some idea of the conscious capability of real genius:—

What, though I am not wealthy in the dower
Of spanning wisdom; though I do not know
The shifting of the mighty winds that blow
Hither and thither all the changing thoughts
Of man: though no great minist'ring reason sorts
Out the dark mysteries of human souls
To clear conceiving: *yet there ever rolls*
A vast idea before me; and I glean
Therefrom my liberty; thence too I've seen
The end and aim of Poesy.

—*Sleep and Poetry.*

This is no common language. It is the under-breath of a 'master-spirit.' It is the deep yearning of genius after the beautiful and fair. It is, as it were, the brooding of an earthquake. It is 'the first virgin passion of a soul communing with the glorious universe.'

I could say much more but must desist for the present. I beg, however, to add, that I am impelled by no unworthy motive in recommending *Endymion* to the public. I am confident of its extraordinary merit, and cannot compromise my firm opinion out of respect to the mere 'forms, modes, and shows,' of the world. I call upon the age to countenance and encourage this rising genius, and not to let him pine away in neglect, lest his memory to after ages speak trumpet-tongued the disgrace of this. I love my country, and admire our literature. Our poets are our glory. I am no bookseller's tool; I am no pandar to poetical vanity; but I would not for worlds witness the insensibility of Old England to her own glory, in the neglect of the vernal genius of her sons.

In my last I gave a very hasty and imperfect sketch of John Keats, the author of *Endymion*. I took the liberty of recommending that poem in very strong and confident terms to the public. Far from retracting anything I there advanced, I shall be rather induced to add to it. I referred to his first volume as a book of great promise, wherein might be observed the seeds of genius, swelling, as it were, like the seeds, in the bosom of the earth at spring time, to rise into 'the paths of upper air,' and 'dwell not unvisited of heaven's fair light.' *Endymion* is but that second child of great promise. It will shew that, in so short a space, the author has 'plumed his feathers, and let grow his wings.' We may see in it the germs of immortality. What Milton, with the modest, yet confident tone of a deathless mind, said in a letter to his friend Deodati, when very young, I can imagine *this* young poet to have *felt*, though he may not have given it utterance:

'*Multa solicitè quaeris etiam, quid cogitem. Audi, Theodote, verum in aurem ut ne rubeam, et sinito paulisper apud te grandia loquar; quid cogitam? Ita me bonus Deus, immortalitatem.*'[1]—You may perhaps think, Sir, I am culpable in making this allusion. I am not going to compare him with Milton as a full-grown man whose 'stature reached the sky,' but with Milton as a young enthusiast panting for fame;—not with Milton,

[1] 'You are very anxious to know what I have in mind. Listen, Theodotus, but in private so that I don't blush; and let me talk to you grandiosely for a minute. What do you think I have in mind? With God's help—immortal fame.'

when, in his blindness and old age, he speaks of fame as 'that last *infirmity* of noble minds,'—but with him who said, 'Fame is the *spur* that the clear spirit doth raise,' as in his *Comus*, which he wrote at 23. Let it be remembered too, that our great epic poet had many advantages of learning and leisure from his youth upwards; but if, without these advantages, this young poet, 'with his soft pipe and smooth-dittied song,' can come at all within the sphere of that 'mighty orb of song, the divine Milton;' if likewise his genius be found in any respect kindred to our national Glory, Shakespeare, (and I think it is so, more than with Milton);—let not his countrymen withhold from him their suffrages, nor refuse to bind the laurel round his brows.

Suffer me, Sir, to detain you a short while longer before I proceed to the poem of *Endymion* itself.—Before he wrote the poems which comprise his first volume, he had not written above 200 lines of poetry. He was unconscious of his power; it had slumbered in him like 'a stream inaudible by day-light.' To apply a beautiful image of his own,—

> 'Twas might half-slumbering on his own right arm.

He next undertook *Endymion*, a poem of 4000 lines. It was a daring undertaking. Enterprize is the offspring of Genius. He has accomplished it.—I shall now proceed to speak of it more exclusively, and make such extracts as your limits will allow me; but were I to stop at every striking beauty, I must transcribe the whole poem. The flowers of spring do not 'broider the ground with richer inlay' than exquisite passages of poetry float:—

> With many a winding bout
> Of linked sweetness long drawn out

through this poem. For—

> Here be all the pleasures
> That Fancy can beget on youthful thoughts,
> When the fresh blood grows lively; and returns
> Brisk as the April buds in primrose season.

Everyone knows the beautiful story of *Endymion*, of which Keats says,—

> The very music of the name has gone
> Into my being, and each pleasant scene
> Is growing fresh before me as the green
> Of our own vallies.

But it is very wonderful how so long a poem could be constructed upon so simple a fable. Nothing but very original genius could have done it. I can but give your readers a faint idea of his management of the story.—

The Poem is in four books. Endymion is a 'Shepherd King.' In the first book there is a feast to Pan, and an exquisitely fine Pastoral Hymn, to which I must refer the reader, it being too long for quotation. Endymion has a sister, Peona, who is his confidante, and to whom he describes his first two scenes with Diana. In the second book Endymion wanders underneath the earth—

> Through winding passages where sameness breeds
> Vexing conceptions of some hidden change.

In this book he gives a beautiful turn to the Story of Adonis. In the third book he wanders through the sea:

> The visions of the earth are gone and fled,
> He saw the giant sea above his head.

In the fourth book he is again upon the earth—

> and forest green,
> Cooler than all the wonders he had seen.

He meets with, and becomes enamoured, of a beautiful Indian. This gives the poet an opportunity, of which he takes a noble advantage, of describing a procession of Bacchus. I shall extract this, to give the reader some idea of the lyrical beauty of his description—

[Quotes *Endymion*, Book IV, lines 188–267, 'Beneath my palm trees' to 'eye-wink turning pale.']

I fear your limits will not suffer me to make any other extract. The catastrophe of the Poem is this young Indian's being changed into Diana. It is worthy of remark, as a singular, and I am sure, an *unconscious* coincidence on the part of the author of *Endymion*, that the conclusion bears great resemblance to the close of *Paradise Regained*. After the angels, having 'brought him on his way with joy,' have left our Saviour,—

> He unobserved
> Home to his mother's house private returned.

When Diana assumes her own form and person, she and Endymion take their leave of his sister, and 'vanish far away'—

Peona went
Home through the gloomy wood in wonderment.

I must be suffered, Sir, to make a few remarks before I conclude. I am aware of the suspicious and invidious task of thus publicly bestowing such high encomiums upon the productions of any one. It is the vice of this age that literature is a trade. Trade is employed upon the lower interests of the world. A book therefore, is valued, according to the standard of Sir Hudibras, for 'as much as it will bring.'

All I wish to be understood is, that no such petty and paltry motives have induced me to come forward as I have. I do not disguise that I am acquainted with the author, but I was *first* acquainted with his *poetry*, and hence sought the knowledge of himself. I have found that personal acquaintance answerable to my expectations of what a poet should be in *character*. He has the most of that character I ever knew or shall know—I mean not to affirm that his poetry is faultless. Far from it. But his faults are those of an ardent genius, not sufficiently curbed. His youth has not yet 'tempered his tresses in Aquarius' beam.' Let not the cold unfeeling world freeze up his enthusiasm by neglect.—Poetry is no trivial toy, however 'this world's true worldling' may sneer at it. The finest book in the world teems with the sublimest poetry. Nature nourishes it at her bosom, and cherishes it in her heart. It 'goes to bed with the sun, and rises with him.' It is the breath of spring, and 'comes before the swallow dares, and takes the winds of March with beauty.' It is 'sweeter than the lids of Juno's eyes, or Cytherea's breath.' All this is felt by this young poet; and I envy not that man his heartless indifference, though *he* should think it philosophy who *cannot* feel this influence of nature. Poetry is but the language of nature. *Poetasters* swarm 'thick as the motes that people the sunbeam.' Poets, in the true meaning of the title, are very rare. If every fair morning gave smiling promise of a lovely day, I repeat it, that the poems already published by the author of *Endymion* are the germs of future greatness.

Some there be, that by due steps aspire
To lay their just hands on that golden key,
That opes the palace of eternity.

13. A great original work

1818

Unsigned review, *Champion*, 8 June 1818, 362–4.

J. H. Reynolds has been suggested as the author of this remarkable little review, and there may be connections between it and Reynolds's known writings on Keats (Nos. 4 and 18), most obviously in the choice of the same passage for quotation. Its style and content, however, point rather to Richard Woodhouse (see headnote to No. 22 and Introduction pp. 13-14). Certainly the writer must have been a member of Keats's inner circle, with prior knowledge of *Endymion* and of its threatened fate at the hands of the Establishment critics. But of far greater interest is its groping discussion of Keats's ideas of dramatic self-projection, which Keats later outlined to Woodhouse in a letter of 27 October 1818 and on which Woodhouse made notes (*The Keats Circle*, ed. H. E. Rollins, Cambridge, Mass., 1948, i. 57–60).

Although this poem has very lately appeared, the short delay between its publication and our notice, was intentional. We are sincerely anxious for its ultimate success: we were willing that the age should do honour to itself by its reception of it; and cared little for having been the first to notice it. We were fearful, that if we ventured to decide on it, and could induce *the few* to take its consideration into their own hands, our great critical authorities would choose, as usual, to maintain an obstinate silence, or to speak slightingly, perhaps contemptuously, to keep up the etiquette; for they have a spice of Cicero, and 'never follow any thing that other men begin.' Neither have we now altered our opinion, but having seen more than one public notice of the work, do not choose longer to delay it. That the consequences will be pretty nearly as we predict we have little doubt. If the reviews play the sure game and say nothing, to nothing can we object; but if they really notice it, let us have something like a fair and liberal criticism—something that can be subjected to examination itself. Let them refer to principles: let them shew us the philosophic construction of poetry, and point out its errors by instance and application. To this we shall not object: but this we must think they owe to Mr Keats himself, and all those who have written and spoken highly of his talent. If however, they follow their old course, and having tacked the introduction of the first book, to the fag end of the last, swear the whole is an unintelligible jumble, we will at least exert ourselves to stop their chuckling and self congratulation.

We cannot, however, disguise from ourselves that the conduct that may be pursued by these reviews will have its influence, and a great influence, on public opinion: but, excepting as to the effect that opinion may have on the poet himself, we care not two straws for it. Public opinion is not a comprehensive or comprehending thing; it is neither a wit nor a wise man: a poet nor a philosopher: it is the veriest 'king of shadows:' it is nothing but the hollow echoing of some momentary oracle: and if we estimate the work of the reviews themselves, we have it, for they are the things now in authority: they are your only substantials: they give currency to our poets: and what chance has an original genius that differs from all our poets, when nearly all our poets write for one or other of them. These men have it in their own hands, to mete out praise and censure, for half the population. We only hope they do not flatter themselves on the general assent: if they really mistake their popularity for immortality, they trick out an ideot in motley, and having stuck a Bartholomew trumpet in his hand, persuade themselves it is fame. But we do fear even public opinion from our knowledge of human nature. No man ever lived but he had a consciousness of his own power, and if he chose to make a fair estimate was perhaps a better judge than any other of his own ability. If then with this consciousness he find nothing in unison with his own feeling, no fair and liberal estimate made of his worth, no concessions made, no deference paid to him by the opinion that for the time passes current, he is driven by necessity upon his self-love for satisfaction, his indignation lashes his pride, he is unsupported by others [where] he has an undoubted assurance of being right, and he maintains those errors that have been justly objected against him, because they have been urged too far, and refuses to concede any thing because too much has been demanded. This, however, is a speculation, and we trust, it will remain so.

It is ever hazardous to predict the fate of a great original work; and of *Endymion*, all we dare venture in this way is an opinion, that an inferior poem is likely to excite a more general interest. The secret of the success of our modern poets, is their universal presence in their poems—they give to every thing the colouring of their own feeling; and what a man has felt intensely—the impressions of actual existence—he is likely to describe powerfully: what he has felt we can easily sympathize with. But Mr Keats goes out of himself into a world of abstractions:—his passions, feelings, are all as much imaginative as his situations. Neither is it the mere outward signs of passions that are given: there seems ever present some being that was equally conscious of its internal and most secret imaginings. There is another objection to its ever becoming popular, that it is, as the *Venus and Adonis* of Shakespeare, a *representation* and not a *description* of passion. Both these poems would, we think, be more generally admired had the poets been only veiled instead of concealed from us. Mr Keats conceives the scene before him, and represents it as it appears. This is the excellence of dramatic poetry; but to feel its truth and power in any other, we must abandon our ordinary feeling and common consciousness, and identify ourselves with the scene. Few people can do this. In representation, which is the ultimate purpose of dramatic poetry, we should feel something of sympathy though we could merely observe the scene, or the gesticulation, and no sound could reach us; but to make an ordinary *reader* sensible of the excellence of a poem, he must be told what the poet felt; and he is affected by him and not by the scene. Our modern poets are the shewmen of their own pictures, and point out its beauties.

Mr Keats' very excellence, we fear, will tell against him. Each scene bears so actually the immediate impress of truth and nature, that it may be said to be local and peculiar, and to require some extrinsic feeling for its full enjoyment:—perhaps we are not clear in what we say. Every man then, according to his particular habit of mind, not only gives a correspondent colouring to all that surrounds him, but seeks to surround himself with corresponding objects, in which he has more than other people's enjoyment. In every thing then that art or nature may present to man, though gratifying to all, each man's gratification and sympathy will be regulated by the disposition and bent of his mind. Look at Milton's Sonnets. With what a deep and bitter feeling would a persecuted religious enthusiast select and dwell 'On the late Massacre in Piemont.' Has a social man no particular enjoyment in those to Laurence and Skynner? or a patriot in those to Fairfax, Cromwell, and Vane? What is common to humanity we are all readily sensible of, and all men proportioned to their intelligence, will receive pleasure on reading that on his birth day:—it wants nothing exclusive either in persons or age:—but would not a young and fearful lover find a thousand beauties in his address to the nightingale that must for ever escape the majority? In further illustration, we would adduce the first meeting of Endymion and Cynthia in the poem before us; which, though wonderfully told, we do not think most likely to be generally liked. It is so true to imagination, that passion absorbs every thing. Now, as we have observed, to transfer the mind to the situation of another, to feel as he feels, requires an enthusiasm, and an abstraction, beyond the power or the habit of most people. It is in this way eloquence differs from poetry, and the same speech on delivery affects people, [that] on an after reading would appear tame and unimpassioned. We have certain sympathies with the person addressing us, and what he feels, we feel in an inferior degree; but he is afterwards to describe to us his passion; to make us feel by *telling us what he felt:* and this is to be done by calculating on the effect on *others'* feelings, and not by abandoning ourselves to our own. If Mr Keats can do this, he has not done it. When he writes of passion, it seems to have possessed him. This, however, is what Shakespeare did, and if *Endymion* bears any general resemblance to any other poem in the language, it is to *Venus and Adonis* on this very account. In the necessarily abrupt breaking off of this scene of intense passion, however, we think he has exceeded even his ordinary power. It is scarcely possible to conceive any thing more poetically imaginative; and though it may be brought in rather abruptly, we cannot refuse ourselves the pleasure of immediately extracting it.

[Quotes *Endymion*, Book II, lines 827–54, from 'Ye who have yearn'd' to 'former chroniclers', italicizing lines 830–9, 846, 853–4.]

The objection we have here stated is equally applicable to the proper and full appreciation of many other beautiful scenes in this poem; but having acknowledged this, we shall extract the hymn to Pan, that our readers may be satisfied there are others to which universal assent must be given as among the finest specimens of classic poetry in our language.

[Quotes the Hymn to Pan from Book I, complete except for lines 263–78, italicizing lines 232–46, 256–7, 293–6, 299–301.]

We shall trespass a little beyond the hymn itself, and must then postpone our further observations.

[Quotes Book I, lines 307–19, italicizing lines 310–11, 317–19, and ending: '*—not yet dead, But in old marbles ever beautiful.*']

This last line is as fine as that in Shakespeare's Sonnets,

And beauty making beautiful old rhyme:

and there are not a dozen finer in Shakespeare's poems.

14. A monstrously droll poem

1818

Unsigned review, *British Critic* (June 1818), n.s. ix, 649–54. This article (indexed: '*Endymion*, a monstrously droll poem, analysis of') was the first of the critical assaults on the poem, and demonstrates, often very amusingly, how easy it was for readers of orthodox tastes to find Keats's idiom merely ludicrous.

This is the most delicious poem, of its kind, which has fallen within our notice, and if Mr Leigh Hunt had never written, we believe we might have pronounced it to be *sui generis* without fear of contradiction. That gentleman, however, has talked so much about 'daisies and daffodils, clover and sweet peas, blossomings and lushiness,' that we fear Mr Keats must be content to share but half the laurel, provided always, and we can most conscientiously assert it, that the disciple be recognized as not one whit inferior to his mighty master. All the world knows that the moon fell in love with Endymion, just as Aurora intrigued with Cephalus, till, as the author of the *Pursuits of Literature*[1] tells us, she jilted him for Mr Steevens; but it remained for a muse of modern days

[1] In this satirical poem (1795), T. J. Mathias had teased the elderly scholar George Steevens by pretending that Aurora, the dawn, mistook him for her lover Cephalus when he climbed Primrose Hill 'between four and five o'clock every morning' to correct proofs.

to acquaint us with the whole progress of this demi-celestial amour. 'A thing of beauty (as Mr Keats says, or sings, we know not which, in the first line of his poem,) is a joy for ever!' And, 'as the year grows lush in juicy stalks,' 'many and many a verse he hopes to write.' Endymion is a very handsome young man, 'but there were some who feelingly could scan a lurking trouble in his nether lip.'—'then they would sigh and think of yellow leaves and owlets cry and (what else in the name of wonder does the reader expect?) *of logs pil'd solemnly*, (B. I. l. 180.) One day after the priest of Patmos had sung a song to Pan, whom he represents, rather indecorously, we must acknowledge, as a god 'who loves to see the Hamadryads *dress;*' and also, one 'for whose soul-soothing quiet, turtles passion their voices cooingly among myrtles,' with many other things about 'broad leaved fig-trees, freckled butterflies, solitary thinkings, shorn peers, and dodging conceptions;' a shout arises among the multitude, just as 'when Ionian shoals of dolphins *bob* their noses through the brine,' (l. 310.) In consequence of this noise, and 'Niobe's caressing tongue,' which 'lay a lost thing upon her paly lip' (l. 340) Endymion goes to sleep among some 'pouting zephyr-sighs,' where, while his sister sits 'guarding his forehead with her round elbow,' he lies 'aye, e'en as dead still as a marble man, frozen in that old tale Arabian,' (l. 405.) After sleeping this 'magic sleep, O comfortable bird!' for a 'triple hour,' he 'opens his eyelids with a healthier brain.' Peona 'shuts her pure sorrow drops with loud exclaim,' and he explains to her what has made him who used to be able to 'frown a lion into growling,' lose his 'toil-breeding fire;' it seems that one evening when the sun had done driving 'his snorting four,' 'there blossom'd suddenly a magic bed of sacred ditamy,' (Qu. dimity?) and he looked up to the 'lidless-eyed train of planets,' where he saw 'a completed form of all completeness,' 'with gordian'd locks and pearl round ears,' and kissed all these till he fell into a 'stupid sleep,' from which he was roused by 'a gentle creep,' (N.B. Mr Tiffin is the ablest bug-destroyer of our days,) to look at some 'upturn'd gills of dying fish.' This very intelligible communication to his sister relieves him a good deal, but he is not quite easy till 'amid his pains he seem'd to taste a drop of manna dew,' (l. 767.) and he continues to tell her of his wish to 'wipe away all slime left by men-slugs and human serpentry,' and winds up with a passage by far too pathetic not to be given at length:

——————But who, of men, can tell
That flowers would bloom, or that green fruit would swell
To melting pulp, that fish would have bright mail,

The earth its dower of river, wood, and vale,
The meadows runnels, runnels pebble-stones,
The seed its harvest, or the lute its tones,
Tones ravishment, or ravishment its sweet,
If human souls did never kiss and greet? P. 42

'Honey-feels,' 'honey whispers,' which come 'refreshfully,' 'obscure and hot hells,' 'secreter caves,' 'sigh-warm kisses and combing hands which travelling cloy and tremble through labyrinthine hair,' (l. 970.) conclude book the first.

Book the second opens, for the sake of contrast, with 'stiff-holden shields, far-piercing spears, keen blades, struggling, and blood, and shrieks,' and proceeds, without ceremony, to use very foul language to one 'History,' who is represented, like an old country attorney, as a 'swart planet in the universe of deeds.' After this Endymion sets out in search of the moon, and meets with a good-natured young woman, whose calling may be easily guessed by the present she offers to make him, of 'all her clear-eyed fish, golden or rainbow-sided, or purplish, vermilion-tail'd, or finn'd with silv'ry gauze,' but he stands on 'the pebble head of doubt,' and runs 'into the fearful deep to hide his head from the clear moon, (not very wise when he is in pursuit of her,) the trees, and coming madness;' from this he passes into 'a vast antre,' where he 'seeth' (and this rhymes to 'beneath,') many things, 'which misery most drowningly doth sing,' there he wishes to ' 'noint' his eyes (l. 325.) which, perhaps, he would do if the poet could restrain the following burst of inspiration from himself.

O did he ever live, that lonely man,
Who lov'd—and music slew not? 'Tis the pest
Of love, that fairest joys give most unrest;
That things of delicate and tenderest worth
Are swallow'd all, and made a seared dearth,
By one consuming flame: it doth immerse
And suffocate true blessings in a curse. P. 70.

This music introduces Adonis between two cupids 'a slumbering,' with 'a faint damask mouth tenderly unclos'd to slumbery pout.' And we are told of his coyness to Venus, 'when her lips and eyes were clos'd in sullen moisture, and quick sighs came vex'd and pettish through her nostrils small,' (l. 470.) then cupid stands up while 'a sovereign quell is in his waving hands,' and 'new-born *Adon*' springs to life again: the scene very soon shifts, and Endymion finds 'a hurried change' 'working within him into something dreary, vex'd like a morning eagle lost and weary,' (l. 635) till Cybele comforts him; she is described as drawn by four lions, whose 'toothed maws' (we presume these lions are ruminating animals, of a new species, who masticate in the stomach,) are 'solemn,' their 'surly eyes brow hidden,' their 'heavy paws uplifted drowsily,' and their 'nervy tails cowering their tawny brushes.' When she has done speaking, ''bove his head flew a delight half-graspable'—but we must pause here—for Mr Keats is not contented with a half initiation into the school he has chosen. And he can strike from unmeaning absurdity into the gross slang of voluptuousness with as much skill as the worthy prototype whom he has selected. We will assure him, however, that not all the flimsy veil of words in which he would involve immoral images, can atone for their impurity; and we will not disgust our readers by retailing to them the artifices of vicious refinement, by which, under the semblance of 'slippery blisses, twinkling eyes, soft completion of faces, and smooth excess of hands,' he would palm upon the unsuspicious and the innocent imaginations better adapted to the stews.

> How he does love me; his poor temples beat,
> To the very tune of love! how sweet, sweet, sweet.
>
> B. II. l. [764–5]

To recur to the story: Endymion next goes into a 'cool wonder' where 'whales arbour close to brood and *sulk*;' and there he has an interview with Arethusa in the shape of 'a misty spray.'

The third book begins in character, with a jacobinical apostrophe to 'crowns, turbans, and tiptop nothings;' we wonder how mitres escaped from their usual place. Then we have 'thunder-tents, abysm-births, gentlier-mightiest, and eterne Apollo;' and are told that the moon makes 'old boughs feel palpitations, and lisp out a holier din,' that she is 'a relief to the poor patient oyster,' and teaches 'far-spooming ocean' how to bow. Moreover, that when Mr Keats was a very young man, she (the moon) was all the following things to him:

> ————Thou wast the deep glen;
> Thou wast the mountain-top—the sage's pen—
> The poet's harp—the voice of friends—the sun*;
> Thou wast the river—thou wast glory won;
> Thou wast the clarion's blast—thou wast my steed—
> My goblet full of wine—my topmost deed:—
> Thou wast the charm of women, lovely moon! P. 113.

* A very odd thing for the moon to be.

Now all this reads very like a rebus, but we have not yet found any solution to it. After his last adventure Endymion meets with a very strange old man, who is right glad to see him, because, as he says,

> To northern seas I'll in a twinkling sail,
> And mount upon the snortings of a whale. P. 117.

This elderly stranger is an acute physiognomist, and informs him that he knows

> He cannot feel a drouth,
> By the melancholy corners of his mouth. P. 124.

He warbles to him 'for very joy mellifluous sorrow,' gives him a history of some 'nectarous camel-draughts' which he had drank, and concludes with an account of some 'sights too fearful for the feel of fear,' which, as far as we can understand, were nothing more than

> A tooth, a tusk, and venom-bag, and sting,
> Laughing and wailing, grovelling, serpenting. P. 129.

Against 'whose *eyes* (i.e. the eyes of the tooth, tusk, venom-bag, and sting) Circe whisked a sooty oil.'

> Until their grieved bodies 'gan to bloat
> And puff, from the tail's end to stifled throat. P. 130.

And then,

> The whole herd, as by a whirlwind writhen,
> Went through the dismal air like one huge Python
> Antagonizing Boreas. P. 130.

Soon after this there is 'a mighty consummation;' 'death falls a weeping in his charnel house,' and

> When each their old love found, a murmuring rose,
> Like what was never heard in *all the throes*
> *Of wind and waters:* 'tis past human wit
> To tell; 'tis dizziness to think of it. P. 144.

'Large Hercules' and 'large Neptune' join the assembly; Cupid, 'empire-sure,' 'flutters and laughs;' 'Eolus skulks to his cavern 'mid the gruff complaint of all his rebel tempests,' and the third book comes to an end.

In the beginning of the last book we are informed of a new discovery in natural history, namely, that there is 'no authentic dew but in the eye of love.' Somebody sings a very pitiful song to sorrow; and somebody else gets upon horseback with Endymion, to 'win an immortality ere a lean bat could plump his wintry skin.' While he was on horseback with this lady, the poet tells us, 'so fond, so beauteous was his *bed-fellow*, he could not help but kiss her.' We suspect that some confusion must have arisen here between a pillion and a pillow. When 'vespers begin to throe,' the hero 'drops hawkwise to the earth,' where he listens to another song about some 'tender bibbers of the rain and dew,' and raves about his saddle-bed-fellow, who he calls his 'Indian bliss, and river-lily bud,' and asks her for 'one gentle squeeze warm as a dove's nest among summer trees;' but finding himself 'enlarged to his hunger, and caught in trammels of perverse deliciousness, he could bear no more, and so bent his soul fiercely like a spiritual bow, and twang'd it inwardly,' till he was able to 'trip lightly on in sort of deathful glee.' In the conclusion 'Cynthia bright Peona kiss'd, and bless'd with fair good night;' Endymion falls into a swoon, and 'Peona went home through the gloomy wood in wonderment;' a feeling which we are by no means surprized that she should entertain after all that had happened.

We do most solemnly assure our readers that this poem, containing 4074 lines, is printed on very nice hot-pressed paper, and sold for nine shillings, by a very respectable London bookseller. Moreover, that the author has put his name in the title page, and told us, that though he is something between man and boy, he means by and by to be 'plotting and fitting himself for verses fit to live.' We think it necessary to add that it is all written in rhyme, and, for the most part, (when there are syllables enough) in the heroic couplet.

15. Lockhart's attack in *Blackwood's*

1818

Review signed 'Z', *Blackwood's Edinburgh Magazine* (August 1818), iii, 519–24.

John Gibson Lockhart (1794–1854), clergyman's son and advocate, was a friend of Walter Scott, whose daughter he married in 1820. He was a clever, unstable young man with a compulsive turn for satire: his own associates nicknamed him 'the scorpion which delighteth to sting the faces of men.' At this time he was just twenty-four, only a year older than Keats himself, and had very recently assumed a leading role, with John Wilson and others, in a new (and at first unsuccessful) magazine. He was an able linguist, and prided himself on his classical scholarship. For details of Lockhart's dealings with Keats, see Introduction, pp. 16–24. The review is given here unabridged.

The references at the end of the review are to Sangrado in Le Sage's novel *Gil Blas* (completed 1735), prototype of doctors who use the same remedies for all requirements.

COCKNEY SCHOOL OF POETRY

No. IV

——————— OF KEATS,
THE MUSES' SON OF PROMISE, AND WHAT FEATS
HE YET MAY DO, &C.

CORNELIUS WEBB.

Of all the manias of this mad age, the most incurable, as well as the most common, seems to be no other than the *Metromanie*. The just celebrity of Robert Burns and Miss Baillie has had the melancholy effect of turning the heads of we know not how many farm-servants and unmarried ladies; our very footmen compose tragedies, and there is scarcely a superannuated governess in the island that does not leave a roll of lyrics behind her in her band-box. To witness the disease of any human understanding, however feeble, is distressing; but the spectacle of an able mind reduced to a state of insanity is of course ten times more afflicting. It is with such sorrow as this that we have contemplated the case of Mr John Keats. This young man appears to have received from nature talents of an excellent, perhaps even of a superior order—talents which, devoted to the purposes of any useful profession, must have rendered him a respectable, if not an eminent citizen. His friends, we understand, destined him to the career of medicine, and he was bound apprentice some years ago to a worthy apothecary in town. But all has been undone by a sudden attack of the malady to which we have alluded. Whether Mr John had been sent home with a diuretic or composing draught to some patient far gone in the poetical mania, we have not heard. This much is certain, that he has caught the infection, and that thoroughly. For some time we were in hopes, that he might get off with a violent fit or two; but of late the symptoms are terrible. The phrenzy of the *Poems* was bad enough in its way; but it did not alarm us half so seriously as the calm, settled, imperturbable drivelling idiocy of *Endymion*. We hope, however, that in so young a person, and with a constitution originally so good, even now the disease is not utterly incurable. Time, firm treatment, and rational restraint, do much for many apparently hopeless invalids; and if Mr Keats should happen, at some interval of reason, to cast his eye upon our pages, he may perhaps be convinced of the existence of his malady, which, in such cases, is often all that is necessary to put the patient in a fair way of being cured.

The readers of the *Examiner* newspaper were informed, some time ago, by a solemn paragraph, in Mr Hunt's best style, of the appearance of two new stars of glorious magnitude and splendour in the poetical horizon of the land of Cockaigne. One of these turned out, by and by, to be no other than Mr John Keats. This precocious adulation confirmed the wavering apprentice in his desire to quit the gallipots, and at the same time excited in his too susceptible mind a fatal admiration for the character and talents of the most worthless and affected of all the versifiers of our time. One of his first productions was the following sonnet, '*written on the day when Mr Leigh Hunt left prison.*' It will be recollected, that the cause of Hunt's confinement was a series of libels against his sovereign, and that its fruit was the odious and incestuous *Story of Rimini*.

What though, for shewing truth to flattered state,
  Kind Hunt was shut in prison, yet has he,
  In his immortal spirit been as free
As the sky-searching lark, and as elate.
Minion of grandeur! think you he did wait?
  Think you he nought but prison walls did see,
  Till, so unwilling, thou unturn'dst the key?
Ah, no! far happier, nobler was his fate!
In Spenser's halls! he strayed, and bowers fair,
  Culling enchanted flowers; and he flew
With daring Milton! through the fields of air;
  To regions of his own his genius true
Took happy flights. Who shall his fame impair
  When thou art dead, and all thy wretched crew?

The absurdity of the thought in this sonnet is, however, if possible, surpassed in another, '*addressed to Haydon*' the painter, that clever, but most affected artist, who as little resembles Raphael in genius as he does in person, notwithstanding the foppery of having his hair curled over his shoulders in the old Italian fashion. In this exquisite piece it will be observed, that Mr Keats classes together WORDSWORTH, HUNT, and HAYDON, as the three greatest spirits of the age, and that he alludes to himself, and some others of the rising brood of Cockneys, as likely to attain hereafter an equally honourable elevation. Wordsworth and Hunt! what a juxta-position! The purest, the loftiest, and, we do not fear to say it, the most classical of living English poets, joined together in the same compliment with the meanest, the filthiest, and the most vulgar of Cockney poetasters. No wonder that he who could be guilty of this should class Haydon with Raphael, and himself with Spencer.

Great spirits now on earth are sojourning;
  He of the cloud, the cataract, the lake,
  Who on Helvellyn's summit, wide awake,
Catches his freshness from Archangel's wing:
He of the rose, the violet, the spring,
  The social smile, the chain for Freedom's sake:
  And lo!—whose stedfastness would never take
A meaner sound than Raphael's whispering.
And other spirits there are standing apart
  Upon the forehead of the age to come;
These, these will give the world another heart,
  And other pulses. *Hear ye not the hum*

Of mighty workings?——————
Listen awhile ye nations, and be dumb.

The nations are to listen and be dumb! and why, good Johnny Keats? because Leigh Hunt is editor of the *Examiner*, and Haydon has painted the judgment of Solomon, and you and Cornelius Webb, and a few more city sparks, are pleased to look upon yourselves as so many future Shakspeares and Miltons! The world has really some reason to look to its foundations! Here is a *tempestas in matulâ* with a vengeance. At the period when these sonnets were published, Mr Keats had no hesitation in saying, that he looked on himself as '*not yet* a glorious denizen of the wide heaven of poetry,' but he had many fine soothing visions of coming greatness, and many rare plans of study to prepare him for it. The following we think is very pretty raving.

Why so sad a moan?
Life is the rose's hope while yet unblown;
The reading of an ever-changing tale;
The light uplifting of a maiden's veil;
A pigeon tumbling in clear summer air;
A laughing school-boy, without grief or care,
Riding the springing branches of an elm.

O for ten years, that I may overwhelm
Myself in poesy; so I may do the deed
That my own soul has to itself decreed.
Then will I pass the countries that I see
In long perspective, and continually
Taste their pure fountains. First the realm I'll pass
Of Flora, and old Pan: sleep in the grass,
Feed upon apples red, and strawberries,
And choose each pleasure that my fancy sees.
Catch the white-handed nymphs in shady places,
To woo sweet kisses from averted faces,—
Play with their fingers, touch their shoulders white
Into a pretty shrinking with a bite
As hard as lips can make it: till agreed,
A lovely tale of human life we'll read.
And one will teach a tame dove how it best
May fan the cool air gently o'er my rest;
Another, bending o'er her nimble tread,
Will set a green robe floating round her head,
And still will dance with ever varied ease,
Smiling upon the flowers and the trees:

Another will entice me on, and on
Through almond blossoms and rich cinnamon;
Till in the bosom of a leafy world
We rest in silence, like two gems upcurl'd
In the recesses of a pearly shell.

Having cooled a little from this 'fine passion,' our youthful poet passes very naturally into a long strain of foaming abuse against a certain class of English Poets, whom, with Pope at their head, it is much the fashion with the ignorant unsettled pretenders of the present time to undervalue. Begging these gentlemens' pardon, although Pope was not a poet of the same high order with some who are now living, yet, to deny his genius, is just about as absurd as to dispute that of Wordsworth, or to believe in that of Hunt. Above all things, it is most pitiably ridiculous to hear men, of whom their country will always have reason to be proud, reviled by uneducated and flimsy striplings, who are not capable of understanding either their merits, or those of any other *men of power*—fanciful dreaming tea-drinkers, who, without logic enough to analyse a single idea, or imagination enough to form one original image, or learning enough to distinguish between the written language of Englishmen and the spoken jargon of Cockneys, presume to talk with contempt of some of the most exquisite spirits the world ever produced, merely because they did not happen to exert their faculties in laborious affected descriptions of flowers seen in window-pots, or cascades heard at Vauxhall; in short, because they chose to be wits, philosophers, patriots, and poets, rather than to found the Cockney school of versification, morality, and politics, a century before its time. After blaspheming himself into a fury against Boileau, &c. Mr Keats comforts himself and his readers with a view of the present more promising aspect of affairs; above all, with the ripened glories of the poet of *Rimini*. Addressing the manes of the departed chiefs of English poetry, he informs them, in the following clear and touching manner, of the existence of 'him of the Rose,' &c.

From a thick brake,
Nested and quiet in a valley mild,
Bubbles a pipe; fine sounds are floating wild
About the earth. Happy are ye and glad.

From this he diverges into a view of 'things in general.' We smile when we think to ourselves how little most of our readers will understand of what follows.

Yet I rejoice: a myrtle fairer than
E'er grew in Paphos, from the bitter weeds
Lifts its sweet head into the air, and feeds
A silent space with ever sprouting green.
All tenderest birds there find a pleasant screen,
Creep through the shade with jaunty fluttering,
Nibble the little cupped flowers and sing.
Then let us clear away the choaking *thorns*
From round its gentle stem; let the young *fawns*,
Yeaned in after times, when we are flown,
Find a fresh sward beneath it, overgrown
With simple flowers: let there nothing be
More boisterous than a lover's bended knee;
Nought more ungentle than the placid look
Of one who leans upon a closed book;
Nought more untranquil than the grassy slopes
Between two hills. All hail delightful hopes!
As she was wont, th' imagination
Into most lovely labyrinths will be gone,
And they shall be accounted poet kings
Who simply tell the most heart-easing things.
O may these joys be ripe before I die.
Will not some say that I presumptuously
Have spoken? that from hastening disgrace
'Twere better far to hide my foolish face?
That whining boyhood should with reverence bow
Ere the dread thunderbolt could reach? How!
If I do hide myself, it sure shall be
In the very fane, the light of poesy.

From some verses addressed to various amiable individuals of the other sex, it appears, notwithstanding all this gossamer-work, that Johnny's affections are not entirely confined to objects purely etherial. Take, by way of specimen, the following prurient and vulgar lines, evidently meant for some young lady east of Temple-bar.

Add too, the sweetness
Of thy honied voice; the neatness
Of thine ankle lightly turn'd:
With those beauties, scarce discern'd,
Kept with such sweet privacy,
That they seldom meet the eye
Of the little loves that fly
Round about with eager pry.

Saving when, with freshening lave,
Thou dipp'st them in the taintless wave;
Like twin water lilies, born
In the coolness of the morn.
O, if thou hadst breathed then,
Now the Muses had been ten.
Couldst thou wish for lineage *higher*
Than twin sister of *Thalia?*
At last for ever, evermore,
Will I call the Graces four.

Who will dispute that our poet, to use his own phrase (and rhyme),

Can mingle music fit for the soft *ear*
Of Lady *Cytherea.*

So much for the opening bud; now for the expanded flower. It is time to pass from the juvenile *Poems*, to the mature and elaborate *Endymion, a Poetic Romance.* The old story of the moon falling in love with a shepherd, so prettily told by a Roman Classic, and so exquisitely enlarged and adorned by one of the most elegant of German poets, has been seized upon by Mr John Keats, to be done with as might seem good unto the sickly fancy of one who never read a single line either of Ovid or of Wieland. If the quantity, not the quality, of the verses dedicated to the story is to be taken into account, there can be no doubt that Mr John Keats may now claim Endymion entirely to himself. To say the truth, we do not suppose either the Latin or the German poet would be very anxious to dispute about the property of the hero of the 'Poetic Romance.' Mr Keats has thoroughly appropriated the character, if not the name. His Endymion is not a Greek shepherd, loved by a Grecian goddess; he is merely a young Cockney rhymester, dreaming a phantastic dream at the full of the moon. Costume, were it worth while to notice such a trifle, is violated in every page of this goodly octavo. From his prototype Hunt, John Keats has acquired a sort of vague idea, that the Greeks were a most tasteful people, and that no mythology can be so finely adapted for the purposes of poetry as theirs. It is amusing to see what a hand the two Cockneys make of this mythology; the one confesses that he never read the Greek Tragedians, and the other knows Homer only from Chapman, and both of them write about Apollo, Pan, Nymphs, Muses, and Mysteries, as might be expected from persons of their education. We shall not, however, enlarge at present upon this subject, as we mean to dedicate an entire paper to the classical attainments and attempts of the Cockney poets.

As for Mr Keats' *Endymion*, it has just as much to do with Greece as it has with 'old Tartary the fierce;' no man, whose mind has ever been imbued with the smallest knowledge or feeling of classical poetry or classical history, could have stooped to profane and vulgarise every association in the manner which has been adopted by this 'son of promise.' Before giving any extracts, we must inform our readers, that this romance is meant to be written in English heroic rhyme. To those who have read any of Hunt's poems, this hint might indeed be needless. Mr Keats has adopted the loose, nerveless versification, and Cockney rhymes of the poet of *Rimini*; but in fairness to that gentleman, we must add, that the defects of the system are tenfold more conspicuous in his disciple's work than in his own. Mr Hunt is a small poet, but he is a clever man. Mr Keats is a still smaller poet, and he is only a boy of pretty abilities, which he has done every thing in his power to spoil.

The poem sets out with the following exposition of the reasons which induced Mr Keats to compose it.

A thing of beauty is a joy for ever:
Its loveliness increases; it will never
Pass into nothingness; but still will keep
A bower quiet for us, and a sleep
Full of sweet dreams, and health, and quiet breathing,
Therefore, on every morrow, are we wreathing
A flowery band to bind us to the earth,
Spite of despondence, of the inhuman dearth
Of noble natures, of the gloomy days,
Of all the unhealthy and o'er-darkened ways
Made for our searching: yes, in spite of all,
Some shape of beauty moves away the pall
From our dark spirits. Such the sun, the moon,
Trees old and young, sprouting a shady boon
For simple sheep; and such are daffodils
With the green world they live in; and clear rills
That for themselves a cooling covert make
'Gainst the hot season; the mid forest brake,
Rich with a sprinkling of fair musk-rose blooms:
And such too is the grandeur of the dooms
We have imagined for the mighty dead;
All lovely tales that we have heard or read;
An endless fountain of immortal drink,
Pouring unto us from the heaven's brink.

Nor do we merely feel these essences
For one short hour; no, even as the trees
That whisper round a temple become soon
Dear as the temple's self, so does the moon,
The passion poesy, glories infinite,
Haunt us till they become a cheering light
Unto our souls, and bound to us so fast,
That, whether there be shine, or gloom o'ercast,
They alway must be with us, or we die.

Therefore 'tis with full happiness that I
Will trace the story of Endymion! ! !

After introducing his hero to us in a procession, and preparing us, by a few mystical lines, for believing that his destiny has in it some strange peculiarity, Mr Keats represents the beloved of the Moon as being conveyed by his sister Peona into an island in a river. This young lady has been alarmed by the appearance of the brother, and questioned him thus:

'Brother, 'tis vain to hide
That thou dost know of things mysterious,
Immortal, starry; such alone could thus
Weigh down thy nature. Hast thou sinn'd in aught
Offensive to the heavenly powers? Caught
A Paphian dove upon a message sent?
Thy deathful bow against some deer-herd bent,
Sacred to Dian? Haply, thou hast seen
Her naked limbs among the alders green;
And that, alas! is death. No, I can trace
Something more high perplexing in thy face!'

Endymion replies in a long speech, wherein he describes his first meeting with the Moon. We cannot make room for the whole of it, but shall take a few passages here and there.

'There blossom'd suddenly a magic bed
Of sacred ditamy, and poppies red:
At which I wonder'd greatly, knowing well
That but one night had wrought this flowery spell;
And, sitting down close by, began to muse
What it might mean. Perhaps, thought I, Morpheus,
In passing here, his owlet pinions shook;
Or, it may be, ere matron Night uptook

Her ebon urn, young Mercury, by stealth,
Had dipt his rod in it: such garland wealth
Came not by common growth. Thus on I thought,
Until my head was dizzy and distraught.
Moreover, through the dancing poppies stole
A breeze, most softly lulling to my soul,' &c.

'Methought the lidless-eyed train
Of planets all were in the blue again.
To commune with those orbs, once more I rais'd
My sight right upward: but it was quite dazed
By a bright something, sailing down apace,
Making me quickly veil my eyes and face:
Again I look'd, and, O ye deities,
Who from Olympus watch our destinies!
Whence that completed form of all completeness?
Whence came that high perfection of all sweetness?
Speak, stubborn earth, and tell me where, O where
Hast thou a symbol of her golden hair?
Not oat-sheaves drooping in the western sun;
Not—thy soft hand, fair sister! let me shun
Such follying before thee—yet she had,
Indeed, locks bright enough to make me mad;
And they were simply gordian'd up and braided,
Leaving, in naked comeliness, unshaded,
Her pearl round ears,' &c.

'She took an airy range,
And then, towards me, like a very maid,
Came blushing, waning, willing, and afraid,
And press'd me by the hand: Ah! 'twas too much;
Methought I fainted at the charmed touch,
Yet held my recollection, even as one
Who dives three fathoms where the waters run
Gurgling in beds of coral: for anon,
I felt upmounted in that region
Where falling stars dart their artillery forth,
And eagles struggle with the buffeting north
That balances the heavy meteor-stone;—
Felt too, I was not fearful, nor alone,' &c.

Not content with the authentic love of the Moon, Keats makes his hero captivate another supernatural lady, of whom no notice occurs in any of his predecessors.

It was a nymph uprisen to the breast
In the fountain's pebbly margin, and she stood
'Mong lilies, like the youngest of the brood.
To him her dripping hand she softly kist,
And anxiously began to plait and twist
Her ringlets round her fingers, saying, 'Youth!
Too long, alas, hast thou starv'd on the ruth,
The bitterness of love: too long indeed,
Seeing thou art so gentle. Could I weed
Thy soul of care, by Heavens, I would offer
All the bright riches of my crystal coffer
To Amphitrite; all my clear-eyed fish,
Golden, or rainbow-sided, or purplish,
Vermilion-tail'd, or finn'd with silvery gauze;
Yea, or my veined pebble-floor, that draws
A virgin light to the deep; my grotto-sands
Tawny and gold, ooz'd slowly from far lands
By my diligent springs; my level lilies, shells,
My charming rod, my potent river spells;
Yes, every thing, even to the pearly cup
Meander gave me,—for I bubbled up
To fainting creatures in a desert wild.
But woe is me, I am but as a child
To gladden thee; and all I dare to say,
Is, that I pity thee: that on this day
I've been thy guide; that thou must wander far
In other regions, past the scanty bar
To mortal steps, before thou can'st be ta'en
From every wasting sigh, from every pain,
Into the gentle bosom of thy love.
Why is thus, one knows in heaven above:
But, a poor Naiad, I guess not. Farewell!
I have a ditty for my hollow cell.'

But we find that we really have no patience for going over four books filled with such amorous scenes as these, with subterraneous journeys equally amusing, and submarine processions equally beautiful; but we must not omit the most interesting scene of the whole piece.

Thus spake he, and that moment felt endued
With power to dream deliciously; so wound
Through a dim passage, searching till he found
The smoothest mossy bed and deepest, where
He threw himself, and just into the air

Stretching his indolent arms, he took, O bliss!
A naked waist: 'Fair Cupid, whence is this?'
A well-known voice sigh'd, 'Sweetest, here am I!'
At which soft ravishment, with doting cry
They trembled to each other.—Helicon!
O fountain'd hill! Old Homer's Helicon!
That thou wouldst spout a little streamlet o'er
These sorry pages: then the verse would soar
And sing above this gentle pair, like lark
Over his nested young: but all is dark
Around thine aged top, and thy clear fount
Exhales in mists to heaven. Aye, the count
Of mighty poets is made up; the scroll
Is folded by the Muses; the bright roll
Is in Apollo's hand: our dazed eyes
Have seen a new tinge in the western skies:
The world has done its duty. Yet, oh yet,
Although the sun of poesy is set,
These lovers did embrace, and we must weep
That there is no old power left to steep
A quill immortal in their joyous tears.
Long time in silence did their anxious fears
Question that thus it was; long time they lay
Fondling and kissing every doubt away;
Long time ere soft caressing sobs began
To mellow into words, and then there ran
Two bubbling springs of talk from their sweet lips.
'O known Unknown! from whom my being sips
Such darling essence, wherefore may I not
Be ever in these arms,' &c.

After all this, however, the 'modesty,' as Mr Keats expresses it, of the Lady Diana prevented her from owning in Olympus her passion for Endymion. Venus, as the most knowing in such matters, is the first to discover the change that has taken place in the temperament of the goddess. 'An idle tale,' says the laughter-loving dame,

'A humid eye, and steps luxurious,
When these are new and strange, are ominous.'

The inamorata, to vary the intrigue, carries on a romantic intercourse with Endymion, under the disguise of an Indian damsel. At last, however, her scruples, for some reason or other, are all overcome, and the Queen of Heaven owns her attachment.

She gave her fair hands to him, and behold,
Before three swiftest kisses he had told,
They vanish far away!—Peona went
Home through the gloomy wood in wonderment.

And so, like many other romances, terminates the 'Poetic Romance' of Johnny Keats, in a patched-up wedding.

We had almost forgot to mention, that Keats belongs to the Cockney School of Politics, as well as the Cockney School of Poetry.

It is fit that he who holds *Rimini* to be the first poem, should believe the *Examiner* to be the first politician of the day. We admire consistency, even in folly. Hear how their bantling has already learned to lisp sedition.

There are who lord it o'er their fellow-men
With most prevailing tinsel: who unpen
Their baaing vanities, to browse away
The comfortable green and juicy hay
From human pastures; or, O torturing fact!
Who, through an idiot blink, will see unpack'd
Fire-branded foxes to sear up and singe
Our gold and ripe-ear'd hopes. With not one tinge
Of sanctuary splendour, not a sight
Able to face an owl's, they still are dight
By the blear-eyed nations in empurpled vests,
And crowns, and turbans. With unladen breasts,
Save of blown self-applause, they proudly mount
To their spirit's perch, their being's high account,
Their tiptop nothings, their dull skies, their thrones—
Amid the fierce intoxicating tones
Of trumpets, shoutings, and belaboured drums,
And sudden cannon. Ah! how all this hums,
In wakeful ears, like uproar past and gone—
Like thunder clouds that spake to Babylon,
And set those old Chaldeans to their tasks.—
Are then regalities all gilded masks?

And now, good-morrow to 'the Muses' son of Promise;' as for 'the feats he yet may do,' as we do not pretend to say, like himself, 'Muse of my native land am I inspired,' we shall adhere to the safe old rule of *pauca verba*. We venture to make one small prophecy, that his bookseller will not a second time venture £50 upon any thing he can write. It is a better and a wiser thing to be a starved apothecary than a starved poet; so back to the shop Mr John, back to 'plasters, pills, and ointment boxes,' &c. But, for Heaven's sake, young Sangrado, be a little more sparing of extenuatives and soporifics in your practice than you have been in your poetry.

16. Croker's attack in the *Quarterly*

1818

Unsigned review, *Quarterly Review* (dated April 1818, published September 1818), xix, 204–8.

John Wilson Croker (1780–1857), an efficient and high-principled Secretary of the Admiralty, had been a co-founder of the *Quarterly* in 1809 with Canning and George Ellis. In the same year he had written a popular but derivative poem *The Battle of Talavera* (see No. 17), and in 1817 *Stories for Children from the History of England.* Cyrus Redding was expressing a widely-held view when he wrote that Croker 'spared nobody, and I should imagine never had a real friend'; but most people at the time, and for long afterwards, assumed that the *Quarterly's* editor, Gifford, was the author of this review. It is here reprinted unabridged.

Reviewers have been sometimes accused of not reading the works which they affected to criticise. On the present occasion we shall anticipate the author's complaint, and honestly confess that we have not read his work. Not that we have been wanting in our duty—far from it—indeed, we have made efforts almost as superhuman as the story itself appears to be, to get through it; but with the fullest stretch of our perseverance, we are forced to confess that we have not been able to struggle beyond the first of the four books of which this Poetic Romance consists. We should extremely lament this want of energy, or whatever it may be, on our parts, were it not for one consolation—

namely, that we are no better acquainted with the meaning of the book through which we have so painfully toiled, than we are with that of the three which we have not looked into.

It is not that Mr Keats, (if that be his real name, for we almost doubt that any man in his senses would put his real name to such a rhapsody,) it is not, we say, that the author has not powers of language, rays of fancy, and gleams of genius—he has all these; but he is unhappily a disciple of the new school of what has been somewhere called Cockney poetry; which may be defined to consist of the most incongruous ideas in the most uncouth language.

Of this school, Mr Leigh Hunt, as we observed in a former Number, aspires to be the hierophant. Our readers will recollect the pleasant recipes for harmonious and sublime poetry which he gave us in his preface to *Rimini*, and the still more facetious instances of his harmony and sublimity in the verses themselves; and they will recollect above all the contempt of Pope, Johnson, and such like poetasters and pseudo-critics, which so forcibly contrasted itself with Mr Leigh Hunt's self-complacent approbation of

—all the things itself had wrote,
Of special merit though of little note.

This author is a copyist of Mr Hunt, but he is more unintelligible, almost as rugged, twice as diffuse, and ten times more tiresome and absurd than his prototype, who, though he impudently presumed to seat himself in the chair of criticism, and to measure his own poetry by his own standard, yet generally had a meaning. But Mr Keats had advanced no dogmas which he was bound to support by examples; his nonsense therefore is quite gratuitous; he writes it for its own sake, and, being bitten by Mr Leigh Hunt's insane criticism, more than rivals the insanity of his poetry.

Mr. Keats's preface hints that his poem was produced under peculiar circumstances.

Knowing within myself (he says) the manner in which this Poem has been produced, it is not without a feeling of regret that I make it public.—What manner I mean, will be *quite clear* to the reader, who must soon perceive great inexperience, immaturity, and every error denoting a feverish attempt, rather than a deed accomplished.—*Preface*, p. vii.

We humbly beg his pardon, but this does not appear to us to be *quite so clear*—we really do not know what he means—but the next passage is more intelligible.

The two first books, and indeed the two last, I feel sensible are not of such completion as to warrant their passing the press.—*Preface*, p. vii.

Thus 'the two first books' are, even in his own judgment, unfit to appear, and 'the two last' are, it seems, in the same condition—and as two and two make four, and as that is the whole number of books, we have a clear and, we believe, a very just estimate of the entire work.

Mr Keats, however, deprecates criticism on this 'immature and feverish work' in terms which are themselves sufficiently feverish; and we confess that we should have abstained from inflicting upon him any of the tortures of the '*fierce hell*' of criticism, which terrify his imagination, if he had not begged to be spared in order that he might write more; if we had not observed in him a certain degree of talent which deserves to be put in the right way, or which, at least, ought to be warned of the wrong; and if, finally, he had not told us that he is of an age and temper which imperiously require mental discipline.

Of the story we have been able to make out but little; it seems to be mythological, and probably relates to the loves of Diana and Endymion; but of this, as the scope of the work has altogether escaped us, we cannot speak with any degree of certainty; and must therefore content ourselves with giving some instances of its diction and versification:—and here again we are perplexed and puzzled.—At first it appeared to us, that Mr Keats had been amusing himself and wearying his readers with an immeasurable game at *bouts—rimés*; but, if we recollect rightly, it is an indispensable condition at this play, that the rhymes when filled up shall have a meaning; and our author, as we have already hinted, has no meaning. He seems to us to write a line at random, and then he follows not the thought excited by this line, but that suggested by the *rhyme* with which it concludes. There is hardly a complete couplet inclosing a complete idea in the whole book. He wanders from one subject to another, from the association, not of ideas but of sounds, and the work is composed of hemistichs which, it is quite evident, have forced themselves upon the author by the mere force of the catchwords on which they turn.

We shall select, not as the most striking instance, but as the least liable to suspicion, a passage from the opening of the poem.

——————— Such the sun, the moon,
Trees old and young, sprouting a shady boon
For simple sheep; and such are daffodils
With the green world they live in; and clear rills

That for themselves a cooling covert make
'Gainst the hot season; the mid forest brake,
Rich with a sprinkling of fair musk-rose blooms:
And such too is the grandeur of the dooms
We have imagined for the mighty dead; &c. &c.—pp. 3, 4.

Here it is clear that the word, and not the idea, *moon* produces the simple sheep and their shady *boon*, and that 'the *dooms* of the mighty dead' would never have intruded themselves but for the '*fair musk-rose blooms*.'

Again.

For 'twas the morn: Apollo's upward fire
Made every eastern cloud a silvery pyre
Of brightness so unsullied, that therein
A melancholy spirit well might win
Oblivion, and melt out his essence fine
Into the winds: rain-scented eglantine
Gave temperate sweets to that well-wooing sun;
The lark was lost in him; cold springs had run
To warm their chilliest bubbles in the grass;
Man's voice was on the mountains; and the mass
Of nature's lives and wonders puls'd tenfold,
To feel this sun-rise and its glories old.—p. 8.

Here Apollo's *fire* produces a *pyre*, a silvery pyre of clouds, *wherein* a spirit might *win* oblivion and melt his essence *fine*, and scented *eglantine* gives sweets to the *sun*, and cold springs had *run* into the *grass*, and then the pulse of the *mass* pulsed *tenfold* to feel the glories *old* of the new-born day, &c.

One example more.

Be still the unimaginable lodge
For solitary thinkings; such as dodge
Conception to the very bourne of heaven,
Then leave the naked brain: be still the leaven,
That spreading in this dull and clodded earth
Gives it a touch ethereal—a new birth.—p. 17.

Lodge, dodge—heaven, leaven—earth, birth; such, in six words, is the sum and substance of six lines.

We come now to the author's taste in versification. He cannot indeed write a sentence, but perhaps he may be able to spin a line. Let us see. The following are specimens of his prosodial notions of our English heroic metre.

Dear as the temple's self, so does the moon,
The passion poesy, glories infinite.—p. 4.

So plenteously all weed-hidden roots.—p. 6.

Of some strange history, potent to send.—p. 18.

Before the deep intoxication.—p. 27.

Her scarf into a fluttering pavilion.—p. 33.

The stubborn canvass for my voyage prepared——.—p. 39.

'Endymion! the cave is secreter
Than the isle of Delos. Echo hence shall stir
No sighs but sigh-warm kisses, or light noise
Of thy combing hand, the while it travelling cloys
And trembles through my labyrinthine hair.'—p. 48.

By this time our readers must be pretty well satisfied as to the meaning of his sentences and the structure of his lines: we now present them with some of the new words with which, in imitation of Mr Leigh Hunt, he adorns our language.

We are told that 'turtles *passion* their voices,' (p. 15); that 'an arbour was *nested*,' (p. 23); and a lady's locks '*gordian'd* up,' (p. 32); and to supply the place of the nouns thus verbalized Mr Keats, with great fecundity, spawns new ones; such as 'men-slugs and human *serpentry*,' (p. 41); the '*honey-feel* of bliss,' (p. 45); 'wives prepare *needments*,' (p. 13)—and so forth.

Then he has formed new verbs by the process of cutting off their natural tails, the adverbs, and affixing them to their foreheads; thus, 'the wine out-sparkled,' (p. 10); the 'multitude up-followed,' (p. 11); and 'night up-took,' (p. 29). 'The wind up-blows,' (p. 32); and the 'hours are down-sunken,' (p. 36.)

But if he sinks some adverbs in the verbs he compensates the language with adverbs and adjectives which he separates from the parent stock. Thus, a lady 'whispers *pantingly* and close,' makes '*hushing* signs,' and steers her skiff into a '*ripply* cove,' (p. 23); a shower falls '*refreshfully*,' (p. 45); and a vulture has a '*spreaded* tail,' (p. 44).

But enough of Mr Leigh Hunt and his simple neophyte.—If any one should be bold enough to purchase this 'Poetic Romance,' and so much more patient, than ourselves, as to get beyond the first book, and so much more fortunate as to find a meaning, we entreat him to make us acquainted with his success; we shall then return to the task which we now abandon in despair, and endeavour to make all due amends to Mr Keats and to our readers.

17. A protest against the *Quarterly*

1818

Letter signed 'J.S.' to the Editor of the *Morning Chronicle*, 3 October 1818.

The writer was presumably John Scott (1783–1821), who was killed less than three years later in a duel arising out of his counter-attack on *Blackwood's* in the *London Magazine*, which he edited (see Introduction, pp. 21–2). Scott had been at school with Byron in Aberdeen. He was well summed up as 'a perfect gentleman'—disliking Keats's Radical attachments, but deeply angered by any kind of meanness or injustice. A brief letter supporting Scott's, with many quotations from *Endymion*, signed 'R.B.', appeared in the *Morning Chronicle* five days later.

The 'Translator of Juvenal' was William Gifford, editor of the *Quarterly*; the 'Biographer of Kirke White' was Robert Southey; and the 'Admiralty Scribe' was Croker—who was the true culprit.

Although I am aware that literary squabbles are of too uninteresting and interminable a nature for your Journal, yet there are occasions when acts of malice and gross injustice towards an author may be properly brought before the public through such a medium.—Allow me, then, without further preface, to refer you to an article in the last Number of *The Quarterly Review*, professing to be a Critique on 'The Poems of John Keats.' Of John Keats I know nothing; from his Preface I collect that he is very young—no doubt a heinous sin; and I have been informed that he has incurred the additional guilt of an acquaintance with Mr Leigh Hunt. That this latter Gentleman and the Editor of *The Quarterly Review* have long been at war, must be known to every one in the least acquainted with the literary gossip of the day. Mr L. Hunt, it appears, has thought highly of the poetical talents of Mr Keats; hence Mr K. is doomed to feel the merciless tomahawk of the Reviewers, termed Quarterly, I presume from the modus operandi. From a perusal of the criticism, I was led to the work itself. I would,

Sir, that your limits would permit a few extracts from this poem. I dare appeal to the taste and judgment of your readers, that beauties of the highest order may be found in almost every page—that there are also many, very many passages indicating haste and carelessness, I will not deny; I will go further, and assert that a real friend of the author would have dissuaded him from an immediate publication.

Had the genius of Lord Byron sunk under the discouraging sneers of an *Edinburgh Review* the nineteenth century would scarcely yet have been termed the Augustan æra of Poetry. Let Mr Keats too persevere—he has talents of no common stamp; this is the hastily written tribute of a stranger, who ventures to predict that Mr K. is capable of producing a poem that shall challenge the admiration of every reader of true taste and feeling; nay if he will give up his acquaintance with Mr Leigh Hunt, and apostatise in his friendships, his principles and his politics (if he have any), he may even command the approbation of the *Quarterly Review*.

I have not heard to whom public opinion has assigned this exquisite morceau of critical acumen. If the Translator of Juvenal be its author, I would refer him to the manly and pathetic narrative prefixed to that translation, to the touching history of genius oppressed by and struggling with innumerable difficulties, yet finally triumphing under patronage and encouragement. If the Biographer of Kirke White have done Mr Keats this cruel wrong, let him remember his own just and feeling expostulation with the Monthly Reviewer, who 'sat down to blast the hopes of a boy, who had confessed to him all his hopes and all his difficulties.' If the 'Admiralty Scribe' (for he too is a Reviewer) be the critic, let him compare the *Battle of Talavera* with *Endymion*.

18. Reynolds also protests

1818

Unsigned review, the *Alfred, West of England Journal and General Advertiser*, 6 October 1818.

J. H. Reynolds's article was reprinted in the *Examiner*, 11 October, 648–9, with an introduction calling the *Quarterly* 'that half-witted, half-hearted Review'.

We have met with a singular instance, in the last number of the *Quarterly Review*, of that unfeeling arrogance, and cold ignorance, which so strangely marked the minds and hearts of Government sycophants and Government writers. The Poem of a young man of genius, which evinces more natural power than any other work of this day, is abused and cried down, in terms which would disgrace any other pens than those used in the defence of an Oliver or a Castles.[1] We have read the Poetic Romance of *Endymion* (the book in question) with no little delight; and could hardly believe that it was written by so young a man as the preface infers. Mr Keats, the author of it, is a genius of the highest order; and no one but a Lottery Commissioner and Government Pensioner (both of which Mr William Gifford, the Editor of the *Quarterly Review*, is) could, with a false and remorseless pen, have striven to frustrate hopes and aims, so youthful and so high as this young Poet nurses. The Monthly Reviewers, it will be remembered, endeavoured, some few years back, to crush the rising heart of young Kirk White;[2] and indeed they in part generated that melancholy which ultimately destroyed him; but the world saw the cruelty, and, with one voice, hailed the genius which malignity would have repressed, and lifted it to fame. Reviewers are creatures 'that stab men in the dark:'—young and enthusiastic spirits are their dearest prey. Our

[1] 'William Oliver' (W. J. Richards) was the Government *agent provocateur* who engineered several hangings by means of the Pentridge Rising (June 1817); and John Castle, another Home Office spy, was exposed in the trial following the Spa Fields Riots (also June 1817).

[2] The poems of Henry Kirke White, who died in 1806 aged 21, had been criticized two years earlier in the *Monthly Review* (lxi. 71–6).

readers will not easily forget the brutality with which the Quarterly Reviewers, in a late number of their ministerial book, commented on the work of an intelligent and patriotic woman, whose ardour and independence happened to be high enough to make them her enemies.[1] The language used by these Government critics, was lower than man would dare to utter to female ears; but Party knows no distinctions,—no proprieties,—and a woman is the best prey for its malignity, because it is the gentlest and the most undefended. We certainly think that Criticism might vent its petty passions on other subjects; that it might chuse its objects from the vain, the dangerous, and the powerful, and not from the young and the unprotected.

It should strike hearts of age and care,
And spare the youthful and the fair.

The cause of the unmerciful condemnation which has been passed on Mr Keats, is pretty apparent to all who have watched the intrigues of literature, and the wily and unsparing contrivances of political parties. This young and powerful writer was noticed, some little time back, in the *Examiner*; and pointed out, by its Editor, as one who was likely to revive the early vigour of English poetry. Such a prediction was a fine, but dangerous compliment, to Mr Keats: it exposed him instantly to the malice of the *Quarterly Review*. Certain it is, that hundreds of fashionable and flippant readers, will henceforth set down this young Poet as a pitiable and nonsensical writer, merely on the assertions of some single heartless critic, who has just energy enough to despise what is good, because it would militate against his pleasantry, if he were to praise it.

The genius of Mr Keats is peculiarly classical; and, with the exception of a few faults, which are the natural followers of youth, his imaginations and his language have a spirit and an intensity which we should in vain look for in half the popular poets of the day. Lord Byron is a splendid and noble egotist.—He visits Classical shores; roams over romantic lands, and wanders through magnificent forests; courses the dark and restless waves of the sea, and rocks his spirit on the midnight lakes; but no spot is conveyed to our minds, that is not peopled by the gloomy and ghastly feelings of one proud and solitary man. It is as if he and the world were the only two things which the air clothed.—His

[1] In its review of Lady Morgan's *France* (1817), the *Quarterly* had repeated, 'with increased severity and earnestness', earlier charges of 'licentiousness, profligacy, irreverence, blasphemy, libertinism, disloyalty, and atheism' (xvii. 260–86).

lines are majestic vanities;—his poetry always is marked with a haughty selfishness;—he writes loftily, because he is the spirit of an ancient family;—he is liked by most of his readers, because he is a Lord. If a common man were to dare to be as moody, as contemptuous, and as misanthropical, the world would laugh at him. There must be a coronet marked on all his little pieces of poetical insolence, or the world would not countenance them. Mr Keats has none of this egotism—this daring selfishness, which is a stain on the robe of poesy—His feelings are full, earnest, and original, as those of the olden writers were and are; they are made for all time, not for the drawing-room and the moment. Mr Keats always speaks of, and describes nature, with an awe and a humility, but with a deep and almost breathless affection.—He knows that Nature is better and older than he is, and he does not put himself on an equality with her. You do not see him, when you see her. The moon, and the mountainous foliage of the woods, and the azure sky, and the ruined and magic temple; the rock, the desert, and the sea; the leaf of the forest, and the embossed foam of the most living ocean, are the spirits of his poetry; but he does not bring them in his own hand, or obtrude his person before you, when you are looking at them. Poetry is a thing of generalities—a wanderer amid persons and things—not a pauser over one thing, or with one person. The mind of Mr Keats, like the minds of our older poets, goes round the universe in its speculations and its dreams. It does not set itself a task. The manners of the world, the fictions and the wonders of other worlds, are its subjects; not the pleasures of hope, or the pleasures of memory. The true poet confines his imagination to no one thing—his soul is an invisible ode to the passions—He does not make a home for his mind in one land—its productions are an universal story, not an eastern tale. The fancies of Moore are exquisitely beautiful, as fancies, but they are always of one colour;—his feelings are pathetic, but they are 'still harping on my daughter.' The true pathetic is to be found in the reflections on things, not in the moods and miseries of one person. There is not one poet of the present day, that enjoys any popularity that will live; each writes for his booksellers and the ladies of fashion, and not for the voice of centuries. Time is a lover of old books, and he suffers few new ones to become old. Posterity is a difficult mark to hit, and few minds can send the arrow full home. Wordsworth might have safely cleared the rapids in the stream of time, but he lost himself by looking at his own image in the waters. Coleridge stands bewildered in the cross-road of fame;—his genius will commit suicide, and be buried in it. Southey is Poet Laureate, 'so there is no heed to be taken of him.' Campbell has relied on two stools, *The Pleasures of Hope*, and *Gertrude of Wyoming*, but he will come to the ground, after the fashion of the old proverb. The journey of fame is an endless one; and does Mr Rogers think that pumps and silk stockings (which his genius wears) will last him the whole way? Poetry is the coyest creature that ever was wooed by man: she has something of the coquette in her; for she flirts with many, and seldom loves one.

Mr Keats has certainly not perfected anything yet; but he has the power, we think, within him, and it is in consequence of such an opinion that we have written these few hasty observations. If he should ever see this, he will not regret to find that all the country is not made up of Quarterly Reviewers. All that we wish is, that our Readers could read the Poem, as we have done, before they assent to its condemnation—they will find passages of singular feeling, force, and pathos. We have the highest hopes of this young Poet. We are obscure men, it is true, and not gifted with that perilous power of mind, and truth of judgment which are possessed by Mr Croker, Mr Canning, Mr Barrow, or Mr Gifford, (all 'honourable men', and writers in the *Quarterly Review*). We live far from the world of letters,—out of the pale of fashionable criticism,—aloof from the atmosphere of a Court; but we are surrounded by a beautiful country, and love Poetry, which we read out of doors, as well as in. We think we see glimpses of a high mind in this young man, and surely the feeling is better that urges us to nourish its strength, than that which prompts the Quarterly Reviewer to crush it in its youth, and for ever. If however, the mind of Mr Keats be of the quality we think it to be of, it will not be cast down by this wanton and empty attack. Malice is a thing of the scorpion kind—It drives the sting into its own heart. The very passages which the *Quarterly Review* quotes as ridiculous, have in them the beauty that sent us to the Poem itself. We shall close these observations with a few extracts from the romance itself:—If our Readers do not see the spirit and beauty in them to justify our remarks, we confess ourselves bad judges, and never more worthy to be trusted.

The following address to Sleep, is full of repose and feeling:—

O magic sleep! Oh comfortable bird,
That broodest o'er the troubled sea of the mind,
Till it is hush'd and smooth! O unconfined
Restraint! Imprisoned Liberty! Great key
To golden palaces, strange minstrelsy,

Fountains grotesque, new trees, bespangled caves,
Echoing grottoes, full of tumbling waves,
And moonlight!

This is beautiful—but there is something finer,

—That men, who might have tower'd in the van
Of all the congregated world to fan
And winnow from the coming step of time,
All chaff of custom, wipe away all slime
Left by men slugs and human serpentry;
Have been content to let occasion die,
Whilst they did sleep in Love's Elysium.
And truly I would rather be struck dumb,
Than speak again this ardent listlessness:
For I have ever thought that it might bless
The world with benefits unknowingly;
As does the nightingale up-perched high,
And cloister'd among cool and bunched leaves,
She sings but to her love, nor e'er conceives
How tiptoe night holds back her dark grey hood.

The turn of this is truly Shakesperian, which Mr Keats will feel to be the highest compliment we can pay him, if we know any thing of his mind. We cannot refrain from giving the following short passage, which appears to us scarcely to be surpassed in the whole range of English Poetry. It has all the naked and solitary vigour of old sculpture, with all the energy and life of Old Poetry:—

—At this, with madden'd stare,
And lifted hands, and trembling lips he stood,
Like old Deucalion mounted o'er the flood.
Or blind Orion hungry for the morn.

Again, we give some exquisitely classical lines, clear and reposing as a Grecian sky—soft and lovely as the waves of Ilyssus.

—Here is wine,
Alive with sparkles—Never I aver,
Since Ariadne was a vintager,
So cool a purple; taste these juicy pears,
Sent me by sad Vertumnus, when his fears
Were high about Pomona: here is cream,
Deepening to richness from a snowy gleam;
Sweeter than that nurse Amalthea skimm'd
For the boy Jupiter.

This is the very fruit of poetry.—A melting repast for the imagination. We can only give one more extract—our limits are reached. Mr Keats is speaking of the story of Endymion itself. Nothing can be more imaginative than what follows:—

—Ye who have yearn'd
With too much passion, will here stay and pity,
For the mere sake of truth; as 'tis a ditty
Not of these days, but long ago 'twas told
By a cavern'd wind unto a forest old;
And then the forest told it in a dream
To a sleeping lake, whose cool and level gleam
A Poet caught as he was journeying
To Phoebus' shrine and in it he did fling
His weary limbs, bathing an hour's space,
And after, straight in that inspired place
He sang the story up into the air,
Giving it universal freedom.

We have no more room for extracts. Does the author of such poetry as this deserve to be made the sport of so servile a dolt as a Quarterly Reviewer?—No. Two things have struck us on the perusal of this singular poem. The first is, that Mr Keats excels, in what Milton excelled—the power of putting a spirit of life and novelty into the Heathen Mythology. The second is, that in the structure of his verse, and the sinewy quality of his thoughts, Mr Keats greatly resembles old Chapman, the nervous translator of Homer. His mind has 'thews and limbs like to its ancestors.' Mr Gifford, who knows something of the old dramatists, ought to have paused before he sanctioned the abuse of a spirit kindred with them. If he could not feel, he ought to know better.

19. Shelley on Keats

1819, 1820, 1821, 1822

Percy Bysshe Shelley (1792–1822) was regarded by Keats, who met him through Leigh Hunt, as a well-intentioned rival, and their friendship never went much beyond verse-writing competitions (*Endymion* and *The Revolt of Islam* were probably begun in this way). Shelley, a perceptive critic, saw Keats's greatness from the outset and defended even *Endymion*, mildly at first (Extract (c)—though this letter was never sent), then with passionate indignation in *Adonais* (Extract (g)). If the chaotic Medwin can be trusted (Extract (k)), Shelley was finally converted to admiring Keats's other later poems besides *Hyperion*. The 'Epitaph' (Extract (j)) has not previously been published in full.

(a) Extract from letter, 6 September 1819, to Charles Ollier: 'I have read your Altham, & Keats' Poem & Lambs Works—For the second in this list much praise is due to me for having read, the Authors intention appearing to be that no person should possibly get to the end of it. Yet it is full of some of the highest & the finest gleams of poetry; indeed every thing seems to be viewed by the mind of a poet which is described in it. I think if he had printed about 50 pages of fragments from it I should have been led to admire Keats as a poet more than I ought, of which there is now no danger.—' (*The Letters of Percy Bysshe Shelley*, ed. F. L. Jones, 1964, ii. 117.)

(b) Extract from letter, 27 July 1820, to John Keats: 'I have lately read your *Endymion* again & ever with a new sense of the treasures of poetry it contains, though treasures poured forth with indistinct profusion. This, people in general will not endure, & that is the cause of the comparatively few copies which have been sold. I feel persuaded that you are capable of the greatest things, so you but will. . . . In poetry *I* have sought to avoid system and mannerism; I wish those who excel me in genius, would pursue the same plan.—' (ii. 221.)

(c) Extract from draft of letter, *c.* 20 October 1820, to the Editor of the *Quarterly Review*: 'The case is different with the unfortunate subject of this letter, the Author of *Endymion*, to whose feelings & situation I intreat you to allow me to call your attention. I write considerably in the dark, but if it is Mr Gifford that I am addressing, I am persuaded that in an appeal to his humanity & justice he will acknowledge the *fas ab hoste doceri.*[1] I am aware that the first duty of a Reviewer is towards the public, and I am willing to confess that the *Endymion* is a poem considerably defective, & that perhaps it deserved as much censure as the pages of your review record against it. But not to mention that there is a certain contemptuousness of phraseology from which it is difficult for a critic to abstain, in the Review of *Endymion*,—I do not think that the writer has given it its due praise. Surely the poem with all its faults is a very remarkable production for a man of Keats's age and the promise of ultimate excellence is such as has rarely been afforded even by such as have afterwards attained high literary eminence. Look at Book 2. line 833 &c. & Book 3. line 113. to 120—read down that page & then again from line 193—I could cite many other passages to convince you that it deserved milder usage. Why it should have been reviewed at all, excepting for the purpose of bringing its excellencies into notice I cannot conceive, for it was very little read, & there was no danger that it should become a model to the age of that false taste with which I confess that it is replenished—' (ii. 252.)

(d) Extract from letter, 29 October 1820, to Marianne Hunt: 'Keats's new volume has arrived to us, & the fragment called *Hyperion* promises for him that he is destined to become one of the first writers of the age.—His other things are imperfect enough, & what is worse written in the bad sort of style which is becoming fashionable among those who fancy that they are imitating Hunt & Wordsworth.' (ii. 239.)

(e) Extract from letter, 15 February 1821, to T. L. Peacock: 'Among your anathemas of the modern attempts in poetry, do you include Keats's *Hyperion*? I think it very fine. His other poems are worth little; but if the *Hyperion* be not grand poetry, none has been produced by our contemporaries.' (ii. 262.)

(f) Extract from letter, 4 May 1821, to Lord Byron: 'The account of Keats is, I fear, too true. Hunt tells me that in the first paroxysms of his disappointment he burst a blood-vessel; and thus laid the foundation of a rapid consumption. There can be no doubt but that the irritability

[1] 'The divine law to be taught by an enemy.'

which exposed him to this catastrophe was a pledge of future sufferings, had he lived. And yet this argument does not reconcile me to the employment of contemptuous and wounding expressions against a man merely because he has written bad verses; or, as Keats did, some good verses in a bad taste. Some plants, which require delicacy in rearing, might bring forth beautiful flowers if ever they should arrive at maturity. . . . As to Keats's merits as a poet, I principally repose them upon the fragment of a poem entitled *Hyperion*, which you may not, perhaps, have seen, and to which I think you would not deny high praise. The energy and beauty of his powers seem to disperse the narrow and wretched taste in which (most unfortunately for the real beauty which they hide) he has clothed his writings. . . . I did not know that Keats had attacked Pope; I had heard that Bowles had done so, and that you had most severely chastised him therefor. Pope, it seems, has been selected as the pivot of a dispute in taste, on which, until I understand it, I must profess myself neuter.' (ii. 289–90.)

(g) Extract from the preface to *Adonais*, published July 1821: 'It is my intention to subjoin to the London edition of this poem, a criticism upon the claims of its lamented object to be classed among the writers of the highest genius who have adorned our age. My known repugnance to the narrow principles of taste on which several of his earlier compositions were modelled, prove, at least that I am an impartial judge. I consider the fragment of *Hyperion*, as second to nothing that was ever produced by a writer of the same years. . . .

The genius of the lamented person to whose memory I have dedicated these unworthy verses, was not less delicate and fragile than it was beautiful; and where canker-worms abound, what wonder, if it's young flower was blighted in the bud? The savage criticism on his *Endymion*, which appeared in the *Quarterly Review*, produced the most violent effect on his susceptible mind; the agitation thus originated ended in the rupture of a blood-vessel in the lungs; a rapid consumption ensued, and the succeeding acknowledgements from more candid critics, of the true greatness of his powers, were ineffectual to heal the wound thus wantonly inflicted.

It may be well said, that these wretched men know not what they do. They scatter their insults and their slanders without heed as to whether the poisoned shaft lights on a heart made callous by many blows, or one, like Keats's composed of more penetrable stuff. One of their associates, is, to my knowledge, a most base and unprincipled calumniator. As to *Endymion*; was it a poem, whatever might be it's defects, to be treated contemptuously by those who had celebrated with various degrees of complacency and panegyric, *Paris*, and *Woman*, and a *Syrian Tale*, and Mrs Lefanu, and Mr Barrett, and Mr Howard Payne, and a long list of the illustrious obscure? Are these the men, who in their venal good nature, presumed to draw a parallel between the Rev. Mr Milman and Lord Byron? What gnat did they strain at here, after having swallowed all those camels? Against what woman taken in adultery, dares the foremost of these literary prostitutes to cast his opprobrious stone? Miserable man! you, one of the meanest, have wantonly defaced one of the noblest specimens of the workmanship of God. Nor shall it be your excuse, that, murderer as you are, you have spoken daggers, but used none.'

(h) Extract from letter, 16 July 1821, to Lord Byron: 'Although I feel the truth of what I have alleged about his *Hyperion*, and I doubt, if you saw that particular poem, whether you would not agree with me; yet I need not be told that I have been carried too far by the enthusiasm of the moment; by my piety, and my indignation, in panegyric. But if I have erred, I console myself by reflecting that it is in defence of the weak—not in conjunction with the powerful. And perhaps I have erred from the narrow view of considering Keats rather as he surpassed *me* in particular than as he was inferior to others: so subtle is the principle of self!' (*Letters*, ii. 308–9.)

(i) Extract from letter, 29 November 1821, to Joseph Severn: 'In spite of his transcendent genius Keats never was nor ever will be a popular poet, & the total neglect & obscurity in which the astonishing remnants of his mind still lie, was hardly to be dissipated by a writer, who, however he may differ from Keats in more important qualities, at least resembles him in that accidental one, a want of popularity. . . . But for these considerations it had been my intention to have collected the remnants of his compositions & to have published them with a life & criticism.—' (ii. 366.)

(j) From Bodl. MS. Shelley adds.e.7, f. 246 [256], composed *c.* 3 December 1821:

'Epitaph
"Here lieth one whose name was writ on water"
But ere the breath that could erase it, blew,
Death in remorse for that fell slaughter,
Death, the immortalizing Winter, flew

Athwart the stream, and Times printless torrent grew
  A scroll of Chrystal blazoning the name
Of Adonais: till all recognized and knew
  The sentence of his fame—'

(k) From notes on conversations with Shelley, 22 October 1820 to 27 February 1821, and 14 November 1821 to April 1822: 'I will state what Shelley's opinions were of his poetry. Those he entertained respecting *Endymion*, are already before the public. He often lamented that, under the adoption of false canons of taste, he spoiled by their affectation his finest passages. But in the volume that Keats published in 1820, he perceived in every one of these productions a marked and continually progressing improvement, and hailed with delight his release from his leading-strings, his emancipation from what he called "a perverse and limited school." The "Pot of Basil", and the "Eve of St. Agnes", he read and re-read with ever new delight, and looked upon *Hyperion* as almost faultless, grieving that it was but a fragment, and that Keats had not been encouraged to complete a work worthy of Milton. He used to say that "the scenery and drawing of his Saturn Dethroned, and the fallen Titans, surpassed those of Satan and his rebellious angels in the *Paradise Lost*,—possessing more human interest; that the whole poem was supported throughout with a colossal grandeur equal to the subject." Shelley had this little volume continually in his pocket, the best proof of his appreciation of its merits. Nothing more deeply affected Shelley than the premature removal from a world, that deserved to lose him, of Keats. Shelley thought that he died too soon for his fame, great as it is; had he lived to bask in the warm south, to drink deep of the warm south, to draw his inspiration from purer sources; had he not been flattered and stimulated into writing from false models, turned as he was daily become more and more from the error of his ways, what might he not have produced?' (Thomas Medwin, *Life of Percy Bysshe Shelley*, 1847, ii. 109–11.)

(l) Extract from letter, 18 June 1822, to John Gisborne: '. . . Keats, who was a poet of great genius, let the classic party say what it will.' (*Letters*, ii. 434.)

20. Byron on the 'Trash of Keats'

1820, 1821–2

In finding Keats's poetry distasteful, George Gordon, Lord Byron (1788–1824), took an opposite view to 'the Snake' (Shelley); but he was strongly influenced both by Shelley and by the reviews in *Blackwood's*, as well as by jealousy of his idol, Pope; and his irritable inconsistency is shown in these critical extracts. On the sexual pathology of some comments, see Introduction, p. 35 (Robert Graves has suggested that what Byron actually wrote in Extract (b) was not *Mankin* but *manecon*, i.e. catamite).

(a) Extract from 'Some Observations upon an Article in *Blackwood's Magazine* No. xxix August 1819', dated 15 March 1820: 'I will conclude with two quotations. . . . The second is from the volume of a young person learning to write poetry, and beginning by teaching the art. Hear him—*

[Quotes 'Sleep and Poetry', lines 193–206, 'But ye were dead' to 'The name of one Boileau!']

A little before, the manner of Pope is termed,

A *scism*,
Nurtured by *foppery* and barbarism,
Made great Apollo blush for this his land.

. . . The writer of this is a tadpole of the Lakes, a young disciple of the six or seven new schools, in which he has learnt to write such lines and such sentiments as the above. He says "easy was the task" of imitating Pope, or it may be of equalling him, I presume. I recommend him to

* [MS. note, dated 12 November 1821]: . . . My indignation at Mr Keats's depreciation of Pope has hardly permitted me to do justice to his own genius, which, malgré all the fantastic fopperies of his style, was undoubtedly of great promise. His fragment of *Hyperion* seems actually inspired by the Titans, and is as sublime as Aeschylus. He is a loss to our literature; and the more so, as he himself before his death, is said to have been persuaded that he had not taken the right line, and was reforming his style upon the more classical models of the language.

try before he is so positive on the subject, and then compare what he will have *then* written and what he has *now* written with the humblest and earliest compositions of Pope, produced in years still more youthful than those of Mr Keats when he invented his new "*Essay on Criticism*," entitled "Sleep and Poetry" (an ominous title,) from whence the above canons are taken. Pope's was written at nineteen, and published at twenty-two.' (*The Works of Lord Byron: Letters and Journals*, ed. R. E. Prothero, 1898–1901, iv. 491–3.)

(b) Extract from letter, 12 August 1820, to John Murray: 'Here are Johnny Keats's *p–ss a bed* poetry. . . . There is such a trash of Keats and the like upon my tables, that I am ashamed to look at them. . . . No more Keats, I entreat:—flay him alive; if some of you don't, I must skin him myself: there is no bearing the drivelling idiotism of the Mankin.' (*Letters and Journals*, v. 93–6.)

(c) Extract from letter, 4 September 1820, to John Murray: 'The *Edinburgh* praises Jack Keats or Ketch, or whatever his names are: why, his is the * of Poetry—something like the pleasure an Italian fiddler extracted out of being suspended daily by a Street Walker in Drury Lane. This went on for some weeks: at last the Girl went to get a pint of Gin—met another, chatted too long, and Cornelli was *hanged outright before she returned*. Such like is the trash they praise, and such will be the end of the *outstretched* poesy of this miserable Self-polluter of the human mind.' (*Byron: A Self-Portrait*, ed. P. Quennell, 1950, ii. 533.)

(d) Extract from letter, 9 September 1820, to John Murray: 'Mr Keats, whose poetry you enquire after, appears to me what I have already said: such writing is a sort of mental masturbation— * * * * * * * * his *Imagination*. I don't mean he is *indecent*, but viciously soliciting his own ideas into a state, which is neither poetry nor any thing else but a Bedlam vision produced by raw pork and opium.' (*Byron: A Self-Portrait*, ii. 536.)

(e) Extract from letter, 18 September 1820, to John Murray: 'P.S.—Of the praises of that little dirty blackguard Keates in the *Edinburgh*, I shall observe as Johnson did when Sheridan the actor got a *pension*: "What! has *he* got a pension? Then it is time that I should give up *mine*!" . . . Why don't they review and praise *Solomon's Guide to Health*? it is better sense and as much poetry as Johnny Keates.' (*Letters and Journals*, v. 120–1.)

(f) Extract from 'A Second Letter to John Murray, Esq., on the Rev. W. L. Bowles's Strictures on the Life & Writings of Pope' (1835), dated 25 March 1821. The passage in brackets was sent on later for insertion in the original Letter: '. . . the personages who decry Pope. One of them, a Mr John Ketch, has written some lines against him, of which it were better to be the subject than the author. [As Mr K. does not want imagination nor industry, let those who have led him astray look to what they have done. Surely they must feel no little remorse in having so perverted the taste and feelings of this young man, and will be satisfied with one such victim to their Moloch of Absurdity.] . . . The grand distinction of the under forms of the new school of poets is their *vulgarity*. By this I do not mean that they are *coarse*, but "shabby-genteel," as it is termed. A man may be *coarse* and yet not *vulgar*, and the reverse. Burns is often coarse, but never *vulgar*. Chatterton is never vulgar, nor Wordsworth, nor the higher of the Lake school, though they treat of low life in all its branches. It is in their *finery* that the new under school are *most* vulgar, and they may be known by this at once; as what we called at Harrow "a Sunday blood" might be easily distinguished from a gentleman. . . . In the present case, I speak of writing, not of persons. . . . They may be honourable and *gentlemanly* men, for what I know; but the latter quality is studiously excluded from their publications. . . . Far be it from me to presume that there ever was, or can be, such a thing as an *aristocracy* of *poets*: but there *is* a nobility of thought and of style, open to all stations, and derived partly from talent, and partly from education,—which is to be found in Shakespeare, and Pope, and Burns, no less than in Dante and Alfieri, but which is nowhere to be perceived in the mock birds and bards of Mr Hunt's little chorus. . . . In poetry, as well as writing in general, it will never *make* entirely a poet or a poem; but neither poet nor poem will ever be good for any thing without it. It is the *salt* of society, and the seasoning of composition. *Vulgarity* is far worse than downright *blackguardism*; for the latter comprehends wit, humour, and strong sense at times; while the former is a sad abortive attempt at all things, "signifying nothing." It does not depend upon low themes, or even low language, for Fielding revels in both;—but is he ever *vulgar*? No. You see the man of education, the gentleman, and the scholar, sporting with his subject,—its master, not its slave. Your vulgar writer is always most vulgar the higher his subject, as the man who showed the menagerie at Pidcock's was wont to say,—"This, gentlemen, is the *eagle* of the *sun*, from Archangel, in Russia; the *otterer* it is the *igherer* he flies." But to the proof. It is a thing to be felt more than explained. Let any man take up a volume of Mr Hunt's subordinate writers, read (if possible) a couple of pages, and pronounce for himself, if they contain not the kind of writing which may be likened to "shabby-genteel" in actual life. When he has done this, let him take up Pope; and when he has laid him down, take up the cockneys again—if he can.' (*Letters and Journals*, v. 591–2.)

(g) Extract from letter, 26 April 1821, to Shelley: 'I am very sorry to hear what you say of Keats—is it *actually* true? I did not think criticism had been so killing. Though I differ from you essentially in your estimate of his performances, I so much abhor all unnecessary pain, that I would rather he had been seated on the highest peak of Parnassus than have perished in such a manner. Poor fellow! though with such inordinate self-love he would probably have not been very happy. I read the review of *Endymion* in the *Quarterly*. It was severe,—but surely not so severe as many reviews in that and other journals upon others. . . . You know my opinion of *that second-hand* school of poetry. . . . I have published a pamphlet on the Pope controversy, which you will not like. Had I known that Keats was dead—or that he was alive and so sensitive—I should have omitted some remarks upon his poetry, to which I was provoked by his *attack* upon *Pope*, and my disapprobation of *his own* style of writing.' (*Byron: A Self-Portrait*, ii. 601–2.)

(h) Extract from letter, 30 July 1821, to John Murray: 'Are you aware that Shelley has written an elegy on Keats, and accuses the *Quarterly* of killing him?

"Who killed John Keats?"
"I", says the Quarterly,
So savage and Tartarly;
" 'Twas one of my feats."

"Who shot the arrow?"
"The poet-priest Milman
(So ready to kill man),
Or Southey or Barrow."

You know very well that I did not approve of Keats's poetry, or principles of poetry, or of his abuse of Pope; but, as he is dead, omit *all* that is said *about him* in any *MSS*. of mine, or publication. His *Hyperion* is a fine monument, and will keep his name. I do not envy the man who wrote the article: your review people have no more right to kill than any other foot pads. However, he who would die of an article in a review would probably have died of something else equally trivial.

The same thing nearly happened to Kirke White, who afterwards died of a consumption.' (*Byron: A Self-Portrait*, ii. 661.)

(i) Extract from letter, 4 August 1821, to John Murray: 'You must . . . omit the whole of the observations against the *Suburban School*: they are meant against Keats, and I cannot war with the dead—particularly those already killed by Criticism. Recollect to omit all that portion in *any case*.' (*Letters and Journals*, v. 337.)

(j) From notes on conversations with Byron, 1821–2: ' "I know no two men," said he, "who have been so infamously treated, as Shelley and Keats. . . . Then as to Keats, though I am no admirer of his poetry, I do not envy the man, whoever he was, that attacked and killed him. . . . As Keats is now gone, we may speak of him. I am always battling with *the Snake* about Keats, and wonder what he finds to make a god of, in that idol of the Cockneys: besides, I always ask Shelley why he does not follow his style, and make himself one of the school, if he thinks it so divine. He will, like me, return some day to admire Pope, and think *The Rape of the Lock* and its sylphs worth fifty *Endymions*, with their faun and satyr machinery. I remember Keats some where says that 'flowers would not blow, leaves bud,' &c. if man and woman did not kiss. How sentimental!"

I remarked that *Hyperion* was a fine fragment, and a proof of his poetical genius.

"*Hyperion!*" said he: "why a man might as well pretend to be rich who had one diamond. *Hyperion* indeed! *Hyperion* to a satyr!" ' (Thomas Medwin, *Conversations of Lord Byron*, 1824, 292–5.)

21. Not a poem, but a dream of poetry

1820

Unsigned review, *London Magazine* (Baldwin's), (April 1820), ii, 380–9.

Peter George Patmore (1786–1855), father of the poet Coventry Patmore (No. 61), had a foot in both literary camps, being a friend of Hazlitt and Lamb as well as a former correspondent for *Blackwood's*. He acted as John Scott's second in the duel with Christie, and has been blamed (unjustly it now appears) for the mistake that led to Scott's death (see Introduction pp. 21–2).

Despite the flowery expressions (ridiculed in No. 29), this is the most interesting and perceptive of the answers to the attacks on *Endymion*; for instance, in its suggestion that a new concept of what constitutes 'a poem' is needed, in its recognition of the characteristics of dream-work in *Endymion*, and in asserting that the good and bad qualities of Keats's style 'are inextricably linked together.'

That the periodical criticism of the present day, *as* criticism, enjoys but a slender portion of public respect,—except among mere book-buyers and blue-stockings,—cannot be denied. It would be unjust not to confess that it has its uses. But, in return, it has its reward. The public, and public critics, mutually serve and despise each other; and if both, for the most part, know that this is the case, the latter are too politic to complain of injustice, and the former too indolent to resent it. Each party is content to accept the evil with the good.

But a feeling much stronger than that of contempt has attached itself to this part of the public press, in consequence of certain attempts of modern criticism to blight and wither the maturity of genius; or—still worse—to change its youthful enthusiasm into despair, and thus tempt it to commit suicide; or—worst of all—to creep to its cradle, and strangle it in the first bloom and beauty of its childhood. To feel that all this has been attempted, and most of it effected, by modern criticism, we need only pronounce to ourselves the names of Chatterton and Kirke White among the dead, of Montgomery, and Keats, and Wordsworth among the living;—not to mention Byron, Shelley, Hunt, &c. It is only necessary to refer, in particular, to the first four of these names; for the others, with an equal share of poetic 'ambition,' have less of 'the illness does attend it;'—less of its over-refined and morbid sensibility.

The miraculous boy, Chatterton, might have been alive, glorying in, and glorifying himself, his country, and his age, at this day, if he had not encountered a shallow-thoughted and cold-blooded critic: for though he was one of the true 'children of the sun' of poetry, his more than human power was linked to more than human weakness. Poor Kirke White, too! different as they were in almost every thing—the one a star, the other a flower—yet both received their light and beauty from the same sun, and both participated in the same fate. To think that the paltry drudge of a bookseller should be permitted to trample in the dirt of a review such an amaranthine flower as this—worthy as it was, to have bloomed in the very Eden of Poetry!—And what had the brilliant, and witty, and successful creator of a new era in criticism to do with the plaintive and tender Montgomery?—If he was too busy or too happy to discover any music in sighs, or any beauty in tears, at least he might have been too philosophical, or too good-natured, to laugh at them. Suppose the poet did indulge a little too much in the 'luxury of grief,'—if it was weakness, at least it was not hypocrisy; and there was small chance of its infecting either the critic or his readers—so that he exhibited little either of skill or courage in going out of his way to pick a quarrel with it. The poet, with all his fine powers, has scarcely yet recovered from the effects of that visitation; and the critic, with all his cleverness, never will.

It would lead us too far from our present purpose,—and indeed does not belong to it,—to do more than refer to the exploits of the same work against the early attempts of the two writers who at present share the poetic throne of the day. Whatever else they might want, these attacks had at least boldness; and they could do little mischief, for the objects of them were armed at all points against the assault. It is not to these latter, but to such as those on Kirke White and Montgomery, and a late one on the work which we are about to notice, that the periodical criticism of the day owes that resentment and indignation which is at present felt against it, by the few whose praise (in matters of literature) is not censure. To make criticism subservient to pecuniary or ambitious views is poor and paltry enough; but there is some natural motive, and therefore some excuse, for this: but to make it a means of depressing true genius, and defrauding it of its dearest reward—its fair fame—is unnaturally, because it is gratuitously, wicked. It is a wickedness, however, that might safely be left to work out its own punishment, but that its anonymous offspring too frequently do their mischievous bidding for a time, and thus answer the end of their birth.

In thinking of these things we are tempted to express an opinion which perhaps it would be more prudent to keep to ourselves,—viz. that poetical criticism is, for the most part, a very superfluous and impertinent business; and is to be tolerated at all only when it is written in an unfeigned spirit of admiration and humility. We must therefore do ourselves the justice to disclaim, for once, any intention of writing a regular critique in the present instance. Criticism, like every thing else, is very well in its place; but, like every thing else, it does not always know where that is. Certainly a poet, properly so called, is beyond its jurisdiction;—for *good* and *bad*, when applied to poetry, are words without a meaning. One might as well talk of good or bad virtue. That which *is* poetry must be good. It may differ in kind and in degree, and therefore it may differ in value; but if it *be* poetry, it is a thing about which criticism has no concern, any more than it has with other of the highest productions of Fine Art. The sublimities of Michael Angelo are beyond the reach of its ken—the divine forms of Raphael were not made to be meddled with by its unhallowed fingers—the ineffable expressions of Corregio must not be sullied by its earthy breath. These things were given to the world for something better than to be written and talked about; and they have done their bidding hitherto, and will do it till they cease to exist. They have opened a perpetual spring of lofty thoughts and pure meditations; they have blended themselves with the very existence, and become a living principle in the hearts of mankind;—and they are, now, no more fit to be touched and tampered with than the stars of heaven—for like them

Levan di terra al cielo nostr' intelletto.[1]

We will not shrink from applying these observations, prospectively, to the young poet whose work we are about to notice. *Endymion*, if it be not, technically speaking, a poem, is poetry itself. As a *promise*, we know of nothing like it, except some things of Chatterton. Of the few

[1] 'They raise our minds from earth to heaven' (Petrarch, *Rime* X, 9).

others that occur to us at the moment, the most remarkable are Pope's Pastorals, and his *Essay on Criticism*;—but these are proofs of an extraordinary precocity, not of genius, but of taste, as the word was understood in his day; and of a remarkably early acquaintance with all the existing common-places of poetry and criticism. It is true that Southey's *Joan of Arc*, and Campbell's *Pleasures of Hope*, were both produced before their authors were one-and-twenty. But *Joan of Arc*, though a fine poem, is diffuse, not from being rich, but from being diluted; and the *Pleasures of Hope* is a delightful work—but then it *is* a work—and one cannot help wishing it had been written at thirty instead of twenty.

Endymion is totally unlike all these, and all other poems. As we said before, it is not *a poem* at all. It is an ecstatic dream of poetry—a flush—a fever—a burning light—an involuntary out-pouring of the spirit of poetry—that will not be controuled. Its movements are the starts and boundings of the young horse before it has felt the bitt—the first flights of the young bird, feeling and exulting in the powers with which it is gifted, but not yet acquainted with their use or their extent. It is the wanderings of the butterfly in the first hour of its birth; not as yet knowing one flower from another, but only that all *are* flowers. Its similitudes come crowding upon us from all delightful things. It is the May-day of poetry—the flush of blossoms and weeds that start up at the first voice of spring. It is the sky-lark's hymn to the day-break, involuntarily gushing forth as he mounts upward to look for the fountain of that light which has awakened him. It is as if the muses had steeped their child in the waters of Castaly, and we beheld him emerging from them, with his eyes sparkling and his limbs quivering with the delicious intoxication, and the precious drops scattered from him into the air at every motion, glittering in the sunshine, and casting the colours of the rainbow on all things around.

Almost entirely unknown as this poem is to general readers, it will perhaps be better to reserve what we have further to say of its characteristics, till we have given some specimens of it. We should premise this, however, by saying, that our examples will probably exhibit almost as many faults as beauties. But the reader will have anticipated this from the nature of the opinion we have already given—at least if we have succeeded in expressing what we intended to express. In fact, there is scarcely a passage of any length in the whole work, which does not exhibit the most glaring faults—faults that in many instances amount almost to the ludicrous: yet positive and palpable as they are, it may be said of them generally, that they are as much collateral evidences of poetical power, as the beauties themselves are direct ones. If the poet had had time, or patience, or we will even say taste, to have weeded out these faults as they sprang up, he could not have possessed the power to create the beauties to which they are joined. If he had waited to make the first half dozen pages of his work faultless, the fever—the ferment of mind in which the whole was composed would have subsided for ever. Or if he had attempted to pick out those faults afterwards, the beauties must inevitably have gone with them—for they are inextricably linked together.

The title of *Endymion* will indicate the subject of it. It is, in one word, the story of the mutual loves of Endymion and the Moon,—including the trials and adventures which the youthful shepherd was destined to pass through, in order to prepare and fit him for the immortality to which he at last succeeds.

It is not part of our plan to follow the poet and his hero—for they go hand in hand together—through their adventures; for, as a tale, this work is nothing. There is no connecting interest to bind one part of it to another. Almost any two parts of it might be transposed, without disadvantage to either, or to the whole. We repeat, it is not a poem, but a dream of poetry; and while many of its separate parts possess that vivid distinctness which frequently belongs to the separate parts of a dream, the impression it leaves as a whole is equally indistinct and confused.—The poet begins by noticing the delightful associations we are accustomed to attach to beautiful thoughts and objects, and continues,

> ——— therefore 'tis that I
> Will trace the story of Endymion.
> The very music of his name has gone
> Into my being.

Then, after dallying a little with the host of beautiful images which are conjured up by that name, he exclaims

> And now at once, adventuresome, I send
> My herald thought into a wilderness.

These two lines are very characteristic. It is the bold boy plunging for the first time into the stream, without knowing or caring whither it may carry him. The story, such as it is, commences with the description of a procession and festival, in honour of the god Pan. The following are parts of this description:

[Quotes Book I, lines 107–21, 'Now while the silent workings' to 'murmurs of the lonely sea'; and Book I, lines 135–52, 'Leading the way' to 'his sacred vestments swept.']

After these comes Endymion, the 'Shepherd Prince.'

> A smile was on his countenance; he seem'd,
> To common lookers on, like one who dream'd
> Of idleness in groves Elysian:
> But there were some who feelingly could scan
> A lurking trouble in his nether lip,
> And see that oftentimes the reins would slip
> Through his forgotten hands.

The following are parts of a hymn to Pan, sung by a chorus of shepherds. We direct the reader's attention to the imagery as well as the rythm of these extracts in particular. They are, likewise, almost entirely free from the writer's characteristic faults.

[Quotes Book I, lines 232–46, 'O thou whose mighty palace roof' to 'Hear us, great Pan!'; and Book I, lines 279–92, 'O Hearkener' to 'With leaves about their brows!']

After this hymn the sports begin, and—

> ——— They danc'd to weariness,
> And then in quiet circles did they press
> The hillock turf, and caught the latter end
> Of some strange history, potent to send
> A young mind from its bodily tenement.

The love-stricken Endymion cannot partake in the sports, but is led, by his sister Peona, to her own favourite bower, where

> Soon was he quieted to slumbrous rest:
> But, ere it crept upon him, he had prest
> Peona's busy hand against his lips,
> And still, a sleeping, held her finger-tips
> In tender pressure. And as a willow keeps
> A patient watch over the stream that creeps
> Windingly by it, so the quiet maid
> Held her in peace: so that a whispering blade
> Of grass, a wailful gnat, a bee bustling
> Down in the blue-bells, or a wren light rustling
> Among sere leaves and twigs, might all be heard.

Nothing can be more exquisitely beautiful than this—nothing more lulling-sweet than the melody of it.—And let us here, once for all, direct the readers' attention to the rythm of the various extracts we lay before them; and add that, upon the whole, it combines more freedom, sweetness, and variety than are to be found in that of any other long poem written in the same measure, without any exception whatever. In the course of more than four thousand lines it never cloys by sameness, and never flags. To judge of the comparative extent of this praise, turn at random to Pope's Homer, or even Dryden's Virgil, and read two or three pages. Sweetness and variety of music in the versification of a young writer, are among the most authentic evidences of poetical power. These qualities are peculiarly conspicuous in Shakspeare's early poems of *Lucrece*, and *Venus and Adonis*. It should be mentioned, however, that in the work before us, these qualities seem to result from—what shall we say?—a fine natural ear?—from any thing, however, rather than system—for the verse frequently runs riot, and loses itself in air. It is the music of the happy wild-bird in the woods—not of the poor caged piping-bullfinch.

The following description of the impressions Endymion receives from various external objects,—on awaking from an Elysian dream of love, and finding that it was *but* a dream,—is finely passionate and natural:

[Quotes Book I, lines 682–705, 'for lo! the poppies hung' to 'The disappointment.']

Peona succeeds in rousing her brother from the listless trance into which he has fallen, and he again feels the true dignity of his being, and its mysterious bridal with the external forms and influences of Nature. The following strikes us as being exceedingly fine, notwithstanding some obvious faults in the diction.—It is the very faith, the religion, of imaginative passion.

————— Hist, when the airy stress
Of music's kiss impregnates the free winds,
And with a sympathetic touch unbinds
Eolian magic from their lucid wombs:
Then old songs waken from enclouded tombs;
Old ditties sigh above their father's grave;
Ghosts of melodious prophecyings rave
Round every spot where trod Apollo's foot;
Bronze clarions awake, and faintly bruit,

Where long ago a giant battle was;
And, from the turf, a lullaby doth pass
In every place where infant Orpheus slept.
Feel we these things?—that moment have we stept
Into a sort of oneness, and our state
Is like a floating spirit's.

They who do not find poetry in this, may be assured that they will look for it in vain elsewhere.—At the end of the first book, Endymion confides the secret of his mysterious passion, and all the circumstances attending it, to his sister Peona; and at the beginning of the second book we find him wandering about, without end or aim,

Through wilderness, and woods of mossed oaks;
Counting his woe-worn minutes, by the strokes
Of the lone wood-cutter;

till at length he meets with a winged messenger, who seems commissioned from heaven to direct his steps; and who leads him

Through buried paths, where sleepy twilight dreams
The summer time away. One track unseams
A wooded cleft, and, far away, the blue
Of ocean fades upon him; then, anew,
He sinks adown a solitary glen,
Where there was never sound of mortal men,
Saving, perhaps, some snow-light cadences
Melting to silence, when upon the breeze
Some holy bark let forth an anthem sweet,
To cheer itself to Delphi.

'Snow-light cadences,' &c. may be a little fantastical, perhaps; but it is very delicate and poetical, nevertheless. The passage in italics is also very still and lonely.—The following delightful little picture of cool quietude is placed in contrast to the restless fever of Endymion's thoughts, when his winged conductor leaves him:—

Hereat, she vanished from Endymion's gaze,
Who brooded o'er the water in amaze:
The dashing fount poured on, and where its pool
Lay, half asleep, in grass and rushes cool,
Quick waterflies and gnats were sporting still,
And fish were dimpling, as if good nor ill
Had fallen out that hour.

After this he yields up his whole soul to the dominion of passion and imagination, and they at last burst forth with an extatic address to his unearthly mistress, the moon—though he does not yet know her as such. The latter part of this address follows: and amidst numerous faults, both of thought and diction, the reader will not fail to detect much beauty. In the picture which follows the close of this address there is great power, and even sublimity.

> '———— Though the playful rout
> Of Cupids shun thee, too divine art thou,
> Too keen in beauty, for thy silver prow
> Not to have dipp'd in love's most gentle stream.
> O be propitious, nor severely deem
> My madness impious; for, by all the stars
> That tend thy bidding, I do think the bars
> That kept my spirit in are burst—that I
> Am sailing with thee through the dizzy sky!
> How beautiful thou art! The world how deep!
> How tremulous-dazzlingly the wheels sweep
> Around their axle! Then these gleaming reins,
> How lithe! When this thy chariot attains
> Its airy goal, haply some bower veils
> Those twilight eyes? Those eyes!—my spirit fails—
> Dear goddess, help! or the wide-gaping air
> Will gulph me—help!'—At this with madden'd stare,
> And lifted hands, and trembling lips he stood;
> Like old Deucalion mountain'd o'er the flood,
> Or blind Orion hungry for the morn.

At this moment a caverned voice is heard, bidding the young lover descend into the hollows of the earth; and adding

> ———— He ne'er is crown'd
> With immortality who fears to follow
> Where airy voices lead.

From this time Endymion quits the surface of the earth, and passes through a multitude of strange adventures in 'the sparry hollows of the world,' and in the other mysterious regions of the air, the sea, and the sky—meeting, in the course of his journeyings, with Glaucus and Scylla, Alpheus and Arethusa, Adonis, &c. part of whose stories are related. Till at length, having fulfilled the measure of his destinies, we find him once more on the earth, and near his own home; where, after an interview with his sister Peona, his immortal mistress appears to him under her proper form, and they ascend the sky together.

It will be seen that here is a rich fund of materials, fitted for almost every variety and degree of poetical power to work upon. And if the young builder before us has not erected from them a regular fabric, which will bear to be examined by a professional surveyor, with his square and rule and plumb-line,—he has at least raised a glittering and fantastic temple, where we may wander about, and delightedly lose ourselves while gazing on the exquisite pictures which every here and there hang on its sun-bright walls—the statues and flower-vases which ornament its painted niches—the delicious prospects opening upon us from its arabesque windows—and the sweet airs and romantic music which come about us when we mount upon its pleasant battlements. And it cannot be denied that the fabric is at least as well adapted to the airy and fanciful beings who dwell in it, as a regular Epic Palace—with its grand geometrical staircases, its long dreary galleries, its lofty state apartments, and its numerous *sleeping-rooms*—is to its kings and heroes.

The whole of the foregoing extracts are taken from the first and the beginning of the second book. We had marked numerous others through the rest of the work; but the little space that we have left for quotations must be given to a few of the fancies, images, and detached thoughts and similes—the pictures, statues, flowers, &c.—which form the mere ornaments of the building, and are scattered here and there, almost at random.

The little cabinet gems which follow may take their place in any collection. The first might have been cut out of a picture by Salvator:

> Echoing grottos, full of tumbling waves
> And moonlight. p. 25.

The next we can fancy to have formed a part of one of Claude's delicious skies. It is Venus ascending from the earth.

> ——— At these words up flew
> The impatient doves, up rose the floating car,
> Up went the hum celestial. High afar
> The Latmian saw them 'minish into nought.

The third reminds us of a sublime picture of the Deluge, by Poussin. It is a lover who loses his mistress, he knows not how, and afterwards, while swimming, finds her dead body floating in the sea.

Upon a dead thing's face my hand I laid;
I look'd—'twas Scylla————
———— Cold, O cold indeed
Were her fair limbs, *and like a common weed*
The sea-swell took her hair.

The fourth picture has all the voluptuous beauty of Titian:

Do not those curls of glossy jet surpass
For tenderness the arms so idly lain
Amongst them? Feelest not a kindred pain,
To see such lovely eyes in swimming search
After some warm delight, *that seems to perch*
Dovelike in the dim cell lying beyond
Their upper lids?

The following are a few of the wild flowers of Fancy that are scatter'd up and down.

When last the wintry gusts gave over strife
With the conquering sun of spring, and left the skies
Warm and serene, *but yet with moistened eyes*
In pity of the shatter'd infant buds.—

A brook running between mossy stones

'Mong which it gurgled blythe adieus, to mock
Its own sweet grief at parting.

The little flowers felt his pleasant sighs,
And stirr'd them faintly.

LOVER'S TALK.

———— And then there ran
Two bubbling springs of talk from their sweet lips.

The following are a few of the detached thoughts which float about like clouds, taking their form and colour from the position and the medium through which they are seen.

SUPPOSED EMPLOYMENTS OF DISEMBODIED SPIRITS.

—————— To nightly call
Vesper, the beauty-crest of summer weather;
To summon all the downiest clouds together
For the sun's purple couch:———
To tint her pallid cheek with bloom, who cons
Sweet poesy by moon-light.

A POET

——— One who through this middle earth should pass
Most like a sojourning demi-god, *and leave*
His name upon the harp-string.

THE END OF UNREQUITED LOVE.

And then the ballad of his sad life closes
With sighs, and an alas!

LOVE.

——— Awfully he stands,—
No sight can bear the lightning of his bow;
His quiver is mysterious, none can know
What themselves think of it.———

A scowl is sometimes on his brow, but who
Look full upon it feel anon the blue
Of his fair eyes run liquid through their souls.

REMEMBRANCE OF PAST YEARS.

————— Is it then possible
To look so plainly through them? to dispel
A thousand years with backward glance sublime?
To breathe away as 'twere all scummy slime
From off a crystal pool, to see its deep,
And one's own image from the bottom peep?

The following similes are as new as they are beautiful:

——— his eyelids
Widened a little, as when Zephyr bids
A little breeze to creep between the fans
Of careless butterflies.

—— As delicious wine doth, sparkling, dive
In nectar'd clouds and curls though water fair,
So from the arbour roof down swell'd an air
Odorous and enlivening.

——— like taper-flame
Left sudden by a dallying breath of air,
He rose in silence.

One more cluster of beautiful thoughts, fancies, and images meeting together, and one example of a totally different style of composition,—and we have done with quotations. The first is part of an address to the Moon, by the poet in his own character:

[Quotes Book III, lines 42, 44–71, 'Eterne Apollo! . . . When thy gold breath' to 'his forehead's cumbrous load.']

If there be such a thing as inspiration, breathed forth by the forms and influences of the external world, and echoed back again from the inner shrine of the poet's breast—this is it. The image of the wren, is, in its kind, not to be surpassed in the whole circle of poetry. We remember nothing equal to it, except Burns's morning picture, which is an exact companion to it, and probably suggested it.

Just when the lark,
'Twixt light and dark,
Awakens, by the daisy's side.

Our last extract shall be part of a song, supposed to be sung by an Indian maid, who has wandered far away from her own native streams:

[Quotes Book IV, lines 146–63, 'O Sorrow' to 'the cold dews among?'; lines 182–7, 'Beneath my palm trees' to 'Cold as my fears'; and lines 279–90, 'Come then, Sorrow!' to 'her wooer in the shade.']

This is, to be sure

——— Silly sooth,
And dallies with the innocence of grief;

but it is very touching and pathetic, nevertheless. Perhaps we like it the better from its reminding us (we do not very well know why) of two little elegies that are especial favourites with us,—one by Chatterton, beginning 'O sing unto my roundelay;'—and the other by Kirke White, 'Edwy, Edwy, ope thine eye!' It was perhaps suggested by Fletcher's divine song to Melancholy, in the *Passionate Madman*.

We cannot refrain from asking, Is it credible that the foregoing extracts are taken, almost at random, from a work in which a writer in the most popular—we will say *deservedly* the most popular—critical journal of the day, has been unable to discover any thing worthy to redeem it from mere contempt? Those who have the most respect for the *Quarterly Review* will feel most pain at seeing its pages disgraced by such an article as that to which we allude. Almost anywhere else it would have been harmless, and unworthy of particular notice; but *there* it cannot fail to gain a certain degree of credit from the company which it keeps. It would be foolish to doubt or to deny the extensive effect which such an article is likely to produce, appearing as it does in a work which is read by tens of thousands, nine-tenths of whom are not able to judge for themselves, and half of the other tenth will not take the trouble of doing so. Its chief mischief, however, is likely to take effect on the poet himself, whose work is the subject of it. Next to the necessity of pouring forth that which is within him, the strongest active principle in the mind of a young poet is the love of fame. Not fame weighed and meted out by the scales of strict justice. Not fame, properly so called. But *mere* fame—mere praise and distinction. He loves it for itself alone. During a certain period, this love exists almost in the form of an instinct in a poet's nature; and seems to be given him for the purpose of urging or leading him on to that 'hereafter' which is to follow. If it is not the food and support of his poetical life, it is at least the *stimulus* without which that life would be but too apt to flag and faulter in its appointed course. Woe to the lovers of poetry, when poets are content merely to *deserve* fame! Let that pest of the literary republic, the mere versifier, be derided and put down as a common nuisance. But let us, even for our own sakes, beware of withholding from youthful poets the fame which they covet;—let us beware of heaping ridicule even upon their faults; lest, in revenge, they learn to keep to themselves the gift which was bestowed on them for the benefit of their fellow-beings, and be satisfied with finding in poetry 'its own reward.' But we willingly return to our more immediate subject. We at first intended to have accompanied the foregoing extracts by a few of a contrary description, shewing the peculiar faults and deficiencies of the work before us. But as, in the present instance, we disclaim any intention of writing a regular criticism, we feel that this would be superfluous. It is not our object to give a distinct idea of the work as a whole; and we repeat, it is not a fit one to be judged of by rules and axioms. We only wish to call the public notice to the great and remarkable powers which it indicates,—at the same time giving encouragement—as far as our sincere suffrage is of any value—to the poet himself; and bespeaking,—not favour,—but attention,—to any thing that he may produce hereafter. It is, therefore, surely sufficient—for it is saying a great deal—to confess that *Endymion* is as full of faults as of beauties. And it is the less needful to point out those faults, as they are exactly of such a description that any one who has a relish for the amusement may readily discover them for himself. They will not hide themselves from his search. He need only open a page at random, and they will look him boldly, but not impudently, in the face—for their parent is, as yet, too inexperienced himself to know how to teach them better.

The same reasons which make it unnecessary to point out the peculiar faults of this work, make it difficult, if not impossible, to state its peculiar beauties as a whole, in any other than general terms. And, even so, we may exhaust all the common-places of criticism in talking about the writer's active and fertile imagination, his rich and lively fancy, his strong and acute sensibility, and so forth,—without advancing one step towards characterising the work which all these together have produced: because, though the writer possesses all these qualities in an eminent degree, his poetical character has not yet taken up any tangible or determinate ground. So that, though we know of no poetical work which differs from all others more than *Endymion* does, yet its distinguishing feature is perhaps nothing more than that exuberant spirit of youth,—that transport of imagination, fancy, and sensibility—which gushes forth from every part, in a glittering shower of words, and a confused and shadowy pomp of thoughts and images, creating and hurrying each other along like waves of the sea. And there is no egotism in all this, and no affectation. The poet offers himself up a willing sacrifice to the power which he serves: not fretting under, but exulting and glorying in his bondage. He plunges into the ocean of Poetry before he has learned to stem and grapple with the waves; but they 'bound beneath him as a steed that knows its rider;' and will not let him sink. Still, however, while they bear him along triumphantly, it is, evidently, at *their* will and pleasure, not at his. He 'rides on the whirlwind' safely; but he cannot yet 'direct the storm.'

We have spoken of this work as being richer in promise than any other that we are acquainted with, except those of Chatterton. It by no means follows that we confidently anticipate the fulfilment of that promise to its utmost extent. We are not without our fears that it may be like that flush of April blossoms which our fine soil almost always sends forth, but which our cloudy and uncertain skies as often prevent from arriving at maturity. Notwithstanding the many living poets that we possess, the times in which we live are essentially un-poetical; and powerful and resolute indeed must that spirit be, which, even in its youth, can escape their influence. When the transports of enthusiasm are gone by, it can hardly dare hope to do so. It must submit to let 'the years bring on the inevitable yoke.' This has been one strong inducement for us to notice the young writer before us; and we cannot conclude these slight and desultory remarks without entreating him not to be cast down or turned aside from the course which nature has marked out for him. He is and must be a poet—and he may be a great one. But let him never be tempted to disregard this first evidence of that power which at present rules over him—much less affect to do so: and least of all let him wish or attempt to make it any thing but what it is. Nothing can ever tame and polish this wild and wayward firstling, and make it fit to be introduced to 'mixed company;' but let him not therefore be ashamed to cherish and claim it for his own. He may live to see himself surrounded by a flourishing family, endowed with all sorts of polite accomplishments, and able not only to make their own way in the world, but to further *his* fortunes too. But *this*—the first-born of his hopes—the child of his youth—whatever he may say or think to the contrary—must ever be the favourite. He may admire those which are to come, and pride himself upon them; but he will never love them as he has loved this; he will never again watch over the infancy and growth of another with such full and unmixed delight: for *this* was born while his muse was his mistress, and he her rapturous lover. He will marry her by and by—or perhaps he has already—and then he may chance to love her *better* than ever; but he will cease to be *her lover.*

LAMIA, ISABELLA, THE EVE OF ST AGNES, AND OTHER POEMS

June 1820

22. Keats's indelicacy alarms his friends

1819

Richard Woodhouse (1788–1834), a lawyer eight years older than Keats, was the admirer who did more than anyone to collect and preserve Keats's manuscripts. John Taylor (1781–1864), a generous friend, with his partner James Hessey published Keats's second and third volumes. He was very devout: Shelley's friend Hogg dismissed him characteristically as 'a vile Methodist'.

(a) Extract from letter, 20 September 1819, from Richard Woodhouse to John Taylor: '—Keats was in Town the day before I left . . . I was much gratified with his Company. He wanted I believe to publish the "Eve of St Agnes" & "Lamia" *immediately*: but Hessey told him it could not answer to do so now. I wondered why he said nothing of "Isabella": & assured him it would please more [than] the "Eve of St Agnes"—He said he could not bear the former now. It appeared to him mawkish. This certainly cannot be so. The feeling is very likely to come across an [au]thor on review of a former work of his own, particularly where the objects of his present meditations are of a more sobered & unpassionate Character. The feeling of mawkishness seems to me to be that which comes upon us where any thing of great tenderness & excessive simplicity is met with when we are not in a sufficiently tender & simple frame of mind to bear it: when we experience a sort of revulsion, or resiliency (if there be such a word) from the sentiment or expression. Now I believe there is nothing in any of the most passionate parts of "Isabella" to excite this feeling. It may, as may *Lear*, leave the reader far behind: but there is none of that sugar & butter sentiment, that cloys & disgusts.—He had the "Eve of St A." copied fair: He has made trifling alterations, inserted an additional stanza early in the poem to make the *legend* more intelligible, and correspondent with what afterwards takes place, particularly with respect to the supper & the playing on the Lute.—he retains the name of Porphyro—has altered the last 3 lines to leave on the reader a sense of pettish disgust, by bringing Old Angela in (only) dead stiff & ugly.—He says he likes that the poem should leave off with this Change of Sentiment—it was what he aimed at, & was glad to find from my objections to it that he had succeeded.—I apprehend he had a fancy for trying his hand at an attempt to play with his reader, & fling him off at last—I sho^{d} have thought, he affected the *Don Juan* style of mingling up sentiment & sneering: but that he had before asked Hessey if he co^{d} procure him a sight of that work, as he had not met with it, and if the "E. of St A." had not in all probability been altered before his Lordship had thus flown in the face of the public. There was another alteration, which I abused for "a full hour by the *Temple* clock." You know if a thing has a decent side, I generally look no further—As the Poem was orig^{y} written, *we* innocent ones (ladies & myself) might very well have supposed that Porphyro, when acquainted with Madeline's love for him, & when "he arose, Etherial flush^{d}" &c. &c. (turn to it) set himself at once to persuade her to go off with him, & succeeded & went over the "Dartmoor black" (now changed for some other place) to be married, in right honest chaste & sober wise. But, as it is now altered, as soon as M. has confessed her love, P. winds by degrees his arm round her, presses breast to breast, and acts all the acts of a bonâ fide husband, while she fancies she is only playing the part of a Wife in a dream. This alteration is of about 3 stanzas; and tho' there are no improper expressions but all is left to inference, and tho' profanely speaking, the Interest on the reader's imagination is greatly heightened, yet I do apprehend it will render the poem unfit for ladies, & indeed scarcely to be mentioned to them among the "things that are."—He says he does not want ladies to read his poetry: that he writes for men, & that if in the former poem there was an opening for a doubt what took place, it was his fault for not writing clearly & comprehensibly—that he sh^{d} despise a man who would be such an eunuch in sentiment as to leave a maid, with that Character about her, in such a situation: & sho^{d} despise himself to write about it &c &c &c—and all this sort of Keats-like rhodomontade.—But you will see the work I dare say.—

He then read to me "Lamia," which he has half fair copied: the rest is rough. I was much pleased with it. I can use no other terms for you know how badly he reads his own poetry: & you know how slow I am in Catching, even the sense of poetry read by the best reader for the 1st time. And his poetry really must be studied to be properly appretiated. The Story is to this effect—Hermes is hunting for a Nymph, when from a wood he hears his name & a song relating to his loss—Mercury finds out that it comes from a serpent, who promises to shew him his Nymph if he will turn the serpent into a Woman; This he agrees to: upon which the serpent breathes on his eyes when he sees his Nymph who had been beside them listening invisibly—The serpent had seen a young Man of Corinth with whom she had fallen desperately in Love—She is metamorphosed into a beautiful Woman, the Change is quite Ovidian, but better,—She then finds the Youth, & they live together in a palace in the Middle of Corinth (described, or rather pictured out in very good costume) the entrance of which no one can see (like the Cavern Prince Ahmed found in the *Arabian Nights*, when searching for his lost arrow)—Here they live & love, "the world forgetting; of the world forgot." He wishes to marry her & introduce her to his friends as his Wife. But this would be a forfeiture of her immortality & she refuses but at length (for says K.—"Women love to be forced to do a thing, by a fine fellow—*such as this*—I forget his name—*was*") she consents. The Palace door becomes visible—to the "astonishment of the Natives"—the friends are invited to the wedding feast—& K. wipes the Cits & the low lived ones: of some of whom he says "who make their mouth a napkin to their thumb" in the midst of this Imperial splendour.—The lover had seen his tutor Appollonius that morning, while in a car with his Lamia; he had a scowl on his brow, which makes the hearts of the lovers sink: & she asks him, who that frowning old fellow was, as soon as A. passed.—He appears at the feast: damps the joy of the two by his presence—sits over against the woman: He is a Magician—He looks earnestly at the woman: so intently & to such effect, that she reads in his eyes that she is discovered: & vanishes away, shrieking.—The lover is told she was a "Lamia" & goes mad for the loss of her, & dies. You may suppose all these Events have given K. scope for some beautiful poetry: which even in this cursory hearing of it, came every now & then upon me, & made me "start, as tho' a Sea Nymph quired." The metre is Drydenian heroic—with many triplets, & many alexandrines. But this K. observed, & I agreed, was required, or rather quite in character with the language &

sentiment in those particular parts.—K. has a fine feeling when & where he may use poetical licences with effect—' (*The Keats Circle*, ed. H. E. Rollins, 1948, i. 90–4.)

(b) Extract from letter, 25 September 1819, from John Taylor to Richard Woodhouse: '—This Folly of Keats is the most stupid piece of Folly I can conceive.—He does not bear the ill opinion of the World calmly, & yet he will not allow it to form a good Opinion of him & his Writings. He repented of this Conduct when *Endymion* was published as much as a Man can repent, who shews by the accidental Expression of Disappointment, Mortification & Disgust that he has met with a Result different from that which he had anticipated—Yet he will again challenge the same Neglect or Censure, & again (I pledge my Discernment on it) be vexed at the Reception he has prepared for himself.—This Vaporing is as far from sound Fortitude, as the Conduct itself in the Instances before us, is devoid of good Feeling & good Sense.—I don't know how the Meaning of the new Stanzas is wrapped up, but I will not be accessary (I can answer also for H. I think) towards publishing any thing which can only be read by Men, since even on their Minds a bad Effect must follow the Encouragement of those Thoughts which cannot be rased without Impropriety—If it was so natural a process in Keats's Mind to carry on the Train of his Story in the way he has done, that he could not write decently, if he had that Disease of the Mind which renders the Perception too dull to discover Right from Wrong in Matters of moral Taste, I should object equally then as now to the Sanctioning of the Infirmity by an act of cool Encouragement on my part, but then he would be personally perhaps excusable—As it is, the flying in the Face of all Decency & Discretion is doubly offensive from its being accompanied with so preposterous a Conceit on his part of being able to overcome the best founded Habits of our Nature.—Had he known truly what the Society and what the Suffrages of Women are worth, he would never have thought of depriving himself of them.—So far as he is unconsciously silly in this Proceeding I am sorry for him, but for the rest I cannot but confess to you that it excites in me the Strongest Sentiments of Disapprobation—Therefore my dear Rich^{d} if he will not so far concede to my Wishes as to leave the passage as it originally stood, I must be content to admire his Poems with some other Imprint, & in so doing I can reap as much Delight from the Perusal of them as if they were our own property, without having the disquieting Consideration attached to them of our approving, by the "Imprimatur," those Parts which are unfit for publication.—

You will think me too severe again. Well then,—I will suspend my Judgment till I see or hear more, but if then my present Views are shewn to be no Illusion I must act as I have described.—How strange too that he should have taken such a Dislike to "Isabella"—I still think of it exactly as you do, & from what he copied out of "Lamia" in a late Letter I fancy I shall prefer it to that poem also.—The Extract he gave me was from the Feast. I did not enter so well into it as to be qualified to criticise, but whether it be a want of Taste for such Subjects as Fairy Tales, or that I do not perceive true Poetry except it is in Conjunction with good Sentiment, I cannot tell, but it did not promise to please me.—' (*The Keats Circle*, i. 96–7.)

23. Clare on Keats

1820, 1821, 1825–37

Keats and the Northamptonshire peasant poet John Clare (1793–1864) narrowly missed meeting, but their common publishers, Taylor and Hessey, reported Keats's criticisms to Clare and no doubt passed on Clare's comments to Keats. Through Hessey, Clare was enabled to read some of Keats's work before publication.

(a) Extract from letter, 4 July 1820, to James Hessey: 'I began on our friend Keats new Vol—find the same fine flowers spread if I can express myself in the wilderness of poetry—for he launches on the sea without compass—& mounts pegassus without saddle or bridle as usual & if those cursd critics coud be shood out of the fashion with their rule & compass & cease from making readers believe a Sonnet cannot be a Sonnet unless it be precisely 14 lines & a long poem as such unless one first sits down to wiredraw out regular argument & then plod after it in a regular manner the same as a Taylor cuts out a coat for the carcase—I say then he may push off first rate—but he is a child of nature warm and wild. . . . I have skimd over Keats & noticed the following as striking

Often times
She askd her brothers with an eye all pale
Striving to be itself
'Isabel'

Season of mists & mellow fruitfulness
Then in a wailful choir the small knats mourn
'Autumn'

& joy whose hand is ever at his lips
Bidding adieu
'Mel':

No stir of air was there
Not so much life as on a summers day
Robs not one light seed from the featherd grass
But where the dead leaf fell there did it rest
Hyp:

A stream went voiceless by
Hyp:

Let the maid
Blush keenly as with some warm kiss surprised
Hyp:

& poplars & lawn shading palms & beach
In which the zepher breaths its loudest song
Hyp:

I think this volume not so warm as *Endymion* why did you not print some of his Sonnets I like them much—I should like *Endymion* bound with his autograph inserted if he pleases & shall send my copy up purposely the first opertunity—' (*The Letters of John Clare*, ed. J. W. and Anne Tibble, 1951, 56–7.)

(b) Extract from letter, July 1820, to James Hessey: 'I like Keats last poem the best *Hyp*:—' (*Letters*, 59.)

(c) Extract from letter, June 1821, to John Taylor: 'I have been reading his "Eve of St Agnes" agen—were Madeline is describd undressing herself it is beautiful & luscious to describe how much so—

—her vespers done
Of all its weatherd pearl her hair she frees
Unclasps her *warmed jewels* one by one
Loosens her *fragrant boddice:* by degrees
Her rich attire creeps *rustling to her knees*
Half hidden like a mermaid in sea weed
Pensive awhile she *dreams awake,* & sees
In fancy fair St Agnes in her bed
But dares not look behind or all the charm is fled.

Look for such a description throughout Barry Cornwalls endless amusements—& were will you find it—you may as well look for the graces of simplicity at a night throughout the painted ranks & files of Drury Lane or Covent Garden & you will meet with equal success—' (*Letters*, 116–17.)

(d) From *The Village Minstrel* (1821):

'To the Memory of John Keats

The world, its hopes, and fears, have pass'd away;
  No more its trifling thou shalt feel or see;
Thy hopes are ripening in a brighter day,
  While these left buds thy monument shall be.
When Rancour's aims have past in naught away,
  Enlarging specks discern'd in more than thee,
And beauties 'minishing which few display—
  When these are past, true child of Poesy,
Thou shalt survive. Ah, while a being dwells,
  With soul, in nature's joys, to warm like thine,
With eye to view her fascinating spells,
  And dream entranced o'er each form divine,
Thy worth, Enthusiast, shall be cherish'd here,
Thy name with him shall linger, and be dear.'
  (*The Poems of John Clare*, ed. J. W. Tibble, 1935, i. 283.)

(e) Extract from 'Fragments 1825–37': 'He keeps up a constant alusion or illusion to the grecian mythology & there I cannot follow—yet when he speaks of woods Dryads & Fawns are sure to follow & the brook looks alone without her naiads to his mind yet the frequency of such classical accompaniment make it wearisome to the reader where behind every rose bush he looks for a Venus & under every laurel a thrumming Apollo—In spite of all this his descriptions of scenery are often very fine but as it is the case with other inhabitants of great cities he often described nature as she appeared to his fancies & not as he would have described her had he witnessed the things he describes—Thus it is he has often undergone the stigma of Cockneyism & what appears as beautys in the eyes of a pent-up citizen are looked upon as consciets by those who live in the country—these are merely errors but even here they are merely the errors of poetry—he is often mystical but such poetical liscences have been looked on as beauties in Wordsworth & Shelley & in Keats they may be forgiven' (*The Prose of John Clare*, ed. J. W. and Anne Tibble, 1951, 223.)

24. Prodigal phrases

1820

Unsigned review by Charles Lamb, *New Times*, (19 July 1820) No. 6210.

The essayist and poet Charles Lamb (1775–1834) was an accountant in the East India Company. He shared Keats's enthusiasm for Elizabethan literature, and had taken a conspicuous, if somewhat inebriated, part in the 'immortal dinner' of 28 December 1817 given by Haydon, when Keats and Lamb agreed that 'Newton had destroyed all the Poetry of the rainbow, by reducing it to a prism'. Three days after this review, *New Times* reprinted 'To Autumn' (complete), part of the 'Ode to a Nightingale', and an extract from *Hyperion*, under the heading 'Further extracts from poems, by John Keats.'

The two non-Keatsian quotations are from Shakespeare's sonnets (CVI and XXX (misquoted)).

[Quotes 'Eve of St. Agnes', stanzas 24–7, 'A casement high' to 'be a bud again', omitting lines 224–6, 'Porphyro grew faint' to 'his heart revives'.]

Such is the description which Mr Keats has given us, with a delicacy worthy of 'Christabel', of a high-born damsel, in one of the apartments of a baronial castle, laying herself down devoutly to dream, on the charmed Eve of St Agnes; and like the radiance, which comes from those old windows upon the limbs and garments of the damsel, is the almost Chaucer-like painting, with which this poet illumes every subject he touches. We have scarcely any thing likc it in modern description. It brings us back to ancient days, and

Beauty making-beautiful old rhymes.

The finest thing in the volume is the paraphrase of Boccaccio's story of the Pot of Basil. Two Florentines, merchants, discovering that their sister Isabella has placed her affections upon Lorenzo, a young factor in their employ, when they had hopes of procuring for her a noble match, decoy Lorenzo, under pretence of a ride, into a wood, where they suddenly stab and bury him. The anticipation of the assassination is wonderfully conceived in one epithet, in the narration of the ride—

So the two brothers, and their *murder'd* man,
    Rode past fair Florence, to where Arno's stream
Gurgles—

Returning to their sister, they delude her with a story of their having sent Lorenzo abroad to look after their merchandises; but the spirit of her lover appears to Isabella in a dream, and discovers how and where he was stabbed, and the spot where they have buried him. To ascertain the truth of the vision, she sets out to the place, accompanied by her old nurse, ignorant as yet of her wild purpose. Her arrival at it, and digging for the body, is described in the following stanzas, than which there is nothing more awfully simple in diction, more nakedly grand and moving in sentiment, in Dante, in Chaucer, or in Spenser:—

[Quotes 'Isabella', stanzas 46–8, 'She gaz'd into the fresh-thrown mould' to 'stamp and rave.']

To pursue the story in prose.—They find the body, and with their joint strengths sever from it the head, which Isabella takes home, and wrapping it in a silken scarf, entombs it in a garden-pot, covers it with mould, and over it she plants sweet basil, which, watered with her tears, thrives so that no other basil tufts in all Florence throve like her basil. How her brothers, suspecting something mysterious in this herb, which she watched day and night, at length discover the head, and secretly convey the basil from her; and how from the day that she loses her basil she pines away, and at last dies, we must refer our readers to the poem, or to the divine germ of it in Boccaccio. It is a great while ago since we read the original; and in this affecting revival of it we do but

weep again a long-forgotten woe.

More exuberantly rich in imagery and painting is the story of the Lamia. It is of as gorgeous stuff as ever romance was composed of. Her first appearance in serpentine form—

—a beauteous wreath with melancholy eyes—

her dialogue with Hermes, the *Star of Lethe*, as he is called by one of those prodigal phrases which Mr Keats abounds in, which are each a poem in a word, and which in this instance lays open to us at once, like a picture, all the dim regions and their inhabitants, and the sudden coming of a celestial among them; the charming of her into woman's shape again by the God; her marriage with the beautiful Lycius; her magic palace, which those who knew the street, and remembered it complete from childhood, never remembered to have seen before; the few Persian mutes, her attendants,

——who that same year
Were seen about the markets: none knew where
They could inhabit;—

the high-wrought splendours of the nuptial bower, with the fading of the whole pageantry, Lamia, and all, away, before the glance of Apollonius,—are all that fairy land can do for us. They are for younger impressibilities. To *us* an ounce of feeling is worth a pound of fancy; and therefore we recur again, with a warmer gratitude, to the story of Isabella and the pot of basil, and those never-cloying stanzas which we have cited, and which we think should disarm criticism, if it be not in its nature cruel; if it would not deny to honey its sweetness, nor to roses redness, nor light to the stars in Heaven; if it would not bay the moon out of the skies, rather than acknowledge she is fair.

25. Unsigned review, *Monthly Review*

July 1820, n.s. xcii, 305–10

This little volume must and ought to attract attention, for it displays the ore of true poetic genius, though mingled with a large portion of dross. Mr Keats is a very bold author, bold perhaps because (as we learn) he has yet but little more than touched the 'years of discretion;' and he has carried his peculiarities both of thought and manner to an extreme which, at the first view, will to many persons be very displeasing. Yet, whatever may be his faults, he is no *Della Crusca* poet; for, though he is frequently involved in ambiguity, and dressed in the affectation of quaint phrases, we are yet sure of finding in all that he writes the proof of deep thought and energetic reflection. Poetry is now become so antient an art, and antiquity has furnished such a storehouse of expression and feeling, that we daily meet with new worshippers of the Muse who are content to repeat for the thousandth time her prescriptive language. If any one would deviate from this beaten track, and from those great landmarks which have so long been the guides of the world in all matters of taste and literary excellence, he will find that it requires no timid foot to strike into new paths, and must deem himself fortunate if he be not lost amid the intricacies of a region with which he is unacquainted. Yet, even should this be partially the case, the wild and beautiful scenery, which such an excursion is frequently the means of developing, is a fair remuneration for the inequalities and obstructions which he may chance to experience on his ramble. We must add that only by attempts like these can we discover the path of true excellence; and that, in checking such efforts by illiberal and ill-timed discouragement, we shut out the prospect of all improvement. Innovations of every kind, more especially in matters of taste, are at first beheld with dislike and jealousy, and it is only by time and usage that we can appreciate their claims to adoption.

Very few persons, probably, will admire Mr Keats on a short acquaintance; and the light and the frivolous never will. If we would enjoy his poetry, we must think over it; and on this very account, which is perhaps the surest proof of its merit, we are afraid that it will be slighted. Unfortunately, Mr Keats may blame himself for much of this neglect; since he might have conceded something to established taste, or (if he will) established prejudice, without derogating from his own originality of thought and spirit. On the contrary, he seems to have written directly in despite of our preconceived notions of the *manner* in which a poet ought to write; and he is continually shocking our ideas of poetical decorum, at the very time when we are acknowledging the hand of genius. In thus boldly running counter to old opinions, however, we cannot conceive that Mr Keats merits either contempt or ridicule; the weapons which are too frequently employed when liberal discussion and argument would be unsuccessful. At all events, let him not be pre-judged without a candid examination of his claims.—A former work by this very young poet, (*Endymion*,) which escaped our notice, cannot certainly be said to have had a fair trial before the public; and now that an opportunity is afforded for correcting that injustice, we trust that the candour of all readers will take advantage of it.

For ourselves, we think that Mr Keats is very faulty. He is often laboriously obscure; and he sometimes indulges in such strange intricacies of thought, and peculiarities of expression, that we find considerable difficulty in discovering his meaning. Most unluckily for him, he is a disciple in a school in which these peculiarities are virtues: but the praises of this small *coterie* will hardly compensate for the disapprobation of the rest of the literary world. Holding, as we do, a high opinion of his talents, especially considering his youth and few advantages, we regret to see him sowing the seeds of disappointment where the fruit should be honour and distinction. If his writings were the dull common-places of an every-day versifier, we should pass them by with indifference or contempt: but, as they exhibit great force and feeling, we have only to regret that such powers are misdirected.

The wild and high imaginations of antient mythology, the mysterious being and awful histories of the deities of Greece and Rome, form subjects which Mr Keats evidently conceives to be suited to his own powers: but, though boldly and skilfully sketched, his delineations of the immortals give a faint idea of the nature which the poets of Greece attributed to them. The only modern writer, by whom this spirit has been completely preserved, is Lord Byron, in his poem of 'Prometheus.' In this mould, too, the character of Milton's Satan is cast.

The fragment of *Hyperion*, the last poem in the volume before us, we consider as decidedly the best of Mr Keats's productions; and the power of both heart and hand which it displays is very great. We think, too, that it has less conceit than other parts of the volume. It is the fable of the antient gods dethroned by the younger.

[Quotes *Hyperion*, Book I, lines 1–14, 'Deep in the shady sadness' to 'closer to her lips'; and lines 22–36, 'It seem'd no force' to 'more beautiful than Beauty's self.']

The appearance of Saturn among the Titans is splendidly told:

[Quotes Book II, lines 105–28, 'So Saturn, as he walk'd' to 'vibrating silverly.']

The description of Hyperion also is really fine:

[Quotes Book II, lines 371–91, 'Golden his hair' to 'the name of "Saturn!" ']

The story of 'Isabella, or the Pot of Basil,' from Boccaccio, is the worst part of the volume; and Mr Barry Cornwall's versification of this fable in his *Sicilian Story* is in some respects superior to Mr Keats's attempt. The latter gentleman seems inclined, in this poem, to shew us at once the extent of his simplicity and his affectation; witness the following *tirade* against the mercantile pride of the brothers of Isabella:

Why were they proud? Because their marble founts
  Gush'd with more pride than do a wretch's tears?—
Why were they proud? Because fair orange-mounts
  Were of more soft ascent than lazar stairs?—
Why were they proud? Because *red lin'd accounts*
  Were richer than the songs of Grecian years?—
Why were they proud? *again we ask aloud,*
Why in the name of Glory were they proud?

Mr Keats displays no great nicety in his selection of images. According to the tenets of that school of poetry to which he belongs, he thinks that any thing or object in nature is a fit material on which the poet may work; forgetting that poetry has a nature of its own, and that it is the destruction of its essence to level its high being with the triteness of every-day life. Can there be a more pointed *concetto* than this address to the Piping Shepherds on a Grecian Urn?

Heard melodies are sweet, but those *unheard*
  Are sweeter; therefore, ye soft pipes, play on;
Not to the sensual ear, but, more endear'd,
  Pipe to the spirit *ditties of no tone:*

but it would be irksome to point out all the instances of this kind which are to be found in Mr K.'s compositions.

Still, we repeat, this writer is very rich both in imagination and fancy; and even a superabundance of the latter faculty is displayed in his lines 'On Autumn,' which bring the reality of nature more before our eyes than almost any description that we remember.

[Quotes 'To Autumn' in full.]

If we did not fear that, young as is Mr K., his peculiarities are fixed beyond all the power of criticism to remove, we would exhort him to become somewhat less strikingly original,—to be less fond of the folly of too new or too old phrases,—and to believe that poetry does not consist in either the one or the other. We could then venture to promise him a double portion of readers, and a reputation which, if he persist in his errors, he will never obtain. Be this as it may, his writings present us with so many fine and striking ideas, or passages, that we shall always read his poems with much pleasure.

26. Unsigned notice, *Literary Chronicle and Weekly Review*

29 July 1820, ii, 484–5

It is customary in Paris and some other places, to present their friends on New Year's Day with some expressive wishes for their future happiness, wealth, or success, in such matters as may be deemed most agreeable. Following this example, we will, at Midsummer instead of Christmas, offer Mr Keats our wishes, and, whether they may be agreeable or not, we assure him they are sincere. First, then, we wish that he would renounce all acquaintance with our metropolitan poets. Secondly, that he would entirely abandon their affected school, instead of being a principal supporter of it; and, exiling himself for twelve months to North Wales or the Highlands of Scotland, trust to nature's ever varying scene and his own talents. And, lastly, until he does all this, we wish that he would never write any poem of more than an hundred verses at the utmost. Of the propriety of this last piece of advice, we believe all who have read his works will become sensible, and were any other argument wanting, the volume before us would furnish it.

We believe there is a sort of fashion observed by authors or booksellers, to place the longest poems at the commencement of a volume, although we are convinced it is often an injudicious one; we would rather tempt the reader by some short and delicate morceau than run the hazard of exhausting his patience or exciting his disgust, by putting the worst piece in the front ranks, because it is largest. 'Lamia' and 'Isabella', and the 'Eve of St. Agnes' have some fine passages, but we can award them no higher praise. Among the minor poems, many of which possess considerable merit, the following appears to be the best:—

[Quotes 'Ode on a Grecian Urn' in full.]

There is a pretty idea, happily expressed, in the following ode:—

[Quotes 'Bards of Passion and of Mirth' in full.]

We confess this volume has disappointed us; from Mr Keats's former productions, we had augured better things, and we are confident he can do better; let him avoid all sickly affectation on one hand, and unintelligible quaintness on the other. Let him avoid coining new words, and give us the English language as it is taught and written in the nineteenth century, and he will have made considerable progress towards improvement. These poems contain many beautiful passages, but they are too thickly strewed with the faults we have noticed, to entitle them to more than a very qualified approval.

27. Leigh Hunt displays Keats's 'calm power'

1820

Review, *The Indicator* (2 August 1820), No. xliii, 337–44, and 9 August 1820, No. xliv, 345–52.

A characteristically full, fair, and thoughtful account of Keats's work, including a sympathetic discussion of 'poetic divinities' in *Hyperion* and in *Paradise Lost*. Keats's misuse of Greek myth was a very sore point with traditionalist critics trained in the classics. The last paragraph should dispel any notion of Hunt's supposed 'vanity' in relation to Keats's talent.

In laying before our readers an account of another new publication, it is fortunate that the nature of the work again falls in with the character of our miscellany; part of the object of which is to relate the stories of old times. We shall therefore abridge into prose the stories which Mr Keats has told in poetry, only making up for it, as we go, by cutting some of the richest passages out of his verse, and fitting them in to our plainer narrative. They are such as would leaven a much greater lump. Their drops are rich and vital, the essence of a heap of fertile thoughts.

The first story, entitled 'Lamia', was suggested to our author by a passage in Burton's *Anatomy of Melancholy*, which he has extracted at the end of it. We will extract it here, at the beginning, that the readers may see how he has enriched it. Burton's relation is itself an improvement on the account in Philostratus. The old book-fighter with melancholy thoughts is speaking of the seductions of phantasmata.

Philostratus, in his fourth book *De Vita Apollonii*, hath a memorable instance in this kind, which I may not omit, of one Menippus Lycius, a young man twenty-five years of age, that going betwixt Cenchreas and Corinth, met such a phantasm in the habit of a fair gentlewoman, which taking him by the hand, carried him home to her house, in the suburbs of Corinth, and told him she was a Phœnician by birth, and if he would tarry with her, he should hear her sing and play, and drink such wine as never any drank, and no man should molest him; but she, being fair and lovely, would live and die with him, that was fair and lovely to behold. The young man, a philosopher, otherwise staid and discreet, able to moderate his passions, though not this of love, tarried with her awhile to his great content, and at last married her, to whose wedding, amongst other guests, came Apollonius; who, by some probable conjectures, found her out to be a serpent, a lamia; and that all her furniture was, like Tantalus' gold, described by Homer, no substance but mere illusions. When she saw herself descried, she wept, and desired Apollonius to be silent, but he would not be moved, and therefore she, plate, house, and all that was in it, vanished in an instant: many thousands took notice of this fact, for it was done in the midst of Greece.—*Anat. of Mel.* Part 3, Sect. 2.

According to our poet, Mercury had come down from heaven, one day, in order to make love to a nymph, famous for her beauty. He could not find her; and he was halting among the woods uneasily, when he heard a lonely voice, complaining. It was

A mournful voice,
Such as once heard, in gentle heart, destroys
All pain but pity: thus the lone voice spake.
'When from this wreathed tomb shall I awake!
When move in a sweet body fit for life,
And love, and pleasure, and the ruddy strife
Of hearts and lips! Ah, miserable me!'

Mercury went looking about among the trees and grass,

Until he found a palpitating snake,
Bright, and cirque-couchant in a dusky brake.

The admiration, pity, and horror, to be excited by humanity in a brute shape, were never perhaps called upon by a greater mixture of beauty and deformity than in the picture of this creature. Our pity and suspicions are begged by the first word: the profuse and vital beauties with which she is covered seem proportioned to her misery and natural rights; and lest we should lose sight of them in this gorgeousness, the 'woman's mouth' fills us at once with shuddering and compassion.

[Quotes 'Lamia', Part I, lines 47–63, 'She was a gordian shape' to 'her Sicilian air.']

The serpent tells Mercury that she knows upon what quest he is bound, and asks him if he has succeeded. The god, with the usual eagerness of his species to have his will, falls into the trap; and tells her that he will put her in possession of any wish she may have at heart, provided she can tell him where to find his nymph. As eagerly, she accepts his promise, making him ratify it by an oath, which he first pronounces with an earnest lightness, and afterwards with a deeper solemnity.

> Then once again the charmed God began
> An oath, and through the serpent's ears it ran
> Warm, tremulous, devout, psalterian.

The creature tells him that it was she who had rendered the nymph invisible, in order to preserve her from the importunities of the ruder wood gods. She adds, that she was a woman herself, that she loves a youth of Corinth and wishes to be a woman again, and that if he will let her breathe upon his eyes, he shall see his invisible beauty. The god sees, loves, and prevails. The serpent undergoes a fierce and convulsive change, and flies towards Corinth,

> A full-born beauty, new and exquisite.

Lamia, whose liability to painful metamorphosis was relieved by a supernatural imagination, had been attracted by the beauty of Lycius, while pitching her mind among the enjoyments of Corinth. By the same process, she knew that he was to pass along, that evening, on the road from the sea-side to Corinth; and there accordingly she contrives to have an interview, which ends in his being smitten with love, and conducting her to her pretended home in that city. She represents herself as a rich orphan, living 'but half-retired,' and affects to wonder that he never saw her before. As they enter Corinth, they pass the philosopher Apollonius, who is Lycius's tutor, and from whom he instinctively conceals his face. Lamia's hand shudders in that of her lover; but she says she is only wearied; and at the same moment, they stop at the entrance of a magnificent house:—

> A pillar'd porch, with lofty portal door,
> Where hung a silver lamp, whose phosphor glow
> Reflected in the slabbed steps below,
> Mild as a star in water.

Here they lived for some time, undisturbed by the world, in all the delight of a mutual passion. The house remained invisible to all eyes, but those of Lycius. There were a few Persian mutes, 'seen that year about the markets;' and nobody knew whence they came; but the most inquisitive were baffled in endeavouring to track them to some place of abode.

But all this while, a god was every night in the house, taking offence. Every night

> With a terrific glare,
> Love, jealous grown of so complete a pair,
> Hovered and buzzed his wings with fearful roar
> Above the lintel of their chamber door,
> And down the passage cast a glow upon the floor.

Lycius, to the great distress of his mistress, who saw in his vanity a great danger, persuaded her to have a public wedding-feast. She only begged him not to invite Apollonius; and then, resolving to dress up her bridals with a sort of despairing magnificence, equal to her apprehensions of danger, she worked a fairy architecture in secret, served only with the noise of wings and a restless sound of music—

> A haunting music, sole perhaps and lone
> Supportress of the faery-roof, made moan
> Throughout, as fearful the whole charm might fade.

This is the very quintessence of the romantic. The walls of the long vaulted room were covered with palms and plantain-trees imitated in cedar-wood, and meeting over head in the middle of the ceiling; between the stems were jasper pannels, from which 'there burst forth creeping imagery of slighter trees;' and before each of these 'lucid pannels'

> Fuming stood
> A censer filled with myrrh and spiced wood,
> Whose slender feet wide-swerv'd upon the soft
> Wool-woofed carpets: fifty wreaths of smoke
> From fifty censers their light voyage took
> To the high roof, still mimick'd as they rose
> Along the mirror'd walls by twin-clouds odorous.

Twelve tables stood in this room, set round with circular couches, and on every table was a noble feast and the statue of a god.

> Lamia, regal drest,
> Silently faced about, and as she went,
> In pale contented sort of discontent,
> Mission'd her viewless servants to enrich
> The fretted splendour of each nook and niche.

* * * * * * * *

Approving all, she faded at self-will,
And shut the chamber up, close, hush'd, and still,
Complete and ready for the revels rude,
When dreadful guests would come to spoil her solitude.

The guests came. They wondered and talked; but their gossiping would have ended well enough, when the wine prevailed, had not Apollonius, an unbidden guest, come with them. He sat right opposite the lovers, and

—Fixed his eye, without a twinkle or stir
Full on the alarmed beauty of the bride,
Brow-beating her fair form, and troubling her sweet pride.

Lycius felt her hand grow alternately hot and cold, and wondered more and more both at her agitation and the conduct of his old tutor. He looked into her eyes, but they looked nothing in return: he spoke to her, but she made no answer: by degrees the music ceased, the flowers faded away, the pleasure all darkened, and

A deadly silence step by step increased,
Until it seemed a horrid presence there,
And not a man but felt the terror in his hair.

The bridegroom at last shrieked out her name; but it was only echoed back to him by the room. Lamia sat fixed, her face of a deadly white. He called in mixed agony and rage to the philosopher to take off his eyes; but Apollonius, refusing, asked him whether his old guide and instructor who had preserved him from all harm to that day, ought to see him made the prey of a serpent. A mortal faintness came into the breath of Lamia at this word; she motioned him, as well as she could, to be silent; but looking her stedfastly in the face, he repeated Serpent! and she vanished with a horrible scream. Upon the same night, died Lycius, and was swathed for the funeral in his wedding-garments.

Mr Keats has departed as much from common-place in the character and moral of this story, as he has in the poetry of it. He would see fair play to the serpent, and makes the power of the philosopher an ill-natured and disturbing thing. Lamia though liable to be turned into painful shapes had a soul of humanity; and the poet does not see why she should not have her pleasures accordingly, merely because a philosopher saw that she was not a mathematical truth. This is fine and good. It is vindicating the greater philosophy of poetry. At the same time, we wish that for the purpose of his story he had not appeared to give in to the common-place of supposing that Apollonius's sophistry must always prevail, and that modern experiment has done a deadly thing to poetry by discovering the nature of the rainbow, the air, &c.: that is to say, that the knowledge of natural history and physics, by shewing us the nature of things, does away the imaginations that once adorned them. This is a condescension to a learned vulgarism, which so excellent a poet as Mr Keats ought not to have made. The world will always have fine poetry, as long as it has events, passions, affections, and a philosophy that sees deeper than this philosophy. There will be a poetry of the heart, as long as there are tears and smiles: there will be a poetry of the imagination, as long as the first causes of things remain a mystery. A man who is no poet, may think he is none, as soon as he finds out the physical cause of the rainbow; but he need not alarm himself:—he was none before. The true poet will go deeper. He will ask himself what is the cause of that physical cause; whether truths to the senses are after all to be taken as truths to the imagination; and whether there is not room and mystery enough in the universe for the creation of infinite things, when the poor matter-of-fact philosopher has come to the end of his own vision. It is remarkable that an age of poetry has grown up with the progress of experiment; and that the very poets, who seem to countenance these notions, accompany them by some of their finest effusions. Even if there were nothing new to be created,—if philosophy, with its line and rule, could even score the ground, and say to poetry 'Thou shalt go no further,' she would look back to the old world, and still find it inexhaustible. The crops from its fertility are endless. But these alarms are altogether idle. The essence of poetical enjoyment does not consist in belief, but in a voluntary power to imagine.

The next story, that of the Pot of Basil, is from Boccaccio. After the narrative of that great writer, we must make as short work of it as possible in prose. To turn one of his stories into verse, is another thing. It is like setting it to a more elaborate music. Mr Keats is so struck with admiration of his author, that even while giving him this accompaniment, he breaks out into an apology to the great Italian, asking pardon for this

—Echo of him in the [n]orth-wind sung.

We might waive a repetition of the narrative altogether, as the public have lately been familiarized with it in the *Sicilian Story* of Mr Barry

Cornwall: but we cannot help calling to mind that the hero and heroine were two young and happy lovers, who kept their love a secret from her rich brothers; that her brothers, getting knowledge of their intercourse, lured him into a solitary place, and murdered him; that Isabella, informed of it by a dreary vision of her lover, found out where he was buried, and with the assistance of her nurse, severed the head from the body that she might cherish even that ghastly memorial of him as a relic never to be parted with; that she buried the head in a pot of earth, and planting basil over it, watered the leaves with her continual tears till they grew into wonderful beauty and luxuriance; that her brothers, prying into her fondness for the Pot of Basil, which she carried with her from place to place, contrived to steal it away; that she made such lamentations for it, as induced them to wonder what could be its value, upon which they dug into it, and discovered the head; that the amazement of that discovery struck back upon their hearts, so that after burying the head secretly, they left their native place, and went to live in another city; and that Isabella continued to cry and moan for her Pot of Basil, which she had not the power to cease wishing for; till, under the pressure of that weeping want, she died.

Our author can pass to the most striking imaginations from the most delicate and airy fancy. He says of the lovers in their happiness,

> Parting they seemed to tread upon the air,
> Twin roses by the zephyrs blown apart
> Only to meet again more close, and share
> The inward fragrance of each other's heart.

These pictures of their intercourse terribly aggravate the gloom of what follows. Lorenzo, when lured away to be killed, is taken unknowingly out of his joys, like a lamb out of the pasture. The following masterly anticipation of his end, conveyed in a single word, has been justly admired:—

> So the two brothers and their *murder'd* man
> Rode past fair Florence, to where Arno's stream
> Gurgles through straitened banks.
> They passed the water
> Into a forest quiet for the slaughter.

When Mr Keats errs in his poetry, it is from the ill management of a good thing,—exuberance of ideas. Once or twice, he does so in a taste positively bad, like Marino or Cowley, as in a line in his 'Ode to Psyche'

> At tender eye-dawn of aurorean love;

but it is once or twice only, in his present volume. Nor has he erred much in it in a nobler way. What we allude to is one or two passages in which he over-informs the occasion or the speaker; as where the brothers, for instance, whom he describes as a couple of mere 'money-bags,' are gifted with the power of uttering the following exquisite metaphor:—

> 'To-day we purpose, ay, this hour we mount
> To spur three leagues towards the Apennine:
> Come down, we pray thee, ere the hot sun count
> His dewy rosary on the eglantine.'

But to return to the core of the story.—Observe the fervid misery of the following.

[Quotes 'Isabella', stanzas 46–8, 'She gaz'd into the fresh-thrown mould' to 'did not stamp and rave.']

It is curious to see how the simple pathos of Boccaccio, or (which is the same thing) the simple intensity of the heroine's feelings, suffices our author more and more, as he gets to the end of his story. And he has related it as happily, as if he had never written any poetry but that of the heart. The passage about the tone of her voice,—the poor lost-witted coaxing,—the 'chuckle,' in which she asks after her Pilgrim and her Basil,—is as true and touching an instance of the effect of a happy familiar word, as any in all poetry. The poet bids his imagination depart,

[Quotes 'Isabella', line 486 to the end, 'For Isabel' to 'away from me!']

'The Eve of St. Agnes', which is rather a picture than a story, may be analysed in a few words. It is an account of a young beauty, who going to bed on the eve in question to dream of her lover, while her rich kinsmen, the opposers of his love, are keeping holiday in the rest of the house, finds herself waked by him in the night, and in the hurry of the moment agrees to elope with him. The portrait of the heroine, preparing to go to bed, is remarkable for its union of extreme richness and good taste; not that those two properties of description are naturally distinct; but that they are too often separated by very good poets, and that the passage affords a striking specimen of the sudden and strong maturity of the author's genius. When he wrote *Endymion* he could not have resisted doing too much. To the description before us, it would be a great injury either to add or diminish. It falls at once gorgeously and delicately upon us, like the colours of the painted glass. Nor is Madeline hurt by all her encrusting jewelry and rustling silks. Her gentle, unsophisticated heart is in the midst, and turns them into so many ministrants to her loveliness.

[Quotes 'Eve of St Agnes', stanzas 24–7, 'A casement high' to 'be a bud again.']

Is not this perfectly beautiful?

As a specimen of the Poems, which are all lyrical, we must indulge ourselves in quoting entire the 'Ode to a Nightingale'. There is that mixture in it of real melancholy and imaginative relief, which poetry alone presents us in her 'charmed cup,' and which some over-rational critics have undertaken to find wrong because it is not true. It does not follow that what is not true to them, is not true to others. If the relief is real, the mixture is good and sufficing. A poet finds refreshment in his imaginary wine, as other men do in their real; nor have we the least doubt, that Milton found his grief for the loss of his friend King, more solaced by the allegorical recollections of 'Lycidas', (which were exercises of his mind, and recollections of a friend who would have admired them) than if he could have anticipated Dr Johnson's objections, and mourned in nothing but broadcloth and matter of fact. He yearned after the poetical as well as social part of his friend's nature; and had as much right to fancy it straying in the wilds and oceans of romance, where it had strayed, as in the avenues of Christ's College where his body had walked. In the same spirit the imagination of Mr Keats betakes itself, like the wind, 'where it listeth,' and is as truly there, as if his feet could follow it. The poem will be the more striking to the reader, when he understands what we take a friend's liberty in telling him, that the author's powerful mind has for some time past been inhabiting a sickened and shaken body, and that in the mean while it has had to contend with feelings that make a fine nature ache for its species, even when it would disdain to do so for itself;—we mean, critical malignity,—that unhappy envy, which would wreak its own tortures upon others, especially upon those that really feel for it already.

[Quotes 'Ode to a Nightingale' in full.]

The *Hyperion* is a fragment,—a gigantic one, like a ruin in the desart, or the bones of the mastodon. It is truly of a piece with its subject, which is the downfall of the elder gods. It opens with Saturn, dethroned, sitting in a deep and solitary valley, benumbed in spite of his huge powers with the amazement of the change.

[Quotes *Hyperion*, Book I, lines 1–41, 'Deep in the shady sadness' to 'thunder labouring up.']

By degrees, the Titans meet in one spot, to consult how they may regain their lost empire; but Clymene the gentlest, and Oceanus the most reflective of those earlier deities, tell them that it is irrecoverable. A very grand and deep-thoughted cause is assigned for this by the latter. Intellect, he gives them to understand, was inevitably displacing a more brute power.

[Quotes *Hyperion*, Book II, lines 182–90, 'Great Saturn, thou' to 'nor the end'; and Book II, lines 202–15, 'Now comes the pain' to 'that old Darkness'.]

The more imaginative parts of the poem are worthy of this sublime moral. Hyperion, the God of the Sun, is the last to give way; but horror begins to visit his old beautitude with new and dread sensations. The living beauty of his palace, whose portals open like a rose, the awful phænomena that announce a change in heaven, and his inability to bid the day break as he was accustomed,—all this part, in short, which is the core and inner diamond of the poem, we must enjoy with the reader.

[Quotes *Hyperion*, Book I, lines 176–304, 'His palace bright' to 'in grief and radiance faint.']

The other Titans, lying half lifeless in their valley of despair, are happily compared to

A dismal cirque
Of Druid stones, upon a forlorn moor,
When the chill rain begins at shut of eve,
In dull November, and their chancel vault,
The Heaven itself, is blinded throughout night.

The fragment ends with the deification of Apollo. It strikes us that there is something too effeminate and human in the way in which

Apollo receives the exaltation which his wisdom is giving him. He weeps and wonders somewhat too fondly; but his powers gather nobly on him as he proceeds. He exclaims to Mnemosyne, the Goddess of Memory,

> Knowledge enormous makes a God of me,
> Names, deeds, gray legends, dire events, rebellions,
> Majesties, sovran voices, agonies,
> Creations and destroyings, all at once
> Pour into the wide hollows of my brain,
> And deify me, as if some blithe wine
> Or bright elixir peerless I had drunk,
> And so become immortal.

After this speech, he is seized with a glow of aspiration, and an intensity of pain, proportioned to the causes that are changing him; Mnemosyne upholds her arms, as one who prophesied; and

> At length
> Apollo shrieked;—and lo! from all his limbs
> Celestial * * * * * *

Here the poem ceases, to the great impatience of the poetical reader.

If any living poet could finish this fragment, we believe it is the author himself. But perhaps he feels that he ought not. A story which involves passion, almost of necessity involves speech; and though we may well enough describe beings greater than ourselves by comparison, unfortunately we cannot make them speak by comparison. Mr Keats, when he first introduces Thea consoling Saturn, says that she spoke

> Some mourning words, which in our feeble tongue
> Would come in these like accents; O how frail
> To that large utterance of the early Gods!

This grand confession of want of grandeur is all that he could do for them. Milton could do no more. Nay, he did less, when according to Pope he made

> God the father turn a school divine.

The moment the Gods speak, we forget that they did not speak like ourselves. The fact is, they feel like ourselves; and the poet would have to make them feel otherwise, even if he could make them speak otherwise, which he cannot, unless he venture upon an obscurity which would destroy our sympathy: and what is sympathy with a God, but turning him into a man? We allow, that superiority and inferiority are, after all, human terms, and imply something not so truly fine and noble as the levelling of a great sympathy and love; but poems of the present nature, like *Paradise Lost*, assume a different principle; and fortunately perhaps, it is one which it is impossible to reconcile with the other.

We have now to conclude the surprise of the reader, who has seen what solid stuff these poems are made of, with informing him of what the book has not mentioned,—that they were almost all written four years ago, when the author was but twenty. Ay, indeed! cries a critic, rubbing his hands delighted (if indeed even criticism can do so, any longer); 'then that accounts for the lines you speak of, written in the taste of Marino.'—It does so; but, sage Sir, after settling the merits of those one or two lines you speak of, what accounts, pray, for a small matter which you leave unnoticed, namely, all the rest?—The truth is, we rather mention this circumstance as a matter of ordinary curiosity, than any thing else; for great faculties have great privileges, and leap over time as well as other obstacles. Time itself, and its continents, are things yet to be discovered. There is no knowing even how much duration one man may crowd into a few years, while others drag out their slender lines. There are circular roads full of hurry and scenery, and straight roads full of listlessness and barrenness; and travellers may arrive by both, at the same hour. The Miltons, who begin intellectually old, and still intellectual, end physically old, are indeed Methusalems; and may such be our author, their son.

Mr Keats's versification sometimes reminds us of Milton in his blank verse, and sometimes of Chapman both in his blank verse and rhyme; but his faculties, essentially speaking, though partaking of the unearthly aspirations and abstract yearnings of both these poets, are altogether his own. They are ambitious, but less directly so. They are more social, and in the finer sense of the word, sensual, than either. They are more coloured by the modern philosophy of sympathy and natural justice. *Endymion*, with all its extraordinary powers, partook of the faults of youth, though the best ones; but the reader of *Hyperion* and these other stories would never guess that they were written at twenty. The author's versification is now perfected, the exuberances of his imagination restrained, and a calm power, the surest and loftiest of all power, takes place of the impatient workings of the younger god within him. The character of his genius is that of energy and voluptuousness, each able at will to take leave of the other, and possessing, in their union, a high feeling of humanity not common to the best authors who can less combine them. Mr Keats undoubtedly takes his seat with the oldest and best of our living poets.

We have carried our criticism to much greater length than we intended; but in truth, whatever the critics might think, it is a refreshment to us to get upon other people's thoughts, even though the rogues be our contemporaries. Oh! how little do those minds get out of themselves, and what fertile and heaven-breathing prospects do they lose, who think that a man must be confined to the mill-path of his own homestead, merely that he may avoid seeing the abundance of his neighbours! Above all, how little do they know of us eternal, weekly, and semi-weekly writers! We do not mean to say that it is not very pleasant to run upon a smooth road, seeing what we like, and talking what we like; but we do say, that it is pleasanter than all, when we are tired, to hear what we like, and to be lulled with congenial thoughts and higher music, till we are fresh to start again upon our journey. What we would not give to have a better *Examiner* and a better *Indicator* than our own twice every week, uttering our own thoughts in a finer manner, and altering the world faster and better than we can alter it! How we should like to read our present number, five times bettered; and to have nothing to do, for years and years, but to pace the green lanes, forget the tax-gatherer, and vent ourselves now and then in a verse.

28. Unsigned review, *Guardian*

6 August 1820, i, No. 33

We open this volume with an indescribable feeling of reverence and curiosity. We approach it as a gentleman from the country takes his seat in the third row of the pit at the Lyceum, to banquet upon the sweets of '*Woman's Will—a Riddle*,' after being told in the play-bills that 'it has received the decided approbation of the first critics of the day.' Mr Keats has been praised by all 'men of mark,' from the Editor of the *New Times* to the Editor of the *Examiner*. Principles the most opposite unite in lauding this 'Muses' Son of Promise:'—He is 'a fresh and true poet,' says one; and 'No criticism can deny his merits,' proclaims another, 'but such as would disprove that moonlight is beautiful, or roses fragrant.' This is oracular—and we bow to it.

What a blessing it is to be a poet now-a-days! Ten years ago we rhyming aspirants used to give an entertainment to our friends if the monopolizing dulness of the *Monthly Review* or the *British Critic* afforded us half a page of notice, with some parting *formula* of benediction; such as 'Mr. —— is a young man of promising talents, and we hope that when experience has matured his imagination,' &c. &c.—But now the sun of criticism is ever shining upon us. We have a perfect polar quarter of never-failing light. The long day of brightness first beams in extracts in *The Morning Post*, or eulogies in *The New Times*;—(the *Old* is, very properly, above such things.) This blaze is gradually diffused over the country by the Evening *Suns*. The three times a-week journals reflect the diurnal brightness; and the flame at last lights the whole land through the potential agency of the Sunday prints. But it does not yet die. There is a new tribe of Illuminati sprung up, under the names of Indicators, and Honeycombs, and Talismans, and Citizens, and Londoners, and Critics, and Mouse-Traps, and—look on the walls—all devoted to 'Literature and the Arts.' For a week or two there may be an eclipse—but then come the Magazines—here is a new-born day. The *Ephemeron* yet lives—and if, after six weeks, his wings tire, and his buzzing is no longer heard—if darkness gather round him, and the world fade from his sight—there is a gleam of hope in the rising of the *Quarterly* or the *Edinburgh*, who may confer on him immortality by not suffering him to die a natural death. Thus we are 'nothing if not critical;'—thus we preserve 'flies in amber;'—thus we will not let a modest man, like Mr Keats, commit the sin of scribbling in secret;—thus—but to our vocation.

The first great merit of Mr Keats' poetry consists in the exercise which it affords to the thinking faculties. It is not to be classed with those commonplace performances which tell us what every body has seen, in language which every body can understand. It is deep and mystical—it has all the stimulating properties of a Christmas riddle—it is a nosegay of enigmas. And then, what is most delightful, the mysterious is so mixed up with the simple, that the mind is not exhausted by its own conjectures—'*est modus in* REBUS.'[1] He never

[1] 'There is a method in things—punning on "rebus," a word-puzzle.'

begins 'riddle-me, riddle-me, ree,' with a solemn face; but offers his problems with the utmost gentility in the midst of the most agreeable and easy narrative. This is very well for a poet, but it will never do for a critic. It is our province to digest and systematize; and we also are determined to revive the much-neglected practice of calling forth juvenile industry and invention, in the manner of the primitive magazines, or the last Ladies' Diary. We therefore hereby offer two splendid prizes for the first and second best solutions of the following Enigmas, viz:—a copy of *Endymion* in yellow morocco; and of the Volume before us, in double extra calf, or red basil.

RIDDLE I

Yet were these Florentines as self-retired
  In hungry pride and gainful cowardice,
As two close Hebrews, in that land inspired,
  Paled-in and vineyarded from beggar-spies;
The hawks of ship-mast forests; the untired
  And pannier'd mules for ducats and old lies—
Quick cats'-paws on the generous stray-away—
Great wits in Spanish, Tuscan, and Malay.

RIDDLE II

So the two brothers and their *murdered* man
Rode past fair Florence.

RIDDLE III

Soon she turn'd up a soiled glove, whereon
  Her silk had play'd in purple phantasies—
She kiss'd it with a lip more cold than stone,
  And put it in her bosom, where it dries,
And freezes utterly unto the bone
  Those dainties made to still an infant's cries.

But why are we, to use Mr Keats' own words, to

look
Like puzzled urchin, on an aged crone,
Who keepeth close a wondrous riddle-book,

and not endeavour to make some guesses ourselves? Our readers shall not have all the honours of discovery, and all the rewards of perseverance.—Spirits of Scaliger and Heyne, assist us!

A palpitating snake,
Bright, and cirque-couchant,

means a snake curled up.

'The brilliance feminine' means a brightness neither masculine nor neuter.

'I took compassion on her, bade her steep
Her hair in weïrd syrops that would keep
Her loveliness invisible,'

means that the lady should buy a bottle of 'Essence of Tyre,' for changing red hair to black.

'A swooning love' is a love that falls into a swoon; beautiful, but uncommon.

'A pillowy cleft' is certainly an indention that the nose has made in a pillow.

Divine liquids come with odorous ooze
Through *the cold-serpent pipe*,

are strong waters made in a portable still.

But there are some passages, which, with all our pains, must remain, for us, in their own mystical beauty. We cannot understand 'a milder-mooned body;'—or 'the ruddy strife of hearts and lips;'—or how 'Love'

buzz'd his wings, with fearful roar,
Above the lintel of their chamber-door,
And down the passage cast a glow upon the floor.

But we do not offer any reward for their explanation.

However we may have dwelt upon the power which Mr Keats thus possesses of setting us to think, we cannot pass over the equally happy influence with which he sways us to laughter. We think that our language cannot furnish any *conceits* half so agreeable, and airy, and provoking, as the following:—

In Cupid's college she had spent
Sweet days, a lovely graduate;

or,

Love in a hut, with water and a crust,
Is—Love forgive us—cinders, ashes, dust;

or two lovers reposing

with eyelids clos'd,
Saving a tithe which love still open kept,
That they might see each other while they almost slept;

or,

He answer'd, bending to her open eyes,
Where he was mirror'd small, in Paradise;

or,

'My voice is not a bellows unto ire!'

Our readers will by this time conclude that Mr Keats is a very original poet. We perfectly accord with them. But he yet has his faults;—he sometimes descends to write naturally, and to use the common language of humanity in the expression of pleasure or grief. We hope he may correct this fault ere the Cockney chair shall become vacant.

29. Unsigned review, *London Magazine and Monthly Critical and Dramatic Review* (Gold's)

August 1820, ii, 160–73

We do not think the poetical merits of Mr Keats have been duly estimated; and that apparently for the worst of all reasons—because he is said to be a disciple of Leigh Hunt's. Now this said Leigh Hunt may write some very quaint articles—and to many perhaps objectionable articles—in his *Examiner*; but no man can pretend to assert with truth that he is devoid of talent. To be sure, there may be some little follies chargeable on the master and his disciple—they may have be-praised each other a little over-much; and the purity of their taste in composition generally may be made a matter of question; but with these *trivial* subtractions from their fame, we have no doubt of their obtaining an exalted place in the temple of our literary benefactors.

It is known to our readers, that Mr Keats belongs to the Cockney School of Poetry—a school, we suppose, so denominated, from the fact of its writers having been educated in the city, and taking their pictures of rural life from its immediate environs. This school, like others, has its opponents and admirers: amongst the former, the *Quarterly Review*, is the most able and the most unjust; amongst the latter, and more amiable, is Baldwin's *Magazine*. Mr Keats, however, has suffered from both; less, perhaps, from the malicious hostility of his open opponent, than from the perverted, strange, and affected friendship of his admirer. Every one who has read 'the review,' as it is termed, of *Endymion*, in the *Quarterly* Journal, must be satisfied of the truth of our remark; and not less so, if they have had patience to peruse a notice of the same work in the pseudo *London Magazine*. The foul injustice of the one needs no comment; but the vicious tone of incongruous remark in the other demands especial censure. When a critic avows determined enmity—when he avows he has not read the work he condemns—the reputation of an author cannot be much endangered. But when we find such a character of a man's work as the following presents, we can scarcely hesitate to pronounce it as damning to the last degree:—

Endymion is totally unlike all these, and all other poems.—(Alluding to Southey's and Campbell's.)—As we said before, it is not *a poem* at all. It is an ecstatic dream of poetry—a flush—a fever—a burning light—an involuntary out-pouring of the spirit of poetry—that will not be controlled. Its movements are the starts and boundings of the young horse before it has felt the bitt—the first flights of the young bird, feeling and exulting in the powers with which it is gifted, but not yet acquainted with their use or their extent. It is the wanderings of the butterfly in the first hour of its birth; not as yet knowing one flower from another, but only that all *are* flowers. Its similitudes come crowding upon us from all delightful things. It is the May-day of poetry—the flush of blossoms and weeds that start up at the first voice of spring. It is the sky-lark's hymn to the day-break, involuntarily gushing forth as he mounts upward to look for the fountain of that light which has awakened him. It is as if the muses had steeped their child in the waters of Castaly, and we beheld him emerging from them, with his eyes sparkling and his limbs quivering with the delicious intoxication, and the precious drops scattered from him into the air at every motion, glittering in the sunshine, and casting the colours of the rainbow on all things around.[1]

We are ready to believe all this was sincerely meant, but nothing short of lunacy could have dictated such expressions. Here we have a poem, styled a *dream—a fever—a burning light—not a poem at all.* Its

[1] See No. 21.

movements are likened to those of a *young horse—a roving bird—a butterfly*. It is called the *May-day of poetry—the sky-lark's hymn—a child steeped in the waters of Castaly ! ! !* Now in the name of common sense was ever such a farrago heaped together before? The virulent condemnation of the *Quarterly* is at all events intelligible; but this is beyond the power of censure, and, what is worse, of cure. Mr Keats between these reviewers has been sadly abused, and treated with a cruelty more mad than ever was inflicted on the vilest heretic by the Spanish Inquisition. Stephen, when stoning to death, or Laurence, broiling on the gridiron, had not half so much reason to complain, as our young and gifted author.

We shall endeavour to act differently by Mr Keats; we shall not, with a dash of a pen, consign his labours to contempt; or, with an idiot's praise, make him a subject for laughter or for pity. We shall allow him to speak in his own person, and enable the public to decide more correctly on his powers and pretensions. We frankly confess our dislike of his rhythm, and his intolerable affectation, and mistaken stringing-together of compound epithets. But still we feel he often *thinks* like a poet. His knowledge of Greek and mythology seems to mystify him on every occasion; and his mode of expression is seldom natural. He does not trust himself to his naturally strong and vivid impressions: he says nothing like other men, and appears always on the stretch for words to shew his thoughts are of a different texture from all other writers. He looks as if he mistook affectation for originality—as some men do dirty linen and unreaped chins as proofs of genius. Mr Keats, however, is young, and may in time learn the folly of so misjudging. His *Endymion* led us, with all its blemishes, to expect from him higher things; and though disappointed, on this occasion, we are still sanguine of his success. We are sure Leigh Hunt never corrected his exercises in 'Lamia' or the 'Basil Pot', or else they would have appeared to more advantage. We shall now proceed to give some account of the work before us; and shall be the more extended, inasmuch as we wish to deal fairly by a clever young man, to whom we would recommend a little country air, to strengthen his nerves; and a change of diet, as necessary to the preservation of his health. The waters of Lymington might prove of essential benefit towards the re-establishment of his constitution; or, if these failed, he might be able to procure a letter of introduction to the *retreat* at York,[1] which would be much more certain, though more tedious and expensive.

[1] A famous private madhouse.

The first of the poems in this volume, which is a fair specimen of the whole, is a misti-mithological *Fantasie*, whose story, if we understand it rightly, is as follows:

The *ever-smitten* Hermes empty left
His golden throne, *bent warm on amorous theft:*

and made a retreat into a forest on the shores of Crete, to look after a nymph, at whose feet we are told was a world of love; at least—

So Hermes thought, and a celestial heat
Burnt from his winged heels to *either ear!*

In his search for this beauty, who caused his very ears to burn, he meets with

——— a *palpitating* snake,
Bright, and *cirque-couchant in a dusky* brake.

She was besides

So rainbow-sided, touch'd with miseries,
She seem'd, at times, some penanced lady elf,
Some demon's mistress, or the demon's *self!*

This snake addresses herself to Hermes, and tells him, that she has had a 'splendid dream' of him the night before, in which she saw him among the gods: the only sad one, as he neither heard the 'lute-fingered muses,'

Nor even Apollo when he sang alone,
Deaf to his throbbing throat's long, long *melodious moan.*

She then proceeds to ask him, with rather a coquetish air, what she knew well herself, if he had found the maid.

Whereat the *star* of Lethe not delay'd
His *rosy eloquence*, and thus inquired:

And when he had finished his speech, we are told,

Light flew his earnest words, among the blossoms blown.

* * * * *

Then thus again the *brilliance feminine:*

Who in this new capacity hath condescended to inform him that she has rendered the Nymph invisible—

'To keep her unaffronted, unassailed
By the love-glances of unlovely eyes,
Of Satyrs, Fauns, and blear'd *Silenus' sighs.*
Pale grew her immortality, for woe
Of all these lovers.'——

The tenure by which she held her immortality must indeed be curious, and its nature not less so, when all at once she could render it invisible. She however requires Hermes to swear he will grant her a boon, if she allows him to behold his Nymph; to which of course he assents, as in duty bound, and

—— Once again the charmed God began
An oath, and through the serpent's ears it ran
Warm, tremulous, devout, psalterian.

With an air of pathetic gravity she says she was a woman once, and wishes to be so again; and as if 'wishing and the deed were one,' she breathes on the brow of Hermes, and swift was seen

Of both the *guarded* nymph *near-smiling* on the green.

A very singular effect, indeed: but the transformation seems still incomplete. But in consequence of this,

One *warm, flush'd moment*, hovering, it might seem
Dash'd by the wood-nymph's beauty, *so he burn'd;*
Then, lighting on the printless verdure, turn'd
To the *swoon'd serpent*, and with *languid arm,*
Delicate, put to proof the lythe Caducean charm.
So done, upon the nymph his eyes he bent
Full of *adoring tears and blandishment,*
And towards her stept: she, like a moon in wane,
Faded before him, *cower'd*, nor could restrain
Her fearful sobs, self-folding like a flower
That *faints* into itself at evening hour:
But the God *fostering her chilled hand,*
She felt the warmth, her eyelids *open'd bland! !*

There seems something of the incomprehensible in this passage: we must not, however, stop at trifles. The serpent now changes, but not before

Her mouth foam'd, and the grass therewith besprent,
Wither'd at dew so sweet and virulent; (! ! !)

while, strange to say,

> Her *eyes in torture fix'd, and anguish drear,*
> Hot, glaz'd, and *wide*, with *lid-lashes all sear,*
> *Flash'd phosphor and sharp sparks, without one cooling tear.*

This is Epic sublimed, but nothing in point of grandeur to the continued effect of the change thus heroically described—

> ——— *Convuls'd with scarlet pain:*
> A deep volcanian yellow took the place
> *Of all her milder-mooned body's grace;*

Still unsatisfied with this usurpation, its daring not only

> ——————— lick'd up her stars: (! ! !)

but also undrest her of her 'rubious argent.'

> ——————— That vanish'd, also she
> Melted and disappear'd as suddenly;
> And in the air, her *new voice* luting soft,
> Cried, 'Lycius! gentle Lycius!'—Borne aloft
> With the bright mists about the mountains hoar
> These words dissolv'd: Crete's forests heard no more.

Lamia, 'now a lady bright,' does not change her character without some reason; and we suppose, in order to wash her clean of her snake-ship, fled to

> ——— a *clear pool* wherein she *passioned*
> To see herself escap'd from so sore ills,
> While her robes flaunted with the daffodils.

Lycius it appears was a happy fellow, or we will suppose him to be so, for his own sake; and she was

> A virgin purest lipp'd, yet in the lore
> Of love deep learned to the red heart's core:
> Not one hour old, yet of sciential brain
> *To unperplex bliss from its neighbour pain.*

She must indeed have a very vivid imagination to effect the purpose of the last line, and not less so to 'intrigue' effectually with 'the *specious* chaos.' One deduction, however, we must make from her *amiable* qualities, for she was a loiterer; but being newly converted, we must wonder the less at her retaining some of her old propensities.

But first 'tis fit to tell how she could muse
And dream, when in the serpent prison-house,
Of all she list, strange or magnificent:
How, ever, where she will'd, her spirit went.

* * * * * * *

And once, while among mortals dreaming thus,
She saw the young Corinthian Lycius.

* * * * * * *

And fell into a *swooning* love of him. ! ! !

Her object for lingering by 'the way side' is now explained to us, for

——— on the moth-time of that evening dim
He would return that way, ———

on his road to Corinth. Jove inspires him to leave his companions,

——————— and set forth to walk,
Perhaps grown wearied of their Corinth talk:

He now takes a turn or two over some solitary hills; on which occasion,

His phantasy was lost where reason fades;

and certainly but for the author's kindness in pointing out where it escaped, few would have been able to discover; it was

In the calm'd twilight of Platonic shades. ! ! !

In despite, however, of this, Lycius was not doomed to be invisible; and

Lamia beheld him coming, near, more near—
Close to her passing, in *indifference drear,*
His *silent sandals swept* the mossy green;
——————————————— while her eyes
Follow'd his steps, and her *neck regal white*
Turn'd—syllabling thus, 'Ah, Lycius bright,
And will you leave me on the hills alone?
Lycius, look back! and be some pity shown.'
He did; not with cold wonder fearingly.

For in fact his eyes

——————— had drunk her beauty up,
Leaving no drop in the bewildering cup.

And with

> Due adoration, thus began to adore;—
> Her soft look growing coy, she saw his chain so sure. [qy. so sore.]

His adoration, however, appeared to have but little effect; for, after stating her reasons for not yielding to his passion,

> ———————— she rose
> Tiptoe with white arms spread. He, sick to lose
> The *amorous promise* of her *lone complain,*
> Swoon'd, murmuring of love, and pale with pain.

And how did the cruel lady then treat 'the life' she 'tangled in her mesh,' seeking

> With brighter eyes and slow amenity,
> Put her new lips to his, and gave afresh
> The life she had entangled in her mesh.

And then she began to sing to such a tune, that

> ——— like held breath, the stars drew in their panting fires.

But still, to relieve his apprehensions of her 'melting,' she tells him a plumper—

> ———————— That the self-same pains
> Inhabited her frail-strung heart as his.

and that she saw him first

> ——————— 'mid baskets heap'd
> Of amorous herbs and flowers. ————

Pity she did not put him in her pocket, but perhaps she then wore none: however, she entices him on

> To unperplex'd delight, and pleasure known.

For Lamia judged,

> ———————— and judg'd aright,
> That Lycius could not love in half a fright.
>
> * * * * *
>
> Lycius to all made eloquent reply,
> Marrying to every word a twinborn sigh.

In fine, this notable matrimony induces the lady to go to Corinth, but she, in her 'eagerness,'

> Made, by a spell, the triple league decrease
> To a few paces; not at all surmised
> By blinded Lycius, so in her comprized.

Entering Corinth, they met an old man, 'slow-stepp'd,' at whose approach 'Lycius shrank closer,'

> Into his mantle, adding wings to haste,
> While hurried Lamia trembled: 'Ah,' said he,
> 'Why do you shudder, love, so ruefully?'
> * * * * *
> While yet he spake they had arrived before
> ——————— a place unknown

(Yet having a gate whose hinges breathed 'Æolian Sounds.')

> Some time to any, but those two alone,
> And a few Persian mutes, who that same year
> Were seen about the markets. ————

The most curious could not find out their place of retreat; but the 'flitter-wing'd verse' is not likely to keep the secret; and we shall ascertain the fact by and by.

The Second Part of this exquisite Poem thus very sublimely opens:—

> Love in a hut, with water and a crust,
> Is—Love, forgive us!—cinders, ashes, dust; (The deuce it is.)
> Love in a palace is perhaps at last
> More grievous torment than a hermit's fast.

And in the following lines the author truly says:

> That is a doubtful tale from faery land,
> Hard for the non-elect to understand. (! ! !)

Bliss is but transitory, for it seems,

> Love, jealous grown of so complete a pair,
> Hover'd and buzz'd his wings, with *fearful roar*,
> Above the lintel of their chamber door,
> And down the passage *cast a glow upon the floor*.

They were reposing (not withering from the 'fearful roar' and buzzing of love's wings) in this chamber, when

Deafening the swallow's twitter, came a thrill
Of trumpets—Lycius started—the sounds fled,
But left a thought, a buzzing in his head. (! ! !)

* * * * *

The lady, ever watchful, penetrant,
Saw this with pain, so arguing a want
Of something more, more than her empery
Of joys; ———————

'Began to moan and sigh.'

'Why do you sigh, fair creature?' whispered he:
'Why do you think?' returned she tenderly.

He then tells her he wishes his neighbours and friends to see what bliss he enjoys, and that it is his determination to wed her publicly. This does not appear to have suited the lady's taste; and so much did she feel,—that, in beseeching him to change his purpose, she

——————————— wept a rain
Of sorrows at his words. ————

But it was of no avail (barbarous man); and

His passion, cruel grown, took on a hue
Fierce and sanguineous as 'twas possible
In one whose brow had *no dark veins to swell*. ! !

She reluctantly consented; when a very natural inquiry is made by the lover, namely, what she was called, and where were her relations. This inquiry the lady contrives to elude; and requests him, if his 'vision rests with any pleasure on her,' not to bid old Apollonius to the feast: for what reason we know not.

Lycius, perplex'd at words so blind and *blank*,
Made close inquiry; from whose touch she shrank,
Feigning a sleep; and he to the dull shade
Of deep sleep in a moment was betray'd.

and thus we see how much the snake was an over-match for the lover. After an account of Lamia's preparation for the bridal feast, in which she was assisted by 'subtle servitors,' but it is doubtful how and whence they came, 'the day arrived,' and 'the herd approached,' and 'entered marvelling,'

Save one, who look'd thereon with eye severe,
And with *calm-planted* steps walk'd in *austere;*
'Twas Apollonius: something too *he laughed,*
As though some knotty problem, that had *daft*
His patient thought, had now begun to thaw,
And solve and melt:—'twas just as he foresaw.

This is a description of a philosopher perhaps unequalled in our language: but we cannot refrain from saying, that the passage, though possessing considerable poetical beauty, is not entirely new; for we remember the Baron Munchausen's trumpet also played an admirably fine flourish when the thaw came on. The author perhaps had a 'perplexed' recollection of the circumstance, and thus unintentionally subjected himself to the charge of plagiarism. Apollonius, however, after apologizing for coming uninvited to the feast, is led into the house by Lycius, who went,

With reconciling words and courteous mien
Turning into *sweet milk* the sophist's spleen.

We hope in a second edition of this work to learn by what chemical process this was effected. After sundry preparations, the guests are seated, and

Soft went the music the *soft air* along,
While *fluent Greek* a vowel'd undersong
Kept up among the guests. ———

And,

—— when the wine had done its rosy deed,
And every soul from human trammels freed,

the company felt themselves quite at home. Garlands of flowers were then brought in, that every guest

——————— as he did please,
Might *fancy-fit his brow, silk-pillow'd at his ease.*

Lycius was in the mean time sitting by Lamia, and wishing to take wine with Apollonius, when he found

——————— The bald-head philosopher
Had fix'd his eye, without a twinkle or stir
Full on the alarmed beauty of the bride,
Brow-beating her fair form, and troubling her sweet pride.

Rather ungenerous treatment every one will admit. But this look has the effect of taking recognition from 'the orbs' of Lamia; the loud revelry grew hushed——

> A *deadly* silence *step* by *step* INCREASED,
> Until it seem'd a horrid presence there,
> And not a man but felt the terror in his hair.

Lycius upbraids Apollonius for his impoliteness in staring his wife to death—

> 'Fool!' said the sophist, in an under-tone
> Gruff with contempt; which a dead-sighing moan
> From Lycius answer'd, as heart-struck and lost,
> He sank supine beside the aching ghost.
> * * * * *
> Then Lamia breath'd death-breath; the sophist's eye,
> Like a sharp spear, went through her utterly,
> Keen, cruel, perceant, stinging: she, as well
> As her weak hand could any meaning tell,
> Motion'd him to be silent; vainly so,
> He look'd and look'd again *a level—No!*
> 'A Serpent!' echoed he; no sooner said,
> Than with a frightful scream she vanished.

The least that Lycius could do after this disappointment was to die, which he accordingly does, and the Poem concludes.

It is impossible to have perused the interesting tale we have just concluded, without admitting ourselves much indebted to Mr Keats. The precision of his remark, the depth of his foresight, the imagery which abounds throughout the whole narrative, and the intensity of feeling which he throws into the catastrophe, are unequalled by any thing ever written by Mr Coleridge, or Mr Fitzgerald, or Monk Lewis. We had determined after the perusal of 'Lamia,' to have left the remainder of the volume untouched, and not rifle it of those jewels—fevered flushes—hawthorn blooms, butterfly colorings, and young birds' wanderings into the skies (as the writer in Baldwin's publication would have described them), but yet we could not resist taking advantage of the last opportunity that may possibly be afforded us of ever seeing this *Bijou* again, and giving to our reader such a feast, as Endymion never found on the brow of Latmos.

The Second Tale in this Volume is called 'Isabella, or the Pot of Basil.' The story is told in about two hundred and fifty lines; but as many of our readers may fear to undertake the task of wading through it, we shall epitomize it for their edification. 'Lorenzo, a young palmer in Love's eye,' 'would not in the self-same mansion dwell' with *Isabel*, 'without some stir of heart, some *malady*;

> They could not, sure, beneath the same roof sleep
> But to each other dream, and nightly weep.

Their love encreased—

> ——————— but, alas,
> Honeyless days and days did he let pass;
> Until sweet Isabella's untouch'd cheek
> Fell thin as a young mother's,———
>
> * * * * *
>
> 'How ill she is,' said he, 'I may not speak,
> And yet I will, and tell my love all plain:
> If looks speak *love-laws*, I will drink her tears,
> And at the least 'twill startle off her cares.

This is in truth a fine vein of poetry. That 'looks' should, however, 'speak *love-laws*,' is not very original; but that their influence should have prompted Lorenzo to 'drink her tears,' which as yet had not reached farther than her pillow, is a discovery reserved for the ingenuity of our author. But again, how could drinking '*her tears*' '*startle* off her cares'? Mr Keats leaves us not altogether in doubt as to the fact; for he informs us, that this was said 'one fair morning,' and, as we must suppose, when his head suffered a little after the applications to his lips of the night before—*Quem non fecundi calices fecere disertum!*[1] But to proceed: the lover 'anguished' out

> A dreary night of love *and* misery,

and matters would have been a great deal worse,

> If Isabel's quick eye had not been wed
> To every symbol on his forehead high;
> And ——————— so, lisped tenderly,
> 'Lorenzo!' ———————

This acted like a talisman upon the 'palmer;' and after telling his love he would not 'grieve' her hand by 'unwelcome pressing,' or '*fear* her

[1] 'Whom flowing cups have not made eloquent.'

eyes by gazing on them,' adds, in a strain of the most moving pathos,

> '———————— but I cannot live
> Another night, and not my passion *shrive*.'
> *   *   *   *   *
> So said, his erewhile timid lips grew bold.
> And *poesied* with hers in dewy rhyme:

No wonder then that

> Great bliss was with them, and great happiness
> Grew like a lusty flower in June's caress.

Happiness, however, in this world is but very short lived, and the 'dewy rhyme' did not prevent their parting. But the manner in which they so parted is told us in happier lines than we elsewhere recollect so heart-rending a scene to have been described:—

> Parting they seem'd to *tread* upon the air,
> Twin roses by the zephyr blown apart.

As soon as they reach home, they are once more in their proper persons, and occupy themselves as befits those over whom the zephyr had no more influence than is ascribed to it by our poet.

> She, to her chamber gone, a ditty fair
> Sang, of delicious love and honey'd dart;
> He with light steps went up a western hill,
> And bade the sun farewell, and joy'd his fill.

We presume the 'sun' was the first object of his love, and in gratitude for the past favours of the Deity, Lorenzo determined, as he was 'blown apart' from 'simple Isabel' not only corporally but mentally, to give evidence of the distance to which they were separated, by climbing up a 'western hill,' where no doubt he very poetically 'joy'd his fill.' They soon met again—

> ———————— before the dusk
> Had taken from the stars its *pleasant* veil,
> Close in a bower of hyacinth and musk,
> Unknown of any, free from whispering tale.

'At such a place as this,' we should have imagined the lovers to be pleasantly, if not happily situated, if it were not that our author starts a doubt upon the subject, and asks,

> Were they unhappy then?———

True, we have an immediate answer—

——————— It cannot be.—

But to us the reasons are not at all satisfactory.

Too many tears for lovers have been shed,
  Too many sighs give we to them in fee,
Too much of pity after they are dead,
  Too many doleful stories do we see,
Whose matter in bright gold were best be read;
Except in such a page where Theseus' spouse
Over the *pathless* waves towards him bows.

Now with all due respect to Mr Keats, we think, neither 'tears that *have been* shed,' nor 'sighs given *in fee*,' nor 'pity *after* they are dead,' nor all the 'doleful stories' in the world could prove the 'Palmer' and his 'simple Isabel' were *not* unhappy. We may not be clear-sighted enough in affairs of love to see the matter otherwise, and in differing with our author, we feel the delicate ground on which we tread, and offer our remarks with all that humility which becomes us.

But the 'fair Lady,' we are informed, lived with her two brothers, who were

Enriched from *ancestral* merchandize;

and the verses in which we are told of the agents by which they obtained their wealth, are amongst the most nervous in the poem. Here and there we are a little at a loss to comprehend their meaning, but our more intelligent readers will no doubt at the first glance divine it:

For them the Ceylon diver held his breath,
For them his ears gush'd blood; for them in death
The seal on the cold ice with *piteous bark*
Lay full of darts; ————

The first line, and the half of the second line of the above extract, are intelligible enough; but for the last line and a half, we confess we are not such skilful naturalists as to be able to discover their beauties.

We have next an apostrophe to Boccaccio, pp. 58–9; and we afterwards find the brothers took it in dudgeon that the 'Palmer' should have won the sister—

When 'twas their plan to *coax* her by degrees
To some high noble and his olive-trees.

At last,

> ——————— these men of cruel clay
> *Cut mercy with a sharp knife to the bone;*
> For they resolved ————

Blush to hear it, ye virgins; hang down your heads and weep, ye children of sentiment and love; shed the tear of pity over the anticipated fate of the poor 'Palmer.'

> For they resolved—(what?)—in some forest dim
> To kill Lorenzo, and—(what? why)—there bury him. ! ! !

They did not, however, choose the assassin-like time of midnight for this dreadful purpose; nor did Lorenzo seem at all suspicious of their murderous intentions. They took a very 'pleasant morning' for the work; and of all times in the world selected that hour when

> ———————————— *he leant*
> *Into the sun-rise;* ————

and when

> ———————— towards him they bent
> Their footing through the dews. ———

Thus we see how respectfully they approached their enemy; and the language in which they addressed him was not less so:

> ———————— and to him said,
> 'You seem there in the quiet of content,
> Lorenzo, *and we are most loth to invade*
> *Calm speculation;'* ————

This might be rather enigmatical; but, under all the circumstances, it must still be considered their notice to him to quit was sufficient, couched as it was in these additional terms:

> '——————— but if you are wise,
> Bestride your steed while *cold* is in the skies.'

But we forgot to state, that when they first saw Lorenzo, he was leaning

> ——————— o'er the balustrade
> Of the garden terrace, ———

and no wonder they should have politely requested him to

'Come down, we pray thee, ere the *hot sun* count
His dewy rosary on the eglantine.'

These powerful entreaties of the *cold*, and the *hot sun*, had their due effect, and

Lorenzo, courteously as he was wont,
Bow'd a fair greeting to these serpents' whinc;
And went *in haste*, to get *in readiness*,
With belt, and spur, and *bracing* huntsman's dress.

What an innocent soul must this Lorenzo have been; but this is not all. He was exceedingly methodical in his pauses; and though the 'hot sun' was out, we find he still sighed to hear his lady's matin song—

—— as he to the court-yard pass'd along,
Each *third* step did he pause, and listen'd oft
If he could hear his lady's matin-song,
Or the light *whisper* of her footstep *soft*;
And as he *thus* over his passion hung,
He heard a *laugh full musical* aloft;
When, looking up, he saw her features bright
Smile through an in-door lattice, all delight.

This happy event enables him

——— to stifle all the heavy sorrow
Of a poor three hours' absence; ———

and to add—

'Good bye! I'll soon be back!' ————

to which,

————————— 'Good bye!' said she;

and, in proof of her *ardent* affection,

——— as he went, *she chanted merrily*.

Well, Lorenzo, who thus went like a sheep to the slaughter, was, without much ceremony or remorse, very speedily slain, and buried in a forest. The brothers, on their return, tell their sister they have shipped off Lorenzo, adding, without much of affection,

To-day thou wilt not see him, nor to-morrow,
And the next day will be a day of sorrow.

The natural result ensued on this; and

Sorely she wept until the night came on,
And then, instead of love, O misery!
She brooded o'er the luxury alone.

*   *   *   *   *

But Selfishness, Love's cousin, held not long
Its fiery vigil in her single breast;

*   *   *   *   *

And,

——— So, sweet Isabel
By gradual decay from beauty fell;

like

——— a roundelay
Of death among the bushes and the leaves;

and the worst of it was, all her uneasiness was excited

Because Lorenzo came not.———

The brothers' consciences were not still callous to remorse, and

——— their crimes
Came on them, like a smoke from Hinmon's vale

Plague take it, that it did not suffocate them at once; but we presume that would be rather an unpoetical sort of death, and hence every night

——— they groan'd aloud,
To see their sister in her *snowy* shroud.

The fact is, however, she was not yet dead, as our author informs us—

And she had died in *drowsy ignorance*;

a singular sort of death by the way, if it were not

——— for a thing more deadly dark than all;

Like a fierce portion, — Like a lance, —

It was a vision.———

And of course it was Lorenzo, who was sadly altered by his new habitation.

——————— The forest tomb
  Had marr'd his glossy hair, which once could shoot
Lustre into the sun, and put cold doom
  Upon his lips, and taken the soft lute
From his lorn voice, and past his loamed ears
Had made a miry channel for his tears.

En passant, we may here remark, that never was hair so much endowed: not all we have ever heard or read of Sampson, could half equal the powers ascribed by Mr Keats to his Lorenzo's 'glossy hair:' let that, however, pass. He tells her he was murdered, and points out the place of his interment; adding, that which she makes no difficulty in believing, that

I am a shadow now, alas! alas!

'If spirits could go mad,' he declares he 'should rage' but Isabel's 'paleness warms' his 'grave,' and 'makes' (him) 'glad;' and on sighing 'adieu,' he

——————— dissolv'd, and left
The *atom* darkness in a slow turmoil;

All this, however, only

—— made sad Isabella's eyelids ache,
And in the dawn (of what?) she started up awake; ! ! !

But was this only for the moment; for with a simplicity worthy of Lorenzo's love, she goes to visit his tomb, and takes

——————— with her an aged nurse,
And went into that dismal forest-hearse.

Of course where he lay buried: she soon turned up one of his soiled gloves,

——————— whereon
Her silk had play'd in *purple phantasies*;

and after laboring for three hours at very 'travail sore,'

At last they felt the *kernel* of the grave,
And Isabella did not stamp and rave.

Mirabile dictu! And then they found his head—

——— and for its tomb did choose
A garden-pot, wherein she laid it by,
And cover'd it with mould, and o'er it set
Sweet Basil, which her tears kept ever wet.

She now forgot the sun, moon, and stars, and thought only of her 'sweet Basil,' which she ever fed with '*thin* tears,'

Whence thick, and green, and beautiful it grew,—
So that the jewel, safely casketed,
Came forth, and in perfumed leafits spread.

But this did not reconcile her to the loss of her lover, whose last relic she was apprehensive would have been stolen from her by her envious brothers. Isabella, however, with all her simplicity, was an over-match for them; for in order to watch it,

——— seldom did she go to *chapel-shrift*,
And seldom felt she any *hunger-pain*.

Excellent sentinels, no doubt—

And, patient as a hen-bird, sat her there
Beside her Basil, *weeping through her hair*.

Unfortunately, however, with all her watching, the Basil was stolen; her brothers went away,

With blood upon their heads, to banishment.

And we are told—

——— Sweet Isabel *will* die;
Will die a death *too lone* and *incomplete*,
Now they have ta'en away her Basil sweet.

In our simplicity we should have imagined her death to be the more complete for the reason assigned in the last line; but our author tells us otherwise; and as those can paint it best who have felt it most, we differ from our author with a proportionate degree of diffidence. The poor girl's senses seemed at length to be exceedingly though strangely fatigued—

And with *melodious chuckle* in the strings
Of her lorn voice, she oftentimes would cry
After the pilgrim in his wanderings,
To ask him where her Basil was. ———

Her tragical fate is now wound up, and she pays the debt of nature—

> Imploring for her Basil to the last.

We have devoted an unusual portion of our Journal to the consideration of Mr Keats's new work, with the hope, that his uncharitable enemies may learn from our extracts to repent them of their enmity, and set that value on his labours, which the perusal of our extracts must induce them to form. To Mr Keats's admirers we have nothing to say; they need no recommendation to peruse his works. On Primrose Hill, as in the Blue Coat School; in the druggist's shop, or by the Paddington Canal, they must guile the reader of many an hour, and often lead him to pause on the extraordinary powers of the human mind, on the wonderful destinies of man, and yet think there exists such gross stupidity, nay so deplorable a want of taste, amongst the bulk of English readers, as not to discover in Mr Keats powers and acquirements that dazzle while they instruct, and astonish while they delight.

30. Jeffrey on Keats

1820, 1829, 1848

Francis Jeffrey (1773–1850), editor of the *Edinburgh Review*, was the most influential and respected critic of the day. Traditionalist in principle, he was deeply affected by the new Romantic sensibility (see headnote to No. 2), although in 1815 the irritated Wordsworth denounced him as 'a depraved Coxcomb; the greatest Dunce, I believe, in this Island, and assuredly the Man who takes most pains to prove himself so.' For the possible genesis of (a), which is almost entirely occupied with *Endymion*, see Introduction, pp. 26–7. When reprinting the article in 1844, Jeffrey expanded the final part, mainly with quotations from 'The Eve of St Agnes' and the Odes. Extract (b) shows him to be somewhat out of touch with contemporary movements of taste. Extract (c) was written after reading Milnes's biography, which had been dedicated to Jeffrey. Keats's friend Brown had been responsible for the plot of *Otho*, which Jeffrey criticizes.

(a) Unsigned article on *Endymion* and *Lamia . . . and Other Poems*: 'We had never happened to see either of these volumes till very lately—and have been exceedingly struck with the genius they display, and the spirit of poetry which breathes through all their extravagance. That imitation of our older writers, and especially of our older dramatists, to which we cannot help flattering ourselves that we have somewhat contributed, has brought on, as it were, a second spring in our poetry;—and few of its blossoms are either more profuse of sweetness or richer in promise, than this which is now before us. Mr Keats, we understand, is still a very young man; and his whole works, indeed, bear evidence enough of the fact. They are full of extravagance and irregularity, rash attempts at originality, interminable wanderings, and excessive obscurity. They manifestly require, therefore, all the indulgence that can be claimed for a first attempt:—but we think it no less plain that they deserve it; for they are flushed all over with the rich lights of fancy, and so coloured and bestrewn with the flowers of poetry, that even while perplexed and bewildered in their labyrinths, it is impossible to resist the intoxication of their sweetness, or to shut our hearts to the enchantments they so lavishly present. The models upon which he has formed himself, in the *Endymion*, the earliest and by much the most considerable of his poems, are obviously the *Faithful Shepherdess* of Fletcher, and the *Sad Shepherd* of Ben Jonson;—the exquisite metres and inspired diction of which he has copied with great boldness and fidelity—and, like his great originals, has also contrived to impart to the whole piece that true rural and poetical air which breathes only in them and in Theocritus—which is at once homely and majestic, luxurious and rude, and sets before us the genuine sights and sounds and smells of the country, with all the magic and grace of Elysium. His subject has the disadvantage of being mythological; and in this respect, as well as on account of the raised and rapturous tone it consequently assumes, his poetry may be better compared perhaps to the *Comus* and the *Arcades* of Milton, of which, also, there are many traces of imitation. The great distinction, however, between him and these divine authors, is, that imagination in them is subordinate to reason and judgment, while, with him, it is paramount and supreme—that their ornaments and images are employed to embellish and recommend just sentiments, engaging incidents, and natural characters, while his are poured out without measure or restraint, and with no apparent design but to unburden the breast of the author, and give vent to the overflowing vein of his fancy. The thin and scanty tissue of his story is merely the light frame work on which his florid wreaths are suspended; and while his imaginations go rambling and entangling themselves everywhere, like wild honeysuckles, all idea of sober reason, and plan, and consistency, is utterly forgotten, and are "strangled in their waste fertility." A great part of the work indeed, is written in the strangest and most fantastical manner that can be imagined. It seems as if the author had ventured everything that occurred to him in the shape of a glittering image or striking expression—taken the first word that presented itself to make up a rhyme, and then made that word the germ of a new cluster of images—a hint for a new excursion of the fancy—and so wandered on, equally forgetful whence he came, and heedless whither he was going, till he had covered his pages with an interminable arabesque of connected and incongruous figures, that multiplied as they extended, and were only harmonized by the brightness of their tints, and the graces of their forms. In this rash and headlong career he has of course many lapses and failures. There is no work, accordingly, from which a malicious critic could cull more matter for ridicule, or select more obscure, unnatural, or absurd passages. But we do not take *that* to be our office;—and just beg leave, on the contrary, to say, that any one who, on this account, would represent the whole poem as despicable, must either have no notion of poetry, or no regard to truth.

It is, in truth, at least as full of genius as of absurdity; and he who does not find a great deal in it to admire and to give delight, cannot in his heart see much beauty in the two exquisite dramas to which we have already alluded, or find any great pleasure in some of the finest creations of Milton and Shakespeare. There are very many such persons, we verily believe, even among the reading and judicious part of the community—correct scholars we have no doubt many of them, and, it may be, very classical composers in prose and in verse—but utterly ignorant of the true genius of English poetry, and incapable of estimating its appropriate and most exquisite beauties. With that spirit we have no hesitation in saying that Mr K. is deeply imbued—and of those beauties he has presented us with many striking examples. We are very much inclined indeed to add, that we do not know any book which we would sooner employ as a test to ascertain whether any one had in him a native relish for poetry, and a genuine sensibility to its intrinsic charm. The greater and more distinguished poets of our country have so much else in them to gratify other tastes and propensities, that they are pretty sure to captivate and amuse those to whom their poetry is but an hindrance and obstruction, as well as those to whom it constitutes their chief attraction. The interest of the stories they tell—the vivacity of the characters they delineate—the weight and force of the maxims and sentiments in which they abound—the very pathos and wit and humour they display, which may all and each of them exist apart from their poetry and independent of it, are quite sufficient to account for their popularity, without referring much to that still higher gift, by which they subdue to their enchantments those whose souls are attuned to the finer impulses of poetry. It is only where those other recommendations are wanting, or exist in a weaker degree, that the true force of the attraction, exercised by the pure poetry with which they are so often combined, can be fairly appreciated—where, without much incident or many characters, and with little wit, wisdom, or arrangement, a number of bright pictures are presented to the imagination, and a fine feeling expressed of those mysterious relations by which visible external things are assimilated with inward thoughts and emotions, and become the images and exponents of all passions and affections. To an unpoetical reader such passages always appear mere raving and absurdity—and to this censure a very great part of the volume before us will certainly be exposed, with this class of readers. Even in the judgment of a fitter audience, however, it must, we fear, be admitted, that, besides the riot and extravagance of his fancy, the scope and substance of Mr K.'s poetry is rather too dreamy and abstracted to excite the strongest interest, or to sustain the attention through a work of any great compass or extent. He deals too much with shadowy and incomprehensible beings, and is too constantly rapt into an extramundane Elysium, to command a lasting interest with ordinary mortals—and must employ the agency of more varied and coarser emotions, if he wishes to take rank with the seducing poets of this or of former generations. There is something very curious too, we think, in the way in which he, and Mr Barry Cornwall also, have dealt with the Pagan mythology, of which they have made so much use in their poetry. Instead of presenting its imaginary persons under the trite and vulgar traits that belong to them in the ordinary systems, little more is borrowed from these than the general conception of their conditions and relations; and an original character and distinct individuality is bestowed upon them, which has all the merit of invention, and all the grace and attraction of the fictions on which it is engrafted. The antients, though they probably did not stand in any great awe of their deities, have yet abstained very much from any minute or dramatic representation of their feelings and affections. In Hesiod and Homer, they are coarsely delineated by some of their actions and adventures, and introduced to us merely as the agents in those particular transactions; while in the Hymns, from those ascribed to Orpheus and Homer, down to those of Callimachus, we have little but pompous epithets and invocations, with a flattering commemoration of their most famous exploits—and are never allowed to enter into their bosoms, or follow out the train of their feelings, with the presumption of our human sympathy. Except the love-song of the Cyclops to his Sea Nymph in Theocritus[1]—the Lamentation of Venus for Adonis in Moschus[2]—and the more recent Legend of Apuleius,[3] we scarcely recollect a passage in all the writings of antiquity

[1] Theocritus, *Idyll* vi.

[2] The writer is confusing Bion's 'Lament for Adonis' (*Idyll* i) with the 'Lament for Bion' himself, attributed to Moschus.

[3] The legend of Cupid and Psyche in Apuleius' Latin prose romance *The Golden Ass*. Mary Tighe's poetic version in English, *Psyche* (1805), had in fact influenced Keats.

in which the passions of an immortal are fairly disclosed to the scrutiny and observation of men. The author before us, however, and some of his contemporaries, have dealt differently with the subject;—and, sheltering the violence of the fiction under the ancient traditionary fable, have created and imagined an entire new set of characters, and brought closely and minutely before us the loves and sorrows and perplexities of beings, with whose names and supernatural attributes we had long been familiar, without any sense or feeling of their personal character. We have more than doubts of the fitness of such personages to maintain a permanent interest with the modern public;—but the way in which they are here managed, certainly gives them the best chance that now remains for them; and, at all events, it cannot be denied that the effect is striking and graceful. But we must now proceed to our extracts.

The first of the volumes before us is occupied with the loves of Endymion and Diana—which it would not be very easy, and which we do not at all intend to analyze in detail. In the beginning of the poem, however, the Shepherd Prince is represented as having had strange visions and delirious interviews with an unknown and celestial beauty; soon after which, he is called on to preside at a festival in honour of Pan; and his appearance in the procession is thus described.

[Quotes *Endymion*, Book I, lines 169–81, 'His youth was fully blown' to 'Through his forgotten hands'.]

There is then a choral hymn addressed to the sylvan deity, which appears to us to be full of beauty; and reminds us, in many places, of the finest strains of Sicilian or English poetry. A part of it is as follows.

[Quotes *Endymion*, Book I, lines 232–87, 'O THOU, whose mighty palace roof' to 'drearily on barren moors', omitting lines 242–6.]

The enamoured youth sinks into insensibility in the midst of the solemnity, and is borne apart and revived by the care of his sister; and, opening his heavy eyes in her arms, says—

[Quotes *Endymion*, Book I, lines 466–97, 'I feel this thine endearing love' to 'So mournful strange'.]

He then tells her all the story of his love and madness; and is afterwards led away by butterflies to the haunts of Naiads, and by them sent down into enchanted caverns, where he sees Venus and Adonis, and great flights of Cupids, and wanders over diamond terraces among beautiful fountains and temples and statues, and all sorts of fine and strange things. All this is very fantastical: But there are splendid pieces of description, and a sort of wild richness on the whole. We cull a few little morsels. This is the picture of the sleeping Adonis.

[Quotes *Endymion*, Book II, lines 393–4, 'In midst of all' to 'fondest beauty'; Book II, lines 403–14, 'Sideway his face repos'd' to 'bugle-blooms divine'; Book II, lines 418–27, 'Hard by' to 'his sleeping eyes'.]

There is another and more classical sketch of Cybele.

[Quotes *Endymion*, Book II, lines 639–49, 'Forth from a rugged arch' to 'another gloomy arch'.]

In the midst of all these spectacles, he has, we do not very well know how, a ravishing interview with his unknown goddess; and, when she melts away from him, he finds himself in a vast grotto, where he overhears the courtship of Alpheus and Arethusa, and, as they elope together, discovers that the grotto has disappeared, and that he is at the bottom of the sea, under the transparent arches of its naked waters. The following is abundantly extravagant; but comes of no ignoble lineage, nor shames its high descent.

[Quotes *Endymion*, Book III, lines 119–36, 'Far had he roam'd' to 'Of nameless monster'.]

There he finds antient Glaucus enchanted by Circe—hears his wild story—and goes with him to the deliverance and restoration of thousands of drowned lovers, whose bodies were piled and stowed away in a large submarine palace. When this feat is happily performed, he finds himself again on dry ground, with woods and waters around him; and cannot help falling desperately in love with a beautiful damsel whom he finds there pining for some such consolations, and who tells a long story of her having come from India in the train of Bacchus, and having strayed away from him into that forest:—so they vow eternal fidelity, and are wafted up to heaven on flying horses, on which they sleep and dream among the stars;—and then the lady melts away, and he is again alone upon the earth; but soon rejoins his Indian love, and agrees to give up his goddess, and live only for her: But she refuses, and says she is resolved to devote herself to the service of Diana; and when she goes to dedicate herself, she turns out to be the goddess in a new shape, and exalts her lover with her to a blest immortality.

We have left ourselves room to say but little of the second volume, which is of a more miscellaneous character. 'Lamia' is a Greek antique story, in the measure and taste of *Endymion*. "Isabella" is a paraphrase of the same tale of Boccacio, which Mr Cornwall has also imitated under the title of *a Sicilian Story*. It would be worth while to compare the two imitations; but we have no longer time for such a task. Mr K. has followed his original more closely, and has given a deep pathos to several of his stanzas. The widowed bride's discovery of the murdered body is very strikingly given.

[Quotes 'Isabella', stanzas 47–8, 'Soon she turn'd up a soiled glove' to 'the kernel of the grave'; stanzas 51–2, 'In anxious secrecy' to 'tears kept ever wet'.]

The following lines from an ode to a Nightingale, are equally distinguished for harmony and feeling.

[Quotes 'Ode to a Nightingale', lines 15–28, 'O for a beaker full' to 'leaden-eyed despairs'; lines 63–70, 'The voice I hear' to 'faery lands forlorn'.]

We must close our extracts with the following lively lines to Fancy.

[Quotes 'Fancy', lines 9–24, 'O sweet Fancy!' to 'banish Even from her sky'; lines 39–66, 'thou shalt hear' to 'autumn breezes sing'.]

There is a fragment of a projected Epic, entitled *Hyperion*, on the expulsion of Saturn and the Titanian deities by Jupiter and his younger adherents, of which we cannot advise the completion: For, though there are passages of some force and grandeur, it is sufficiently obvious, from the specimen before us, that the subject is too far removed from all the sources of human interest, to be successfully treated by any modern author. Mr Keats has unquestionably a very beautiful imagination, and a great familiarity with the finest diction of English poetry; but he must learn not to misuse or misapply these advantages; and neither to waste the good gifts of nature and study on intractable themes, nor to luxuriate too recklessly on such as are more suitable.' (*Edinburgh Review* (August 1820), xxxiv, 203–13.)

(b) Extract from unsigned review 'Felicia Hemans': 'Since the beginning of our critical career, we have seen a vast deal of beautiful poetry pass into oblivion, in spite of our feeble efforts to recall or retain it in remembrance. The tuneful quartos of Southey are already little better than lumber:—And the rich melodies of Keats and Shelley,—and the fantastical emphasis of Wordsworth,—and the plebeian pathos of Crabbe, are melting fast from the field of our vision. The novels of Scott have put out his poetry. Even the splendid strains of Moore are fading into distance and dimness, except where they have been married to immortal music; and the blazing star of Byron himself is receding from its pride of place. . . . The two who have the longest withstood this rapid withering of the laurel, and with the least marks of decay on their branches, are Rogers and Campbell; neither of them, it may be remarked, a voluminous writer, and both distinguished rather for the fine taste and consummate elegance of their writings, than for that fiery passion, and disdainful vehemence, which seemed for a time to be so much more in favour with the public.' (*Edinburgh Review* (October 1829), l, 47.)

(c) Extract from letter, 15 August 1848, to R. M. Milnes: 'There are few names with which I shud so much wish to have my own associated as that of poor Keats.—I never regretted anything more than to have been *too late* with my testimony to his merits: and you may therefore judge how gratifying it now is to me, to find these names united in your pages, and that tardy vindication recognised, by so high an authority, as having contributed to the *rescue* of his fame—

There are touching indications of true genius, and of its irritable temperament, in the letters you have now published—and precious fragments in the literary remains yet there are traits of moodiness that are somewhat painful—and the unbroken gloom of the closing scene is oppressive— The tragedy is a great failure—and makes one wonder that the author shud ever have imagined that it was part of his mission to effect a complete revolution in the dramatic literature of his age!— There are brilliant images—and words of power—scattered thro it, no doubt—but the puerile extravagance and absolute bombast of most of the passionate speeches—(Ludolph's especially)—appear to me more humiliating, than even the palpable and almost inconceivable weakness and absurdity of the dramatic conception—

There are beautiful passages and lines of ineffable sweetness in the minor pieces—and strange outbreaks of redundant fancy, and felicitous expression in the "Cap and Bells"—tho the general extravagance of the fiction is more suited to an Italian than an English taste— The prologue to the "Eve of St Mark" seems to me the most faultless of these relics— and likely, if finished, to have grown into something even more exquisite than the "Eve of St Agnes"—' (*The Keats Circle*, ii. 248–9.)

31. Unsigned review, *Edinburgh Magazine, and Literary Miscellany (Scots Magazine)*

August 1820, vii, 107–10, and October 1820, vii, 313–16

Mr Keats is a poet of high and undoubted powers. He has evident peculiarities, which some of the London critics, who are averse to his style, have seized upon and produced as fair specimens of his writings; and this has operated, of course, to his disadvantage with the public, who have scarcely had an opportunity of judging what his powers really are. Some of his friends, indeed, have put in a word or two of praise, but it has been nearly unqualified; and this, when viewed at the same time with the criticism produced in an opposite spirit, has tended very much to confirm the objections made to his poetry.

Mr Keats has produced three volumes of verse: the first is very inferior in power to the two others, but containing very delightful passages, and some sonnets of great beauty. The second volume consists of the old mythological story of Endymion, and over which is scattered a multitude of thoughts and images, conceived and produced in the highest spirit of poetry. Perhaps the *Endymion*, though it contains more positive faults than the last book, (*Lamia,*) is more completely in Mr Keats's own style; and we think that it contains, at least, as many beauties. It is more careless, perhaps, but there is a greater freshness about it than about the last book, which (in *Hyperion* at least) reminds us occasionally of other writers, but which we must not be understood to speak of otherwise than in terms of the sincerest admiration.

The poem of *Endymion* contains about 4000 lines, and the story of the hero is not, perhaps, very interesting in itself; indeed, it is scarcely possible to endure, with a lively interest, a tale so slight and shadowy as that of the Loves of Diana and the Shepherd of Latmos. While this is stated, however, great praise must be ceded to the author, who, by force of poetry alone, can claim and compel the attention of the reader, for any length of time, to so bare (although graceful) a subject.

Mr Keats commences his poem with an evident delight. Shapes and stories of beauty, he tells us, are joys for ever. They

> Haunt us till they become a cheering light
> Unto our souls.

Therefore, he says, and how beautifully does he say it—

> Therefore, 'tis with full happiness that I
> Will trace the story of Endymion,
> *The very music of whose name has gone*
> *Into my being.* p. 5.

We do not profess to give a summary of the contents of this volume. Our intention is merely to give a few extracts, and to let our readers judge for themselves. It will save a wonderful deal of insisting on our parts; and after all, poetry is a matter of feeling rather than of argument.

The first book opens with a procession in honour of Pan, in which the Latmian Prince Endymion appears. Part of this, and the hymn subsequent to it, are told in words that would shed lustre upon any age of poetry. After damsels, who carry baskets of April flowers, come on

> A crowd of shepherds, with as sunburnt looks
> As may be read of in Arcadian books,
> Such as sate listening round Apollo's pipe,
> When the great deity, for earth too ripe,
> *Let his divinity, o'erflowing, die*
> *In music* thro' the vales of Thessaly. p. 10.

Of Endymion it is said,—

> A smile was on his countenance; he seemed,
> To common lookers on, *like one who dreamed*
> *Of idleness, in groves Elysian;* p. 11.

and yet he had a 'lurking trouble' in his nether lip, which, to a keener observer, would have betrayed his incipient passion. The procession stops at last, and ranges itself in a circle, in the midst of which a venerable priest rises, and invites the 'Men of Latmos' to address their vows to the great god Pan. They obey; and the following hymn is sung. It is worthy of any of the gods.

[Quotes *Endymion*, Book I, lines 232–319 (omitting lines 247–62, 'O thou, for whose soul-soothing quiet' to 'O forester divine'), italicizing lines 238–9, 285–7, 309–10, 317–19.]

We hope that our readers begin to feel that there are some (not ordinary) beauties in the volumes of Mr Keats. He is, perhaps, the poet, above all others, that we should refer to, in case we were challenged to produce *single* lines of extraordinary merit. He is very unequal in his earlier volumes certainly, (and what poet is not?) but there are beauties which might redeem ten times the amount of any defects that they may contain.

Speaking of Zephyr, before sunrise, he says, he

Fondles the flower amid the sobbing rain.

This seems to us very charming, and it is quite in the spirit of that mythology which has invested the west wind and the flowers with such delicate personifications. Again, speaking of Peona, the sister of Endymion, who sits by him while he sleeps, he says,

——————— *as a willow keeps*
A patient watch over the stream that creeps
Windingly by it, so the quiet maid
Held her in peace: so that a whispering blade
Of grass, p. 24,

or any other trivial thing, might be heard.

We have given the title of Mr Keats's second volume of poetry, and it was our intention to notice it, but this we find we must defer doing at present, and we have only space enough to give a few more single lines, or ideas from *Endymion*, but these our readers will, we doubt not, appreciate. It is sufficient to say, that the flowers which we select are by no means rare. Look at the effect of a single word,—

——————— Sometimes
A scent of violets, and blossoming limes,
Loiter'd around us. p. 34.

The following lines were quoted against the author, in a London Review. They are irregular, perhaps, but still very beautiful, we think.

Endymion! the cave is secreter
Than the isle of Delos. Echo hence shall stir
No sighs, but sigh warm kisses, or *light noise*
Of thy combing hand, the while it travelling cloys
And trembles thro' my labyrinthine hair. p. 48.

Endymion wanders for many days

Thro' wilderness and woods of mossed oaks,
Counting his woe-worn minutes, by the strokes
Of the lone wood-cutter. p. 55.

A butterfly is sent to guide him: he follows it

> Thro' the green evening quiet in the sun,
> O'er many a heath, and many a woodland dun,
> *Thro' buried paths, where sleepy twilight dreams*
> *The summer time away.* p. 56, 57.

If this be not poetry, we do not know what is; but we must, per force, leave *Endymion*, begging our readers to refer to it without more ado, both for their sakes and our own.

'Lamia' is the poem in which, in Mr Keats's second volume, the greatest fancy is displayed. It is more in the style of the *Endymion*, and we shall therefore forbear quoting from it, excepting only three lines, which, for the imagination contained in them, and the beauty with which they are executed, have seldom been equalled: the poet is speaking of a palace built by the magic power of Lamia.

> *A haunting music, sole perhaps and lone*
> *Supportress of the faery-roof, made moan*
> *Throughout, as fearful the whole charm might fade.* p. 34.

'Isabella, or the Pot of Basil,' is a story from Boccaccio, and is the same as was given to the public sometime ago by Mr Barry Cornwall, under the title of *A Sicilian Story*. We can safely recommend 'Isabella' as eminently beautiful. What can be sweeter than this? The days pass sadly,

> Until sweet *Isabella's untouched cheek*
> *Fell sick within the rose's just domain,*
> *Fell thin as a young mother's, who doth seek*
> *By every lull to cool her infant's pain.* p. 51.

The progress of the love of Lorenzo and Isabella is told in this delightful manner.

[Quotes 'Isabella', lines 9–26, 'With every morn' to 'break of June'.]

The brothers of Isabella discover that their sister loves Lorenzo: they entice him to a forest, and murder and bury him: his ghost appears to Isabella, who seeks the body, and cutting off the head, buries it beneath a pot of Basil, which she waters with her tears. There are some terms in this poem which Mr Keats inflicts upon the brothers of Isabella, which we think in bad taste. He calls them 'money-bags,' 'ledger-men,' &c. which injures, in some respect, this delightful story. Mr K. indeed, himself seems to have some doubts of this, and in the following beautiful stanzas intreats the forgiveness of his master. They are enough, to say the least, to wipe away the sin committed.

[Quotes 'Isabella', stanzas 19–20.]

What a beautiful picture might not Stothard make from the following exquisite stanza?

And as he to the court-yard pass'd along,
 Each third step did he pause, and listen'd oft
If he could hear his lady's matin-song,
 Or the light whisper of her footstep soft;
And as he thus over his passion hung,
 He heard a laugh full musical aloft;
When, looking up, he saw her features bright
Smile through an in-door lattice, all delight. p. 61.

Isabella, as we have said, buries the head of the lover in the pot of Basil, and weeps over it continually.

And she forgot the stars, the moon, and sun,
 And she forgot the blue above the trees,
And she forgot the dells where waters run,
 And she forgot the chilly autumn breeze;
She had no knowledge when the day was done,
 And the new morn she saw not: but in peace
Hung over her sweet Basil evermore,
And moisten'd it with tears unto the core. p. 75.

The brothers, discovering at last the cause of her grief, take the Basil-pot away: she having nothing then left to console her, pines and dies.

[Quotes 'Isabella', stanzas 62–3.]

The 'Eve of St Agnes' consists merely of one scene. Porphyro, a young cavalier, is in love with, and beloved by Madeline; he enters her chamber on the eve of St Agnes, when she is dreaming of him under the supposed influence of the Saint. He persuades her to fly with him. We have only room for the following stanzas, which will speak for themselves sufficiently.

[Quotes 'Eve of St Agnes', stanzas 24–8.]

Amongst the minor poems we prefer the 'Ode to the Nightingale. Indeed, we are inclined to prefer it beyond every other poem in the book; but let the reader judge. The third and seventh stanzas have a charm for us which we should find it difficult to explain. We have read this ode over and over again, and every time with increased delight.

[Quotes 'Ode to a Nightingale', omitting the first and last stanzas.]

As our object is rather to let Mr Keats's verses be seen in justification of themselves, than to insist upon their positive beauty, we shall quote part of another of the minor poems. It is entitled 'Robin Hood', whose days, the poet says, 'are gone away.'

[Quotes 'Robin Hood', lines 33 to the end, 'Gone, the merry morris din' to 'burden try'.]

The ode to 'Fancy,' and the ode to 'Autumn,' also have great merit. *Hyperion*, we confess, we do not like quite so well, on the whole, as some others; yet there is an air of grandeur about it, and it opens in a striking manner.

> Deep in the shady sadness of a vale
> Far sunken from the healthy breath of morn,
> Far from the fiery noon, and eve's one star,
> Sat grey-hair'd Saturn, quiet as a stone,
> Still as the silence round about his lair;
> Forest on forest hung about his head
> Like cloud on cloud. p. 145.

One expression here reminds us of a line in the old poem called the *Mirror for Magistrates*,

> By him lay heavie sleep, cosen of death,
> Flat on the ground, and *still as any stone*;

and also of another line in Chaucer.

The picture of Thea, in p. 147, is very beautiful, and the effect of a word (it is where Saturn is deploring the loss of his kingdom) is given with exceeding power and simplicity. Saturn speaks,

> Where is another chaos? Where? *That word*
> *Found way unto Olympus.*

The description, too, of Hyperion, '*a vast shade in midst of his own brightness*,' is very fine; though the preceding part of it,

> Golden his hair of short Numidian curl,
> Regal his shape majestic,

is not like Mr Keats, but like Milton.

Upon the whole, we have felt great pleasure from the perusal of Mr Keats's volumes, and we can safely commend them to our readers, as—not faultless books indeed,—but as containing, perhaps, as much absolute poetry as the works of almost any contemporary writer.

32. Unsigned review, *New Monthly Magazine*

1 September 1820, xiv, 245–8

These poems are very far superior to any which their author has previously committed to the press. They have nothing showy, or extravagant, or eccentric about them; but are pieces of calm beauty, or of lone and self-supported grandeur. There is a fine freeness of touch about them, like that which is manifest in the old marbles, as though the poet played at will his fancies virginal, and produced his most perfect works without toil. We have perused them with the heartiest pleasure—for we feared that their youthful author was suffering his genius to be enthralled in the meshes of sickly affectation—and we rejoice to find these his latest works as free from all offensive peculiarities—as pure, as genuine, and as lofty, as the severest critic could desire.

'Lamia', the first of these poems, is founded on the following passage in Burton's *Anatomy of Melancholy*, which is given as a note at its close:

[Quoted in No. 27, pp. 165–6.]

The poem commences with the descent of Mercury to Crete, in search of a nymph of whom he is enamoured. We give the opening passage, as it will enable the reader to feel the airy spirit with which the young poet sets forth on his career.

[Quotes 'Lamia', Part I, lines 1–26.]

After seeking the nymph with vain search through the vales and woods, as he rests upon the ground pensively, he hears a mournful voice, 'such as once heard in gentle heart destroys all pain but pity,' and perceives in a dusky brake a magnificent serpent, with the lips of a woman, who addresses him in human words, and promises to place the nymph before him, if he will set her spirit free from her serpent-form. He consents—his utmost wishes are granted—and the brilliant snake, after a convulsive agony, vanishes, and Lamia's soft voice is heard luting in the air. Having enjoyed power during her degradation to send her spirit into distant places, she had seen and loved Lycius, a youth of Corinth, whom she now hastens to meet in her new, angelic beauty. He sees and loves her; and is led by her to a beautiful palace in the midst of Corinth, which none ever remembered to have seen before, where they live for some time in an unbroken dream of love. But Lycius, at last, becomes restless in his happiness, and longs to shew his beautiful mistress to the world. He resolves to solemnize publicly his marriage festival, against which she tremblingly remonstrates in vain. Finding she cannot win him from his purpose,

> She sets herself high-thoughted how to dress
> Her misery in fit magnificence:

And the following is the beautiful result of her art:

[Quotes 'Lamia', Part II, lines 119–45, 'About the halls' to 'spoil her solitude'.]

The fatal day arrives—the guests assemble—Apollonius, the tutor of Lycius, comes an unbidden guest—but all, for a while, is luxury and delighted wonder.—

[Quotes 'Lamia', Part II, lines 199–220, 'Soft went the music' to 'silk-pillow'd at his ease'.]

The awful catastrophe is, however, at hand. In the midst of the festivities Apollonius fixes his eye upon the cold, pallid, beseeching bride—she vanishes with a frightful scream, and Lycius is found, on his high couch, lifeless! There is, in this poem, a mingling of Greek majesty with fairy luxuriance, which we have not elsewhere seen. The fair shapes stand clear in their antique beauty, encircled with the profuse magnificence of romance, and in the thick atmosphere of its golden lustre!

'Isabella' is the old and sweet tale of the Pot of Basil, from Boccaccio, which forms the groundwork of Barry Cornwall's delicious 'Sicilian Story.' It is here so differently told, that we need not undertake the invidious task of deciding which is the sweetest. The poem of Mr Keats has not the luxury of description, nor the rich love-scenes, of Mr Cornwall; but he tells the tale with a naked and affecting simplicity which goes irresistibly to the heart. The following description of Isabella's visit with her old nurse to her lover's grave, and their digging for the head, is as wildly intense as any thing which we can remember.

[Quotes 'Isabella', stanzas 44–8, 'See, as they creep' to 'did not stamp and rave'.]

'The Eve of St Agnes' is a piece of consecrated fancy, which shews how a young lover, in the purity of heart, went to see his gentle mistress, the daughter of a baron, as she laid herself in her couch to dream in that holy season—and how she awoke and these lovers fled into the storm—while the father and his guests were oppressed with strange night-mare, and the old nurse died smitten with the palsy. A soft religious light is shed over the whole story. The following is part of the exquisite scene in the chamber:

[Quotes 'The Eve of St Agnes', stanzas 24–8, 'A casement high and triple-arch'd' to 'how fast she slept'.]

Hyperion, a fragment, is in a very different style. It shews us old Saturn after the loss of his empire, and the Titans in their horrid cave, meditating revenge on the usurper, and young Apollo breathing in the dawn of his joyous existence. We do not think any thing exceeds in silent grandeur the opening of the poem, which exhibits Saturn in his solitude:

[Quotes *Hyperion*, Book I, lines 1–21.]

The picture of the vast abode of Cybele and the Titans—and of its gigantic inhabitants, is in the sublimest style of Æschylus. Lest this praise should be thought extravagant we will make room for the whole.

[Quotes *Hyperion*, Book II, lines 5–81, 'It was a den' to 'whose names may not be told'.]

We now take leave of Mr Keats with wonder at the gigantic stride which he has taken, and with the good hope that, if he proceeds in the high and pure style which he has now chosen, he will attain an exalted and a lasting station among English poets.

33. Unsigned review, *London Magazine* (Baldwin's)

September 1820, ii, 315–21

John Scott, who had already protested at Keats's handling by the *Quarterly*, was now campaigning against the more unprincipled methods of *Blackwood's*. This article exemplifies the critical candour and fairmindedness he demands from others.

We opened this volume with very considerable anxiety:—an anxiety partly occasioned by the unqualified praises of which the author has been the object,—but more owing to the abuse by which he has been assailed. Perhaps from the whole history of criticism, real and pretended, nothing more truly unprincipled than that abuse can be quoted; nothing more heartless, more vindictive,—more nefarious in design, more pitiful and paltry in spirit. We consider it one of the worst signs of these, the worst times which England, we are afraid, has ever seen, that the miserable selfishness of political party has erected itself into a literary authority, and established, by means of popular channels, the most direct and easy access to the public ear on literary questions. The provocation, we allow, is reciprocal: the vanity of the *Examiner* manifests just as great a deficiency in real candour as is apparent in the bitter spite of the *Quarterly*, or the merry ruffianism of *Blackwood*. But the distinct consciousness of depravity in the two latter, which must accompany them in many of their lucubrations, gives a blacker feature to their conduct. It would be well worthy, we think, of the great talents and lofty principles of the new Edinburgh Professor of Moral Philosophy,[1] to discuss ethically from his comfortable chair,—where he sits, the honour of Scotland, and fit substitute for Dugald Stewart,—the specific difference in moral guilt and personal degradation, which distinguishes

[1] When in June 1820 the distinguished philosopher Dugald Stewart had resigned his Professorship of Moral Philosophy in the University of Edinburgh, John Wilson, one of the editors of *Blackwood's*, had secured the vacant Chair by political influence. He had no qualifications.

the misrepresentations of a blind overweening vanity from those of a sordid and cunning worldly greediness. The young Scotchmen would listen attentively to the arguments of one so well-qualified to handle this point; and the lecture might have blessed effects on their future lives and fortunes.—But to the subject before us, from whence we are wandering.

Mr Keats, though not a political writer, plunged at once, with what we shall take the liberty of calling a boyish petulance, and with an air of rather insulting bravado, into some very delicate subjects;—subjects on which, we have no hesitation to say, those very qualities of his mind which confer on his poetry its most characteristic beauties, incapacitate him fairly to pronounce. There have been, and it is possible there may be even now, great comprehensive intellects, which, to wealthy and voluptuous imaginations, add a far-sightedness sufficient to discern, and a magnanimity inducing them to acknowledge, the deep, internal, and inextricable connection between the pains and penalties of human nature, and its hopes and enjoyments: whose spirits dwell and play in 'the plighted clouds,'—but who understand enough of the philosophy of earthly existence to know, that, as man must cultivate the ground by the sweat of his brow, so he must cultivate his faculties by self-denials and struggles of soul:—who perceive lurking in the common restraints of society, eternal principles of human nature—mysterious instincts, which, through the mortification of desire, the humiliation of feeling, and often in the absence of an active sense of justice or clear view of utility, conduct to the average *maximum*, such as it is, of human good and moral beauty. Such intellects are scornful of none of our necessities while they provide for our delights: in stimulating the strength of human nature, they do not mislead or neglect its weaknesses: they are impartial in their judgments, because their views are commanding, and their motives issue from lofty dispositions. They will not palter, or play false with what they see daily before them, because the conclusions it suggests may chance to reproach some of their own actions. They will have learnt, by degrees, to correct the unfavourable decisions which we are all naturally inclined to found on dissimilarity of habits, and opposition of tastes; and they will at length have been induced to convert these into reasons for self-suspicion, rather than grounds for accusing others. Following human life into its various walks; contemplating it fairly and kindly in all its aspects, they will have been compelled to conclude, that it is not self-abandonment to the favourite themes of touching description, and to those pursuits which seem to lead most directly to the indulgence and excitement of a reflective sensibility, that exclusively proves the fine construction and delicate movements of the mind. In the labyrinth of the world they will have found that appearances are not guides;—that a face cast up towards the moon does not more certainly infer an amiable or susceptible disposition, than a contracted brow cast down over a ledger of bad debts. Selfishness, it will have struck them, is often most active in the whirlwind of passion; and it will have occurred to them that, in the estimation of intelligences altogether superior to this worldly turmoil, fainting away over a fair bosom does not, unless accompanied by other symptoms, prove much more in favour of the refinement of the transported person than clasping a money-bag, or ogling a haunch of venison. A man may smell to a rose, or walk out to admire an effect of sun-set, and yet not have half that complication of the warmer affections stirring within him, which shall move a tradesman of the Strand, seated with his wife, children, and shopman, in his back parlour;—and the said tradesman may take out a writ against a dilatory customer, in no worse spirit than that in which one author pursues another for literary defalcation. It is well to let the imagination contemplate splendours hanging over past times; the soul must stretch itself somehow out of its cramps: but this may be done without committing crying, positive injustice towards the present. It may be allowable in poetry to treat ancient thieves with the respect due to true men; but the poet has no business, more than the police officer, to treat true men, his neighbours, as thieves. If Maid Marian were to come back, and complain in our hearing, as she does in Mr Keats's poetry—

> ———————— Strange! that honey
> Can't be got without hard money—

we would ask her what there is strange in this? and whether it is not quite as well to get things by hard money as by hard blows? and whether more injustice be included in the inequality of purses—a consequence of society—than in that inequality of arms, which is an effect of nature? Of course, we would not have thus selected, for the purpose of argument, a passage bearing an air of pleasantry, if we did not think that Mr Keats's sensibility is diseased in this respect—that his spirit is impregnated with a flippant impatience, (irritated and justified by a false philosophy) of the great phenomena of society, and the varieties of human nature, which hurts his poetry quite as much as it corrupts his sentiments—and which is altogether unworthy of the grandeur of his powers. There are some stanzas introduced into his delicious tale of 'Isabel—poor simple Isabel,' in this volume, which, we think, dreadfully mar the musical tenderness of its general strain. They are no better than extravagant school-boy vituperation of trade and traders; just as if lovers did not trade,—and that, often in stolen goods—or had in general any higher object than a barter of enjoyment! These stanzas in Mr Keats's poem, when contrasted with the larger philosophy of Boccacio, and his more genial spirit, as exemplified with reference to the very circumstances in question, are additionally offensive. Instead of tirading against the brothers as 'money-bags,' 'Baalites of pelf,' 'ledger-men,'—and asking, 'why, in the name of glory, were they proud?' Boccacio describes the honour of the family as actually injured by Lorenzo, whom they employed—he shows us the elder brother, on discovering his sister's dishonour, afflicted with grief and perplexity, and passing a sleepless night on his bed—he even compliments the discretion of this member of the family—and it is thus naturally, and faithfully, and feelingly introduced, that he leads up the dreadful catastrophe to its consummation in Italian revenge, and the broken-heartedness of widowed love. Does the pathos of the tale suffer by thus looking fairly into the face of human nature? Do we pity the lovers less; do we sympathize less with Isabel's bitter tears, because we have both sides of the case thus placed before us? No—our sympathies, being more fairly excited, are more keenly so: the story is in fine keeping, as a painter would say: the effect of truth overpowers us: we weep the more because we feel that human frailty provides for human suffering, and that the best impulses of the heart are not removed from the liability of producing the extremities of agony and of crime. Mr Keats, we are sure, has a sensibility sufficiently delicate to feel this beauty in Boccacio: why then has he substituted for it, in his own composition, a boisterous rhapsody, which interrupts the harmony of the sorrowful tale,—repels sympathy by the introduction of caricature,—and suggests all sorts of dissenting, and altercating prejudices and opinions? His device is a clumsy one: Boccacio's delicate and true. That most beautiful Paper, (by a correspondent of course) in our last number, on the 'ledger-men,' of the South Sea House,[1] is an elegant reproof of such short-sighted views of character; such idle hostilities against the realities of life. How free from intolerance of every sort must the spirit be, that conceived that paper,—or took off so fair and clear an impression from facts! It would not be prone to find suggestion of invective in the sound of

[1] The first of Charles Lamb's 'Essays of Elia'.

Sabbath bells, as Mr Keats has done in a former work. The author of *Endymion* and *Hyperion* must delight in that Paper;—and, to give another example of what we mean, he must surely feel the gentle poetical beauty which is infused into the star-light tale of *Rosamund Grey*, through its vein of 'natural piety.' What would that tale be without the Grandmother's Bible? How eclipsed would be the gleaming light of such a character as Rosamund's, in a re-modelled state of society, where it should be the fashion for wives to be considered as dainties at a pic-nic party, each man bringing his own with him—but ready to give and take with those about him! Creeds here are out of the question altogether;—we only speak with reference to the wants and instincts of the human soul. We mention these things, not because we desire to see Mr Keats playing the hypocrite, or enlisted as a florid declaimer on the profitable side of things; but because, with our admiration of his powers, we are loath to see him irrecoverably committed to a flippant and false system of reasoning on human nature;—because to his picturesque imagination, we wish that he would add a more pliable, and, at the same time, a more magnanimous sensibility. Nor need his philosophy be a whit more condescending to what is grovelling and base. Let him write, as much as he pleases, in the bold indignant style of Wordsworth's glorious Sonnet!

The world is too much with us!

Here the poet speaks—not the malcontent;—it is not mortification, but inspiration he feels;—it is not classes of men, but crawling minds he anathematizes. We must positively give this magnificent Sonnet entire, now we have accidentally been brought to it by the current of our writing. It cannot be deemed out of place any where—for it is a high animation to noble thoughts.

[Quotes Wordsworth's sonnet 'The world is too much with us'.]

From what we have said, in the way of objection to the fashion of Mr Keats's thinking, on certain important questions, it will easily be seen that he has very much, and very incautiously exposed himself to attack;—and his chivalry, as it will be guessed, has done him but little service in his contest with the windmills in Albemarle-street. These things, that go furiously with the breeze of the time, have beaten his lance out of its rest, battered his helmet, and overturned in the dirt himself and his steed. It is impossible,—however we may regret the extravagant course his Knight-errantry has taken,—not to feel our wishes and sympathies on the side of the knight of the Sorrowful countenance in this encounter. His spirit is a gallant one; his brain is full of high feats; his heart beats in real devotion to a Dulcinea whom he has clad with fine attributes in his imagination, though, certainly, we believe her to be much less a lady than he imagines her. His delusion, however, is the offspring of a romantic temperament; whereas his maulers are but things of brute matter, machines for grinding grist;—'plates hung on pins to turn with the wind,'—acquiring a murderous power from their specific levity.

The injustice which has been done to our author's works, in estimating their poetical merit, rendered us doubly anxious, on opening his last volume, to find it likely to seize fast hold of general sympathy, and thus turn an overwhelming power against the paltry traducers of a talent, more eminently promising in many respects, than any that the present age has been called upon to encourage. We have not found it to be quite all that we wished in this respect—and it would have been very extraordinary if we had, for our wishes went far beyond reasonable expectations. But we have found it of a nature to present to common understandings the poetical power with which the author's mind is gifted, in a more tangible and intelligible shape than that in which it has appeared in any of his former compositions. It is, therefore, calculated to throw shame on the lying, vulgar spirit, in which this young worshipper in the temple of the Muses has been cried-down; whatever questions it may still leave to be settled as to the kind and degree of his poetical merits. Take for instance, as a proof of the justice of our praise, the following passage from an Ode to the Nightingale:—it is distinct, noble, pathetic, and true: the thoughts have all chords of direct communication with naturally-constituted hearts: the echoes of the strain linger about the depths of human bosoms.

[Quotes 'Ode to a Nightingale', last two stanzas, italicizing lines 65–7.]

Let us take also a passage of another sort altogether—the description of a young beauty preparing for her nightly rest, overlooked by a concealed lover, in which we know not whether most to admire the magical delicacy of the hazardous picture, or its consummate, irresistible attraction. 'How sweet the moonlight sleeps upon this bank,' says Shakspeare; and sweetly indeed does it fall on the half undressed form of Madeline:—it has an exquisite moral influence, corresponding with the picturesque effect.

[Quotes 'Eve of St Agnes', stanzas 23, 25–8, italicizing lines 201–2, 222–5, 229–31.]

One more extract,—again varying entirely the style of the composition. It shall be taken from a piece called *Hyperion*; one of the most extraordinary creations of any modern imagination. Its 'woods are ruthless, dreadful, deaf, and dull:' the soul of dim antiquity hovers, like a mountain-cloud, over its vast and gloomy grandeur: it carries us back in spirit beyond the classical age; earlier than 'the gods of the Greeks;' when the powers of creation were to be met with visible about the young earth, shouldering the mountains, and with their huge forms filling the vallies. The sorrows of this piece are 'huge;' its utterance 'large;' its tears 'big.'—Alas, centuries have brought littleness since then,—otherwise a crawling, reptile of office, with just strength enough to leave its slimy traces on the pages of a fashionable Review, could never have done a real mischief to the poet of the Titans! It is but a fragment we have of *Hyperion*: an advertisement tells us that 'the poem was intended to have been of equal length with *Endymion*, *but the reception given to that work discouraged the author from proceeding*.' Let Mr Croker read the following sublime and gorgeous personification of Asia, and be proud of the information thus given him—and of that superior encouragement to which it is owing that we have his *Talavera* in a complete state!

————— Nearest him
Asia, born of most enormous Caf,
Who cost her mother Tellus keener pangs,
Though feminine, than any of her sons:
More thought than woe was in her dusky face,
For she was prophesying of her glory;
And in her wide imagination stood
Palm-shaded temples, and high rival fanes,
By Oxus or in Ganges' sacred isles.
Even as Hope upon her anchor leans,
So lent she, not so fair, upon a tusk
Shed from the broadest of her elephants.

This is not the extract, however, which we were about to make: it was the opening of the poem we thought of. The dethronement of Saturn by Jupiter, and the later gods taking the places of the early powers of heaven and earth, form its subject. We seem entering the awful demesne of primeval solitude as the poet commences:

[Quotes *Hyperion*, Book I, lines 1–71, italicizing lines 1–7, 10, 13–17, 24, 31–3, 37–41.]

Will not our readers feel it as a disgrace attaching to the character of the period, that a dastardly attempt should have been made to assassinate a poet of power equal to these passages: that one should come like a thief to steal his 'precious diadem;'—a murder and a robbery 'most foul and horrible?' Cold-blooded conscious dishonesty, we have no hesitation to say, must have directed the pen of the critic of *Endymion* in the *Quarterly Review*: making every allowance for the callousness of a worldly spirit, it is impossible to conceive a total insensibility to the vast beauties scattered profusely over that disordered, ill-digested work. The author provokes opposition, as we have already fully said: not unfrequently he even suggests angry censure. We cannot help applying the word *insolent*, in a literary sense, to some instances of his neglectfulness, to the random swagger of occasional expressions, to the bravado style of many of his sentiments. But, coupling these great faults with his still greater poetical merits, what a fine, what an interesting subject did he offer for perspicacious, honourable criticism! But he was beset by a very dog-kennel; and he must be more than human if he has not had his erroneous tendencies hardened in him in consequence.

What strike us as the principal faults of his poetry, impeding his popularity, we would venture thus to specify.

1. His frequent obscurity and confusion of language. As an instance of the latter, we may mention, that he attaches the epithet of '*leaden-eyed*,' to despair, considered as a quality or sentiment. Were it a personification of despair, the compound would be as finely applied, as, under the actual circumstances, it is erroneously so. There are many, many passages too, in his last volume, as well as in his earlier ones, from which we are not able, after taking some pains to understand them, to derive any distinct notion or meaning whatever.

2. He is too fond of running out glimmerings of thoughts, and indicating distant shadowy fancies: he shows, also, a fondness for dwelling on features which are not naturally the most important or prominent. His imagination coquets with, and mocks the reader in this respect; and plain earnest minds turn away from such tricks with disgust. The greatest poets have always chiefly availed themselves of the plainest and most palpable materials.

3. He affects, in bad taste, a quaint strangeness of phrase; as some folks affect an odd manner of arranging their neckcloths, &c. This

'shows a most pitiful ambition.' We wish Mr Keats would not talk of *cutting mercy with a sharp knife to the bone*; we cannot contemplate the *skeleton* of mercy. Nor can we familiarize ourselves pleasantly with the *dainties made to still an infant's cries*:—the latter is indeed a very round about way of expression,—and not very complimentary either, we think. Young ladies, who know, of course, little or nothing of the economy of the nursery, will be apt, we imagine, to pout at this periphrasis, which puts their charms on a level with baby-corals!

But we are by this time tired of criticism; as we hope our readers are:—let us then all turn together to the book itself. We have said here what we have deemed it our duty to say: we shall there find what it will be our delight to enjoy.

34. Unsigned notice, *Monthly Magazine*

September 1820, l, 166

We have read with pleasure a volume of Poems, lately published by Mr Keats, the author of *Endymion*. There is a boldness of fancy and a classical expression of language in the poetry of this gentleman, which, we think, entitle him to stand equally high in the estimation of public opinion, as the author of *Rimini*, or as he of the *Dramatic Scenes*. Our pleasure, however, was not unmingled with sentiments of extreme disapprobation. The faults characteristic of his school, are still held up to view with as much affectation, by Mr K., as if he were fearful of not coming in for his due share of singularity, obscurity, and conceit. But though of the same genus, his poetic labours are specifically different from those of his fellow labourers in the same vineyard. There is more reach of poetic capacity, more depth and intenseness of thought and feeling, with more classical power of expression, than what we discover in the writings of his master, or of his fellow pupil Mr Cornwall. Mr C. is compounded of imitation—of Shakespeare and of Mr Leigh Hunt. Mr H. is a familiar copier of Dryden, with the manner, only a more sparkling one, but without the pathos, of Crabbe. Mr K., on the contrary, is always himself, and as long as fair originality shall be thought superior to good imitation, he will always be preferred. The Poems consist of various Tales, 'Lamia', 'Isabella', 'The Eve of St Agnes', of which we think the first is the best. *Hyperion*, however, is the most powerful.

35. Unsigned review, *British Critic*

September 1820, n.s. xiv, 257–64

If there be one person in the present day, for whom we feel an especial contempt, it is Mr Examiner Hunt; and we confess that it is not easy for us to bring our minds to entertain respect for any one whose taste, whether in morals, in poetry, or politics, is so exceedingly corrupt as that person's must be supposed to be, who is willing to take such a man for his model. It was for this reason that Mr Keats fell under our lash, so severely, upon the occasion of his poem of *Endymion*. Upon recurring to the poem, we are not unwilling to admit, that it possesses more merit, than upon a first perusal of it we were able to perceive, or rather than we were in a frame of mind to appreciate. We can hardly doubt as to that poem having been corrected by our modern Malvolio, and projected by his advice and under his superintendence;—so full was it, of all the peculiarities of that ingenious gentleman's ideas. The effect of this upon Mr Keats's poetry, was like an infusion of ipecacuanha powder in a dish of marmalade. It created such a sickness and nausea, that the mind felt little inclination to analyse the mixture produced, and to consider, whether after all, the dose might not have been mixed with some ingredients that were in themselves agreeable. In the poems before us, the same obstacle to a dispassionate judgment, is still to be encountered—not perhaps to so great a degree, as upon the former occasion, but still in such a degree, as to reflect great praise, we think, upon our impartiality for the commendation which we feel willing to bestow.

We cannot approve of the morality of the principal poems in this little collection. One of them is from Boccacio, and the others upon exactly the same sort of subjects as the Florentine too generally chose. However, there is nothing in the details of either poem, that would appear calculated to wound delicacy, and this, in cases whether the temptation to the contrary may be supposed to have existed, is certainly deserving of praise.

The first tale is in two parts, and called 'Lamia'. The subject of it is taken from the following passage in Burton's *Anatomy of Melancholy*; and we extract it as conveying a very agreeable fiction, and which loses none of its merit in the hands of Mr Keats.

[Quoted in No. 27, pp. 165–6.]

We shall now present our readers with some specimens of the manner in which our poet has dressed up the materials here afforded him; and we think those which we shall give, will prove that Mr Keats is really a person of no ordinary genius; and that if he will only have the good sense to take advice, making Spenser or Milton his model of poetical diction, instead of Mr Leigh Hunt, he need not despair of attaining to a very high and enviable place in the public esteem.—The poem opens with a description of Hermes seeking a nymph, of whom he was enamoured. In the course of his pursuit through the woods, he is addressed by a voice which issues from a creature in the form of a serpent, who tells him that she is a woman in love with a youth of Corinth, and that if he will restore her, as he is able to do, to her natural shape, she will give him accounts of the nymph whom he seeks. This being premised, the reader will be able to enter into the beauty of the following specimen of the manner in which this part of the poem is managed, and from thence to form some judgment of the whole.

[Quotes 'Lamia', Part I, lines 1–37, 'Upon a time' to 'lone voice spake'.]

After some explanation, the Lamia thus addresses Hermes on the object of his chase.

[Quotes 'Lamia', Part I, lines 93–111, 'Too frail of heart!' to 'grant my boon!']

The god having agreed to the terms upon which his assistance was asked, immediately destroys the spell, by which the Lamia described herself as being bound.

[Quotes 'Lamia', Part I, lines 134–45, 'So done,' to 'as mortal lovers do.']

Hermes and the Lamia then depart different ways, and soon the [latter] meets the Corinthian youth, of whom she was enamoured. Having changed a few looks and words, the youth, of course, becomes entranced with admiration, and addresses the Lamia.

[Quotes 'Lamia', Part I, lines 261–87, 'Stay! though a Naiad' to 'Tiptoe with white arms spread.']

The Lamia then accompanies the youth to Corinth; and the remainder of the story displays the same richness of fancy, only as the scene becomes less peculiarly poetical, the interest, in consequence, is not sustained. The next tale is from Boccacio, and possesses less merit; nor is there much to admire in the 'Eve of St Agnes;' but the last poem, which is unfinished, and is called *Hyperion*, contains some very beautiful poetry, although the greater part of it appears not to have been executed with much success; nor do we think that Mr Keats has evinced any want of taste in leaving it incomplete; for it is plainly projected upon principles that would infallibly lead to failure, even supposing the subject were not, which we think it is, somewhat above the pitch of Mr Keats' peculiar genius, which lies altogether in the region of fancy and description. The fable of the poem seems to be, the wars of the Titans: Saturn is described sitting alone, in despair for the loss of his celestial dominions, and afterwards Thea and Cœlus, and others belonging to the Saturnian dynasty in heaven, are severally introduced. The opening of this poem struck us as very beautiful indeed.

[Quotes *Hyperion*, Book I, lines 1–51, 'Deep in the shady sadness' to 'large utterance of the early Gods!']

We pass over the speech which ensues; but the following lines, which come immediately after it, are, we think, strikingly fine.

[Quotes *Hyperion*, Book I, lines 72–92, 'As when, upon a tranced summer night,' to 'and then spake'.]

We think that the specimens which we have now given of Mr Keats' talents, are quite decisive as to his poetical powers. That a man who can write so well, should produce such absurd lines, and fall into such ridiculous modes of expression, as are to be met with in almost every page, is really lamentable. An example or two will be sufficient to convince our readers of the forbearance which we have exerted, in giving these poems the praise which is their due; for if we were to strike a balance between their beauties and absurdities, many would probably be disposed to doubt as to which side the scale inclined.

Thus we are told that

> ———————— charmed God
> Began an *oath*, and through the serpent's ears it ran
> *Warm, tremulous, devout, psalterian*. P. 10.

In another place the Lamia, as we are told,

> Writh'd about, convuls'd with *scarlet* pain:
> A deep *volcanian* yellow took the place
> Of all her *milder-mooned* body's grace. P. 12.

We hear also of 'a clear pool, wherein she *passioned*, to see herself escaped.' P. 14. And likewise of this same person's pacing about 'in a pale contented sort of discontent.' P. 35. In another poem,[1] we have the following exquisite nonsense to describe a kiss:

> So said, his erewhile timid lips grew bold,
> And *poesied* with her's in *dewy rhyme*. P. 53.

Thus likewise we hear of *pleasuring* a thing, and a *mirroring* a thing; of doing a thing *fearingly* and *fairily*; of *leafits*; of walking '*silken* hush'd and *chaste*;' and innumerable other such follies, which are really too contemptible to criticise. If all this nonsense is mere youthful affectation, perhaps as Mr Keats gets more sense, he will learn to see it in its true light; such innovations in language are despicable in themselves, and disgusting to the imagination of every man of virtue and taste, from having been originally *conceited*, as Mr Keats would say, in the brain of one of the most profligate and wretched scribblers that we can remember to have ever either heard or read of.

[1] *Isabella*, lines 69–70.

36. A mischief at the core

1820

Unsigned review, *Eclectic Review* (September 1820), n.s. xiv, 158–71 (second pagination).

Josiah Conder, who reviewed Keats's *Poems* in 1817 (No. 8), now concedes a stylistic advance in his latest volume, but deplores his apparent lack of moral purpose and his celebration of the 'happy pieties' of Paganism, identifying his fatal weakness as a want of 'the regulating principle of religion'. This attitude to Keats remained a very important one throughout the Victorian period (see Introduction, pp. 9, 33-66).

It is just three years since we were called upon to review Mr Keats's first production. We then gave it as our opinion, that he was not incapable of writing good poetry, that he possessed both the requisite fancy and skill; but we regretted that a young man of his vivid imagination and promising talents should have been flattered into the resolution to publish verses of which he would probably be glad a few years after to escape from the remembrance. It is our practice, when a young writer appears for the first time as a candidate for public favour, to look to the indications of ability which are to be detected in his performance, rather than to its intrinsic merits. There is a wasteful efflorescence that must be thrown off before the intellect attains its maturity. The mind is then at a critical period: there is equal danger of its lavishing all its strength in the abortive promise of excellence, and of its being blighted by unjust discouragement. Such appeared to us to be then the situation of Mr Keats; and in the spirit of candour and of kindness, we made those remarks on his volume which were designed at once to guide and to excite his future exertions, but for which he manfully disdained to be the wiser. His next production had the good fortune to fall into the hands of critics who rarely deal in either half-praise or half-censure, and whose severity of censure can at least confer notoriety upon the offender. According to his own account, the Author of *Endymion* must, while smarting under their unsparing lash, have claimed pity almost equally on account of his mortified feelings and his infidel creed; for, in the preface to that 'feverish attempt,' he avows his conviction 'that there is not a fiercer hell than the failure in a great object.' How complete was his failure in that matchless tissue of sparkling and delicious nonsense, his Publishers frankly confess in an Advertisement prefixed to the present volume, wherein they take upon themselves the responsibility of printing an unfinished poem in the same strain, from proceeding with which the Author was discouraged by the reception given to that poem. And yet, under the sanction, we presume, of the same advisers, Mr Keats has ventured to proclaim himself in his title-page as the unfortunate 'Author of *Endymion*.' Are we to gather from this, that he is vain and foolish enough to wish that production not to be forgotten?

The present volume, however, we have been assured, contains something much better. Startled as we were at the appearance of the ghost of *Endymion* in the title, we endeavoured, on renewing our acquaintance with its Author, to banish from our recollection the unpropitious circumstances under which we had last met, and, as it is now too late to expect that he will exhibit any material change as the result of further intellectual growth, to take a fresh and final estimate of his talents and pretensions as they may be judged of from the volume before us. The evidence on which our opinion is formed, shall now be laid before our readers. One naturally turns first to the shorter pieces, in order to taste the flavour of the poetry. The following ode to Autumn is no unfavourable specimen.

[Quotes 'To Autumn' in full.]

Fancy has again and again been hymned in lays Pindaric or Anacreontic, but not often in more pleasing and spirited numbers than the following.

[Quotes 'Fancy', lines 1–66.]

The lines addressed to a friend, on Robin Hood, are in the same light and sportive style.

[Quotes 'Robin Hood' in full.]

Of the longer pieces, 'Lamia' is decidedly the best. The story on which it is built, is taken from the rich repository of old Burton, who cites from Philostratus the memorable account of one Menippus Lycius.

[Quoted in No. 27, pp. 165–6.]

This sort of semi-allegorical legend is of the same family of fictions as the Vampire. The plain matter of fact which it envelops, would seem to be, the case of a young man of good talents and respectable connexions, that falls in love with a rich courtezan who has the address to persuade him to marry her. The spell of her charms and her ill-gotten wealth naturally enough dissolve together, and her victim at last discovers her to be—*a lamia.* The story thus interpreted is not without a moral; though Mr Keats does not make use of it. His account of the transaction is as follows. 'Upon a time,' or, as Mother Bunch has it with stricter precision, once upon a time,

> before the faery broods
> Drove Nymph and Satyr from the prosperous woods,
> The *ever-smitten* Hermes

left Olympus for a forest in the isle of Crete, in search of an invisible mistress who lived somewhere or other in that neighbourhood; where, his god-ship could not tell. Here his attention is arrested by a mournful voice that issues from 'a palpitating snake,'

[Quotes 'Lamia', Part I, lines 47–65, 'a gordian shape' to 'for Love's sake'.]

This feminine incarnation of the Evil Principle is fortunately acquainted with what Hermes wants to know, and a bargain is soon struck between them, by which, as a reward for her obligingly acting as a procuress, she is restored, by virtue of 'the Caducean charm,' to the shape of woman, according to the tenour of her demand:

> 'I love a youth of Corinth—O the bliss!
> Give me my woman's form, and place me where he is.'

All this, not being in Burton, we take it for granted is out of Mr Keats's own head, as the children say; except so far as Mr Coleridge may have helped him to the portrait of the serpent-elf, in his *Christabel.* The metamorphose is thus described.

[Quotes 'Lamia', Part I, lines 146–69, 'Left to herself' to '"Lycius! gentle Lycius!"']

Away she flies, to waylay the said Lycius, who, as a matter of course, is deeply smitten with her, mistakes her for a naiad, or a dryad, or a pleïad, he cannot tell which, till she throws off the assumed goddess, and 'wins his heart more pleasantly by playing woman's part:' in short, he goes home with her. In the enchanted palace to which she conducts him, he lies, like most heroes in similar toils, all dissolved in luxury, till he begins to be tired of doing nothing but being happy, and is one day roused by 'a thrill of trumpets,' into the desire to revisit the noisy world. He wishes, in plain English, to drive his lady out through the streets of Corinth, that his friends may see her beauty and envy him; and he talks of a bridal feast. His lady reluctantly consents, on the condition that old Apollonius should not be invited; and she proceeds to fit up the hall accordingly, by the help of her demon-servitors, for the occasion. The day arrives, the gossip rout of guests enter, and among the rest, but self-invited, the philosopher; the feast, however, goes forward, the music floats along the perfumed air,—but

Philosophy will clip an Angel's wings,
Conquer all mysteries by rule and line,
Empty the haunted air and gnomed mine—
Unweave a rainbow, as it erewhile made
The *tender-person'd* Lamia melt into a shade.

Lycius pledges his old master in a bumper; father bald-head makes no answer, but fixes his eye 'without a twinkle' on the alarmed beauty of the bride,

Browbeating her fair form and troubling her sweet pride.

Her lover, seeing her start and turn pale, asks her a very silly and insulting question, considering the previous warning she had given him; to wit, whether she knew that man.

[Quotes 'Lamia', Part II, line 255 to the end, 'Poor Lamia answer'd not' to 'the heavy body wound.']

'Isabella, or the Pot of Basil', is founded on a tale in the Decameron. A poetical rival of Mr Keats, whose volumes are now on our table, has taken the same subject in his *Sicilian Story*; and in a future Number, we shall, perhaps, afford our readers the opportunity of comparing the different versions. 'The Eve of St Agnes', is the story of a young damsel of high degree, who loves the son of her father's foe. Having heard that upon St Agnes' eve, young virgins might, if they would go to bed supperless, and perform certain other rites, enjoy a vision of their lovers, she determines to try the spell; and Young Porphyro, who learns her purpose from her Duenna, resolves to fulfil the legend *in propriâ personâ*. Every thing succeeds to admiration; Madeline is quite delighted when she finds the supposed vision is a palpable reality; and while all in the castle are asleep, they elope together; the old nurse dies in the night; and thus endeth the tale. A few stanzas must suffice for further extracts:—

[Quotes 'The Eve of St Agnes', stanzas 25, 27–8, 33–5, 40–2.]

We have laid before our readers these copious extracts from Mr Keats's present volume, without any comment, in order that he might have the full benefit of pleading his own cause: there they are, and they can be made to speak neither more nor less in his favour than they have already testified.

Mr Keats, it will be sufficiently evident, is a young man—whatever be his age, we must consider him as still but a young man,—possessed of an elegant fancy, a warm and lively imagination, and something above the average talents of persons who take to writing poetry. Poetry is his mistress,—we were going to say, his *Lamia,* for we suspect that she has proved a syren, that her wine is drugged, and that her treasures will be found to be like the gold of Tantalus. Mr Keats has given his whole soul to 'plotting and fitting himself for verses fit to live;' and the consequence is, that he has produced verses which, if we mistake not, will not live very long, though they will live as long as they deserve. The exclusive cultivation of the imagination is always attended by a dwindling or contraction of the other powers of the mind. This effect has often been remarked upon: it is the penalty which second-rate genius pays for the distinction purchased by the exhaustion of its whole strength in that one direction, or upon that one object, that has seized upon the fancy; and it is the true source of affectation and eccentricity. In no other way can we account for the imbecility of judgement, the want of sober calculation, the intense enthusiasm about mean or trivial objects, and the real emptiness of mind, which are sometimes found connected with distinguishing talents. Poetry, after all, if pursued as an end, is but child's play; and no wonder that those who seem not to have any higher object than to be poets, should sometimes be very childish. What better name can we bestow on the nonsense that Mr Keats, and Mr Leigh Hunt, and Mr Percy Bysshe Shelley, and some other poets about town, have been talking of 'the beautiful mythology of Greece?' To some persons, although we would by no means place Mr Keats among the number, that mythology comes recommended chiefly by its grossness—its alliance to the sensitive pleasures which belong to the animal. With our Author, this fondness for it proceeds, we very believe, from nothing worse than a school boy taste for the stories of the Pantheon and Ovid's *Metamorphoses*, and the fascination of the word *classical*. Had he passed through the higher forms of a liberal education, he would have *shed* all these puerilities; his mind would have received the rich alluvial deposit of such studies, but this would only have formed the soil for its native fancies; and he would have known that the last use which a full-grown scholar thinks of making of his classical acquirements, is to make a parade of them either in prose or verse. There is nothing gives a greater richness to poetry, we admit, than classical allusions, if they are not of a common-place kind; but they will generally be found to please in proportion to their slightness and remoteness: it is as illustrations, sometimes highly picturesque illustrations of the subject, not as distinct objects of thought,—it is as metaphor, never in the broad and palpable shape of simile, that they please. It was reserved for the Author of *Endymion* to beat out the gold of ancient fable into leaf thin enough to cover four long cantos of incoherent verse. And now, in the present volume, we have *Hyperion*, books one, two, and three! We do not mean to deny that there is a respectable degree of inventive skill and liveliness of fancy displayed in this last poem, but they are most miserably misapplied; nor should we have imagined that any person would have thrown away his time in attempting such a theme, unless it were some lad with his fancy half full of Homer and half full of Milton, who might, as a school exercise, try to frame something out of the compound ideas of the Titan and the Demon, of Olympus and Pandemonium. But Mr Keats, seemingly, can think or write of scarcely any thing else than the 'happy pieties' of Paganism. A Grecian Urn throws him into an ecstasy: its 'silent form,' he says, 'doth tease us out of thought as doth Eternity,'—a very happy description of the bewildering effect which such subjects have at least had upon his own mind; and his fancy having thus got the better of his reason, we are the less surprised at the oracle which the Urn is made to utter:

> 'Beauty is truth, truth beauty,'—that is all
> Ye know on earth, and all ye need to know.

That is, all that Mr Keats knows or cares to know.—But till he knows much more than this, he will never write verses fit to live.

We wish to say little of the affectation which still frequently disfigures Mr Keats's phraseology, because there is very much less of it in the present volume than in his former poems. We are glad to notice this indication of *growth.* An imperfect acquaintance with the genuine resources of the language, or an impatience of its poverty and weakness as a vehicle for his teeming fancies, is still occasionally discernible in the violence he lays upon words and syllables forced to become such: *e. g.* 'rubious-argent?' 'milder-moon'd;' 'frail-strung heart;' a 'tithe' of eye-sight,—

——— With eye-lids closed,
Saving a tythe which love still open kept.

(N. B. An American Keats would have said, '*a balance*;') 'trembled blossoms;' 'honey'd middle of the night;' and other splendid novelties.

We would, however, be the last persons to lay great stress on such *minutiæ*, in estimating the merits of a writer; but we feel it our duty to warn off all persons who are for breaking down the fences which language interposes between sense and nonsense.

The true cause of Mr Keats's failure is, not the want of talent, but the misdirection of it; and this circumstance presents the only chance there is that some day or other he will produce something better: whether he ever does or not, is a matter of extreme insignificance to the public, for we have surely poets enough; but it would seem to be not so to himself. At present, there is a sickliness about his productions, which shews there is a mischief at the core. He has with singular ingenuousness and correctness described his own case in the preface to *Endymion*: 'The imagination of a boy,' he says, 'is healthy, and the *mature* imagination of a man is healthy; but there is a space of life between, in which the soul is in a ferment, the character undecided, the way of life uncertain, the ambition thick-sighted: thence proceeds mawkishness.' The diagnosis of the complaint is well laid down; his is a diseased state of feeling, arising from the want of a sufficient and worthy object of hope and enterprise, and of the regulating principle of religion. Can a more unequivocal proof of this be given, than that there does not occur, if our recollection serves us, throughout his present volume, a single reference to any one object of *real* interest, a single burst of virtuous affection or enlightened sentiment, a single reference, even of the most general kind, to the Supreme Being, or the slenderest indication that the Author is allied by any one tie to his family, his country, or his kind? Mr Keats, we doubt not, *has* attachments and virtuous feelings, and we would fain hope, notwithstanding the silly expressions which would justify a presumption to the contrary, that he is a Christian: if he is not, it will matter very little to him in a few years what else he may or may not be. We will, however, take it for granted that he is an amiable and well principled young man; and then we have but one piece of advice to offer him on parting, namely, to let it appear in his future productions.

37. Error and imagination

1820

Extract from unsigned article, 'An Essay on Poetry, with Observations on the Living Poets', *London Magazine and Monthly Critical and Dramatic Review* (Gold's) (December 1820), ii, 559–61.

There is a young man of the name of John Keats, whom it has lately become the fashion to abuse, because he has been bepraised by Leigh Hunt and abused by the *Quarterly Review*. He is a poet of excessive imagination; perhaps as much so as any writer of the present day; but abounds in errors both of taste and sentiment. His fragment of *Hyperion*, wild and unconnected as it is, is a giant in ruins,—grand, vast, and sublime, and a fine specimen of original thinking, that is at no great lapse of time destined to achieve wonders in the poetical world. The prevailing foibles of Mr Keats' system are, first, a strained inversion of sentiment; and, secondly, an intense, earnest affectation, that is intimately linked with the poetry, and cannot without injury be eradicated. But he has a happy facility of expressing apt images by individual expression, and of hitching the faculty of imagination on a single word; such as that exquisitely imaginative line—

> She stood in tears amid the *alien* corn.

For those who have hitherto treated the writings of Keats with scorn, and discovered nothing in his poetry but endless affectation and inverted sentiment, we shall extract the following lines; not because we consider them as the happiest effusions of the Author's muse, but because they abound less in the peculiarities of his style than almost any other of his writings, and come forcibly home to the imaginations of the thoughtful and romantic:—

[Quotes 'Robin Hood' in full.]

OBITUARIES

38. The death of Mr John Keats

1821

Obituary notice ('Town Conversation. No. IV'), signed 'L', *London Magazine* (Baldwin's) (April 1821), iii, 426–7.

'Barry Cornwall', or Bryan Waller Procter (1787–1874), a solicitor by profession, was a poet whose verses were sloppy but whose generous nature gained him a large circle of literary friends—including Keats. Substantial parts of this notice were reproduced in the *Imperial Magazine* (December 1821), iii, columns 1077–8; in *Time's Telescope for 1822* under 23 February 1821; and in American journals.

We commence our article this month with but a melancholy subject—*the death of Mr John Keats.*—It is, perhaps, an unfit topic to be discussed under this head, but we knew not where else to place it, and we could not reconcile ourselves to the idea of letting a poet's death pass by in the common obituary. He died on the 23rd of February, 1821, at Rome, whither he had gone for the benefit of his health. His complaint was a consumption, under which he had languished for some time, but his death was accelerated by a cold caught in his voyage to Italy.

Mr Keats was, in the truest sense of the word, A POET.—There is but a small portion of the public acquainted with the writings of this young man; yet they were full of high imagination and delicate fancy, and his images were beautiful and more entirely his own, perhaps, than those of any living writer whatever. He had a fine ear, a tender heart, and at times great force and originality of expression; and notwithstanding all this, he has been suffered to rise and pass away almost without a notice: the laurel has been awarded (for the present) to other brows: the bolder aspirants have been allowed to take their station on the slippery steps of the temple of fame, while he has been nearly hidden among the crowd during his life, and has at last died, solitary and in sorrow, in a foreign land.

It is at all times difficult, if not impossible, to argue others into a love of poets and poetry: it is altogether a matter of feeling, and we must leave to time (while it hallows his memory) to do justice to the reputation of Keats. There were many, however, even among the critics living, who held his powers in high estimation; and it was well observed by the Editor of the *Edinburgh Review*, that there was no other Author whatever, whose writings would form so good a test by which to try the love which any one professed to bear towards poetry.

When Keats left England, he had a presentiment that he should not return: that this has been too sadly realized the reader already knows.—After his arrival in Italy, he revived for a brief period, but soon afterwards declined, and sunk gradually into his grave. He was one of three English poets who had been compelled by circumstances to adopt a foreign country as their own. He was the youngest, but the first to leave us. His sad and beautiful wish is at last accomplished: it was that he might drink 'of the warm south,' and 'leave the world unseen,'—and—(he is addressing the nightingale)—

And with thee fade away.

[Quotes stanza 3 of 'Ode to a Nightingale', italicizing line 6.]

A few weeks before he died, a gentleman who was sitting by his bed-side, spoke of an inscription to his memory, but he declined this altogether,—desiring that there should be no mention of his name or country; 'or if any,' said he, 'let it be—*Here lies the body of one whose name was writ in water*!' —There is something in this to us most painfully affecting; indeed the whole story of his later days is well calculated to make a deep impression.—It is to be hoped that his biography will be given to the world, and also whatever he may have left (whether in poetry or prose) behind him. The public is fond of patronizing poets: they are considered in the light of an almost helpless race: they are bright as stars, but like meteors

Short-lived and self-consuming.

We do not claim the *patronage* of the public for Mr Keats, but we hope that it will now cast aside every little and unworthy prejudice, and do justice to the high memory of a young but undoubted poet.

39. The death of genius

1821

Unsigned obituary, *New Monthly Magazine and Literary Journal* (1 May 1821), iii, 256–7.

Died at Rome, on the 23rd of February last, Mr John Keats, well known for his poetical productions. He left England for the benefit of his health, having exhibited marks of a consumptive disorder, which appeared to be rapidly increasing. A cold, caught on his journey to Italy, hurried him still faster to the tomb; and though for a short time after his arrival there he seemed to revive, it was only to confirm the fallacy of a hope too often indulged in similar disorders; for he soon languished into an untimely grave. He often talked of his approaching death, with the resignation of one who contemplated its certainty without anxiety, and seemed to wish to 'steal from the world' into silence and repose. From a contemporary writer we learn, that when a friend was sitting by his bed, and talking of an inscription to his memory, he desired there might be no notice taken of him, 'or if any,' to be '*Here lies the body of one whose name was writ in water*!' The temperament and feeling of the poet, which is always 'much nearer allied to melancholy than to jollity or mirth,' seem to have been the heritage of Keats: the deep susceptibility to external beauty, the intense vividness of mental impressions, and the rich colouring of thought, which are seen in genius, were all his. Though young, and his taste leaning towards an extravagance which maturer years would no doubt have corrected, his poetry displays throughout those breathing thoughts which so peculiarly identify the presence of the poetical spirit. He was an original writer, his productions were his own; and no pen of the present age can lay claim to the epithet of poetical, on the ground of a powerful fancy, freshness of colouring, and force of expression, if Keats be not allowed a claim far from humble, on those distinguishing characteristics of the sons of song. A name richer in promise England did not possess, and the mind insensible to the sweetness of his productions must indeed be a miserable one—the very climax of heartlessness. The subject of *Endymion*, his principal poem, is perhaps less attractive than one more natural and more agreeable to the general taste: mythological fictions do not now interest mankind; yet it does not follow therefrom that they should not be told in strains of exquisite poetry. His other poems possess sufficient attraction to interest every class of readers, and they will still be read when the sneers of ephemeral critics shall have long expired on the gross lips which impudently arrayed themselves against acknowledged truth, and the whole suffrage of the literary world. The base attack made with the hope of crushing the rising genius of young Keats, can never be forgotten: it was made against a youthful, friendless, virtuous, highly-gifted character, by a pen, equally reckless of veracity and justice, from the mean motive of a dislike to his political tenets. It appears that Keats had a presentiment he should never return to England, and that he communicated it to more than one person. He is said to have wished to drink 'of the warm South,' and 'leave the world unseen;' and his wish was accordingly fulfilled. There is something very impressive about the death of genius, and particularly of youthful genius. Poets, perhaps, have shared most of this feeling from mankind; indeed their labours which survive themselves are for ever creating it. Not only

By fairy hands *their* knell is rung,
By forms unseen *their* dirge is sung,

but the beautiful, the tender, and the wise, are perpetual sorrowers over their obsequies.

40. The death of a radically presumptuous profligate

1821

Extract from an unsigned review of Shelley's *Adonais*, in the *Literary Gazette and Journal of Belles Lettres* (8 December 1821), No. cclv, 772.

The allusion to South America in this typically tasteless passage derives from a letter signed 'Y' in the *Morning Chronicle*, 27 July 1821, where the writer (probably Charles Cowden Clarke) mentioned that Keats 'once said, that if he should live a few years, he would go over to South America, and write a Poem on Liberty.'

Adonais is an elegy after *the manner of Moschus*, on a foolish young man, who, after writing some volumes of very weak, and, in the greater part, of very indecent poetry, died some time since of a consumption: the breaking down of an infirm constitution having, in all probability, been accelerated by the discarding his neckcloth, a practice of the cockney poets, who look upon it as essential to genius, inasmuch as neither Michael Angelo, Raphael nor Tasso are supposed to have worn those antispiritual incumbrances. In short, as the vigour of Sampson lay in his hair, the secret of talent with these persons lies in the neck; and what aspirations can be expected from a mind enveloped in muslin. Keats caught cold in training for a genius, and, after a lingering illness, died, to the great loss of the Independents of South America, whom he had intended to visit with an English epic poem, for the purpose of exciting them to liberty. But death, even the death of the radically presumptuous profligate, is a serious thing; and as we believe that Keats was made presumptuous chiefly by the treacherous puffing of his cockney fellow gossips, and profligate in his poems merely to make them saleable, we regret that he did not live long enough to acquire common sense, and abjure the pestilent and perfidious gang who betrayed his weakness to the grave, and are now panegyrising his memory into contempt. For what is the praise of the cockneys but disgrace, or what honourable inscription can be placed over the dead by the hands of notorious libellers, exiled adulterers, and avowed atheists.

POSTHUMOUS REPUTATION

41. Hazlitt on Keats

1821, 1822, 1824

The essayist William Hazlitt (1778–1830) was a friend of Keats, who sympathized with his radical views and greatly admired his critical lectures and writings; but Hazlitt did not equally admire Keats's work, which seemed to lack the forceful qualities of his own, and never committed himself on it at any length. 'When Keats was living,' Haydon complained in 1823, 'I could not get Hazlitt to admit Keats had common talents!'

(a) Extract from essay 'On Reading Old Books': 'Books have in a great measure lost their power over me; nor can I revive the same interest in them as formerly. I perceive when a thing is good, rather than feel it. It is true,

Marcian Colonna is a dainty book;[1]

and the reading of Mr Keats's "Eve of St Agnes" lately made me regret that I was not young again. The beautiful and tender images there conjured up, "come like shadows—so depart." The "tiger-moth's wings," which he has spread over his rich poetic blazonry, just flit across my fancy; the gorgeous twilight window which he has painted over again in his verse, to me "blushes" almost in vain "with blood of queens and kings." I know how I should have felt at one time in reading such authors; and that is all. The sharp luscious flavour, the fine *aroma* is fled, and nothing but the stalk, the bran, the husk of literature is left.' (*London Magazine* (February 1821), iii, 132.)

[1] From Charles Lamb's 'Sonnet to the Author of Poems Published under the Name of Barry Cornwall'.

(b) Extract from essay 'On Effeminacy of Character': 'I cannot help thinking that the fault of Mr Keats's poems was a deficiency in masculine energy of style. He had beauty, tenderness, delicacy, in an uncommon degree, but there was a want of strength and substance. His *Endymion* is a very delightful description of the illusions of a youthful imagination, given up to airy dreams—we have flowers, clouds, rainbows, moonlight, all sweet sounds and smells, and Oreads and Dryads flitting by—but there is nothing tangible in it, nothing marked or palpable—we have none of the hardy spirit or rigid forms of antiquity. He painted his own thoughts and character; and did not transport himself into the fabulous and heroic ages. There is a want of action, of character, and so far, of imagination, but there is exquisite fancy. All is soft and fleshy, without bone or muscle. We see in him the youth, without the manhood of poetry. His genius breathed "vernal delight and joy."—"Like Maia's son he stood and shook his plumes," with fragrance filled. His mind was redolent of spring. He had not the fierceness of summer, nor the richness of autumn, and winter he seemed not to have known, till he felt the icy hand of death!' (*Table-Talk; or, Original Essays* (1822), ii. 215–16.)

(c) 'Mr KEATS is also dead. He gave the greatest promise of genius of any poet of his day. He displayed extreme tenderness, beauty, originality, and delicacy of fancy; all he wanted was manly strength and fortitude to reject the temptations of singularity in sentiment and expression. Some of his shorter and later pieces are, however, as free from faults as they are full of beauties.' ('A Critical List of Authors Contained in this Volume', in *Select British Poets, or New Elegant Extracts from Chaucer to the Present Time, with Critical Remarks* (1824), xv.)

42. Leigh Hunt : retrospective views of Keats

1828, 1859

The entry in Gorton's *Biographical Dictionary* is anonymous, but as H. E. Rollins says, 'Hunt's authorship is unmistakable' (*The Keats Circle*, i. xcv), and some of its material is quoted in (b). In turn, much of the material in *Lord Byron* was later incorporated in Hunt's *Autobiography* (1850, revised 1859), with some additions elicited by a reading of Milnes's *Life*. The most notable of these additions is printed as (c).

(a) Extracts from article signed 'Original Com.': 'KEATS (John) a young English poet, of extraordinary promise, and almost as extraordinary performance. . . . Mr Keats's poetical faculty was of a nature to make its way into notice under any circumstances, and would unquestionably have done so; but the political and other opinions to which his attention had been early directed, the public connexions to which he was introduced, and the generous enthusiasm, natural to great talents, which would not allow him to conceal either, soon brought on him a host of critics, some of whom were but too happy to mask their political hostility under the guise of public zeal. . . . Mr Keats had a very manly, as well as delicate spirit. He was personally courageous in no ordinary degree, and had the usual superiority of genius to little arts and the love of money. His patrimony, which was inconsiderable, he freely used in part, and even risqued altogether, to relieve the wants of others, and farther their views. He could be hot now and then; and perhaps was a little proud, owing to the humbleness of his origin, and the front he thought it necessary to present to vulgar abuse. He was handsome, with remarkably beautiful hair, curling in natural ringlets. Mr Keats's poems have been so often criticized both by friends and enemies, and have succeeded, since his death, in securing him so unequivocal a reputation as a highly promising genius, that it will be necessary to say comparatively little of them here. If it was unlucky for his immediate success, that he came before the public recommended by a political party, it was fortunate for him with posterity, that he began to write at a period when original thinking, and a dependance on a man's own resources, were earnestly inculcated on all sides. Of his standing with posterity we have no doubt. He will be considered, *par excellence*, as *the young poet*; as the one who poured forth at the earliest age the greatest unequivocal exuberance, and who proceeded very speedily to show that maturity brought him a judgment equal to the task of pruning it, and rendering it immortal. He had the two highest qualities of a poet, in the highest degree—sensibility and imagination. His *Endymion*, with all its young faults, will be a store-house for the lovers of genuine poetry, both young and old; a wood to wander in; a solitude inhabited by creatures of superhuman beauty and intellect; and superabundant in the luxuries of a poetical domain, not omitting "weeds of glorious feature." Its most obvious fault was a negligence of rhyme ostentatiously careless, which, by the common law of extremes, produced the very effect he wished to avoid—a pressure of itself on the reader. The fragment of *Hyperion*, which was his last performance, and which extorted the admiration of Lord Byron, has been compared to those bones of enormous creatures which are occasionally dug up, and remind us of extraordinary and gigantic times.' (*A General Biographical Dictionary*, by John Gorton (1828), ii. 241–2.)

(b) Extracts from *Lord Byron*: 'Modern criticism has made the public well acquainted with the merits of Chapman. . . . Mr Keats's epithets of "loud and bold", showed that he understood him thoroughly. The men of Cortez staring at each other, and the eagle eyes of their leader looking out upon the Pacific, have been thought too violent a picture for the dignity of the occasion; but it is a case that requires the exception. Cortez's "eagle eyes" are a piece of historical painting, as the reader may see by Titian's portrait of him. The last line,

> Silent—upon a peak in Darien,

makes the mountain a part of the spectacle, and supports the emotion of the rest of the sonnet upon a basis of gigantic tranquillity.

The volume containing this sonnet was published in 1817, when the author was in his twenty-first year. The poem with which it begins, was suggested to him by a delightful summer-day, as he stood beside the gate that leads from the Battery on Hampstead Heath into a field by Caen Wood; and the last poem, the one on "Sleep and Poetry," was occasioned by his sleeping in one of the cottages in the Vale of Health, the first one that fronts the valley, beginning from the same quarter. I mention these things, which now look trivial, because his readers will not think them so twenty years hence. It was in the beautiful lane, running from the road between Hampstead and Highgate to the foot of Highgate Hill, that, meeting me one day, he first gave me the volume . . .

> A drainless shower
> Of light is poesy; 'tis the supreme of power;
> *'Tis might half slumb'ring on its own right arm.*

These are some more of the lines in a book, in which feeble critics thought they saw nothing but feebleness . . . *Endymion*, it must be allowed, was not a little calculated to perplex the critics. It was a wilderness of sweets, but it was truly a wilderness; a domain of young, luxuriant, uncompromising poetry, where the "weeds of glorious feature" hampered the petty legs accustomed to the lawns and trodden walks, in vogue for the last hundred years; lawns, as Johnson says, "shaven by the scythe, and levelled with the roller;" walks, which, being public property, have been re-consecrated, like Kensington Gardens, by the beadles of authority, instead of the Pans and Sylvans. Mr Wordsworth knew better than the critics, but he did not choose to say anything. . . . "Such sights as youthful poets dream" must cease, when their predecessors grow old; when they get jealous as fading beauties, and have little annuities for behaving themselves.

The great fault of *Endymion*, next to its unpruned luxuriance, (or before it, rather, for it was not a fault on the right side,) was the wilfulness of its rhymes. The author had a just contempt for the monotonous termination of every-day couplets; he broke up his lines in order to distribute the rhyme properly; but going only upon the ground of his contempt, and not having yet settled with himself any principle of versification, the very exuberance of his ideas led him to make use of the first rhymes that offered; so that, by a new meeting of extremes, the effect was as artificial, and much more obtrusive than the one under the old system. Dryden modestly confessed, that a rhyme had often helped him to a thought. Mr Keats, in the tyranny of his wealth, forced his rhymes to help him, whether they would or not; and they obeyed him, in the most singular manner, with equal promptitude and ungainness. *Endymion*, too, was not without its faults of weakness, as well as of power. Mr Keats's natural tendency to pleasure, as a poet, sometimes degenerated, by reason of his ill health, into a poetical effeminacy.

There are symptoms of it here and there in all his productions, not excepting the gigantic grandeur of *Hyperion*. His lovers grow "faint" with the sight of their mistresses; and Apollo, when he is superseding his divine predecessor, and undergoing his transformation into a Divus Major, suffers a little too exquisitely among his lilies. But Mr Keats was aware of this contradiction to the real energy of his nature, and prepared to get rid of it. What is more, he said as much in the Preface to *Endymion*, and in a manner calculated to conciliate all critics who were worth touching his volume; but not such were those, from whom the public were to receive their notions of him. Let the reader see it, and wish, if he has hitherto read nothing but criticism upon him, that he had seen it before.

[Quotes preface to *Endymion* in full.]

An organised system of abuse had come up at this period, of a nature with which it was thought no department of literature had hitherto been polluted . . .

The contrivers of this system of calumny thought that it suited their views, trading, political, and personal, to attack the writer of the present work. They did so, and his friends with him, Mr Keats among the number. . . . I have since regretted, on Mr Keats's account, that I did not take a more active part. The scorn which the public and they would feel for one another, before long, was evident enough; but, in the meantime, an injury, in every point of view, was done to a young and sensitive nature, to which I ought to have been more alive. The truth was, I never thought about it; nor, I believe, did he, with a view to my taking any farther notice. I was in the habit, though a public man, of living in a world of abstractions of my own, and I regarded him as a nature still more abstracted, and sure of unsought renown. . . . Our whole talk was made up of idealisms. In the streets we were in the thick of the old woods. I little suspected at that time, as I did afterwards, that the hunters had struck him; that a delicate organization, which already anticipated a premature death, made him feel his ambition thwarted by these fellow; and that the very impatience of being impatient was resented by him, and preyed on his mind. Had he said but a word to me on the subject, I would have kept no measures with them. . . . On Mr Brown's leaving England, a second time . . . Mr Keats, who was too ill to accompany him, came to reside with me, when his last and best volume of poems appeared, containing "Lamia", "Isabella", the "Eve of St Agnes", and the noble fragment of *Hyperion*.

I remember Charles Lamb's delight and admiration on reading this work; how pleased he was with the designation of Mercury as "the star of Lethe" (rising, as it were, and glittering, as he came upon that pale region); with the fine daring anticipation in that passage of the second poem,—

> So the two brothers and *their murdered man*
> Rode past fair Florence;

and with the description, at once delicate and gorgeous, of Agnes praying beneath the painted window. This last (which should be called, *par excellence*, the Prayer at the Painted Window) has often been quoted; but . . . I cannot resist repeating it. It throws a light upon one's book.

[Quotes 'Eve of St Agnes', lines 208–24, 'A casement high' to 'Save wings, for heaven'.]

The whole volume is worthy of this passage. Mr Keats is no half-painter, who has only distinct ideas occasionally, and fills up the rest with commonplaces. He feels all as he goes. In his best pieces, every bit is precious; and he knew it, and laid it on as carefully as Titian or Giorgione. Take a few more samples

LOVERS.

> Parting they seem'd to tread upon the air,
> Twin roses by the zephyr blown apart,
> Only to meet again more close, and share
> The inward fragrance of each other's heart.

BEES,

> Bees, the little almsmen of spring bowers.

A DELICATE SUPPER,

> And still she slept an azure-lidded sleep,
> In blanched linen, smooth, and lavender'd,
> While he from forth the closet brought a heap
> Of candied apple, quince, and plum, and gourd
> With jellies soother than the creamy curd,
> And lucent syrops, tinct with cinnamon;
> Manna and dates, in argosy transferr'd
> From Fez; and spiced dainties, every one,
> From silken Samarcand to cedar'd Lebanon.

These are stanzas, for which Persian kings would fill a poet's mouth with gold. I remember Mr Keats reading these lines to me with great relish and particularity, conscious of what he had set forth. The melody is as sweet as the subject, especially at

Lucent syrops tinct with cinnamon,

and the conclusion. Mr Wordsworth would say that the vowels were not varied enough; but Mr Keats knew where his vowels were *not* to be varied. On the occasion above alluded to [see No. 70], Mr Wordsworth found fault with the repetition of the concluding sound of the participles in Shakspeare's line about bees:—

The *singing* masons *building* roofs of gold.

This, he said, was a line which Milton would never have written. Mr Keats thought, on the other hand, that the repetition was in harmony with the continued note of the singers, and that Shakspeare's negligence (if negligence it was) had instinctively felt the thing in the best manner. . . . It was Mr Keats who observed to me, that Milton, in various parts of his writings, has shown himself a bit of an epicure, and loves to talk of good eating. . . .

CALAMITIES FOLLOWING CALAMITIES

There was a listening fear in her regard,
As if calamity had but begun;
As if the vanward clouds of evil days
Had spent their malice, *and the sullen rear*
Was with its stored thunder labouring up.

This is out of the fragment of *Hyperion*, which is truly like the fragment of a former world. There is a voice in it grander than any that has been uttered in these times, except in some of Wordsworth's Sonnets. . . .

[Quotes further fragments from *Hyperion* and from 'Ode on a Grecian Urn', and quotes 'Ode to a Nightingale' in full.]

It was Lord Byron, at that time living in Italy, drinking its wine, and basking in its sunshine, who asked me what was the meaning of a beaker "full of the warm south." It was not the word beaker that puzzled him: College had made him intimate enough with that. But the sort of poetry in which he excelled, was not accustomed to these poetical concentrations. At the moment also, he was willing to find fault, and did not wish to discern an excellence different from his own. . . .

So much for the mortal life of as true a man of genius as these latter times have seen; one of those who are too genuine and too original to be properly appreciated at first, but whose time for applause will infallibly arrive with the many, and has already begun in all poetical quarters.' (*Lord Byron and Some of His Contemporaries* (1828), i. 411–42.)

(c) 'I had not known the young poet long, when Shelley and he became acquainted under my roof. Keats did not take to Shelley as kindly as Shelley did to him. Shelley's only thoughts of his new acquaintance were such as regarded his bad health, with which he sympathized, and his poetry, of which he has left such a monument of his admiration in *Adonais*. Keats, being a little too sensitive on the score of his origin, felt inclined to see in every man of birth a sort of natural enemy. Their styles in writing also were very different; and Keats, notwithstanding his unbounded sympathies with ordinary flesh and blood, and even the transcendental cosmopolitics of *Hyperion*, was so far inferior in universality to his great acquaintance, that he could not accompany him in his dædal rounds with nature, and his Archimedean endeavours to move the globe with his own hands. I am bound to state thus much; because, hopeless of recovering his health, under circumstances that made the feeling extremely bitter, an irritable morbidity appears even to have driven his suspicions to excess; and this not only with regard to the acquaintance whom he might reasonably suppose to have had some advantages over him, but to myself, who had none; for I learned the other day, with extreme pain, such as I am sure so kind and reflecting a man as Mr Monckton Milnes would not have inflicted on me could he have foreseen it, that Keats at one period of his intercourse with us suspected both Shelley and myself of a wish to see him undervalued! Such are the tricks which constant infelicity can play with the most noble natures. For Shelley, let *Adonais* answer. For myself, let every word answer which I uttered about him, living and dead, and such as I now proceed to repeat. I might as well have been told that I wished to see the flowers or the stars undervalued, or my own heart that loved him.' (*Autobiography* (1859), ed. J. E. Morpurgo, 1949, 273–4.)

43. A Titan in spirit

1828

Extract from article entitled 'Recollections of Books and their Authors.—No. 6. John Keats, The Poet', signed 'Iluscenor', in *The Olio* (28 June 1828), i. 391–4.

'Barry Cornwall' (B. W. Procter) has been suggested by Professor MacGillivray as a possible author.

I never think of John Keats, but I regret that I knew him, for if I had not known him, the sorrow that I feel for his death would be less, and perhaps little more than that felt for the loss of any young man of genius, who did not live to complete the glorious task set down for him.

John Keats was handsome, indeed his face might be termed intellectually beautiful; it expressed more of poetry than even his poetry does, beautiful as it is, with all its faults, and these are not few. It was such a face as I never saw before nor since. Any one who had looked on it would have said 'That is no common man.' There was a lustre in his look which gave you the idea of a mind of exquisite refinement, and high imagination; yet, to an observing eye, the seeds of early death were sown there; it was impossible to look at him, and think him long-lived. Jeremy Taylor says, in one of his admirable sermons, that 'there are but few persons upon whose foreheads every man can read the sentence of death, written in the lines of a lingering sickness;' but on his forehead it was written sufficiently palpable for some to read it as they ran.

These signs were somewhat contradicted by a look of strength and durability about his chest and shoulders, which might have deceived a casual looker-on; but he who could perceive the inner-workings, who could estimate the wear and wasting which an ardent, ambitious, and restless intellect makes in the 'human form divine,' must have felt persuaded that the flame burning within would shortly consume the outward shell. His spirit was like burning oil in a vessel of some precious and costly wood, which when the flame has consumed its nutriment, will then burn that which contained it. Unlike the pyre that consumes the devoted widow of the Hindoo husband, where we may see the fire but not the victim, in him we saw the fire and the victim too. *He*, however, was a self-devoted martyr to intellect, and not to a senseless and brutal custom; and if literature had its army of martyrs, as Religion gloriously has, his name would not be forgotten in its calends.

Poor fellow, I shall never forget him; those who did not know him, and who have only read his too early productions may; but those who knew him well never can, if there be any fellowship in man, and human kindness be anything more than a word. He was kind, affectionate, a delightful friend, an excellent companion, a young man wiser than his years, a true and tender brother (this affection it was that sacrificed his life,) a boy in look, but a man in mind, a mortal in seeming, but a titan in spirit. Shelley, who with all his liberal opinions, was at heart an aristocrat (and I speak this not offensively) slighted him till he knew his worth, but knew it too late. He afterwards made some amends in his *Adonais*, an extravagant rhapsody; and yet there is in it a true portrait of that young man of genius, who, if he had lived, would have proved himself the only mind worthy to be placed side by side with Milton in blank verse and epic genius.

His fragment called *Hyperion* is the noblest piece of blank verse that has appeared since Milton's. It would be difficult to produce a passage of equal length from Young, or from Blair's *Grave*, or from Cumberland's *Calvary*, or Townsend's *Armageddon* (which is a fine and undeservedly neglected work), or from Wordsworth's *Excursion*, that might compete with it. It was an overpowering avalanche from the very mountain of the Muses, which ought to have crushed and buried those poor blind moles and miners who are still uselessly labouring to underwork his fame. It was fortunate for his reputation that his booksellers persuaded him to publish it, for there were but two or three pieces in his last volume ('Isabel,' the 'Eve of St Agnes,' and one of his Odes) which could have added to his reputation. His publishers, however, should have spared such a silly excuse for the fragment-like appearance of *Hyperion*: the poet who could write so noble a fragment ought to have been above the idle criticism of the day: he should have finished what he had so nobly began, though a million of reviewers had cried 'hold!' Would Shakspeare, had he lived in these days, have cared to please such never-pleasable cynicks? Would Milton? The only poet of this time who has placed himself with those great names, set himself above criticism, and then criticism, instead of trampling him under foot, as it would have done, had he been humble, seeing that his spirit would not bow to it, bowed even to prostration to him. This was what John Keats should have done, and he might have lived.

There are few errors in *Hyperion*. I do not like this simile in it:—

> For as in crowded theatres of men
> Hubbub increases more they call out 'Hush!'

It is a very poor anachronism, and what is worse, has in it an air of vulgarity: to come back to earth from the 'highest heaven of invention,' for such a simile, was as illustrative of sinking as it would have been in Michael Angelo to leave working out his sublime and colossal Moses to carve a cherry stone. It may be excuse enough for so young a poet that Milton has sinned in the same manner; though some may say that the error of a great, will not warrant the error of a lesser, poet. It is, of course, inevitable and unavoidable, that we should describe things with which we are not familiar by things with which we are. But what is classical should only be illustrated by classical comparisons; or else should be left alone.

Hyperion will do more, in more candid times, to preserve his name, than all the rest of his poetry. It is, to be sure, but a fragment; so is the Theseus among the Elgin marbles; but we may judge by that portion what the entire work must have been. Would to heaven that he had been urged by some one who had influence over his mind to finish it: he should have left the pretty and the fantastic to others; he had sublimer powers, which should not have been wasted in minor efforts.—But it is now too late to accuse him of the error of neglecting his own reputation. A certain crew among critics did their best to nip his genius in the bud, and it is but justice to them to say that they succeeded.

When we think of the abused and ferocious power which those canker-worms of literature exert upon authors, it makes one envy the good old writers. Then if a man had merit in his works he was read for that merit, and praised without fear and without deduction; he was not damned and made a bye-word of reproach, for scorn to point his filthy finger at, because he was unfortunate enough to know a brother author, who was hostile in taste or politics to the self-created critic; nor was he excommunicated because he was guilty of the literary heterodoxy of publishing in the city instead of Albemarle-street, or in London instead of Edinburgh.

44. Landor on Keats

1828, 1846, 1848, 1850, undated

Walter Savage Landor (1775–1864), essayist and poet. Although his taste had a strong classical bias (Extract (d)), and although he avoided Shelley when both were living in Pisa, Landor came to have a great admiration for the new Romantic poets. His insistence on Keats's affinities with Chaucer is especially interesting, and it is a pity he nowhere develops the comparison in greater detail.

(a) Extract from 'Conversation XIV. Landor, English Visitor, and Florentine Visitor', in *Imaginary Conversations of Literary Men and Statesmen* (1828):

'ENGLISH VISITOR. But certainly there are blemishes, which strike the most incurious and inobservant beholder.

LANDOR. If so, why expose them? why triumph over them? In Keats, I acknowledge, there are many wild thoughts, and there are expressions which even outstrip them in extravagance: but in none of our poets, with the sole exception of Shakespeare, do we find so many phrases so happy in their boldness.

ENGLISH VISITOR. There is a more vivid spirit, more genuine poetry, in him than in any of his contemporaries; in whom it has rarely its full swing; but the chords (excepting in Burns and Moore) are flattened, as it were, by leaves or feathers on them.

Since the time of Chaucer there have been only two poets who at all resemble him: and these two are widely dissimilar from each other, Burns and Keats. The accuracy and truth with which Chaucer has described the manners of common life with the fore-ground and background, are also to be found in Burns, who delights in broader strokes of external nature, but equally appropriate. He has parts of genius which Chaucer has not in the same degree; the animated and pathetic Keats in his *Endymion* is richer in imagery than either: and there are passages in which no poet has arrived at the same excellence on the same ground. Time alone was wanting to complete a poet, who already far surpassed all his contemporaries in this country in the poet's most noble attributes.' (iii. 426–31.)

(b) Extract from 'Imaginary Conversations. Southey and Landor. Second Conversation': 'LANDOR. Young poets imagine feelings to which in reality they are strangers. . . . Both feelings and images fly from distant coverts into their own little field, without their consciousness whence they come, and rear young ones there which are properly their own . . . Keats is the most imaginative of our poets, after Chaucer, Spenser, Shakspeare, and Milton.' (*The Works of Walter Savage Landor* (1846), ii. 164.)

(c) Extract from letter to R. M. Milnes, 29 August 1848: 'Of all our poets, excepting Shakspeare and Milton, and perhaps Chaucer, he has most of the poetical character—fire, fancy, and diversity. He has not indeed overcome so great a difficulty as Shelley in his *Cenci*, nor united so many powers of the mind as Southey in *Kehama*—but there is an effluence of power and light pervading all his works, and a freshness such as we feel in the glorious dawn of Chaucer.' (*The Keats Circle*, ii. 257.)

(d) Extract from letter to John Forster, 24 March 1850: 'Keats is our Ariel of poetry, Scott our Prospero. The one commands, the other captivates: the one controls all the elements, the other tempers and enlivens them. And yet this wonderful creature Keats, who in his felicities of expression comes very often near to Shakespeare, has defects which his admirers do not seem to understand. Wordsworth called his ode to Pan a very pretty piece of Paganism when my friend Charles Brown read it to him; but Keats was no more pagan than Wordsworth himself. Between you and me, the style of Keats is extremely far removed from the very boundaries of Greece. I wish someone had been near him when he printed his *Endymion*, to strike out, as ruthlessly as you would have done, all that amidst its opulence is capricious and disorderly. The truth is, and indeed I hardly know an exception to it, it is in Selection that we English are most deficient. We lay our hands upon all, and manage very badly our dependencies. A young poet should be bound apprentice to Pindar for three years, whether his business be the ode or anything else. He will find nothing in the workshop which he expected to find, but quite enough of highly-wrought tools and well-seasoned materials.' (John Forster, *Walter Savage Landor* (1879), 497.)

(e) Extract from conversation with 'Barry Cornwall', undated: 'What a poet would poor Keats have been, if he had lived! He had something of Shakespear in him, and (what nobody else ever had) much, very much of Chaucer.' (*B. W. Procter: An Autobiographical Fragment* (1877), 304–5.

45. Memoir in Galignani's edition

1829

Extract from *The Poetical Works of Coleridge, Shelley and Keats*, Paris, 1829, pp. v–vii of the third section.

This anonymous memoir was by Cyrus Redding (1785–1870), Whig editor of the *New Monthly Magazine*. Redding's facts derive largely from Hunt's *Lord Byron* (No. 42(b)), but his presentation of a 'manly and independent' Keats, combining fortitude with pathos, helped to form the American image of the poet. The memoir also included the wording on Keats's tombstone and directions for finding the Protestant Cemetery in Rome.

The short career of JOHN KEATS was marked by the development of powers which have been rarely exhibited in one at so immatured an age. He had but just completed his twenty-fourth year when he was snatched away from the world, and an end put for ever to a genius of a lofty and novel order. Certain party critics, who made it their object to lacerate the feelings, and endeavour to put down by vituperation and misplaced ridicule every effort which emanated not from their own servile dependents or followers, furiously attacked the writings of Keats on their appearance. Their promise of greater excellence was unquestionable, their beauties were obvious,—but so also were defects, which might easily be made available for an attack upon the author;

and which certain writers of the *Quarterly Review* instantly seized upon to gratify party malice,—not against the author so much as against his friends. The unmerited abuse poured upon Keats by this periodical work is supposed to have hastened his end, which was slowly approaching when the criticism before-mentioned appeared. . . .

The juvenile productions of Keats were published in 1817, the author being at that time in his twenty-first year. His favourite sojourn appears to have been Hampstead, the localities of which village were the scenes of his earliest abstractions, and the prompters of many of his best poetical productions: most of his personal friends, too, resided in the neighbourhood. His first published volume, though the greater part of it was not above mediocrity, contained passages and lines of rare beauty. His political sentiments differing from those of the *Quarterly Review*, being manly and independent, were sins never to be forgiven; and as in that party work literary judgment was always dealt out according to political congeniality of feeling, with the known servility of its writers, an author like Keats had no chance of being judged fairly. He was friendless and unknown, and could not even attract notice to a just complaint if he appealed to the public, from his being yet obscure as an author. . . . On the publication of Keats's next work, *Endymion*, Gifford attacked it with all the bitterness of which his pen was capable, and did not hesitate, before he saw the work, to announce his intention of doing so to the publisher. Keats had endeavoured, as much as was consistent with independent feeling, to conciliate the critics at large, as may be observed in his preface to that poem. He merited to be treated with indulgence, not wounded by the envenomed shafts of political animosity for literary errors. His book abounded in passages of true poetry, which were of course passed over; and it is difficult to decide whether the cowardice or the cruelty of the attack upon it, most deserve execration. Of great sensitiveness, as already observed, and his frame already touched by a mortal distemper, he felt his hopes withered, and his attempts to obtain honourable public notice in his own scantily allotted days frustrated. He was never to see his honourable fame: this preyed upon his spirit and hastened his end, as has been already noticed. The third and last of his works was the little volume (his best work) containing 'Lamia', 'Isabella,' 'The Eve of St Agnes,' and *Hyperion*.—That he was not a finished writer, must be conceded; that, like Koerner in Germany, he gave rich promise rather than matured fruit, may be granted; but they must indeed be ill judges of genius who are not delighted with what he left, and do not see that, had he lived, he might have worn a wreath of renown which time would not easily have withered. His was indeed an 'untoward fate,' as Byron observes of him in the eleventh canto of *Don Juan*. . . .

Scattered through the writings of Keats will be found passages which come home to every bosom alive to each nobler and kindlier feeling of the human heart. There is much in them to be corrected, much to be altered for the better; but there are sparkling gems of the first lustre everywhere to be found. It is strange, that in civilized societies writings should be judged of, not by their merits, but by the faction to which their author belongs, though their productions may be solely confined to subjects the most remote from controversy. In England, a party-man must yield up every thing to the opinions and dogmatism of his caste. He must reject truths, pervert reason, misrepresent all things coming from an opponent of another creed in religion or politics. Such a state of virulent and lamentable narrow-mindedness, is the most certain that can exist for blighting the tender blossoms of genius, and blasting the innocent and virtuous hopes of the young aspirant after honest fame. It is not necessary that a young and ardent mind avow principles hostile to those who set up for its enemies —if he be but the friend of a friend openly opposed to them, it is enough; and the worst is, that the hostility displayed is neither limited by truth and candour, sound principles of criticism, humanity, or honourable feeling: it fights with all weapons, in the dark or in the light, by craft, or in any mode to obtain its bitter objects. The critics who hastened the end of Keats, had his works been set before them as being those of an unknown writer, would have acknowledged their talent, and applauded where it was due, for their attacks upon him were not made from lack of judgment, but from wilful hostility. One knows not how to characterize such demoniacal insincerity. Keats belonged to a school of politics which they from their ambush anathematized:—hence, and hence alone, their malice towards him.

Keats was, as a poet, like a rich fruit-tree which the gardener has not pruned of its luxuriance: time, had it been allotted him by Heaven, would have seen it as trim and rich as any brother of the garden. It is and will ever be regretted by the readers of his works, that he lingered no longer among living men, to bring to perfection what he meditated, to contribute to British literature a greater name, and to delight the lovers of true poetry with the rich melody of his musically embodied thoughts.

46. The significance of Keats's work

1831

Extract from signed review entitled 'On Some of the Characteristics of Modern Poetry, and on the Lyrical Poems of Alfred Tennyson', *Englishman's Magazine* (August 1831), i, 616–21.

Arthur Henry Hallam (1811–33), Tennyson's great friend and brilliant member of the Cambridge 'Apostles', was himself a poet who died at the age of twenty-two. In 1829, with R. M. Milnes, he had arranged the publication of the second (Cambridge) edition of *Adonais*.

This important essay, primarily concerned with Tennyson, is the first attempt to provide a *rationale* for the poetry of Keats, seen here as Tennyson's forerunner, and it lays down the aesthetic principles on which Keats's work was already becoming influential among the writers and artists of a new generation. Poetry's first concern is not intellectual contemplation, but immediate sensuous response to the environment: sensations rather than thoughts. 'Whenever the mind of the artist suffers itself to be occupied, during its periods of creation, by any other predominant motive than the desire of beauty, the result is false in art.' The best poetry is 'a sort of magic', working through images and symbols which demand strenuous activity from the participating reader. Hence its limited appeal and slow rise to popularity. The line of argument appealed strongly to the Pre-Raphaelites, and to the young Yeats (see his *Autobiographies*, 1955, 489–90). The conclusion of the article, which concerns Tennyson alone, has been omitted.

So Mr Montgomery's *Oxford*, by the help of some pretty illustrations, has contrived to prolong its miserable existence to a second edition! But this is slow work, compared to that triumphant progress of the *Omnipresence*, which, we concede to the author's friends, was 'truly astonishing.'[1] We understand, moreover, that a new light has broken upon this 'desolator desolate;' and since the 'columns' have begun to follow the example of 'men and gods,' by whom our poetaster has long been condemned, 'it is the fate of genius,' he begins to discover, 'to be unpopular.' Now, strongly as we protest against Mr Montgomery's application of this maxim to his own case, we are much disposed to agree with him as to its abstract correctness. Indeed, the truth which it involves seems to afford the only solution of so curious a phenomenon as the success, partial and transient though it be, of himself, and others of his calibre. When Mr Wordsworth, in his celebrated Preface to the *Lyrical Ballads*, asserted that immediate or rapid popularity was not the test of poetry, great was the consternation and clamour among those farmers of public favour, the established critics. Never had so audacious an attack been made upon their undoubted privileges and hereditary charter of oppression. 'What! *The Edinburgh Review* not infallible!' shrieked the amiable petulance of Mr Jeffrey. '*The Gentleman's Magazine* incapable of decision!' faltered the feeble garrulity of Silvanus Urban. And straightway the whole sciolist herd, men of rank, men of letters, men of wealth, men of business, all the 'mob of gentlemen who think with ease,'[2] and a terrible number of old ladies and boarding-school misses began to scream in chorus, and prolonged the notes of execration with which they overwhelmed the new doctrine, until their wits and their voices fairly gave in from exhaustion. Much, no doubt, they did, for much persons will do when they fight for their dear selves: but there was one thing they could not do, and unfortunately it was the only one of any importance. They could not put down Mr Wordsworth by clamour, or prevent his doctrine, once uttered, and enforced by his example, from awakening the minds of men, and giving a fresh impulse to art. It was the truth, and it prevailed; not only against the exasperation of that hydra, the Reading Public, whose vanity was hurt, and the blustering of its keepers, whose delusion was exposed, but even against the false glosses and narrow apprehensions of the Wordsworthians themselves. It is the madness of all who loosen some great principle, long buried under a snow-heap of custom and superstition, to imagine that they can restrain its operation, or circumscribe it by their purposes. But the right of private judgment was

[1] A devastating article by Macaulay in the *Edinburgh Review* had failed to affect the craze for Robert Montgomery's fourth-rate poems *The Omnipresence of the Deity* (1828) and *Oxford* (1831).

[2] An adaptation of Pope's line on the Restoration wits: 'The Mob of Gentlemen who wrote with Ease' (*Imitations of Horace*, Ep. I, Lib. ii, 108).

stronger than the will of Luther; and even the genius of Wordsworth cannot expand itself to the full periphery of poetic art.

It is not true, as his exclusive admirers would have it, that the highest species of poetry is the reflective: it is a gross fallacy, that, because certain opinions are acute or profound, the expression of them by the imagination must be eminently beautiful. Whenever the mind of the artist suffers itself to be occupied, during its periods of creation, by any other predominant motive than the desire of beauty, the result is false in art. Now there is undoubtedly no reason, why he may not find beauty in those moods of emotion, which arise from the combinations of reflective thought, and it is possible that he may delineate these with fidelity, and not be led astray by any suggestions of an unpoetical mood. But, though possible, it is hardly probable: for a man, whose reveries take a reasoning turn, and who is accustomed to measure his ideas by their logical relations rather than the congruity of the sentiments to which they refer, will be apt to mistake the pleasure he has in knowing a thing to be true, for the pleasure he would have in knowing it to be beautiful, and so will pile his thoughts in a rhetorical battery, that they may convince, instead of letting them glow in the natural course of contemplation, that they may enrapture. It would not be difficult to shew, by reference to the most admired poems of Wordsworth, that he is frequently chargeable with this error, and that much has been said by him which is good as philosophy, powerful as rhetoric, but false as poetry. Perhaps this very distortion of the truth did more in the peculiar juncture of our literary affairs to enlarge and liberalize the genius of our age, than could have been effected by a less sectarian temper. However this may be, a new school of reformers soon began to attract attention, who, professing the same independence of immediate favour, took their stand on a different region of Parnassus from that occupied by the Lakers,* and one, in our opinion, much less liable to perturbing currents of air from ungenial climates. We shall not hesitate to express our conviction, that the Cockney school (as it was termed in derision, from a cursory view of its accidental circumstances) contained more genuine inspiration, and adhered more speedily to that portion of truth which it embraced, than any *form* of art that has existed in this country since the day of Milton. Their *caposetta* was Mr

* This cant term was justly ridiculed by Mr Wordsworth's supporters; but it was not so easy to substitute an inoffensive denomination. We are not at all events the first who have used it without a contemptuous intention, for we remember to have heard a disciple quote Aristophanes in its behalf. *'Οῦτος ὀυ τῶν ἠθάδων τῶνδ' ὧν ὁρᾶθ' ὑμεῖς ἀεὶ ἀλλὰ ΛΙΜΝΑΙΟΣ.* 'This is no common, no barn-door fowl: No, but a *Lakist!*'

Leigh Hunt, who did little more than point the way, and was diverted from his aim by a thousand personal predilections and political habits of thought. But he was followed by two men of a very superior make; men who were born poets, lived poets, and went poets to their untimely graves. Shelley and Keats were, indeed, of opposite genius; that of the one was vast, impetuous, and sublime: the other seemed to be 'fed with honey-dew,' and to have 'drunk the milk of Paradise.' Even the softness of Shelley comes out in bold, rapid, comprehensive strokes; he has no patience for minute beauties, unless they can be massed into a general effect of grandeur. On the other hand, the tenderness of Keats cannot sustain a lofty flight; he does not generalize or allegorize Nature; his imagination works with few symbols, and reposes willingly on what is given freely. Yet in this formal opposition of character there is, it seems to us, a ground-work of similarity sufficient for the purposes of classification, and constituting a remarkable point in the progress of literature. They are both poets of sensation rather than reflection. Susceptible of the slightest impulse from external nature, their fine organs trembled into emotion at colours, and sounds, and movements, unperceived or unregarded by duller temperaments. Rich and clear were their perceptions of visible forms; full and deep their feelings of music. So vivid was the delight attending the simple exertions of eye and ear, that it became mingled more and more with their trains of active thought, and tended to absorb their whole being into the energy of sense. Other poets *seek* for images to illustrate their conceptions; these men had no need to seek; they lived in a world of images; for the most important and extensive portion of their life consisted in those emotions, which are immediately conversant with sensation. Like the hero of Goethe's novel, they would hardly have been affected by what are called the pathetic parts of a book; but the *merely beautiful* passages, 'those from which the spirit of the author looks clearly and mildly forth,' would have melted them to tears. Hence they are not descriptive; they are picturesque. They are not smooth and *negatively* harmonious; they are full of deep and varied melodies. This powerful tendency of imagination to a life of immediate sympathy with the external universe, is not nearly so liable to false views of art as the opposite disposition of purely intellectual contemplation. For where beauty is constantly passing before 'that inward eye, which is the bliss of solitude;' where the soul seeks it as a perpetual and necessary refreshment to the sources of activity and intuition; where all the other sacred ideas of our nature, the idea of good, the idea of perfection, the idea of truth, are habitually contemplated through the medium of this predominant mood, so that they assume its colour, and are subject to its peculiar laws—there is little danger that the ruling passion of the whole mind will cease to direct its creative operations, or the energetic principle of love for the beautiful sink, even for a brief period, to the level of a mere notion in the understanding. We do not deny that it is, on other accounts, dangerous for frail humanity to linger with fond attachment in the vicinity of sense. Minds of this description are especially liable to moral temptations, and upon them, more than any, it is incumbent to remember that their mission as men, which they share with all their fellow-beings, is of infinitely higher interest than their mission as artists, which they possess by rare and exclusive privilege. But it is obvious that, critically speaking, such temptations are of slight moment. Not the gross and evident passions of our nature, but the elevated and less separable desires are the dangerous enemies which misguide the poetic spirit in its attempts at self-cultivation. That delicate sense of fitness, which grows with the growth of artist feelings, and strengthens with their strength, until it acquires a celerity and weight of decision hardly inferior to the correspondent judgments of conscience, is weakened by every indulgence of heterogeneous aspirations, however pure they may be, however lofty, however suitable to human nature. We are therefore decidedly of opinion that the heights and depths of art are most within the reach of those who have received from Nature the 'fearful and wonderful' constitution we have described, whose poetry is a sort of magic, producing a number of impressions too multiplied, too minute, and too diversified to allow of our tracing them to their causes, because just such was the effect, even so boundless, and so bewildering, produced on their imaginations by the real appearance of Nature. These things being so, our friends of the new school had evidently much reason to recur to the maxim laid down by Mr Wordsworth, and to appeal from the immediate judgments of lettered or unlettered contemporaries to the decision of a more equitable posterity. How should they be popular, whose senses told them a richer and ampler tale than most men could understand, and who constantly expressed, because they constantly felt, sentiments of exquisite pleasure or pain, which most men were not permitted to experience? The public very naturally derided them as visionaries, and gibbeted *in terrorem* those inaccuracies of diction, occasioned sometimes by the speed of their conceptions, sometimes by the inadequacy of language to their peculiar conditions of thought. But, it may be asked, does not this line of argument prove too much? Does it not prove that there is a barrier between these poets and all other persons, so strong and immoveable, that, as has been said of the Supreme Essence, we must be themselves before we can understand them in the least? Not only are they not liable to sudden and vulgar estimation, but the lapse of ages, it seems, will not consolidate their fame, nor the suffrages of the wise few produce any impression, however remote or slowly matured, on the judgments of the incapacitated many. We answer, this is not the import of our argument. Undoubtedly the true poet addresses himself, in all his conceptions, to the common nature of us all. Art is a lofty tree, and may shoot up far beyond our grasp, but its roots are in daily life and experience. Every bosom contains the elements of those complex emotions which the artist feels, and every head can, to a certain extent, go over in itself the process of their combination, so as to understand his expressions and sympathize with his state. But this requires exertion; more or less, indeed, according to the difference of occasion, but always some degree of exertion. For since the emotions of the poet, during composition, follow a regular law of association, it follows that to accompany their progress up to the harmonious prospect of the whole, and to perceive the proper dependence of every step on that which preceded, it is absolutely necessary *to start from the same point*, i.e., clearly to apprehend that leading sentiment in the poet's mind, by their conformity to which the host of suggestions are arranged. Now this requisite exertion is not willingly made by the large majority of readers. It is so easy to judge capriciously, and according to indolent impulse! For very many, therefore, it has become *morally* impossible to attain the author's point of vision, on account of their habits, or their prejudices, or their circumstances; but it is never *physically* impossible, because nature has placed in every man the simple elements, of which art is the sublimation. Since then this demand on the reader for activity, when he wants to peruse his author in a luxurious passiveness, is the very thing that moves his bile, it is obvious that those writers will be always most popular, who require the least degree of exertion. Hence, whatever is mixed up with art, and appears under its semblance, is always more favourably regarded than art free and unalloyed. Hence, half the fashionable poems in the world are mere rhetoric, and half the remainder are perhaps not liked by the generality for their substantial merits. Hence, likewise, of the really pure compositions those are most universally agreeable, which take for their primary subject the *usual* passions of the heart, and deal with them in a simple state, without applying the transforming powers of high imagination. Love, friendship, ambition, religion, &c., are matters of daily experience, even amongst imaginative tempers. The forces of association, therefore, are ready to work in these directions, and little effort of will is necessary to follow the artist. For the same reason such subjects often excite a partial power of composition, which is no sign of a truly poetic organization. We are very far from wishing to depreciate this class of poems, whose influence is so extensive, and communicates so refined a pleasure. We contend only that the facility with which its impressions are communicated, is no proof of its elevation as a form of art, but rather the contrary. What then, some may be ready to exclaim, is the pleasure derived by most men from Shakspeare, or Dante, or Homer, entirely false and factitious? If these are really masters of their art, must not the energy required of the ordinary intelligences, that come in contact with their mighty genius, be the greatest possible? How comes it then that they are popular? Shall we not say, after all, that the difference is in the power of the author, not in the tenor of his meditations? Those eminent spirits find no difficulty in conveying to common apprehension their lofty sense, and profound observation of Nature. They keep no aristocratic state, apart from the sentiments of society at large; they speak to the hearts of all, and by the magnetic force of their conceptions elevate inferior intellects into a higher and purer atmosphere. The truth contained in this objection is undoubtedly important; geniuses of the most universal order, and assigned by destiny to the most propitious eras of a nation's literary development, have a clearer and larger access to the minds of their compatriots, than can ever be open to those who are circumscribed by less fortunate circumstances. In the youthful periods of any literature there is an expansive and communicative tendency in mind, which produces unreservedness of communion, and reciprocity of vigour between different orders of intelligence. Without abandoning the ground which has always been defended by the partizans of Mr Wordsworth, who declare with perfect truth that the number of real admirers of what is really admirable in Shakspeare and Milton are much fewer than the number of apparent admirers might lead one to imagine, we may safely assert that the intense thoughts set in circulation by those 'orbs of song,' and their noble satellites, 'in great Eliza's golden time,' did not fail to awaken a proportionable intensity in the natures of numberless auditors. Some might feel feebly, some strongly; the effect would vary according to the character of the recipient; but upon none was the stirring influence entirely unimpressive. The knowledge and power thus imbibed, became a part of national existence; it was ours as Englishmen; and amid the flux of generations and customs we retain unimpaired this privilege of intercourse with greatness. But the age in which we live comes late in our national progress. That first raciness, and juvenile vigour of literature, when nature 'wantoned as in her prime, and played at will her virgin fancies,' is gone, never to return. Since that day we have undergone a period of degradation. 'Every handicraftsman has worn the mark of Poesy.' It would be tedious to repeat the tale, so often related, of French contagion, and the heresies of the Popian school. With the close of the last century came an era of reaction, an era of painful struggle, to bring our overcivilised condition of thought into union with the fresh productive spirit that brightened the morning of our literature. But repentance is unlike innocence: the laborious endeavour to restore has more complicated methods of action, than the freedom of untainted nature. Those different powers of poetic disposition, the energies of Sensitive,* of Reflective, of Passionate Emotion, which in former times were intermingled, and derived from mutual support an extensive empire over the feelings of men, were now restrained within separate spheres of agency. The whole system no longer worked harmoniously, and by intrinsic harmony acquired external freedom; but there arose a violent and unusual action in the several component functions, each for itself, all striving to reproduce the regular power which the whole had once enjoyed. Hence the melancholy, which so evidently characterizes the spirit of modern poetry; hence that return of the mind upon itself, and the habit of seeking relief in idiosyncracies rather than community of interest. In the old times the poetic impulse went along with the general impulse of the nation; in these, it is a reaction against it, a check acting for conservation against a propulsion towards change. We have indeed seen it urged in some of our fashionable publications, that the diffusion of poetry must necessarily be in the direct ratio of the diffusion of machinery, because a highly civilized people must have new objects of interest, and thus a new field will be opened to description. But this notable argument forgets that against this *objective* amelioration may be set the decrease of *subjective* power, arising from a prevalence of social

* We are aware that this is not the right word, being appropriated by common use to a different signification. Those who think the caution given by Cæsar should not stand in the way of urgent occasion, may substitute 'sensuous,' a word in use amongst our elder divines, and revived by a few bold writers in our own time.

activity, and a continual absorption of the higher feelings into the palpable interests of ordinary life. The French Revolution may be a finer theme than the war of Troy; but it does not so evidently follow that Homer is to find his superior. Our inference, therefore, from this change in the relative position of artists to the rest of the community is, that modern poetry, in proportion to its depth and truth, is likely to have little immediate authority over public opinion. Admirers it will have; sects consequently it will form; and these strong under-currents will in time sensibly affect the principal stream. Those writers, whose genius, though great, is not strictly and essentially poetic, become mediators between the votaries of art and the careless cravers for excitement.† Art herself, less manifestly glorious than in her periods of undisputed supremacy, retains her essential prerogatives, and forgets not to raise up chosen spirits, who may minister to her state, and vindicate her title.

One of this faithful Islâm, a poet in the truest and highest sense, we are anxious to present to our readers. He has yet written little, and published less; but in these 'preludes of a loftier strain,' we recognize the inspiring god. Mr Tennyson belongs decidedly to the class we have already described as Poets of Sensation. He sees all the forms of nature with the '*eruditus oculus*,' and his ear has a fairy fineness. There is a strange earnestness in his worship of beauty, which throws a charm over his impassioned song, more easily felt than described, and not to be escaped by those who have once felt it. We think he has more definiteness, and soundness of general conception, than the late Mr Keats, and is much more free from blemishes of diction, and hasty capriccios of fancy. He has also this advantage over that poet, and his friend Shelley, that he comes before the public, unconnected with any political party, or peculiar system of opinions. Nevertheless, true to the theory we have stated, we believe his participation in their characteristic excellencies is sufficient to secure him a share in their unpopularity.

† May we not compare them to the bright, but unsubstantial clouds which, in still evenings, girdle the sides of lofty mountains, and seem to form a natural connexion between the lowly vallies, spread out beneath, and those isolated peaks above, that hold the 'last parley with the setting sun?'

47. The *Quarterly* is unrepentant

1833

Extract from unsigned review of *Poems* by Alfred Tennyson, *Quarterly Review* (April 1833), xlix, 81–2.

For details of this, Croker's second attack on *Endymion*, see Introduction, p. 25. It is agreeable to know that Croker did, in fact, live long enough to see 'many editions' of Keats's works, some of them 'with graphic illustrations'.

We gladly seize this opportunity of . . . introducing to the admiration of our more sequestered readers a new prodigy of genius—another and a brighter star of that galaxy or *milky way* of poetry of which the lamented Keats was the harbinger; and let us take this occasion to sing our palinode on the subject of *Endymion*. We certainly did not* discover in that poem the same degree of merit that its more clear-sighted and prophetic admirers did. We did not foresee the unbounded popularity which has carried it through we know not how many editions; which has placed it on every table; and, what is still more unequivocal, familiarized it in every mouth. All this splendour of fame, however, though we had not the sagacity to anticipate, we have the candour to acknowledge; and we request that the publisher of the new and beautiful edition of Keats's works now in the press, with graphic illustrations by Calcott and Turner, will do us the favour and the justice to notice our conversion in his prolegomena.

Warned by our former mishap, wiser by experience, and improved, as we hope, in taste, we have to offer Mr Tennyson our tribute of unmingled approbation.

[After quoting freely from Tennyson, Croker comments:]

these are beauties which, we do not fear to say, equal anything even in Keats.

* See *Quarterly Review*, vol. xix, p. 204 [i.e. No. 16].

48. A misleading textbook account

1834

Entry 'Keats' in Allan Cunningham's *Biographical and Critical History of the British Literature of the Last Fifty Years*, Paris, 1834, 102–4.

Of John Keats no memoir has been written—which is mentioned to the reproach of good friends and gifted ones, who survive him. He was a native of London, and was born in 1796: he received a good education, and when young, chose the profession of a surgeon, which induced critics to reproach him with walking the hospitals. He gave early indications of courting the muse, and when under twenty, published a singular poem called *Endymion*, which his admirers describe as filled with noble fancies, and dreamy and delightful. His *Hyperion* and other works are less mystical; but they have all more or less of the obscure and the dark, save a remarkably fine fragment, called 'The Eve of St Agnes,' founded on an inland tradition, which says, he that dares to stand at the church-yard gate on that eve, will see all the individuals who are in the following year to die, come trooping to the burial ground, in the order in which they will be buried. The Editor of the *Quarterly Review* happened to be looking out for a victim, when the works of Keats appeared: the stern son of Crispin forgot the arts which caused himself to rise, and, what was worse, overlooked the manifold beauties of the poems—he saw nothing but folly and fine words. To such a review, there was no other mode of reply but a horsewhip or a brace of pistols; and Keats had courage fit for anything: but long before the review appeared, a consumption had begun to sap the functions of life, and the young poet had, in the homely but expressive phrase, 'taken death to him.' A warmer climate was recommended, and he went to Italy; but the sunshine and balmy air of that land, which continues health to the slavish and the undeserving, wrought no change in Keats: he drooped and died, and was buried in the stranger's ground, as consecrated earth must not be polluted with the dust of a heretic.

49. A commentary on two poems

1835, 1844

Hunt opened his *London Journal* for 21 January 1835 (the anniversary of St Agnes) by observing: 'The reader should give us three pearls, instead of three half-pence, for this number of our Journal, for it presents him with the *whole* of Mr Keats's beautiful poem ['The Eve of St Agnes']—to say nothing of our loving commentary.' Despite some tendency to preach or rhapsodize, the importance of this commentary, (a), must not be underrated: it is the first systematic discussion of a poem by Keats, and it shows much sensitive understanding of the way his poetry works, as well as psychological insight.

For his *Imagination and Fancy* nine years later, Hunt reprinted the commentary on 'The Eve of St Agnes' with only minor changes, but also prefixed a general criticism of Keats and appended short passages on the 'Ode to a Nightingale' and 'On First Looking into Chapman's Homer'. The first two of these additions are given below as Extracts (b) and (c).

(a) Article on 'The Eve of St Agnes':

[Quotes 'Eve of St Agnes', stanza 1, italicizing lines 2 and 7.]

'What a complete feeling of winter-time is here, together with an intimation of those Catholic elegancies, of which we are to have more in the poem!

> The owl, with all his feathers, was a-cold.

Could he have selected an image more warm and comfortable in itself, and, therefore, better contradicted by the season? We feel the plump, feathery bird in his nook, shivering in spite of his natural household warmth, and staring out at the strange weather. The hare cringing through the chill grass is very piteous, and the "silent flock" very patient; and how quiet and gentle, as well as winterly, are all these

K

circumstances, and fit to open a quiet and gentle poem! The breath of the pilgrim, likened to "pious incense," completes them, and is a simile in admirable "keeping," as the painters call it; that is to say, is thoroughly harmonious in itself and with all that is going on. The breath of the pilgrim is visible, so is that of a censer; his object is religious, and so is the use of the censer; the censer, after its fashion, may be said to pray, and its breath, like the pilgrim's, ascends to heaven. Young students of poetry may, in this image alone, see what imagination is, under one of its most poetical forms, and how thoroughly it "tells." There is no part of it unfitting. It is not applicable in one point, and the reverse in another.

[Quotes stanza 2, italicizing lines 6 and 9.]

The germ of this thought, or something like it, is in Dante, where he speaks of the figures that perform the part of sustaining columns in architecture. Keats had read Dante in Mr Carey's translation, for which he had a great respect. He began to read him afterwards in Italian, which language he was mastering with surprising quickness. A friend of ours has a copy of Ariosto, containing admiring marks of his pen. But the same thought may have originally struck one poet as well as another. Perhaps there are few that have not felt something like it in seeing the figures upon tombs. Here, however, for the first time, we believe, in English poetry, is it expressed, and with what feeling and elegance! Most wintery as well as penitential is the word "aching," in "icy hoods and mails;" and most felicitous the introduction of the Catholic idea in the word "purgatorial." The very colour of the rails is made to assume a meaning, and to shadow forth the gloom of the punishment—

> *Imprisoned* in *black purgatorial* rails.

[Quotes stanza 3, italicizing '*Flatter'd*'.]

> *Flatter'd to tears* this aged man and poor.

This "flattered" is exquisite. A true poet is by nature a metaphysician; far greater in general than metaphysicians professed. He feels instinctively what the others get at by long searching. In this word "flattered" is the whole theory of the secret of tears; which are the tributes, more or less worthy, of self-pity to self-love. Whenever we shed tears, we take pity on ourselves; and we feel, if we do not consciously say so, that we deserve to have the pity taken. In many cases, the pity is just, and the self-love not to be construed unhandsomely. In many others, it is the reverse; and this is the reason why selfish people are so often found among the tear-shedders, and why they seem even to shed them for others. They imagine themselves in the situation of the others, as indeed the most generous must, before they can sympathize; but the generous console as well as weep. Selfish tears are avaricious of everything but themselves.

"Flatter'd to tears." Yes, the poor old man was moved, by the sweet music, to think that so sweet a thing was intended for his comfort as well as for others. He felt that the mysterious kindness of heaven did not omit even his poor, old, sorry case, in its numerous workings and visitations; and, as he wished to live longer, he began to think that his wish was to be attended to. He began to consider how much he had suffered—how much he had suffered wrongly or mysteriously—and how much better a man he was, with all his sins, than fate seemed to have taken him for. Hence, he found himself deserving of tears and self-pity, and he shed them, and felt soothed by his poor, old, loving self. Not undeservedly either; for he was a pains-taking pilgrim, aged, patient, and humble, and willingly suffered cold and toil, for the sake of something better than he could otherwise deserve; and so the pity is not exclusively on his own side: we pity him too, and would fain see him well out of that cold chapel, gathered into a warmer place than a grave. But it was not to be. We must, therefore, console ourselves with knowing, that this icy endurance of his was the last, and that he soon found himself at the sunny gate of heaven.

[Quotes stanza 4, italicizing '*silver snarling trumpets*', line 34, '*Stared*', and line 36; stanzas 5–6; stanza 7, italicizing line 56; stanza 8, '*Hoodwinked with faery fancy*'; stanzas 9–11; stanza 12, '*More tame for his grey hairs*'; stanza 13, '*in a little moonlight room, Pale, latticed, chill*'.]

The poet does not make his "little moonlight room" comfortable, observe. The high taste of the exordium is kept up. All is still wintery. There is to be no comfort in the poem but what is given by love. All else may be willingly left to the cold walls.

[Quotes stanza 14; stanza 15, italicizing lines 127, 130–1, '*Tears*', and line 135.]

He almost shed tears—of sympathy, to think how his treasure is exposed to the cold—and of delight and pride to think of her sleeping beauty, and her love for himself. This passage "asleep in lap of legends old" is in the highest imaginative taste, fusing together the tangible and the spiritual, the real and the fanciful, the remote and the near. Madeline is asleep in her bed; but she is also asleep in accordance with the legends of the season; and therefore the bed becomes *their* lap as well as sleep's. The poet does not critically think of all this; he feels it: and thus should other young poets draw upon the prominent points of their feelings on a subject, sucking the essence out of them into analogous words, instead of beating about the bush for *thoughts*, and, perhaps, getting very clever ones, but confused—not the best, nor any one better than another. Such, at least, is the difference between the truest poetry and the degrees beneath it.

[Quotes stanza 16, italicizing '*came, like a full-blown rose*'; stanza 17, '*ruffian-passion*'; stanza 18, '*church-yard*'; stanza 19.]

What he means by Merlin's "monstrous debt," we cannot say. Merlin, the famous enchanter, obtained King Uther his interview with the fair Iogerne; but though the son of a devil, and conversant with the race, we are aware of no debt that he owed them.

[Quotes stanza 20; stanza 21, italicizing '*silken, hush'd, and chaste*'; stanza 22; stanza 23, italicizing lines 200, 204–7.]

Its little smoke, in pallid moonshine, died,

is a verse in the taste of Chaucer, full of minute grace and truth. The smoke of the waxen taper seems almost as etherial and fair as the moonlight, and both suit each other and the heroine. But what a lovely line is the seventh, about the heart,

Paining with eloquence her balmy side!

And the nightingale! how touching the simile! the heart a "tongueless nightingale," dying in that dell of the bosom. What thorough sweetness, and perfection of lovely imagery! How one delicacy is heaped upon another! But for a burst of richness, noiseless, coloured, suddenly enriching the moonlight, as if a door of heaven were opened, read the following:—

[Quotes stanza 24, all italicized, 'TWILIGHT' and 'BLUSH'D' in capitals.]

Could all the pomp and graces of aristocracy, with Titian's and Raphael's aid to boot, go beyond the rich religion of this picture, with its "twilight saints," and its 'scutcheons "blushing with the blood of queens?" But we must not stop the reader:—

[Quotes stanza 25, italicizing '*gules*', lines 220–2, and '*a splendid angel, newly drest, Save wings, for heaven*'.]

The lovely and innocent creature, thus praying under the gorgeous painted window, completes the exceeding and unique beauty of this picture,—one that will for ever stand by itself in poetry, as an addition to the stock. It would have struck a glow on the face of Shakspeare himself. He might have put Imogen or Ophelia under such a shrine. How proper, as well as pretty, the heraldic term *gules*, considering the occasion. *Red* would not have been a fiftieth part so good. And with what elegant luxury he touches the "silver cross" with "amethyst," and the fair human hands with "rose-colours," the kin to their carnation! The lover's growing "faint" is one of the few inequalities which are to be found in the later productions of this great, but young and over-sensitive poet. He had, at the time of writing his poems, the seeds of a mortal illness in him, and he, doubtless, wrote as he had felt—for he was also deeply in love; and extreme sensibility struggled in him with a great understanding. But our picture is not finished:—

[Quotes stanza 26, italicizing '*warmed*', '*by degrees*', line 230, and '*like a mermaid in sea-weed*'.]

How true and cordial, the "*warmed* jewels," and what matter of fact also, made elegant, in the rustling downward of the attire; and the mixture of dress and undress, and dishevelled hair, likened to a "mermaid in sea-weed!" But the next stanza is perhaps the most exquisite in the poem.

[Quotes stanza 27, italicizing lines 239–42 and printing line 243 in capitals.]

Can the beautiful go beyond this? We never saw it. And how the imagery rises! Flown like a *thought*—Blissfully *haven'd*—Clasp'd like a missal in a land of *Pagans*: that is to say, where Christian prayer books must not be seen, and are, therefore, doubly cherished for the danger. And then, although nothing can surpass the preciousness of this idea, is the idea of the beautiful, crowning all—

> *Blinded* alike from sunshine and from rain,
> *As though a rose should shut, and be a bud again.*

Thus it is that poetry, in its intense sympathy with creation, may be said to create anew, rendering its words almost as tangible as the objects they speak of, and individually more lasting; the spiritual perpetuity putting them on a level (not to speak it profanely) with the fugitive substance.

But we are to have more luxuries still, presently.

[Quotes stanza 28, italicizing line 250; stanza 29, '*woven crimson, gold, and jet*'; stanza 30, '*an azure-lidded sleep*', line 267, '*and spiced dainties, every one, From silken Samarcand to cedar'd Lebanon*'.]

Here is delicate modulation, and super-refined epicurean nicety!

> Lucent syrups, tinct with cinnamon,

make us read the line delicately, and at the tip-end, as it were, of one's tongue.

[Quotes stanza 31, italicizing line 275; stanzas 32–5.]

Madeline is half-awake, and Porphyro reassures her with living, kind looks, and an affectionate embrace.

[Quotes stanzas 36–7; stanza 38, italicizing line 336.]

With what a pretty wilful conceit the *costume* of the poem is kept up in the third line about the shield! The poet knew when to introduce apparent trifles forbidden to those who are void of real passion, and who, feeling nothing intensely, can intensify nothing.

[Quotes stanza 39; stanza 40, italicizing line 360.]

This is a slip of the memory, for there were hardly carpets in those days. But the truth of the painting makes amends, as in the unchronological pictures of old masters.

[Quotes stanza 41; stanza 42, italicizing '*into the storm*'.]

Here endeth the young and divine Poet, but not the delight and gratitude of his readers; for, as he sings elsewhere—

> A thing of beauty is a joy for ever.'

(*Leigh Hunt's London Journal* (21 January 1835), ii, 17–20.)

(b) Extract from *Imagination and Fancy*: 'Keats was a born poet of the most poetical kind. All his feelings came to him through a poetical medium, or were speedily coloured by it. He enjoyed a jest as heartily as any one, and sympathized with the lowliest common-place; but the next minute his thoughts were in a garden of enchantment, with nymphs, and fauns, and shapes of exalted humanity;

> Elysian beauty, melancholy grace.

It might be said of him, that he never beheld an oak-tree without seeing the Dryad. His fame may now forgive the critics who disliked his politics, and did not understand his poetry. Repeated editions of him in England, France, and America, attest its triumphant survival of all obloquy; and there can be no doubt that he has taken a permanent station among the British Poets, of a very high, if not thoroughly mature, description.

Keats's early poetry, indeed, partook plentifully of the exuberance of youth; and even in most of his later, his sensibility, sharpened by mortal illness, tended to a morbid excess. His region is "a wilderness of sweets,"—flowers of all hue, and "weeds of glorious feature,"—where, as he says, the luxuriant soil brings

> The pipy hemlock to strange overgrowth.

But there also is the "rain-scented eglantine," and bushes of May-flowers, with bees, and myrtle, and bay,—and endless paths into forests haunted with the loveliest as well as gentlest beings; and the gods live in the distance, amid notes of majestic thunder. I do not say that no "surfeit" is ever there; but I do, that there is no end of the "nectared sweets." In what other English poet (however superior to him in other respects) are you so *certain* of never opening a page without lighting upon the loveliest imagery and the most eloquent expressions? Name one. Compare any succession of their pages at random, and see if the young poet is not sure to present his stock of beauty; crude it may be, in many instances; too indiscriminate in general; never, perhaps, thoroughly perfect in cultivation; but there it is, exquisite of its kind, and filling envy with despair. He died at five-and-twenty; he had not revised his earlier works, nor given his genius its last pruning. His *Endymion*, in resolving to be free from all critical trammels, had no versification; and his last noble fragment, *Hyperion*, is not faultless,—but it is nearly so. "The Eve of St Agnes" betrays morbidity only in one instance (noticed in the comment). Even in his earliest productions, which are to be considered as those of youth just emerging from boyhood, are to be found passages of as masculine a beauty as ever were written. Witness the "Sonnet on reading Chapman's Homer",—epical in the splendour and dignity of its images, and terminating with the noblest Greek simplicity. Among his finished productions, however, of any length, the "Eve of Saint Agnes" still appears to me the most delightful and complete specimen of his genius. It stands mid-way between his most sensitive ones (which, though of rare beauty, occasionally sink into feebleness) and the less generally characteristic majesty of the fragment of *Hyperion*. Doubtless his greatest poetry is to be found in *Hyperion*; and had he lived, there is as little doubt he would have written chiefly in that strain; rising superior to those languishments of love which made the critics so angry, and which they might so easily have pardoned at his time of life. But the "Eve of St Agnes" had already bid most of them adieu,—exquisitely loving as it is. It is young, but full-grown poetry of the rarest description; graceful as the beardless Apollo; glowing and gorgeous with the colours of romance. I have therefore reprinted the whole of it in the present volume, together with the comment alluded to in the Preface; especially as, in addition to felicity of treatment, its subject is in every respect a happy one, and helps to "paint" this our bower of "poetry with delight." Melancholy, it is true, will "break in" when the reader thinks of the early death of such a writer; but it is one of the benevolent provisions of nature, that all good things tend to pleasure in the recollection, when the bitterness of their loss is past, their own sweetness embalms them.

A thing of beauty is a joy for ever.

While writing this paragraph, a hand-organ out-of-doors has been playing one of the mournfullest and loveliest of the airs of Bellini—another genius who died young. The sound of music always gives a feeling either of triumph or tenderness to the state of mind in which it is heard: in this instance it seemed like one departed spirit come to bear testimony to another, and to say how true indeed may be the union of sorrowful and sweet recollections.

Keats knew the youthful faults of his poetry as well as any man, as the reader may see by the preface to *Endymion*, and its touching though manly acknowledgement of them to critical candour. I have this moment read it again, after a lapse of years, and have been astonished to think how any body could answer such an appeal to the mercy of strength, with the cruelty of weakness. All the good for which Mr Gifford pretended to be zealous, he might have effected with pain to no one, and glory to himself; and therefore all the evil he mixed with it was of his own making. But the secret at the bottom of such unprovoked censure is exasperated inferiority. Young poets, upon the whole, —at least very young poets,—had better not publish at all. They are pretty sure to have faults; and jealousy and envy are as sure to find them out, and wreak upon them their own disappointments. The critic is often an unsuccessful author, almost always an inferior one to a man of genius, and possesses his sensibility neither to beauty nor to pain. If he does,—if by any chance he is a man of genius himself (and such things have been), sure and certain will be his regret, some day, for having given pains which he might have turned into noble pleasures; and nothing will console him but that very charity towards himself, the grace of which can only be secured to us by our having denied it to no one.

Let the student of poetry observe, that in all the luxury of the "Eve of Saint Agnes" there is nothing of the conventional craft of artificial writers; no heaping up of words or similes for their own sakes or the rhyme's sake; no gaudy common-places; no borrowed airs of earnestness; no tricks of inversion; no substitution of reading or of ingenious thoughts for feeling or spontaneity; no irrelevancy or unfitness of any sort. All flows out of sincerity and passion. The writer is as much in love with the heroine as his hero is; his description of the painted window, however gorgeous, has not an untrue or superfluous word; and the only speck of a fault in the whole poem arises from an excess of emotion.' (*Imagination and Fancy* (1844), 312–17.)

(c) Extract from *Imagination and Fancy*: ' "*Ode to a Nightingale.*"— This poem was written in a house at the foot of Highgate Hill, on the border of the fields looking towards Hampstead. The poet had then his mortal illness upon him, and knew it. Never was the voice of death sweeter.

"*Charm'd magic casements,*" &c.—This beats Claude's "Enchanted Castle,"[1] and the story of King Beder in the *Arabian Nights*. You do not know what the house is, or where, nor who the bird. Perhaps a king himself. But you see the window, open on the perilous sea, and hear the voice from out the trees in which it is nested, sending its warble over the foam. The whole is at once vague and particular, full of mysterious life. You see nobody, though something is heard; and you know not what of beauty or wickedness is to come over that sea. Perhaps it was

[1] Keats was familiar with Claude Lorrain's romantic painting in a contemporary reproduction.

suggested by some fairy tale. I remember nothing of it in the dream-like wildness of things in *Palmerin of England*,[1] a book which is full of colour and home landscapes, ending with a noble and affecting scene of war; and of which Keats was very fond.' (page 344.)

50. A good half-poet

1840

Extracts from unsigned article entitled 'The Poets of England who have died young. No. III—John Keats', *Cambridge University Magazine* (March 1840), i, 213–28.

Although this article is written from somewhat rigid classical presuppositions, it is clear-headed, workmanlike, and well-illustrated. It reflects the hesitance of mid-century critics before finally accepting Keats as a major poet. Only the first three pages of the article, which were partly biographical, have been abridged.

John Keats, the subject of the following pages, has enjoyed a fluctuating reputation and a fluctuating notoriety. The notoriety of a man is the degree to which he is talked of in the world. The reputation of a man is something better—it is the character that the world gives him. Much, as being the friend of Shelley and Leigh Hunt, and more, as being the supposed victim of the *Quarterly Review*, has John Keats been, both by those who judge for themselves, and by those who are swayed by others, talked of and criticized, sneered at and panegyrized. He stood first before the public when the obnoxious Reviewers were at work on him. He stood again before the public when, under the title of *Adonais*, Shelley wrote over his ashes the finest elegy that poet ever sung over poet, or friend over friend. Beyond this, he has shared

[1] A Portuguese romance of chivalry (1544), which Keats had read in a recent English version (1807) by Robert Southey.

the fate of immature talent harshly put down, and of originality mistaken for affectation. . . .

Of late years so thoroughly have we been bothered with the enumeration of this influence and of that influence in the way of inspiring poetry, of the influence of Lake scenery, and of the influence of Scotch scenery, that we welcome the man who (like the honest Charles Lamb) can sing as sweetly from an office in Threadneedle Street, as from a cottage upon the Grampians. Much of this cant about the influences of the scenery around us, and about the inspirations of the face of Nature, comes from Scotland. . . .

We think, if Keats was a man of genius, he was not to be killed by a review; and that if he *was* killed by a review, he was not a man of genius. . . .

I hope I have not in too late a day touched the beautiful mythology of Greece.—This is an extract from the Preface to the *Endymion*, dated April 10, 1818. It cannot be too plainly laid down, that although the mythology of Greece may have first inspired Keats with poetry,—that although it may have furnished him with the subject-matter of his verses,—and that although it may have stood godfather to his poems, giving them the names of *Endymion* and *Hyperion*, it is in no degree the spirit of Greece, that the poetry of Keats represents. This is not said in the way of detraction. The beauties of the poems are not lessened by the circumstance of their not being of a Greek complexion. It is only the *criticism* of the bard that is demurred to.

This is no place for detailing the characteristics of classical poetry as opposed to the romantic—of the Gothic spirit as opposed to the Grecian. Greece, and the spirit of Greece, call up in our minds ideas of the Regular, the Formal, the Defined—of the expression of the visible beauties of the external world—of Harmony in arrangement, of Symmetry in form. Of things Gothic, the characteristic is the Indefinite. In Keats' poem nothing is Grecian but the title-page.

The fact that shews this is, that the images of Keats, beautiful as they often are, and taken from the world around us, (as is almost always the case with them,) are not so much poetical in and of themselves, as they are poetical because they exhibit the peculiarly sensitive and sympathetic mind of the writer. They seldom present to us a picture: they merely raise an impression. This is English rather than Greek. There is in the whole range of Athenian poetry little that reminds us of Keats. There is indeed in the whole range of Athenian poetry little descriptive of rural imagery, such as is found in the chorusses. Let it shock no one if we assert that, of the many characteristic beauties of those chorusses descriptive of rural scenery, *truth* is not one. They exhibit (like the poetry of Keats) rather the poetic sensibilities of the writer, than the face of Nature. Saying, then, that the poetry of Keats is not of a Grecian complexion, is perhaps too wide an assertion. It savours of a *section* of the Greek literature.

The fact is, that when the spirit of any literature differing from that of our mother-tongue comes upon us, it comes upon us not naturally, but by the way of study and thought. It comes as a secondary taste, and as a secondary habit of mind. The *primary* taste and the *primary* habit of mind is the habit that we gain from the land we live in, infused into us with the language of our nurses and mothers. Keats, dying young, had *not time* for the imbibition of a Greek spirit, even if his mind had been prepared for it.

To ascertain the merit of a poem is one thing: to determine the powers of a poet, is another. The present paper aims at the latter. Such being the case, the faults of Keats' poetry may be divided in two classes:—1. those of youth and inexperience; 2. those of deficiency of genius. Out of the former he might (had his life been spared) have grown: the latter he would have kept till his death-bed.

His crying fault is mannerism. Spenser is imitated indifferently: Leigh Hunt too well. The mischief, in the way of his thoughts, is *dilution*: the mischief, in the way of his language, is *incorrectness*: the mischief, in the way of his metres, is *licence overdone*. The writers of the school in question deal, one and all, with the subjects of their poetry in the same way. They tell at length what has already been told compendiously. They *expand*; and as they expand, *dilute*. Dante tells the story of Francesca di Rimini in fourscore lines: Leigh Hunt expands it into three cantos. The effect of this is the substitution of detail for (we use a pictorial phrase) *breadth*. But, mark, where there is no breadth, there is but little poetry.

The following illustrations of the language and the metre of Keats, as they are meant for specimens of his style, are all taken from one portion of his works—the first canto of *Endymion*.

Remark we now upon certain metrical peculiarities characteristic of the writers of the school in question. They, each and all, besides their lyrical measures, delight in the use of the common heroic couplet, the line of ten syllables, the metre of Pope and Dryden. Now, though their metre be that of the poets mentioned above, their versification is different. The heroic couplet of Pope and the heroic couplet of Keats are virtually distinct measures. That of the one is lax—that of the other concise, neat, and defined. The metre of Pope, normal and regular, may be considered the TYPE of the heroic couplet. Let us see what licences Pope denies himself, and Keats (with his school) indulges in.

I. In the time of Pope it was imputed as a fault if the sense closed otherwise than at the end of a couplet: lines such as these were inadmissible—

——They bound to us so fast,
That, whether there be shine, or gloom o'ercast,
They alway must be with us, or we die.
Therefore 'tis with full happiness that I
Will trace the story of Endymion.
The very music of his name hath gone
Into my being——

Versification like the following was admitted, but was not unexceptionable.

Until it came to some unfooted plains
Where fed the herds of Pan: ay, great his gains
Who thus one lamb did lose. Paths there were many,
Winding through palmy fern and rushes fenny.

II. It was bad for the rhyme to fall on an unaccented syllable—*e.g.*

Of their old piety, and of their glee,
In telling of this goodly company—

Such a couplet was objectionable: but it was still more so if the weak rhyme came first—*e.g.*

In telling of this goodly company,
Of their old piety, and of their glee.

In contradistinction, then, to the poets of Queen Anne's time, those of the present time (at least a section of them) indulge in lines that run into each other, and in unaccented rhymes. They differ in points of concatenation, and they differ in points of positive rhyme. Now which of the two styles is preferable? If we take up a Life of either Dryden or Pope, we shall find that before their times, the style of versification was (in the points in question) precisely as it is at present; that Chaucer and Ben Jonson used weak rhymes, and verses running into each other, just as Shelley and Keats do at present; and that the merit of Pope, Dryden, and Waller consisted in the fact of their having abolished these licenses, and of having introduced regularity in their stead. Such being the fact, one of two things is the case: either that our modern versification is the worst—or that Pope, Dryden, and Waller have been unjustly panegyrized. This deduction, however, although it bears the aspect of a dilemma, is scarcely a true one.

Chaucer and Ben Jonson differ from Shelley and Keats in this. Chaucer and B. Jonson wrote inharmoniously out of their ignorance of the laws of metre, and because the art of versification was imperfect; whereas, Shelley and Keats, knowing what rules have been established, and what metrical art teaches, taking what seems to them a higher view than the old metrists, write loosely upon system; for theirs is the negligence not of the boor, but of the sloven. Whether this negligence be graceful, is another question. Whether, also, (presuming that in a certain degree it is so,) it has not been carried too far, is a third point. Upon this we may expatiate anon. The question now to be asked is, how far the style in hand is a creation of our own times; or, in other words, how far the poets of the Georgian era have been the first whose ears (more musical than the ears that went before them) detected this *grace beyond the rules of art.* One poet, and one only, anterior not only to the times of Shelley, but to those of Dryden and Waller, do we at this moment remember, of whom it may be said that no point of this graceful negligence was unknown to him, and that whilst he wrote unsystematically, he wrote so *upon system.* There is no metrical grace in the writers of our own times that is not to be found in the *Faithful Shepherdess* of Fletcher.

Sins against accent—such are the following lines:—

——— Unmew
My soul, that I may dare, *in wayfaring,*
To stammer where old Chaucer used to sing—

Of some strange history, potent to send
A young mind from its bodily tenement.
Or they might watch the quoit-pitchers, intent
On either side; pitying the sad death
Of Hyacinthus—

The archers too, upon a wider plain,
Beside the feathery whizzing of the shaft,
And the dull twanging bow-string, and the raft
Branch down sweeping from a tall ash top,
Call'd up a thousand thoughts to envelope
Those who would watch—

How is the word *envelope* to be pronounced? If as a French word, then is there a sin against the language of England, and still more against the language of Poesy: if as an English one, then is there a sin against metre.

The faults of imperfection in the way of rhyme correspond—

> Who whispers him so pantingly and *close*?
> Peona, his sweet sister: of all *those*,
> His friends, the dearest—
>
> Nor do we merely feel these essences
> For one short hour: no, even as the trees—
>
> ——— to entice
> My stumbling down the monstrous precipice—
>
> No higher bard than simple maidenhood,
> Singing alone, and fearfully—how the blood
> Left his young cheek—
>
> ——— How a ring-dove
> Let fall a sprig of yew-tree in his path;
> And how he died: and then, that love doth scathe—
>
> ——— strands
> With horses prancing o'er them, palaces
> And towers of amethyst,—would I so tease
> My pleasant days—
> &c. &c.

No good poetry can be written where language is violated. It is the crying fault of the mannerist of the present days to coin new words. The language of the people of England is not like the Duke of Newcastle's tenantry. We cannot do what we choose with it, simply because it is our own. If we create new words, we must *coin*—not *forge* them. The words *milky* and *earthy* are good; the word *nervy* (in Keats) is bad. The reason of this is, that *nervy* is a hybrid or bastard word; the termination *y* being of Saxon, the noun *nerve* of Latin origin. If twenty words be coined, nineteen of them shall (as things go) be *hybrid*. Similarly, we may say *penetrable*, because the termination *ilis* and the verb *penetro* are both Latin. *Graspable*, however, we cannot *say*, because *grasp* is Saxon. Yet Keats writes *half-graspable*.

Language.—Simplicity is not the sole element of poetical language. A thought may be essentially vulgar. The language expressive of it may be the same. Of sins in the way of vulgarity, Keats has not a few—*e.g.*

Are not our lowing heifers sleeker than
Night-swollen mushrooms?

That linger'd in the air like dying rolls
Of abrupt thunder, when Ionian shoals
Of dolphins bob their noses through the brine.

——— So that a whispering blade
Of grass, a wailful gnat, a bee bustling
Down in the blue-bells, or a wren light rustling
Among sere leaves and twigs, might all be heard.

——— Our taintless rills
Seem'd sooty, and o'erspread with upturn'd gills
Of dying fish.

Occasionally there is, what the Greeks would call, Oxymoron, and the English, Nonsense: occasionally there is circumlocution combined with harshness,—*e.g.*

O magic sleep! O comfortable bird,
That broodest o'er the troubled sea of the mind
Till it is hush'd and smooth! O *unconfined*
Restraint! imprisoned liberty!—

Hereat Peona in their silver source,
Shut her pure *sorrow-drops*!—

When a word has not only a *common* but a *technical* sense, it is unpoetical to use it in the latter,—it is dangerous to use it with the former. Such are by their very nature excluded from the poet's vocabulary. Why is it that we can talk of the *sweet bean*, but not of the *sweet pea*,—of the *sweet acacia*, but not of the *sweet almond*? The reason is because the latter phrases raise in our minds ideas, not of fragrance and odour, but of horticulture and perfumery, of nurserymen and pomatum-sellers. Yet Keats wrote,

—— Ere yet the bees
Hum about globes of clover and *sweet peas*.

—— They danced to weariness,
And then in quiet circles did they press
The hillock turf, and caught the *latter end*
Of some strange history.

And soon it lightly dipt, and rose, and sank,
And dipt again with the *young couple's* weight.

Does not this savour of a wedding in a newspaper, rather than of the walk of a brother and sister in a poem?

Speaking of the Sun,

> When he doth lighten up the golden reins,
> And paces leisurely down amber plains
> His snorting four——

Do we not almost involuntarily add—*in hand*?

We state again, that all the quotations above are from a single part of a single poem—the first part of the *Endymion*. Such were the demerits of Keats' Poems, Volume II.

Now, upon the story of Endymion, others besides John Keats have written. Read we the *Monastery* of Sir Walter Scott, and therein the speeches of Percie Shafton. The language of these speeches is peculiar, high-flown, metaphorical, and (*pace Shaftoni dixerim*) absurd. Such as it was, it was called Euphuism. Now, John Lily, a poet of the age of Queen Elizabeth, was the inventor of Euphuism. The inventor of Euphuism was a dramatist. Amongst his dramas is the drama of *Endymion, or the Man in the Moon*, written, not like the work of Keats, in verse, but in plain homely (though not unpoetical) prose. The man that reads Lily's *Endymion* shall be gratified. In Hazlitt's Lectures on the Literature of Queen Elizabeth's reign are to be found copious extracts from it: in the Old British Drama is to be found the play itself.

The first of the poems of the third and last volume of his Works is 'Lamia'. The story is taken from an extract in Burton's *Anatomy of Melancholy*, from the *Life of the Sophist Apollonius*, by Philostratus. The facts were as follows:—A young man of the name of Lycius found a fair gentlewoman between Cenchreas and Corinth. With the fair gentlewoman he became enamoured. At last he made her his wife. As she had no friends of her own to invite to the wedding, she thought that she might beg for the exclusion of one of Lycius's, viz. the philosopher Apollonius. Apollonius, however, came uninvited and unwished for. He stared her out of countenance. She begged him to turn aside his eye. The more she begged, the stronger he stared. At length it turned out, not that she was (as the reader may possibly expect) a naughty woman, but a horrible serpent, a Lamia. 'Seeing herself descried, she, plate, house, and all that was in it, vanished in an instant. Many thousands took notice of this fact, for it was done in the midst of Greece.'*

* Burton's *Anatomy of Melancholy*, Part III. sect. 2.

There is something in the poem of 'Lamia' that recalls to our recollection Mr Coleridge's *Christabel*: there is something, also, in the opening of it, reminding us of Shelley's *Witch of Atlas*.

In 'Lamia', the poet waxes practical. His remarks savour of common sense and common life. *e.g.*

> Love in a hut, with water and a crust,
> Is—Love, forgive us!—cinders, ashes, dust;
> Love in a palace is perhaps at last
> More grievous torment than a hermit's fast.

Speaking of the supernatural charms of his serpentine heroine, he writes—

> Let the mad poets say whate'er they please
> Of the sweets of Fairies, Peris, Goddesses,
> There is not such a treat among them all,
> Haunters of cavern, lake, and waterfall,
> As a real woman, lineal indeed
> From Pyrrha's pebbles or old Adam's seed.

Byron thought the same, flesh and blood being compared not with spirit and air, but with chiselled stone:

> I've seen much finer women, ripe and real,
> Than all your beauties of the stone ideal.
>
> *Don Juan.*

The versification is evidently improved: it has gained in vigour.

> Her eyes in torture fix'd, and anguish drear,
> Hot, glazed, and wide, with *lid-lashes* all sear,
> Flash'd phosphor and sharp sparks, without one cooling tear.

Replace the prettyism *lid-lashes* by the plain word *eye-lashes*, and you have lines that Dryden might have written. Dryden, too, might have written the following:—

> ——— No more the stately music breathes;
> The myrtle sickened in a thousand wreaths.
> By faint degrees, voice, lute, and pleasure ceased;
> A deadly silence step by step increased;
> Until it seemed a horrid presence there,
> *And not a man but felt the terror in his hair.*

'The Pot of Basil' is from Boccaccio, a short tale, in the eight-line stanza of *Don Juan*: *simplex munditiis.*

'The Eve of St Agnes' is Spenserian,—at least in the matter of metre. Madeline is the heroine, Porphyro the hero of the tale, son and daughter, respectively, (like Romeo and Juliet,) of hereditary foemen. Now, the retainers of the father of the lady are no tea-totallers; so that Porphyro, taking advantage of this, fills them with Rhenish, and carries off the lady.

For the merits or demerits of *Hyperion*, the publisher (not the poet) is responsible. The work was given to the world at their particular request, and against the wishes of the author. Originally intended to be of the same length with *Endymion* (*i.e.* of four cantos), it was left unfinished, the two first books, and the opening of the third, being all that the author accomplished. Hyperion is a Titan, the last of the race, that wars against Jupiter; and this he does with the bitterness of spirit, and the strength of arm, of a ruined archangel. He is the Satan of the Earth-born. The merits of *Hyperion* are greater than the merits of *Endymion*: the metre (blank verse) is less lax, though not Miltonic, and the language more uniformly poetical.

Take we now, from the first volume of his Poems, the following extract:—

[Quotes 'In a drear-nighted December' in full—not, however, from 'the first volume of his Poems' (the poem was written in late autumn 1818) but from Galignani's edition.]

From Vol. II.

[Quotes *Endymion*, Book I, lines 34–57, 'Therefore, 'tis with full happiness' to 'when I make an end'; Book IV, lines 146–87, 'O Sorrow!' to 'cold as my fears'; Book IV, lines 273–90, 'Young stranger' to 'her wooer in the shade'.]

The second extract was given not so much on account of its poetical merits, as for insight it gives us into the feelings of a peculiarly sensitive mind united to a body physically weak, of whose gradual decay it was conscious, and of which it contemplated the speedy dissolution. Such a mind shrinks with feelings of repugnance (almost of fear) from the cold features of winter, in which it sees only the numb expression, and the wan complexion of death. To the summer it clings as to a kind consoling friend, and it feels life only so long as the summer smiles. Lines like those that have been quoted, express not only a feeling that has had a real place in the bosom of the writer, but one that can find a place in such bosoms only. Poetry inspired (as much poetry is inspired) by strong passions, grounded upon strong physical powers, can no more speak such language than the monk can speak the language of love. The poetry of Keats and the poetry of Kirke White derive many of their charms from one and the same cause.

From Vol. III.

MERCANTILE PRIDE.

Why were they proud? Because their marble founts
Gush'd with more pride than do a wretch's tears?—
Why were they proud? Because fair orange-mounts
Were of more soft ascent than lazar stairs?
Why were they proud? Because red-lined accounts
Were richer than the songs of Grecian years?
Why were they proud? again we ask aloud,
Why in the name of Glory were they proud?

'Isabella, or the Pot of Basil'

[Quotes 'Eve of St Agnes', stanzas 1–4; and *Hyperion*, Book I, lines 227–50, 'O dreams of day and night!' to 'take his throne again'.]

Something this of the Satan of Milton; something, too, of the Prometheus of Shelley; something, however, less than either.

The faults that have been stated above are deficiencies in the way of art. Out of these he might have grown. What, however, are the deficiencies of his genius—the faults out of which he would *not* have grown?

The elements of the poetical spirit are partly moral, partly intellectual. Of the intellectual ones—are command of imagery, command of language, knowledge of the heart of man, knowledge of the external world, and the sense of metrical harmony—of the moral ones, are passion and sensibility. The full poet has both classes of elements, and of each class all the elements. The half poet has one class only, or if both classes, each partially. Keats seems to have been a poet of the latter class. His elements were the moral ones; and of the moral one, sensibility. His preeminent characteristic was a section of the latter class of elements, and of the sections of that class it was not the highest; for, though the poetry of pure sensibility is good, the poetry of pure passion is better. For all this the poetry of Keats is good, and is good because it has one true element: it were better had it more—it is well that it has so much.

51. Elizabeth Barrett Browning on Keats

1841, 1842, 1844, 1856

Elizabeth Barrett Barrett (1806–61), poet and scholar, was treated as a permanent invalid before her romantic elopement with Robert Browning in 1846. Her view of Keats's influence on contemporary poets and their readers is also represented by the next extract (No. 52).

(a) Extract from letter, 27 October 1841, to Mary Russell Mitford: 'Keats—yes—Keats—*he was* a poet. That Jove is recognized by his Thunder. A true true poet, from his first words to his last, when he said he "felt the daisies growing over him." Poor Keats! Do you know, did I ever tell you, that Mr Horne was at school with him, and that they were intimate friends? "The divine Keats"—he says of him—and will not hear the common tale, which I for one thought deteriorative to the dead poet's memory, that he suffered himself to be slain outright and ingloriously by the *Quarterly* reviewer's tomahawk. No, said Mr Horne to me once—"He was already bending over his grave in sweet and solemn contemplation, when the satyrs *hoofed* him into it!" ' (*Elizabeth Barrett to Miss Mitford*, ed. Betty Miller, 1954, 93.)

(b) Extract from letter, 28 December 1842, to Hugh Stuart Boyd: 'My not having recognized them [Keats and Shelley] as poets in your presence, was a mere accident of omission—I love and admire them as poets.' (*Elizabeth Barrett to Mr Boyd*, ed. B. P. McCarthy, 1955, 257.)

(c) Extract from letter [August 1844] to John Kenyon: '. . . agree with me in reverencing that wonderful genius *Keats*, who, rising as a grand exception from among the vulgar herd of juvenile versifiers, was an individual *man* from the beginning, and spoke with his own voice, though surrounded by the yet unfamiliar murmur of antique echoes. Leigh Hunt calls him "the young poet" very rightly.' (*The Letters of Elizabeth Barrett Barrett*, ed. F. G. Kenyon, 1897, i. 188.)

(d) Extract from 'A Vision of Poets', published in *Poems* (1844). An angel exhibits a line of 'God's prophets of the Beautiful', including poets of all nations and ages,

'And Keats the real
Adonis, with the hymeneal

Fresh vernal buds half sunk between
His youthful curls, kissed straight and sheen
In his Rome-grave, by Venus queen.'

(e) Extract from *Aurora Leigh* (1856), Book I, lines 1004–20:

'By Keats's soul, the man who never stepped
In gradual progress like another man,
But, turning grandly on his central self,
Ensphered himself in twenty perfect years
And died, not young (the life of a long life
Distilled to a mere drop, falling like a tear
Upon the world's cold cheek to make it burn
For ever); by that strong excepted soul,
I count it strange and hard to understand
That nearly all young poets should write old,
That Pope was sexagenary at sixteen,
And beardless Byron academical,
And so with others. It may be perhaps
Such have not settled long and deep enough
In trance, to attain to clairvoyance,—and still
The memory mixes with the vision, spoils,
And works it turbid.'

52. 'Orion' Horne on Keats

1844

Extract from essay 'Alfred Tennyson' in *A New Spirit of the Age* (1844), edited by R. H. Horne, ii. 7–11.

Richard Hengist Horne (1803–84), 'a combination of the troubadour and the prize-fighter', turned to writing after a colourful early life which had ranged from hitting Keats with a snowball to serving in the Mexican navy. Between 1839 and 1846 he corresponded with the future Mrs Browning, who was his principal collaborator in the writing of *A New Spirit of the Age*. His nickname arose from his authorship of *Orion, an Epic Poem* (1840), known as 'the farthing epic' because it was first sold at that price as a publicity stunt. Miss Barrett told Horne (7 July 1843) that one of the early readers of *Orion* (John Kenyon) had found in it 'the same sort of pleasure as from Keats's *Endymion* or *Hyperion*; and what particularly charmed him was the versification.'

The essay on Tennyson was written by Horne with (unspecified) interpolations added by Miss Barrett.

A very striking remark was made in *The Times* (December 26th 1842), with reference to the fate and progress of true poets in the mind of the public. Alluding to 'the noble fragment of *Hyperion*,' the writer says, 'Strange as it may appear, it is no less certain that the half-finished works of this young, miseducated, and unripe genius, have had the greatest influence on that which is now the popular poetry. In the eyes of the "young England" of poets, as in those of Shelley—

> The soul of Adonais, like a star,
> Beacons from the abode where the immortals are.'

'What a text,' pursues the same writer, 'for a dissertation on the mutability of popular taste!' True indeed; but we must not be tempted into it, at present. Objecting to the expressions of 'miseducated' and 'unripe,' as only applicable to the errors in *Endymion* and his earlier poems; and to 'half-finished' as only applicable (we believe this is correct?) to *Hyperion*, there can be no sort of doubt of the influence. But there is this peculiarity attached to it, one which stands alone in the history, certainly of all modern influences. It is, that he has not had a single mechanical imitator. There is an excellent reason for this. A mechanical imitation of style, or by choice of similar subjects, would not bear any resemblance to Keats; no one would recognize the intended imitation. When somebody expressed his surprise to Shelley, that Keats, who was not very conversant with the Greek language, could write so finely and classically of their gods and goddesses, Shelley replied 'He *was* a Greek.' . . . The writings of Keats are saturated and instinct with the purest inspiration of poetry; his mythology is full of ideal passion; his divinities are drawn as from 'the life,' nay, from their inner and essential life; his enchantments and his 'faery land' are exactly like the most lovely and truthful records of one who has been a dweller among them and a participator in their mysteries; and his descriptions of pastoral scenery, are often as natural and simple as they are romantic, and tinged all over with ideal beauty. Admitting all the faults, errors in taste, and want of design in his earliest works, but laying our hands with full faith upon his 'Lamia', 'Isabella,' 'The Eve of St Agnes,' the four 'Odes' in the same collection, and the fragment of *Hyperion*, we unhesitatingly say that there is no poet, ancient or modern, upon whom the title of 'Divine' can be more appropriately conferred than upon Keats. While the 'Satanic School' was in its glory, it is no great wonder that Wordsworth should have been a constant laughing-stock, and Keats an object for contemptuous dismissal to the tomb. It must, however, be added that the marked neglect of the public towards the latter has continued down to the present day. The pure Greek wine of Keats has been set aside for the thin gruel of Kirk White. But if there be faith in the pure Ideal, and in the progress of intelligence and refinement, the ultimate recognition of Keats by the public will certainly follow that of the 'fit audience' which he will ever continue to possess. Of all the numerous imitators of Lord Byron, not one now remains. And this may be mentioned as a quiet commentary upon his supercilious fling at the superior genius of John Keats.

How it should happen that the influencer of so many spirits of the present time should himself have been left to the ecstatic solitude of his own charmed shores and 'faery lands forlorn,' while those very spirits have each and all of them made some passage for themselves into the public mind, is one of those problems which neither the common fate of originators, the obduracy or caprice of the public, the clinging poison of bygone malice and depreciation, nor the want of sufficient introduction and championship on the part of living appreciators, can furnish a perfectly satisfactory solution. Such, however, is the fact at this very time.

We have said that Keats has had no imitators; of what nature, then, has been his influence upon the poetry of the present day? It has been spiritual in its ideality; it has been classical in its revivification of the forms and images of the antique, which he inspired with a new soul; it has been romantic in its spells, and dreams, and legendary associations; and it has been pastoral in its fresh gatherings from the wild forests and fields, and as little as possible from the garden, and never from the hot-house and the flower-shows. His imagination identified itself with the essences of things, poetical in themselves, and he acted as the interpreter of all this, by words which eminently possess the prerogative of expressive form and colour, and have a sense of their own by which to make themselves understood. Who shall imitate these peculiarities of genius? It is not possible. But kindred spirits will always recognize the voice from other spheres, will hail the 'vision, and the faculty divine,' come from whom it may, will have their own inherent impulses quickened to look into their own hearts, and abroad upon nature and mankind, and to work out the purposes of their souls.

How much of the peculiar genius of Keats is visible in Alfred Tennyson, must have been apparent to all those who are familiar with their writings; and yet it is equally certain that Tennyson, so far from being an imitator of any one, is undoubtedly one of the most original poets that ever lived.

53. An American dialogue on Keats

1845

Extract from J. R. Lowell's *Conversations on Some of the Old Poets*, Cambridge, Mass., 1845, 101–17.

James Russell Lowell (1819–91), poet, essayist, and diplomat, became Professor of Modern Languages at Harvard in 1855, and was Ambassador to England in the 1880s. Lowell's eventual eminence was such that his approval gave Keats the same sort of official *cachet* in America that Milnes's *Life* gave in England. His criticism is more elegant than profound; but here and in No. 66 he stresses the freshness and rightness of Keats's use of language. 'Keats rediscovered the delight and wonder that lay enchanted in the dictionary.' This dialogue was re-cast from a version in *The Boston Miscellany* (1842).

Philip

Keats and Tennyson are both masters of description, but Keats had the finer ear for all the nice analogies and suggestions of sound, while his eye had an equally instinctive rectitude of perception in color. Tennyson's epithets suggest a silent picture; Keats' the very thing itself, with its sound or stillness. . . . But if Tennyson's mind be more sensitive, Keats' is grander and of a larger grasp. It may be a generation or two before there comes another so delicate thinker and speaker as Tennyson; but it will be centuries before another nature so spontaneously noble and majestic as that of Keats, and so tender and merciful, too, is embodied. What a scene of despair is that of his, where Saturn finds the vanquished Titans!

Scarce images of life, one here, one there,
Lay vast and edgeways, like a dismal cirque
Of Druid-stones upon a forlorn moor,
When the chill rain begins at shut of eve,
In dull November——

And what can be more perfect than this?

> So far her voice flowed on, like timorous brook,
> That, lingering along a pebbled coast,
> Doth fear to meet the sea; but sea it met,
> And shuddered; for the overwhelming voice
> Of huge Enceladus swallowed it in wrath:
> The ponderous syllables, like sullen waves
> In the half-glutted hollows of reef-rocks,
> Came booming thus.

John

The world is not yet aware of the wonderful merit of Keats. Men have squabbled about Chatterton, and written lives of Kirke White, while they have treated with contempt the rival, and, I will dare to say, the sometimes superior, of Milton. The critics gravely and with reverence hold up their bit of smoked glass between you and the lantern at a kite's tail, and bid you behold the sun, undazzled; but their ceremonious fooleries will one day be as ridiculous as those of the Tahitian priests. Keats can afford to wait, and he will yet be sacred to the hearts of all those who love the triumphs and ovations of our noble mother-tongue.

Philip

I must please myself with one more quotation from his *Hyperion*. After the murmur among the Titans at Saturn's entrance has ceased,

> Saturn's voice therefrom
> Grew up like organ, that begins anew
> Its strain, when other harmonies *stopped short,*
> *Leave the dinned air vibrating silverly.*

Could sound and sense harmonize more fitly? In reading it, the voice flows on at first smoothly and equably. At the end of the third verse, it pauses abruptly in spite of itself, and in the last vibrates and wavers in accordance with the meaning. You see the art with which the word 'vibrating' is placed so as to prevent you from reading the verse monotonously. Among the ancient poets, I can detect none of the nice feeling of language which distinguishes many of our own. . . .

I fear that I have spoken too harshly of the letter *s*. It often adds much to the expression of a verse,—in the word 'silence,' for example. It is only by the contrast of some slight noise that we can appreciate silence.

A solitude is never so lonely as when the wind sighs through it. This is suggested to the ear, and so to the imagination, by the sound of the word. Keats, therefore, did well in bringing together such a cohort of *s*-s in the opening of his *Hyperion*:

> Deep in the *s*hady *s*tillne*ss* of a vale,
> Far *s*unken from the healthy breath of morn,
> Far from the fiery noon and eve'*s* one *s*tar,
> *S*at gray-haired *S*aturn, *s*ilent a*s* a *s*tone,
> *S*till a*s* the *s*ilen*c*e round about hi*s* lair.

Do you not feel it? The whole passage, for some distance farther on, is full of this sighing melody, and so impresses me with its utter loneliness and desertion, that, after repeating it to myself when alone, I am relieved to hear the companionable flicker of the fire, or the tinkling fall of an ember.

54. Gilfillan on Keats

1845, 1850, 1854

The Revd. George Gilfillan (1813–78), whose literary activities were tireless, was a Scottish protégé of 'Christopher North'. The first of his 'Portraits' appeared in the *Dumfries Herald* in 1844. His essay on Keats, (a), is given complete except for the first seven pages, which have argued that men of genius are not, as commonly supposed, *always* afflicted by indolence, poverty, or unhappiness.

(a) Extract from article 'John Keats': 'Not unbefitting are these remarks, for at least the sake of contrast, to introducing to us John Keats, the hapless apothecary's boy. Seldom were circumstances less propitious to the growth of genius than those in which this fine spirit was reared. Michael Bruce had Lochleven and its romantic shores to awaken his vein of verse: Chatterton the inspiring environs of Bristol; Kirke

White the placid richness of Nottinghamshire; Keats nothing but the scenery of his own soul! Transient and occasional were his glimpses of nature, but what a load of impression did he carry away with him! A mere boy, he seems an old acquaintance of nature, as if he had seen and studied her features in an antenatal state. His sense of beauty has been well called a disease. Whether, as De Quincey says of Wordsworth, his eye had more than a common degree of organic pleasure from the shows of earth and air, we cannot tell; but to us it appears as if the hue of the tulip were richer and more luscious, and the colour of the "gold cloud metropolitan" more intensely lustrous, and the smell of the bean-flower more arrowy in its odour, and the note of the nightingale more suggestive and sweet, and the shade of the pines productive of a diviner horror to him than to others, even of the inspired sons and daughters of mankind. We find scarcely any where but in his verse and in the minor poems of Milton such lingering luxury of descriptive beauty—such a literal, yet ideal translation of nature. Scarcely second to this painful and torturing sense of the beautiful, which detained and rivetted his young soul to all that was lovely in idealism or reality, was his feeling of the most Eschylean shape of the sublime. He contrived, even through the thin and scraggy pipe of translation, to suck out the genuine spirit of the Grecian drama. The rough mantle, with its studs of gold, which the author of *Prometheus Vinctus* wore so proudly, fell on, without crushing, the Cockney boy! And then, a glorious truant, he turned aside into the heart of the wilderness of the Titans, and saw here Prometheus writhing on his rock, and yonder, in the shady sadness of a vale, "gray-haired Saturn, quiet as a stone;" below "Coeus, and Gyges, and Briareus, Typhon, and Dolor, and Porphyrion, with many more, the brawniest in assault, pent up in regions of laborious breath;" and above "blazing Hyperion on his orbed throne;" here Thea, leaning over the discrowned deity, with "parted lips and posture motionless, like natural sculpture in cathedral cavern;" and there Apollo, in the pangs of his divine birth, as "knowledge enormous makes a god of him." And seeing all this, and shrieking out his last word, "celestial," the pale youth died.

Hyperion is the greatest of poetical Torsos. "Left untold," like *Cambuscan*[1] and *Christabel*, and Burns' speech of Liberty, it is perhaps better that it remains a fragment. Had only the two first Books of *Paradise Lost* come down to us, we question if they had not impressed us with a higher opinion of the author's powers than the completed

[1] Chaucer's *Squire's Tale*.

work. Such magnificent mutilations are regarded with a complex emotion, composed of admiration, expectation, and regret. Short and sustained, they seldom tire or disappoint. And the poem itself is so bold in its conception, so true to the genuine classical spirit, so austerely statuesque in its still or moving figures, so antique to awfulness in its spirit, and, above all, indicates a rise so rapid and so great from his other works, as from Richmond-hill to an Alp, that those who love not Keats are compelled to admire *Hyperion*. It is, says Byron, "as sublime as Eschylus."

Endymion is the dyspeptic dream of a boy of genius. Steeped in Spenserian imagination, it is, on the other hand, stuffed with affectations and poornesses, and pure sillyisms of fancy, thought and language, almost incredible. Yet is there a beseeching innocence in its very weakness, which, while the imagination and beauty of parts ought to have commanded the admiration, might have awakened the pity of the harshest critic. Like a boy lost in a wide wood, who now shrieks for terror under the hollow shade, now shouts for joy as he gains an eminence whence he commands a far view over the surging tree-tops, now weeps aloud as he loses a path which promised to conduct him homewards, or as he stumbles into a morass, now plucks a wild flower or a bunch of blae-berries, and now defiles his hands by the merest fungus—so is Keats led astray through the tangled woodland of the Grecian Mythology, and *Endymion* is precisely such a "boy's progress." Brutal the beadle, who, meeting such a bewildered child, should, notwithstanding the eloquence of his bright eyes, profuse and beauteous hair, bleeding hands and trickling tears, avenge his wanderings by the lash. And surely cruel the *Quarterly* critic, who stripped, and striped, and cut, and branded the muse's Son.

"Isabella" is a versification of one of Boccacio's finest stories; but on the simple thread of the narrative Keats has suspended some of his own richest gems. The story is that of two lovers who loved "not wisely but too well." The brothers of the maiden, seducing the youth away under the guise of a journey, kill and bury him in the forest. Isabella, after long watching, and weeping, and uncertainty as to his fate, is warned of it in a dream, and, repairing to the forest where her true love lies, digs up his head, and hides it in a pot of sweet basil, over which she prays and weeps out her heart incessantly. Her cruel kinsmen, finding out the secret, remove the basil-pot, banish themselves, and their sister pines away. The story is told with exquisite simplicity, pathos, and those quiet quaint touches so characteristic of the author. Two expressions, instinct with poetry, cling to our memories. They occur in the same stanza.

> So the two brothers and their *murdered man*
> Rode past fair Florence to where Arno's stream
> Gurgles through straitened banks.
>
> ——— Sick and wan
> The brothers' faces in the ford did seem—
> Lorenzo's flush with love—they passed the water
> Into a forest *quiet for the slaughter.*

What an awful leap forward of imagination in the first line! Florence saw no gore on Lorenzo's garments as he rode by; but the guilty eye of the brothers, and the purged eye of the poet, saw it all bedropped with gouts of blood—the deed already done—the man murdered. No spectre bestriding spectre-steed, no fiend mounted on black charger, joining a solitary traveller at twilight among trackless woods, was ever such a terrible companion as to the two brothers and to us is the murdered man—his own apparition. And then, how striking the contrast between the wan, sick, corpse-like faces of the brothers and his, shining with the rose-hue of love! They enter an old forest, not swinging its dark cones in the tempest, but "quiet for the slaughter," as if supernaturally hushed for the occasion, as if by a special decree prepared and predestined to the silence of that hour, as if dumbly sympathizing through all its red trunks and black rounded tops, with the "deed without a name."

Much more gorgeous in style, and colouring, and breathing a yet more intensely poetical spirit, is "St Agnes' Eve." It is a dream within a dream. Its every line wears *couleur de rose.* A curious feature of Keats' mind was its elegant effeminacy. No poet describes dress with more gust and beauty. Witness his picture of Madeline kneeling at her devotions, and seeming, in the light of the painted window, "a splendid angel, newly dressed, save wings, for heaven," or "trembling in her soft and chilly nest," after having freed her hair from her "wreathed pearls," "unclasped her warmed jewels," "loosened her fragrant boddice," and,

> by degrees,
> Her rich attire creeps rustling to her knees.

None save Keats, and Tennyson after him, has adventured on the delicate yet lovely theme, the poetry of dress; a subject which, artificial as it is, is capable, in chaste and tender hands, of the most imaginative treatment. Who, following in their footsteps, shall write the rhymed history of dress, from the first reeking lion-hide worn by a warrior of the infant world, down through the coloured skins of the Picts, the flowing toga of the ancients, the "garb of old Gaul," the turban of the Turks, the picturesque attire of the American Indians, the gorgeous vestments of God's ancient people, the kilt, the trews, and the plaid of Caledonia, the sandal or symar, or cloak, or shawl, or head-dress of various ages, to the great-coat of the modern Briton, who, in the description of Cowper, is

> An honest man, close buttoned to the chin,
> Broad-cloth without, and a warm heart within.

The finest of Keats' smaller pieces are, "Lines written on Chapman's Homer," (the only translation which gives the savageism, if not the sublimity of Homer—his wild beasts muzzling and maddening in their fleshy fury, and his heroes "red-wat-shod," and which, in its original folio, Charles Lamb is said once to have kissed in his rapturous appreciation); the "Ode to a Nightingale," or rather to its voice, "singing of summer in full-throated ease;" the "Ode to a Grecian Urn," elegant as that "sylvan historian itself," (what a sigh for eternity in its description of the pair of pictured lovers, whom he congratulates

> that ever thou wilt love, and she be fair;)

the "Ode to Autumn" "sitting careless on a granary floor," "her hair soft-lifted by the winnowing wind;" and the dewy sonnet beginning—

> Happy is England, I could be content
> To see no other verdure but its own.

In originality Keats has seldom been surpassed. His works "rise like an exhalation." His language had been formed on a false system; but, ere he died, was clarifying itself from its more glaring faults, and becoming copious, clear, and select. He seems to have been averse to all speculative thought, and his only creed, we fear, was expressed in the words—

> Beauty is truth,—truth beauty.

His great defect lay in the want, not of a man-like soul or spirit, but of a man-like constitution. His genius lay in his body like sun-fire in a dewdrop, at once beautifying and burning it up. Griffin, the author of the *Collegians*, describes him (in deep consumption the while) hanging over the fatal review in the *Quarterly* as if fascinated, reading it again and again, sucking out every drop of the poison. Had he but had the resolution, as we have known done in similar circumstances, of dashing it against the wall, or kicking it into the fire! Even Percival Stockdale could do this to *The Edinburgh Review* when it cut up his *Lives of the English Poets*; and John Keats was worth many millions of him. But disappointment, disease, deep love, and poverty, combined to unman him. Through his thin materialism he "felt the daisies growing over him." And in this lowly epitaph did his soaring ambitions terminate:—"Here lies one whose name was writ in water." But why mourn over his fate when the lamentation of all hearts has been already enshrined in the verse of "Alastor?" Let *Adonais* be at once his panegyric and his mausoleum.'

[Quotes from stanzas 45–6 of Shelley's *Adonais.*]

(*A Gallery of Literary Portraits*, 1845, 372–85.)

(b) '. . . the occasional languor, the luxury of descriptive beauty, the feminine tone, the tender melancholy, the grand aspirations, perpetually checked and chilled by the access of morbid weakness, and the mannerisms of style which distinguish Keats.' (*A Second Gallery of Literary Portraits*, 1850, 216.)

(c) 'Keats . . . the purest specimen of the ideal—a ball of beautiful foam, "cut off from the water," and not adopted by the air . . .' (Ibid. 284.)

(d) Gilfillan has been saying that Shelley's *Prometheus Unbound* is not as good as Aeschylus, and adds: 'Nor has it the massive strength, the piled-up gold and gems, the barbaric but kingly magnificence of Keats' *Hyperion*'. (*A Third Gallery of Literary Portraits*, 1854, 499.)

55. De Quincey on Keats

1846, 1857

Thomas De Quincey (1785–1859) is best known for his *Confessions of an Opium-Eater* (1821) and *Recollections of the Lake Poets* (1834–40). His rather febrile style and catty manner both influenced later prose-writers, and he begins his discussion of Keats's poetry by asserting that Keats was not really interested in 'the great moving realities of life'. His first reaction to Keats's language in *Endymion* represents an irritably extreme case of the familiar 'classical' objections. Extract (a) runs from after the first three pages of the article, which dismiss the story that Keats was killed by a review, to the end. The footnote, (b), was added when the article was reprinted eleven years later.

(a) Extract from signed article 'Notes on Gilfillan's "Gallery of Literary Portraits." John Keats': 'As a man, and viewed in relation to social objects, Keats was nothing. It was as mere an affectation when he talked with apparent zeal of liberty, or human rights, or human prospects, as is the hollow enthusiasm which many people profess for music, or most poets for external nature. For these things Keats fancied that he cared; but in reality he cared not at all. Upon them, or any of their aspects, he had thought too little, and too indeterminately, to feel for them as personal concerns. Whereas Shelley, from his earliest days, was mastered and shaken by the great moving realities of life, as a prophet is by the burden of wrath or of promise which he has been commissioned to reveal. Had there been no such thing as literature, Keats would have dwindled into a cipher. Shelley, in the same event, would hardly have lost one plume from his crest. It is in relation to literature, and to the boundless questions as to the true and the false arising out of literature and poetry, that Keats challenges a fluctuating interest; sometimes an interest of strong disgust, sometimes of deep admiration. There is not, I believe, a case on record throughout European literature, where feelings so repulsive of each other have centred in the same individual. The very midsummer madness of affectation, of false vapoury sentiment, and of fantastic effeminacy, seemed to me combined in Keats's *Endymion*, when I first saw it near the close of 1821. The Italian poet Marino had been reputed the greatest master of gossamery affectation in Europe. But *his* conceits showed the palest of rosy blushes by the side of Keats's bloody crimson. Naturally, I was discouraged from looking further. But about a week later, by pure accident, my eye fell upon his *Hyperion*. The first feeling was that of incredulity that the two poems could, under change of circumstances or lapse of time, have emanated from the same mind. The *Endymion* displays absolutely the most shocking revolt against good sense and just feeling that all literature does now, or even *can*, furnish. The *Hyperion*, as Mr Gilfillan truly says, "is the greatest of poetical torsos." The first belongs essentially to the vilest collections of wax-work filigree, or gilt gingerbread. The other presents the majesty, the austere beauty, and the simplicity of Grecian temples enriched with Grecian sculpture.

We have in this country a word, viz. the word *Folly*, which has a technical appropriation to the case of fantastic buildings. Any building is called "a folly," which mimics purposes incapable of being realized, and makes a promise to the eye which it cannot keep to the experience.

[He cites for example the Czarina's ice-palace as described in Book v of Cowper's *Task*.]

Now, such a folly, as *would* have been the Czarina's, if executed upon the scale of Versailles, or of the new palace at St Petersburg, *was* the *Endymion*: a gigantic edifice (for its tortuous enigmas of thought multiplied every line of the four thousand into fifty) reared upon a basis slighter and less apprehensible than moonshine. As reasonably, and as hopefully in regard to human sympathies, might a man undertake an epic poem upon the loves of two butterflies. The modes of existence in the two parties to the love-fable of the *Endymion*, their relations to each other and to us, their prospects finally, and the obstacles to the *instant* realization of these prospects,—all these things are more vague and incomprehensible than the reveries of an oyster. Still the unhappy subject, and its unhappy expansion, must be laid to the account of childish years and childish inexperience. But there is another fault in Keats, of the first magnitude, which youth does not palliate, which youth even aggravates. This lies in the most shocking abuse of his mother-tongue. If there is one thing in this world that, next after the flag of his country and its spotless honour, should be holy in the eyes of a young poet,—it is the *language* of his country. He should spend the third part of his life in studying this language, and cultivating its total resources. He should be willing to pluck out his right eye, or to circumnavigate the globe, if by such a sacrifice, if by such an exertion, he could attain to greater purity, precision, compass, or idiomatic energy of diction. This if he were even a Kalmuck Tartar, who by the way *has* the good feeling and patriotism to pride himself upon his beastly language. But Keats was an Englishman; Keats had the honour to speak the language of Chaucer, Shakspere, Bacon, Milton, Newton. The more awful was the obligation of his allegiance. And yet upon this mother tongue, upon this English language, has Keats trampled as with the hoofs of a buffalo. With its syntax, with its prosody, with its idiom, he has played such fantastic tricks as could enter only into the heart of a barbarian, and for which only the anarchy of Chaos could furnish a forgiving audience. Verily it required the *Hyperion* to weigh against the deep treason of these unparalleled offences.' (*Tait's Edinburgh Magazine* (April 1846), xiii, 249–54.)

(b) Footnote (1857): 'In the case of Keats there is something which (after a lapse of several years) I could wish unsaid, or said more gently. It is the denunciation, much too harsh, and disproportioned to the offence, of Keats's licentiousness in the treatment of his mother-tongue: to which venerable mother-tongue Keats certainly *did* approach with too little reverence, and with a false notion of his rights over it as a material servile to his caprices. But the tone of complaint on my part was too vehement and unmeasured,—though still (as I request the reader to observe) not uttered until Keats had been dead for many years, and had notoriously left no representatives interested in his literary pretensions,—which, besides, are able to protect themselves.' (From Preface to volume vi (1857) of *Selections Grave and Gay from the Writings Published and Unpublished by Thomas De Quincey* (1853–60).)

56. Unsurpassed vigour and acumen

1847

Extract from William Howitt's *Homes and Haunts of the Most Eminent British Poets* (1847), i. 425–31.

William Howitt (1792–1879), a Quaker who abandoned his practice as a chemist to become a writer, was converted to Keats's poetry by reading the sonnet on Chapman's Homer in Leigh Hunt's first *Examiner* notice (No. 2). He died very near Keats's house in Rome, and is buried in the same cemetery.

Howitt's essay (partly based on conversations with Leigh Hunt, whom he revered), although highly rhapsodical in expression, in fact stresses the mental energy and judgment of Keats's mature work, and contains one very striking phrase in which Keats's poetry is epitomized as a 'vivid orgasm of the intellect.' The 'ministrations' of the first sentence are those of God, made through Nature and art to vitalize the souls of men.

Of the class of swift but resplendent messengers by whom these ministrations are performed, neither ours nor any other history can furnish a specimen more beautiful than John Keats. He was of feeling and 'imagination all compact.' His nature was one pure mass of the living light of poetry. On this world and its concerns he could take no hold, and they could take none on him. The worldly and the worldly wise could not comprehend him, could not sympathize with him. To them his vivid orgasm of the intellect was madness; his exuberance of celestial gifts was extravagance; his unworldliness was effeminacy; his love of the universal man, and not of gross distinctions of pride and party, was treason. As of the highest and divinest of God's messengers to earth, they cried 'Away with him, he is not fit to live;' and the body, that mere mist-like, that mere shadow-like body, already failing before the fervency of his spiritual functions, fell, 'faded away, dissolved,' and disappeared before the bitter frost-wind of base criticism. . . . The first volume was a volume of immature fancies and unsettled style, but with things which denoted the glorious dawn of a short but illustrious day. The *Endymion* had much extravagance. It was a poetical effervescence. The mind of the writer was haunted by crowds of imaginations, and scenes of wonder, and dreams of beauty, chiefly from the old mythological world, but mingled with the passion for living nature, and the warmest feelings of youth. It brought forward the deities of Greece, and invested them with the passions and tenderness of men, and all the youthful glow which then reigned in the poet's heart. The mind was boiling over from intense heat, but amid the luscious foam rose streams of the richest wine of poetry which ever came from the vintage of this world. The next volume, *Lamia, Isabella, etc.* showed how the heady liquor had cleared itself, and become spirit bright and strong. There was an aim, a settled plan and purpose, in each composition, and a steady power of judgment growing up amid all the vivid impulses of the brain that still remained vivid as ever. The style was wonderfully condensed, and the descriptive as well as conceptive faculty, had assumed a vigour and acumen which was not, and is not, and probably never will be, surpassed by any other poet. For proofs to justify these high terms, it is only necessary to open the little volume, and open it almost anywhere. How powerful and tender is the narrative of 'Isabella': how rich and gorgeous and chaste and well weighed is the whole of 'St Agnes' Eve': how full of the soul of poetry is 'The Ode to the Nightingale'. Perhaps there is no poet, living or dead, except Shakspeare, who can pretend to anything like the felicity of epithet which characterizes Keats. One word or phrase is the essence of a whole description or sentiment. It is like the dull substance of the earth struck through by electric fires and converted into veins of gold and diamonds. For a piece of perfect and inventive description, that passage from 'Lamia', where, Lycius gone to bid the guests to his wedding, Lamia in her uneasy excitement employs herself and her demon powers in adorning her palace, is unrivalled.

[Quotes Part II, lines 106–45, 'It was the custom' to 'spoil her solitude'.]

The description of Lamia undergoing the metamorphosis by which she escaped from the form of a serpent to that of a beautiful woman, is marvellous for its power and precision of language.

[Quotes Part I, lines 146–70, 'Left to herself' to 'Crete's forests heard no more'.]

The most magnificent trophy of his genius, however, is the fragment of

Hyperion. On this poem, which has something vast, colossal, and dreamy about it, giving you a conception of the unfoldings of an almost infinite scope of 'the vision and the faculty divine' in this extraordinary youth, he was employed when the progress of his complaint, and the savage treatment of the critics, sunk his heart, and he abandoned the task, and went forth to die.

MILNES'S *LIFE, LETTERS AND LITERARY REMAINS OF JOHN KEATS*

1848

57. Keats's first biography

August 1848, 1854

Richard Monckton Milnes (1809–85), 'Apostle', politician, and patron of letters, became first Baron Houghton in 1863. It was he who proposed Tennyson ('the most noted, and perhaps the most original, of present poets') for the Laureateship in 1850. By his tact and enthusiasm he won the confidence of the bickering survivors among Keats's friends; and his *Life* proved the decisive turning-point in Keats's reputation—partly because his prestige, moderation, and very formal prose gave the poet an immediate *cachet* of respectability. In the *Life*, Keats was allowed to speak for himself as far as possible through letters and poems. The later memoir, (b), gave Milnes a little more opportunity for criticism. It is significant that by 1854 Milnes is able to discuss Keats's poetic habits historically: that is, as the innovations of established greatness.

(a) Extracts from Milnes's *Life*: 'The impressible nature of Keats would naturally incline him to erotic composition, but his early love-verses are remarkably deficient in beauty and even in passion. Some which remain in manuscript are without any interest, and those published in the little volume of 1817 are the worst pieces in it. The world of personal emotion was then far less familiar to him than that of fancy, and indeed it seems to have been long before he descended from the ideal atmosphere in which he dwelt so happily, into the troubled realities of human love. Not, however, that the creatures even of his young imagination were unimbued with natural affections; so far from it, it may be reasonably conjectured that it was the interfusion of ideal and sensual life which rendered the Grecian mythology so peculiarly congenial to the mind of Keats, and when the *Endymion* comes to be critically considered, it will be found that its excellence consists in its clear comprehension of that ancient spirit of beauty, to which all outward perceptions so excellently ministered, and which undertook to ennoble and purify, as far as was consistent with their retention, the instinctive desires of mankind.

Friendship, generally ardent in youth, would not remain without its impression in the early poems of Keats, and a congeniality of literary disposition appears to have been the chief impulse to these relations. With Mr Felton Mathew, to whom his first published Epistle was addressed, he appears to have enjoyed a high intellectual sympathy. This friend had introduced him to agreeable society, both of books and men, and those verses were written just at the time when Keats became fully aware that he had no real interest in the profession he was sedulously pursuing, and was already in the midst of that sad conflict between the outer and inner worlds, which is too often, perhaps always in some degree, the Poet's heritage in life. That freedom from the bonds of conventional phraseology which so clearly designates true genius, but which, if unwatched and unchastened, will continually outrage the perfect form that can alone embalm the beautiful idea and preserve it for ever, is there already manifest, and the presence of Spenser shows itself not only by quaint expressions and curious adaptations of rhyme, but by the introduction of the words "and make a sun-shine in a shady place," applied to the power of the Muse.' (R. M. Milnes, *Life, Letters and Literary Remains of John Keats* (1848), i. 13–15.)

'Keats did not escape the charge of sacrificing beauty to supposed intensity, and of merging the abiding grace of his song in the passionate fantasies of the moment. Words indeed seem to have been often selected by him rather for their force and their harmony, than according to any just rules of diction; if he met with a word anywhere in an old writer that took his fancy he inserted it in his verse on the first opportunity; and one has a kind of impression that he must have thought aloud as he was writing, so that many an ungainly phrase has acquired its place by its assonance or harmony, or capability to rhyme, (for he took great pleasure in fresh and original rhymes) rather than for its grammatical correctness or even justness of expression. And when to this is added the example set him by his great master Spenser, of whom a noted man of letters has been heard irreverently to assert "that every Englishman might be thankful that Spenser's gibberish had never become part and parcel of the language," the wonder is rather that he sloughed off so fast so many of his offending peculiarities, and in his third volume attained so great a purity and concinnity of phraseology, that little was left to designate either his poetical education or his literary associates.' (i. 22–3.)

'*Endymion* was finished at Burford Bridge, on the 28th of November, 1817; so records the still existing manuscript, written fairly in a book, with many corrections of phrases and some of lines, but with few of sentences or of arrangement. It betrays the leading fault of the composition, namely, the dependence of the matter on the rhyme, but shows the confidence of the Poet in his own profusion of diction, the strongest and most emphatic words being generally taken as those to which the continuing verse was to be adapted. There was no doubt a pleasure to him in this very victory over the limited harmonies of our language, and the result, when fortunate, is very impressive.' (i. 72.)

'I am unwilling to leave this, the last of Keats's literary labours ["The Cap and Bells"] without a word of defence against the objection that might with some reason be raised against the originality of his genius, from the circumstance that it is easy to refer almost every poem he wrote to some suggestion of style and manner derived from preceding writers. From the Spenserian *Endymion*, to these Ariosto-like stanzas, you can always see reflected in the mirror of his intellect the great works he is studying at the time. This is so generally the case with verse-writers, and the test has been so severely and successfully applied to many of the most noted authors of our time, that I should not have alluded to it had I not been desirous to claim for Keats an access to that inmost penetralium of Fame which is solely consecrated to original genius. . . . In the case of Keats, his literary studies were apparently the sources of his productions, and his variety and facility of composition certainly increases very much in proportion to his reading, thus clearly showing how much he owed to those who had preceded him. But let us not omit two considerations:—first, that these resemblances of form or spirit are a reproduction, not an imitation, and that while they often are what those great masters might themselves have contentedly written, they always include something which the model has not—some additional intuitive vigour; and secondly, let us never forget, that wonderful as are the poems of Keats, yet, after all, they are rather the records of a poetical education than the accomplished work of the mature artist. This is in truth the chief interest of these pages; this is what these letters so vividly exhibit. Day by day, his imagination is extended, his fancy enriched, his taste purified; every fresh acquaintance with the motive minds of past generations leads him a step onwards in knowledge and in power; the elements of ancient genius become his own; the skill of faculties long-spent revives in him; ever, like Nature herself, he gladly receives and energetically reproduces. And now we approach the consummation of this laborious work, the formation of a mind of the highest order; we hope to see the perfect fruit whose promise has been more than the perfection of noted men; we desire to sympathize with this realized idea of a great poet, from which he has ever felt himself so far, but which he yet knows he is ever approaching; we yearn to witness the full flow of this great spiritual river, whose source has long lain in the heart of the earth, and to which the streams of a thousand hills have ministered.' (ii. 51–3.)

'Let any man of literary accomplishment, though without the habit of writing poetry, or even much taste for reading it, open *Endymion* at random (to say nothing of the later and more perfect poems,) and examine the characteristics of the page before him, and I shall be surprised if he does not feel that the whole range of literature hardly supplies a parallel phenomenon. As a psychological curiosity, perhaps Chatterton is more wonderful; but in him the immediate ability displayed is rather the full comprehension of and identification with the old model, than the effluence of creative genius. In Keats, on the contrary, the originality in the use of his scanty materials, his expansion of them to the proportions of his own imagination, and above all, his field of diction and expression extending so far beyond his knowledge of literature, is quite inexplicable by any of the ordinary processes of mental education. If his classical learning had been deeper, his seizure of the full spirit of Grecian beauty would have been less surprising; if his English reading had been more extensive, his inexhaustible vocabulary of picturesque and mimetic words could more easily be accounted for; but here is a surgeon's apprentice, with the ordinary culture of the middle classes, rivalling in aesthetic perceptions of antique life and thought the most careful scholars of his time and country, and reproducing these impressions in a phraseology as complete and unconventional as if he had mastered the whole history and the frequent variations of the English tongue, and elaborated a mode of utterance commensurate with his vast ideas.

The artistic absence of moral purpose may offend many readers, and the just harmony of the colouring may appear to others a displeasing monotony, but I think it impossible to lay the book down without feeling that almost every line of it contains solid gold enough to be beaten out, by common literary manufacturers, into a poem of itself. Concentration of imagery, the hitting off a picture at a stroke, the clear decisive word that brings the thing before you and will not let it go, are the rarest distinctions of the early exercise of the faculties. So much more is usually known than digested by sensitive youth, so much more felt than understood, so much more perceived than methodized, that diffusion is fairly permitted in the earlier stages of authorship, and it is held to be one of the advantages, amid some losses, of maturer intelligence, that it learns to fix and hold the beauty it apprehends, and to crystallize the dew of its morning. Such examples to the contrary, as the "Windsor Forest" of Pope, are rather scholastic exercises of men who afterwards became great, than the first-fruits of such genius, while all Keats's poems are early productions, and there is nothing beyond them but the thought of what he might have become. Truncated as is this intellectual life, it is still a substantive whole, and the complete statue, of which such a fragment is revealed to us, stands perhaps solely in the temple of the imagination. There is indeed progress, continual and visible, in the works of Keats, but it is towards his own ideal of a poet, not towards any defined and tangible model. All that we can do is to transfer that ideal to ourselves, and to believe that if Keats had lived, that is what he would have been.

Contrary to the expectation of Shelley, the appreciation of Keats by men of thought and sensibility gradually rose after his death, until he attained the place he now holds among the poets of his country. . . . Nor has Keats been without his direct influence on the poetical literature that succeeded him. The most noted, and perhaps the most original, of present poets, bears more analogy to him than to any other writer.' (ii. 103–6.)

(b) Extracts from memoir: 'The "Epistles" . . . indicate a rapid development of the poetic faculty, especially free from the formalism and imitation which encumber the early writings even of distinguished poets, and full of an easy gaiety, which at times runs into conversational common-place, or helps itself out of difficulties by quaintnesses that look like affectations. But, even in these first efforts, the peculiarity of making the rhymes to rest on the most picturesque and varied words, instead of the conventional resonance of unimportant syllables, is distinctive, and an effect is produced which from its very novelty often mars the force and beauty of the expression, and lowers the sense of poetic harmony into an ingenious concurrence of sounds. It is also a palpable consequence of this mode of composition, that the sense appears too often made for the rhyme, and, while most poets would be loth to allow how frequently the necessity of the rhyme suggests the corresponding thought, here the uncommon prominence of the rhyme keeps this effect constantly before the reader. Yet, when approached with sympathetic feeling and good will, this impression soon vanishes before the astonishing affluence of thought and imagination, which at once explains and excuses the defect, if it be one. Picture after picture seems to rise before the poet's eye in a succession so rapid as to embarrass judgment and limit choice, and fancies and expressions that elsewhere would be strange and far-fetched are here felt to have been the first suggested. . . .

In all these Poems [those of Keats's last volume], in their different styles, the progress in purity and grace of diction was manifest. The simplicity of language which had been inaugurated by Goldsmith and Cowper, formalised into a theory by Wordsworth, and by him and other writers both of the Lake and the London schools carried to extravagance, had been adapted by Keats to a class of subjects to which, according to literary taste and habit, it was especially inappropriate, and where it produced on many minds almost the sensation of a classical burlesque. Such of the Gods as had spoken English up to this time had done so in formal and courtly language, and the familiarity of poetic diction which in any case was novel, here appeared extravagant. Now that *Endymion* has taken its place as a great English Poem, and is in truth become a region of delight in which the youth of every generation finds "a week's stroll in the summer," we can hardly feel the force of these objections . . . if he had lived to maturity, he would probably have had less of peculiarity and mannerism than any other Poet of his time.' (Memoir by R. M. Milnes prefixed to *The Poetical Works of Keats* (1854), xiii–xiv, xxxiv–xxxv.)

58. Justice in the market-place

1848

Extract from unsigned review-article entitled 'The Life of John Keats', *The Times* (19 September 1848), p. 3.

Samuel Phillips (1814–54) was a staff reviewer on *The Times.* His political viewpoint was not very different from Lockhart's, but Keats's supremacy was now publicly plain. 'Do not question the fact with the evidence you have around you. It is the spirit of Keats that at the present moment hovers over the best of our national poesy.'

It is the old story! We are again summoned to admire where once we despised. The citizens of Bristol erect a monument to the memory of Chatterton, who, to save himself from death through hunger, took poison, and was thrown, pauper-like, into the burying ground of Shoe-lane workhouse, London. Keats, spurned and persecuted in his lifetime, is welcomed to-day, and from his distant grave begins to influence thought in the land of his birth, which he quitted in proud, but intolerable despair. The instances are two out of many. The tale did not begin with 'the marvellous boy, the sleepless soul, that perished in his pride;' it has not ended with Adonais, whose soul—

Like a star
Beacons from the abode where the eternal are.

Our present task is a simple one. We cannot recal genius from the tomb to witness the final triumph of its long suffering, and to console itself for its wrongs in the consciousness of our remorse. We may in the public market-place do justice to the citizen whom we ostracised in ignorance and hooted forth in folly.

John Keats was born under an unlucky star. He was beset with evil influences from the moment that he felt his own great strength. Had he been suffered to walk alone, unaided but by the might of his spirit, he would never have been struck down on the way by the fury of men who were waging war to the death against his associates. Keats at starting was the victim of a quarrel between parties who, like most antagonists, were wrong and were right in their respective grounds of opposition. The chosen or forced companions of Keats, when, as a mere boy, he resolved to dedicate his life to the service of poetry, were unfortunately members of a school. Unfortunately, again, the sharpest and cleverest critics of the day were members of another. The author of *Comus* himself would not have escaped scot-free from the encounter. Keats might have sung as an angel, and his voice would have made no impression upon ears that listened to nothing but the promptings of an internal and most vindictive rage.

There is much to be said for and against the belligerents. It is not to be denied that if the critics of the early part of the century were vicious beyond all bounds, the objects of their attack were but too often ridiculous past all hope. The very worthy and, in their way, highly respectable gentlemen who, at the time of Keats' appearance upon the stage, had formed themselves into a snug coterie, and under the unpoetical title of 'Cockneys,' forced public attention to a most ridiculous expression of many rare and noble sentiments, invited satire and laid themselves fairly open to the assaults of the evil-disposed. Grown-up men are not suffered, in the heart of our practical and manly nation, to play the parts of children. Even the madness of our poets must have its method, or be dismissed to the asylum. What could be done with a small family of lyrical aspirants who employed the muse in writing sonnets to one another, and the greengrocer in preparing crowns of ivy for mutual coronations? How was it possible to avoid a laugh at the amiable simplicity of inveterate Londoners, who converted Primrose Hill into Parnassus, and deliberately walked to the Vale of Health at Hampstead—not for health, but inspiration? Two of the earliest productions of poor Keats indicate, in their very titles, how thoroughly he had identified himself at starting with the puerilities of his friends. One is suggested by sleeping in Mr Leigh Hunt's pretty cottage on the Hampstead Road; the other owes its origin to a neighbouring paddock. Hunt, Hazlitt, Shelley, and Godwin were the backers of the boy when he stripped, with a lion's heart, to fight his great battle for fame; and never had mortal deeper reason to pray heaven to save him from his friends. The greatness of the names are beyond all doubt; so is the fact that in the year 1817, or thereabouts, they were sounds to alarm the rising generation, and the veriest bugbears of society. A letter of recommendation from any one of the four was a certain passport, not to neglect—that might have been borne—but to persecution and insult. The failings—the vices, if you will—of one and all were visited on the head of their unfortunate *protégé*, whoever he might be. Keats, chivalrous to a fault, cannot be said to have been caught when his sympathies urged him to the side of individuals whom, in his soul, he believed to be cruelly oppressed.

The critics were far from blameless. They revelled wantonly in their strength, and took unfair advantage of the time. The peace of Europe, the triumph of order, the frightful remembrance of the French Revolution, the downfal of the Corsican despot, gave extraordinary power to the pen advocating Conservatism, and opposing the designs of Democracy. The friends of Keats were politicians as well as poets; one, indeed, the chief and most affectionate, was suffering in prison the penalty of excessive liberality which had been betrayed into a libel upon the then Prince Regent. There can be no doubt whatever that the literary critic, assuming the sword of the political partisan, struck at the fantastic poet through the heart of the uncompromising Radical, and mocked the writing chiefly because he hated the man. The temptation to crush was immense, but the mode of attack was, after all, cowardly. Society, but too willing to stigmatise the conscientious Reformer, needed not the instigations of falsehood to bring its whole scorn to bear upon a few well-meaning and high-hearted, although, in many respects, misguided men. Crimes were imputed to harmless dreamers in the Hampstead fields, in the existence of which the accusers themselves never believed. Practices were hinted at too monstrous for belief—if anything can be too monstrous for prejudice to credit and enjoy. The responsibility and gravity of the literary judge utterly gave way before the necessity of silencing an enemy to Church and State. You opened the critic's pages for a touch of his quality, and found him belabouring, with a heavy cudgel, an unhappy devil lying already half crushed under his foot.

In such a state of things Keats rose—an undoubted poet. Do not question the fact with the evidence you have around you. It is the spirit of Keats that at the present moment hovers over the best of our national poesy, and inspires the poetic genius—such as it is—of our unpoetic age. Had he lived, he would eventually have towered above his contemporaries; dying before he was twenty-six years of age, he took his place at once amongst the examples whom he so passionately loved, and the models he so successfully imitated, and so closely approached. *Endymion*, full of faults, overflows with as many beauties, and both are stamped with greatness. The most unsparing reviewer of the time was not half so conscious of the many defects of this extraordinary composition as the author himself, who, at the beginning of his career, entered upon a system of self-tuition, the effects of which are strikingly apparent at its close, although the interval is spanned by a very few months.

[Quotes Keats's preface to *Endymion* (see No. 10) in full.]

Such was the honest declaration, and such the simple and masculine strength of a mere yearning for earliest adventure; but it did not save him from the wrath he anticipated and deprecated. Even at this distance of time, it is not without a smarting sense of pain that the lover of Keats takes up *Endymion* and becomes conscious of the many opportunities for ridicule which the poem presents, but which tenderness and a simple desire for the honour of the national literature would have known how to appreciate. The intoxication of an imagination that scorned, in its joyous delirium, the promptings of reason and judgment, is visible throughout; but the luxuriance of the highest poetic faculty was in itself a pledge sufficient of the poet's future eminence. For the reasons already given, the essential beauty of the structure was overlooked by the arbiters of the day in their eagerness to expose the grotesqueness, and, it may be, the absurdity of the ornament. It was a huge mistake, but time alone was required to correct it. To attempt the annihilation of genius because of its exaggerations and imperfections, is the most fruitless of all efforts. The exuberant tree must not be upbraided with sterility simply because it needs pruning. In his choice of a subject we believe Keats to have been unfortunate. Against the opinion of his present biographer we are disposed to assert that his first steps would have been safer had they been not on classic ground. Unacquainted with Greek, and deriving his inspiration and knowledge not directly from the primitive sources, a tone and stamp were given to characters and subjects that startled by their novelty, and provoked irresistible mirth from the associations which they suggested. Scholars were offended, and the uninitiated were puzzled. Whilst *Lemprière's Dictionary* lent blocks, John Keats furnished the clothing. The skeleton of Pagan mythology looked strange enough in its modern garb, and the kindly disposed might be pardoned for their smile of wonder as they watched the august visitor of antiquity taking his splendid airing in the Hampstead fields. The minor faults of the composition were certainly not few. It was evident to the lightest reader that the author of

Endymion, instead of adapting rhymes to his subject, very frequently indeed compelled his subject to bend obsequiously to his rhymes. The effect of this high dereliction of the poet's sacred duty is too visible. But sum up all the vices of style, and all the faults inseparable from the nature of the subject, and there remains behind a poem that will live, because it bears the impress of undoubted originality and power, and is redolent of the stuff which makes Milton and Jonson, Fletcher and Shakspeare, the household gods they have become. . . .

In the year 1820, less than two years after the publication of *Endymion*, the poem of *Hyperion* appeared with other compositions. The journey was all but accomplished. The earlier poems of Keats had exhibited striking vigour shrouded in obscurity, and the sinews of thought, though sadly encumbered with fervid mystification. A leap of years had been made in the interval. For simplicity, beauty, grandeur, and the deepest pathos, *Hyperion* is scarcely to be surpassed in the language. With one spring the rejected, but inspired boy had placed himself where he had long hoped and prayed to be. 'I think,' he says in one of his letters, 'I shall be among the English poets after my death.'

Keats wrote no more! On the 23rd of February, 1821, he died at Rome—not 'snuffed out by an article,' as the tradition goes, but the victim of a disease which had already destroyed his mother and his younger brother. It may be seen from the glimpses we have given above that the effect of malignity was not to depress the poet, but rather to rouse him, as a criticism had already roused Byron, to the vindication of his genius, and to the putting forth of his strength. There was nothing of death in the arrows that came from the reviewer's quiver. Had no 'article' ever been written, we question whether Keats, with his foredoomed tendency to physical decay, could at any time of his life have passed muster at a life insurance office; consumption had marked him for her own. He lingered but little, and, after death, the only wonder was that he had lingered so long. Who knows how closely allied, in the case of Keats, were the mother's inheritance and his own intellectual pre-eminence.

59. Arnold on Keats

1848, 1849, 1852, 1853

Matthew Arnold (1822–1888), poet and critic. Extracts (a) and (b) were written soon after reading Milnes's *Life*. Arnold's point at the end of (a) seems to be that young writers should study simplicity, then if they fail as poets they can still cope with life; whereas writers (such as Keats) who cultivate richness and abundance are overwhelmed both as poets and men. Arnold's fuller and more famous estimate of Keats, written thirty-five years later as an introduction to the Keats selection in A. W. Ward's *English Poets* (1880), develops a similar argument to that in the 1853 preface (d): Keats's gift of expression ranks with Shakespeare's, but in the 'faculty of moral interpretation' and the 'architectonics' of poetry he was immature. He had 'flint and iron in him' as well as sensuousness, and 'the elements of high character', but these qualities were still unripe when he died.

(a) Extract from letter of *c.* September/October 1848: 'What harm he has done in English Poetry. As Browning is a man with a moderate gift passionately desiring movement and fulness, and obtaining but a confused multitudinousness, so Keats with a very high gift, is yet also consumed by this desire: and cannot produce the truly living and moving, as his conscience keeps telling him. They will not be patient neither understand that they must begin with an Idea of the world in order not to be prevailed over by the world's multitudinousness: or if they cannot get that, at least with isolated ideas: and all other things shall (perhaps) be added unto them. . . . But what perplexity Keats Tennyson et id genus omne must occasion to young writers of the ὁπλίτης[1] sort: yes and those d——d Elizabethan poets generally. Those who cannot read G[ree]k sh[ou]ld read nothing but Milton and parts of Wordsworth: the state should see to it: for the failures of the σταθμοί[2]

[1] Heavy-armed infantry.
[2] Days' marches; i.e. they cannot keep up the pace as poetical soldiers.

may leave them good citizens enough, as Trench: but the others go to the dogs failing or succeeding.' (*The Letters of Matthew Arnold to Arthur Hugh Clough*, ed. H. F. Lowry, 1932, 97.)

(b) Extract from letter of *c.* 1 March 1849: '. . . there are two offices of Poetry—one to add to one's store of thoughts and feelings—another to compose and elevate the mind by a sustained tone, numerous allusions, and a grand style. What other process is Milton's than this last, in *Comus* for instance. There is no fruitful analysis of character, but a great effect is produced. What is Keats? A style and form seeker, and this with an impetuosity that heightens the effect of his style almost painfully. Nay in Sophocles what is valuable is not so much his contributions to psychology and the anatomy of sentiment, as the grand moral effects produced by *style*. For the style is the expression of the nobility of the poet's character, as the matter is the expression of the richness of his mind: but on men character produces as great an effect as mind.' (pp. 100–1.)

(c) Extract from letter of 28 October 1852: 'More and more I feel that the difference between a mature and a youthful age of the world compels the poetry of the former to use great plainness of speech as compared with that of the latter: and that Keats and Shelley were on a false track when they set themselves to reproduce the exuberance of expression, the charm, the richness of images, and the felicity, of the Elizabethan poets. Yet critics cannot get to learn this, because the Elizabethan poets are our greatest, and our canons of poetry are founded on their works. They still think that the object of poetry is to produce exquisite bits and images—such as Shelley's *clouds shepherded by the slow unwilling wind*, and Keats passim: whereas modern poetry can only subsist by its *contents*: by becoming a complete magister vitae as the poetry of the ancients did: by including, as theirs did, religion with poetry, instead of existing as poetry only, and leaving religious wants to be supplied by the Christian religion, as a power existing independent of the poetical power. But the language, style and general proceedings of a poetry which has such an immense task to perform, must be very plain direct and severe: and it must not lose itself in parts and episodes and ornamental work, but must press forwards to the whole.' (p. 124.)

(d) Extract from the preface to the first edition of Arnold's *Poems* (1853). Arnold has been arguing that Shakespeare is a dangerous model for young writers, because the excellence of his 'poetical actions' tends to be overshadowed by his special gift of 'abundant, and ingenious expression'; hence in most modern poetry 'the details alone are valuable, the composition worthless.' He continues: 'Let me give an instance of what I mean. I will take it from the works of the very chief among those who seem to have been formed in the school of Shakspeare: of one whose exquisite genius and pathetic death render him for ever interesting. I will take the poem of "Isabella, or the Pot of Basil", by Keats. I choose this rather than the *Endymion*, because the latter work (which a modern critic has classed with the *Fairy Queen*!), although undoubtedly there blows through it the breath of genius, is yet as a whole so utterly incoherent, as not strictly to merit the name of a poem at all. The poem of "Isabella", then, is a perfect treasure-house of graceful and felicitous words and images; almost in every stanza there occurs one of those vivid and picturesque turns of expression, by which the object is made to flash upon the eye of the mind, and which thrill the reader with a sudden delight. This one short poem contains, perhaps, a greater number of happy single expressions which one could quote than all the extant tragedies of Sophocles. But the action, the story? The action in itself is an excellent one; but so feebly is it conceived by the Poet, so loosely constructed, that the effect produced by it, in and for itself, is absolutely null. Let the reader, after he has finished the poem of Keats, turn to the same story in the *Decameron*: he will then feel how pregnant and interesting the same action has become in the hands of a great artist, who above all things delineates his object; who subordinates expression to that which it is designed to express.' (Preface to *Poems*, 1853, xxi–xxii.)

60. Extracts from unsigned review of Milnes's *Life*, *Gentleman's Magazine*

November 1848, xxx, 507–10

On the whole, these poems will add no additional sprig to the wreath the poet had won before. They have most of his faults, his exaggeration, his carelessness, his obsolete expressions, his inapplicable epithets, his disjointed numbers, his fanciful analogies, and his mythological subjects, which, to be interesting, must call up an audience that have been departed from earth these two thousand years and more. We can believe that Keats might have gained a circle of auditors while reciting his Odes at the Isthian games, or at a symposium at the Piraeus; but other subjects, and other interests, and other creeds, have succeeded, and an English poet must write for London, not for Athens. What Greek would have read Sophocles and Pindar if they had chosen for their poetical subjects, not their own deities and their own heroes, but had gone to Egypt, and the Pyramids, and the Nile, and brought back histories of Anubis, and Osiris, and Osymandyas, and Amunoph the Second, and Thothrun the Third, and all the crocodile-headed monarchs of Hecatompylos?

61. The sensual school of poetry

1848

Extracts from unsigned review of R. M. Milnes's *Life, Letters and Literary Remains of John Keats*, *North British Review* (November 1848), x, 69–96.

Coventry Kersey Dighton Patmore (1823–96), son of P. G. Patmore (No. 21), wrote a verse-novel *The Angel in the House* (1854–6), celebrating the ideals of Victorian married life. Patmore's long study reveals the dilemma of those Victorians who were afraid of admiring Keats, on moral and religious grounds. Poets are regarded as high authorities on morals, and must fulfil their responsibilities. But Keats had no firm beliefs, and 'a man without a belief is like a man without a backbone'. The argument is less crude than this, however. 'Sensuality', as Patmore defines it, implies an inability to perceive 'true harmony', which entails bad artistic form and slack metre. 'The only true beauty is the beauty of holiness.' This was the line followed by Cardinal Wiseman (No. 67), which called down the angry derision of Leigh Hunt (see Introduction, p. 6).

In order to secure ourselves against being prejudged of injustice to the subject of this notice, we may at once state our opinion, that as surprising powers of merely sensual perception and expression are to be detected in the poems of Keats as in any others within the range of English literature. Herrick surpassed Keats, in his own way, by fits, and in a few single passages; and Chaucer has pieces of brilliant and unmixed word-painting which have no equals in our language; but the power that these great poets attained, or at least exerted, only in moments, was the common manner and easy habit of the wonderful man, who may claim the honour of having assisted more than any other writer, except Mr Wordsworth, in the origination of the remarkable school of poetry which is yet in its vigorous youth, and exhibits indications of capabilities of unlimited expansion. We also anticipate objections that might be urged, with apparent reason, against the following remarks, by stating our conviction, that the shortcomings of which we shall complain, could not have existed in the mature productions of Keats, had he lived to produce them. Indeed, as we shall presently take occasion to show, his mind, which was endowed with a power of growth almost unprecedentedly rapid, was on the eve of passing beyond the terrestrial sphere in which he had as yet moved, when death cut short his marvellous, and only just commenced, career.

To Keats, more deeply perhaps than to any poet born in Christian times,

> Life, like a dome of many coloured glass,
> Stained the white radiance of eternity.

His mind, like Goethe's, was 'lighted from below.' Not a ray of the wisdom that is from above had, as yet, illumined it.

The character of the poet, in as far as it differs from that of other men, is indeed a subject of too much importance to allow of our sacrificing this admirable occasion for extending our knowledge concerning it, to our tenderness, or to that of our readers, for the young writer of whom Mr Monckton Milnes is at once the faithful biographer, and the eloquent apologist. Mr Milnes will pardon us if our deductions from the data with which he has supplied us, do not wholly coincide with his own inferences. We confess that we are unable to detect, even in Keats' latest letters and compositions, anything more than a strong promise of, and aspiration towards many qualities of character and genius, which Mr Milnes regards as already numbered among the constituents of the young poet's life and power.

[It is argued, with illustrations from Keats's letters, that Keats's poetical genius was closely and patently connected with his disease, though this relationship was complicated by factors of temperament and circumstance.]

A co-temporary journal of respectable authority, pronounces the writings of Keats to be distinguished by two of the Miltonic characteristics of poetry, sensuousness and passion, and to be wanting in the third, simplicity. We do not think that Keats' verses are characterized remarkably by either of these qualities, in the sense in which Milton understood them, when he proclaimed his famous rule. That Keats' poems, if we except certain parts of the fragment of *Hyperion*, want simplicity, is too obvious to require proof or illustration. His verses constitute a region of eye-wearying splendour, from which all who can duly appreciate them, must feel glad to escape, after the astonishment and rapture caused by a short sojourn among them. As for sensuousness, it is an excellence which cannot thrive in the presence of sensuality; and it is by sensuality, in the broader, and not in the vulgar and degrading sense of the term, that Keats' poems are most obviously characterized. This charge, for such we admit that it is, must be substantiated; and to this object we devote our second batch of extracts. They will be, not from Keats' poems, but from his letters; since the shortest way of establishing the general prevalence of a quality in a man's writings is to shew it to have been constantly present in his personal character.

The first quotation we make is a very important one. It contains Keats' explicit testimony against himself, with regard to the quality in point. Notwithstanding the young poet's unusual honesty of character, he would probably not have made the following confession and complaint, had he not secretly, though certainly very erroneously, believed them to be a revelation of traits of which he was possessed in common with Shakspeare.

[Quotes from letter to Woodhouse dated 27 October 1818 the passage from 'As to the poetical character itself' to 'no dependence is to be placed on what I said that day', which includes the sentence: 'A poet is the most unpoetical of anything in existence, because he has no identity'.]

Now this want of identity, as Keats calls it, has been more or less the characteristic of artists of all kinds, who have been endowed only with the first, or sensual degree of genius. In Keats, the preponderance of this nature was, however, overwhelming, especially in the earlier portion of his career. A great revolution must have occurred in his views, if not in his character, had he lived a year or two longer than he did; but, as it happened, it was impossible that his poetry, as a general thing, should be other than sensual, or literal, and for the most part, opposed in quality to the sensuous or interpretative. We hold it to be out of the question, that Keats, with such a physical organization as his, could have ever entirely escaped from the preponderance of sense in his character and writings; but a year or two more of reflection and emotion must have led him to the determinate and deliberate adoption of a creed of some sort or other, if it had been no other than the wretched one, that all creeds are worthless; and this would have been an immense accession to his mental power. A man without a belief is like a man without a backbone. Keats made the very common mistake of preferring the true to the good; for his rejection of all opinions was nothing more than his refusal to accept of any but such as seemed demonstrably true. Had he lived to think and feel more deeply than he did; had his thoughts and feelings been more ordinarily occupied than they were, about the interests and mysteries of the immortal spirit, despair must have chased him from the regions of indifference, Goodness would probably have asserted her superiority over formal Truth, to which she is the only guide; and, finally, commanded by her, he would have chosen some star to steer by, although compelled to do so in the full assurance that it was, at best, but an approximation to the, perhaps, undiscoverable pole of absolute verity.

[It is suggested, again by means of quotations from the letters, that Keats's notions of conjugal love were more sensual than spiritual.]

Mr Milnes has perceived the liability of Keats' nature to the charge that we are now making against it, and he defends him upon the plea of youth, and an ardent temperament. Could we have convinced ourselves of the validity of this plea, our readers should have heard nothing of the present complaint; but we are persuaded that the quality under discussion was vitally inherent in the nature of Keats; that is to say, that it not only affected his life and writings, but entered into his ideal of what was desirable. A man is to be judged not so much by what he outwardly is, as by what he wishes to become. Let Keats be judged out of his own mouth: 'I have been hovering for some time between an exquisite sense of the luxurious and a love for philosophy. *Were I calculated for the former, I should be glad;* but as I am not' (his health was then breaking down) 'I shall turn all my soul to the latter.'

Mr Milnes tells us that—

Keats' health does not seem to have prevented him from indulging somewhat in that dissipation which is the natural outlet for the young energies of ardent temperaments, unconscious of how scanty a portion of vital strength had been allotted to him; but a strictly regulated and abstinent life would have appeared to him pedantic and sentimental. He did not, however, to any serious extent, allow wine to usurp on his intellect, or games of chance to impair his means, for in his letters to his brothers he speaks of having drank too much as of a piece of rare jovialty, &c.

We repeat, that we do not believe Keats' dissipation, such as it was, to have been the spontaneous outbreak of the 'young energies of an ardent temperament.' To us, Keats seems to have pursued the pleasures and temptations of sense, rather than to have been pursued by them. We often find him feasting coolly over the imagination of sensual enjoyment. 'Talking of pleasure, this moment I was writing with one hand, and with the other holding to my mouth a nectarine. Good God! how fine! it went down soft, pulpy, slushy, oozy—all its delicious embonpoint melted down my throat like a large beatified strawberry.' He sometimes aspires to be thought a tippler, gamester, &c., but it is with the air of an unripe boy, awkwardly feigning the irregularities of a man.

We have not noticed one-fourth of the passages which we had marked for quotation, as corroborating our views upon this point; but one proof is as good as a thousand, and we are glad to turn from this part of our task to the more agreeable duty of shewing the truth of our assertion that the mind of Keats, before its withdrawal from the world, was upon the eve of a great intellectual and moral alteration.

It must be remembered that our present purpose is to examine the character of Keats, solely in order to the illustration of his poetry, and of the species of poetry to which it belongs. Otherwise we should have gone more fully into the circumstances whereby the moral agency of young Keats is partly unburthened of the responsibility of much temporarily defective feeling, and erroneous thought. As it is, we can only take a hasty glance at two or three of those circumstances. 'His mother, a lively and intelligent woman, was supposed to have prematurely hastened the birth of John *by her passionate love of amusement,* though his constitution at first gave no signs of the peculiar debility of *a seventh month's child.*' Keats was, moreover, unfortunate, we venture to think, in some of the friends, who by their powers and their reputations were calculated to exert the greatest influence upon him, at the most susceptible period of his life. Extremely clever, 'self-educated' men are not often otherwise than very ill adapted to form the standard of moral taste in a young man, unless, indeed, it be by antagonism. We fancy that we hear the voice of some of Keats' distinguished preceptors, in such sentences as the following, 'Failings I am always rather rejoiced to find in a man than sorry for it, they bring us to a level.' John Keats was, however, so vastly superior to even the most gifted of his really intimate friends, that their influence, as far as it was undesirable, could not have endured. It was, in fact, rapidly waning, when he was removed from its sphere by his visit to Italy.

[The letters are copiously quoted to illustrate 'an emphatically transitional state' in Keats's mind; a very long passage is included from the letter to George and Georgiana Keats dated 19 March 1819 which ends with the sonnet 'Why did I laugh tonight?']

The above sonnet is remarkably fine and of extreme interest. 'The cloudy porch that opens on the sun' of Christianity is often made up of such misgivings as are therein expressed. The entire passage is valuable, moreover, as an illustration of the laborious introspection which must have been constantly exercised by the mind of Keats. This introspection or self-consciousness is a very important element of the discipline which every great artist has probably at some time or other undergone, and it is a feature which deserves attentive consideration here, inasmuch as with the peculiar order of poets to which Keats must be said to have belonged, at least up to the time of the composition of *Hyperion*, such self-consciousness becomes an integral portion of the effect, instead of remaining in the background as a subordinated mean of obtaining it. Concerning this characteristic of Keats' poetry we shall presently speak more at large. As a trait of the young poet's personal character, this habitual self-contemplation accounts for the apparent want of heart which sometimes repels us in his letters, and which seems to have rendered precarious such of his friendships as were not founded upon one side or the other, in hero-worship.

[Keats's 'profound sense of the importance of his vocation' is next illustrated at length from the same sources.]

It would have been difficult to hope too much of a man who had done so much as Keats, and who thought so little of it. We must distinguish between a man's confidence in his powers and his valuation of their products. A confidence in his own power is the half of power; whereas an overweening admiration of its results is the surest check upon its further development and exercise. 'Extol not thy *deeds* in the counsel of thine own heart, (for thus) thou shalt eat up thy leaves and lose thy fruit, and leave thyself as a dry tree,' is a precept no less important to the artist than to the moralist—if, indeed, in courtesy to an established error, we still speak of them as two. Keats' confidence in his capacity seems to have had no limit; but we would not hazard the opinion that the first was disproportioned to the last. The severe and subtle critic Coleridge, is known to have regarded the promise exhibited by Keats as something exorbitant, unprecedented, and amazing; although it must be admitted that, judging from what remains to us of his opinions, he seems to have looked upon that promise as being rather gigantic to sense than spiritually great.

From the above passages we also gather that Keats was not likely to have failed for lack of diligence or ambition. 'The sciences,' writes Lord Bacon, 'have been much hurt by pusillanimity, and the slenderness of the tasks men have proposed themselves.' This is equally true of the arts, although the truth may not be equally apparent. Artists, indeed, have often proposed to themselves great subjects, but they have too often neglected to make great tasks of them. This would not have been the case with Keats, who, we see, looked upon six years' practice of expression, after he had already spent several years at it, and had attained therein to astonishing excellence, as a moderate apprenticeship to the Muses, and a necessary completion of his poetical minority.

[A biographical section of three pages is omitted.]

The *Remains*, which occupy the greater part of Mr Milnes' second volume, are of great interest, as illustrating the growth, and suggesting the limits of the poet's power; but they are, for the most part, of little permanent literary value. Before we speak of them in detail, we shall make a few remarks upon some unexamined peculiarities of that school of modern poetry which is best represented by Keats; namely, the sensual and self-conscious. This school has been the offspring of that extraordinary cultivation of the critical faculties which is the grand distinguishing characteristic of our times.

It would be manifest upon reflection, if we did not know the fact from history, that the best periods of art and criticism are never coincident. The critical period is as necessarily subsequent to the best period of the art or arts criticized, as the artistical age is necessarily subsequent to, and not coincident with the age of the emotion, which is by art depicted and embalmed. Great results of art have always been the product of the general movement of a nation or a time; and such a movement could not possibly co-exist in its integrity with that advanced stage of the development of consciousness, which is the first requisite of a profound criticism. An analytical spirit, fatal to the production, though conducive, under certain circumstances, to the enjoyment of the highest art, is the life of criticism. Criticism, in modern times, has attained to an unprecedented excellence; and this has been the result of an unprecedented development of consciousness. Into the question of the general absence of faith, which is the cause, and too often the consequence of such consciousness, we must not enter, although it is closely allied to our subject. The habit of consciousness exists, and we should make the best of it. We are fully aware of its many evils, and of the desirableness of a revolution in the spirit of the time; and we are persuaded that that spirit is essentially self-destructive; but it must become more conscious before it can become less so; let us not, then, endeavour to stifle the critical spirit, which now everywhere prevails; that would not be the way to amend: *on ne rétrograde point vers le bien:* the work which is on hand, though, for the time, we should have been happier and better had it never commenced, must now be finished: Nature, man and his works and his history are undergoing an examination, which is being prosecuted with amazing diligence and insight; the heat of the investigation will not cease while the fuel lasts; but that cannot be for ever; the critical spirit must turn at length to self-examination; the necessity of doing something more than contemplating that which has been done will be seen and felt; and it is confidently to be hoped that the world will then advance anew, and with steadier and straighter steps, for the long pause which will have been taken by it, in order to view and understand the direction and validity of all its former ways.

Although the same period cannot be at once critical and artistical in the highest degree, criticism and true art are, nevertheless, by no means incompatible with each other, up to a certain point. Wordsworth, Goethe, and Coleridge, have been the offspring of our intensely critical era; and there are few, we imagine, who would at present venture to deny the claim of these poets to a high place among the poets who are for all time. Nor have these writers, by any accident of retirement or peculiar studies, been withdrawn from the influence of the prevailing spirit; they themselves have performed the part generally taken by the first poets of the age; they themselves have been the leading instruments of the age's tendency; and, as such, they have acquired a peculiarity which is worthy of our notice: they seem to have attained to the limits of the critical region of the mind, to have beheld the promised land beyond, and to have become inspired by the prospect; so that it is true generally of the best poets of later years, that their Muse has been the daughter of Hope, and not of Memory. The published works of Keats seem indeed to constitute an exception to this remark: we have, however, read an interesting fragment of his which enables us to deny the exceptional nature of this case.[1] The fragment, which we regret that Mr Milnes has not printed, consists of a kind of introduction to *Hyperion*, in which Keats, in the name of the world, bids farewell to the Grecian Mythology, *and to its spirit*. There is no document to inform us, and it is difficult to judge from the fragment itself, whether it was written before or after the publication of that part of *Hyperion* which is in the possession of the public. The question of time, however, does not affect the interest of this production as showing that Keats had begun to feel the necessity of looking to the future for his subject and inspiration.

To take up the thread of our subject where we dropped it, to run our eye over the life of Keats—By the word sensual, when we apply it to an entire school of poetry, we wish to be understood as speaking of a separate activity of sense, whatever may be the sphere in which it acts. The effect of sensuousness is produced when a strong passion of the mind finds its adequate expression in strong imagery of the senses. Deduct the passion, and you destroy the *sensuous*, and leave the *sensual*. Sensuousness, in an entire poem, is rhythm, or harmony; according as the poem is narrative and continuous, or picturesque and dramatic. Take away the passion, and the separate images, constituting, with their connexion, the general rhythmus or harmony, drop as beads from a string, into an inorganic heap, or lie, as beads when the string is more carefully withdrawn, in an order which seems vital only so long as it is unexamined.

[Patmore illustrates by quoting Keats's 'Ode to Apollo' and Thomas Taylor the Platonist's 'To the Rising Sun', finding the latter superior in charm, sincerity, and music to 'the lazy labour of Keats'.]

The characteristic beauties of the sensual school are now so very generally appreciated, that we shall be doing the cause of English poetry the best service in our power by dwelling here almost exclusively upon its less obvious, though still more characteristic faults. Among the principal of these are, imperfect artistical construction, extreme literalness of expression, defective perception of true harmony, and, as a consequence of the last, unskilfulness in the choice and management of metres, and incapacity for the invention of them.

We know not of a single fine measure that is to be attributed to the poets of this order; on the other hand, they have produced a multi-

[1] *The Fall of Hyperion—A Dream*, first published in 1857 (see Appendix: the Principal Early Editions).

plicity of metres which are wholly wanting in law and meaning, and of which the existence can be accounted for only by supposing that the arrangement of rhymes, and of the varying numbers of feet in the lines, arising in the composition of the first few verses, [become] negligently fixed upon as the form of stanza for the whole poem. The only striking proof of the existence of true metrical power in Keats, seems to us to occur in the measure of a little, and almost unknown poem, called 'La belle Dame sans merci,' which appeared first in one of Mr Leigh Hunt's weekly publications, and is reprinted now in the *Remains*. This poem is, indeed, among the most mark-worthy of the productions of Keats; besides being good and original in metre, it is simple, passionate, sensuous, and, above all, truly musical.

Concerning the extreme self-consciousness which characterized Keats, and shewed itself in his poems, we have only space to remark, that this quality was the chief cause of the excess of sense over sentiment, of which we have complained, and to adduce the following additional documentary proof of the existence of this self-consciousness in Keats' habits of thought:—'I think a little change has taken place in my intellect lately. I cannot bear to be uninterested or unemployed; I, who for a long time have been addicted to passiveness. Nothing is finer for the purposes of great productions than a very gradual ripening of the intellectual powers. As an instance of this, observe, I sat down yesterday to read *King Lear* once again. The thing appeared to demand the prologue of a sonnet; I wrote it, and began to read.'

We have already stated our belief that this consciousness is a stage through which the modern mind must pass on its road to excellence; it is not, therefore, the less a defect while it exists. Keats died before he had outgrown this stage, as he certainly must have done, had he lived a few years more. As it was, the best of Keats' poetry, by reason of the quality in question, falls considerably short of the highest beauty, which, whether it be sweet or severe, is always the spontaneous, or unconscious obedience of spirit to law: when the obedience is unopposed, sweetness results, when it meets with opposition, severity is expressed: witness, for example, the 'Venus de Medicis,' and the 'Niobe.' The highest, the only true beauty, is thus the beauty of holiness; and since obedience is essential humility, beauty, by becoming proud and self-conscious, reverses its own nature, and is not the less essential deformity for its assumption of the shape of an angel of light.

It remains for us formally to introduce to our readers the *Remains*, which occupy the bulk of the second of the two little volumes before us. Altogether they will not add to the very high reputation of Keats. The tragedy called *Otho the Great*, is the most important of these productions. It contains extremely little that is truly dramatic; and that little wants originality, being evidently imitated, even to the rhythms of the separate lines, from Shakspeare, and more often from that bad, but very tempting model, Fletcher. There is, however, one passage that strikes us as being finer, in its peculiar way, than anything in the hitherto published writings of Keats. We quote it the more readily, because it stands almost alone, and constitutes the chief right possessed by the tragedy to the time and attention of our readers; for, highly interesting as the work must be to *students* of poetry, and of the poetical character, we are bound to confess that, on the whole, it exhibits a strange dearth even of the author's common excellencies.

The Prince Ludolph, driven mad by the sudden discovery of the guilt of his bride, enters the banquet-room in which the bridal party is assembled:

[Quotes *Otho the Great*, v.v. 21–48, 'A splendid company!' to 'is it not dark?', italicizing lines 24, 35–48; and v.v. 55–72, 'There should be three more here' to 'So taking a disguise', italicizing lines 64–72.]

Next in consideration to *Otho the Great*, stands an attempt in the comic style, called 'The Cap and Bells.' The humour is of a very indifferent vein, depending chiefly upon the introduction of slang, or extremely colloquial phrases, in immediate connexion with more serious expressions. There are, however, frequent touches of charming poetry; for example—

'Good! good!' cried Hum, 'I have known her from a child!
She is a changeling of my management;
She was born at midnight, in an Indian wild;
Her mother's screams with the striped tiger's blent,
While the torch-bearing slaves a halloo sent
Into the jungles; and her palanquin
Rested amid the desert's dreariment,
Shook with her agony, *till fair were seen*
The little Bertha's eyes ope on the stars serene.'

Of the two following stanzas, the first is as good an illustration of the mistakes of the poem as the second is of its beauties:—

[Quotes 'The Cap and Bells', stanzas 63–4.]

Of the lesser poems 'The Song of Four Fairies,' and the fragment called 'The Eve of St Mark,' deserve especial attention, but they are too long to quote. We must close our extracts with a grand and subtle sonnet ON THE SEA.

[Quotes the sonnet 'On the Sea' in full.]

Ere we conclude, we must again entreat that we may not be misunderstood in what has been put forth by us concerning the shortcomings of Keats in his character as a poet. Were we to speak at full all the praise which we believe his writings merit, we should satisfy the blindest of his admirers; but we have dwelt rather upon the faults of Keats, because while they have been very much less generally perceived than his excellencies, the perception of them is by no means of less importance to the health of English literature. When we remember that poets are unconsciously received in the world as the highest authorities upon matters of feeling, and therefore of morals, we cannot think that we have dwelt even fully enough upon the deficiencies of the last phase which our poetry has assumed. We console ourselves with the assurance that it is a phase which cannot be an enduring one. Poetry in England has passed through three great epochs, and is now in the early youth of the fourth, and let us hope the noblest. Natural and religious, almost by compulsion, nearly till the time of Milton, the muse at last endeavoured to be something other and more than these; with Cowley and his train, she affected elaborate, artificial, and meretricious ornament; but the re-action appeared in that school of *sensible* poets, of which Dryden and Pope were the chief doctors; we are now returning to the right path; nothing can be more laudable than have been the *aims* of most of our modern poets, and we found our extraordinary hopes of the final success of the school, less upon any earnest we have received of the harvest than upon the incontrovertible truth that 'whatsoever we desire in youth, in age we shall plentifully obtain.'

It remains for us to assure our readers that Mr Milnes, whose prose style is the completest, in its happy way, that we are acquainted with, has executed his task with accomplished taste. For a poet to have conducted the autobiography of a brother poet, as Mr Milnes has done, without having once overstepped the modest office of an 'editor,' is an exhibition of self-denial which is now as rare as it is worthy of imitation.

62. Shelley, Keats and Tennyson compared

1849

Extract from unsigned review, *Edinburgh Review* (October 1849), xc, 388–433.

Aubrey Thomas de Vere (1814–1902), Irish poet, was a friend of Wordsworth's later life. He became a Roman Catholic within two years of writing this review of Shelley's *Poetical Works* (1847), Milnes's *Life of Keats*, and Tennyson's *Princess* (1847), but unlike Coventry Patmore's, de Vere's sympathetic and perceptive study presents an 'integrated' Keats. 'His body seemed to think.'

Before this extract begins it has been argued that 'The imagination . . . has ever recognized two great offices, distinct though allied—the one, that of representing the actual world; the other, that of creating an ideal region, into which spirits whom this world has wearied may retire.' Thus two schools of poets have arisen, one northern and national (such as Cowper and Burns), the other southern and ideal (such as Spenser, Shakespeare, Milton). Shelley and Keats were both 'poets in whom a southern temperament and more classical ideal prevails', but Shelley's great gifts were vitiated by his moral and artistic rashness. The last three pages of the article, concerned with Tennyson alone, have been omitted.

The genius of Keats was Grecian to a far higher degree than that of Shelley. His sense of beauty was profounder still; and was accompanied by that in which Shelley's poetry was deficient—Repose. Tranquillity is no high merit if it be attained at the expense of ardour; but the two qualities are not incompatible. The ardour of Shelley's nature shows itself in a strong evolution of thought and succession of imagery;—that of Keats in a still intensity. The former was a fiery enthusiasm, the latter was a profound passion. Rushing through regions of unlimited thought, Shelley could but throw out hints which are often suggestive only. His designs are always outline sketches, and the lines of light in which they are drawn remind us of that 'temple of a spirit' described by him, the walls of which revealed

> A tale of passionate change divinely taught,
> Which in their winged dance unconscious genii wrought.

Truth and action may be thus emblemed; but beauty is a thing of shape and of colour, not of light merely, and rest is essential to it. That mystic rapidity of interwoven thought, in which Shelley exulted, was foreign to the deeper temperament of Keats. One of his canons of poetry was, that 'its touches of beauty should never be half-way, thereby making the reader breathless, instead of content. The rise, the progress, the setting of imagery, should, like the sun, come naturally to the poet, shine over him, and set soberly, although in magnificence, leaving him in the luxury of twilight.' He disliked all poetical surprises, and affirmed that poetry 'should strike the reader as a wording of his own highest thoughts, and appear almost a remembrance.' Shelley's genius, like the eagle he describes,

> *Runs down* the slanted sunlight of the dawn.

But, beauty moves ever in curved lines, like the celestial bodies, and even in movement simulates rest. Beauty was the adornment of Shelley's poetry; it was the very essence of Keats's. There is in his poetry not only a constant enjoyment of the beautiful,—there is a thirst for it never to be satisfied, of which we are reminded by his portrait. Shelley admired the beautiful, Keats was absorbed in it; and admired it no more than an infant admires the mother at whose breast he feeds. That deep absorption excluded all consciousness of self,—nay, every intrusion of alien thought; and while the genius of others, too often like a double-reflecting crystal, returns a twofold image, that poetic vision which day by day grew clearer before Keats was an image of beauty only, whole and unbroken. There is a peculiar significance in the expression, 'a child of song,' as applied to him. Not only his outward susceptibilities retained throughout the freshness of infancy, but his whole nature possessed that integrity which belongs but to childhood, or to the purest and most energetic genius. When the poetic mood was not on him, though his heart was full of manly courage, there was much of a child's waywardness, want of self-command, and inexperienced weakness in his nature. His poetry is never *juvenile*. It is either the stammer of the child or the 'large utterance of the early gods.'

Keats possessed eminently the rare gift of invention—as is proved by the narrative poems he has left behind. He had also, though without Shelley's constructive skill as to the architecture of sentences, a depth, significance, and power of diction, which even the imitational affectation to be found in his earliest productions, could not disguise. He instinctively selects the words which exhibit the more characteristic qualities of the objects described. The most remarkable property of his poetry, however, is the degree in which it combines the sensuous with the ideal. The sensuousness of Keats's poetry might have degenerated into the sensual, but for the ideality that exalted it,—a union which existed in consequence of a connexion not less intimate between his sensitive temperament and his wide imagination. Perhaps we have had no other instance of a bodily constitution so poetical. With him all things were more or less sensational; his mental faculties being, as it were, extended throughout the sensitive part of his nature—as the sense of sight, according to the theory of the Mesmerists, is diffused throughout the body on some occasions of unusual excitement. His body seemed to think; and, on the other hand, he sometimes appears hardly to have known whether he possessed aught but body. His whole nature partook of a sensational character in this respect, namely, that every thought and sentiment came upon him with the suddenness, and appealed to him with the reality of a sensation. It is not the lowest only, but also the loftiest part of our being to which this character of unconsciousness and immediateness belongs. Intuitions and aspirations are spiritual sensations; while the physical perceptions and appetites are bodily intuitions. Instinct itself is but a lower form of inspiration; and the highest virtue becomes a spiritual instinct. It was in the intermediate part of our nature that Keats had but a small part. His mind had little affinity with whatever belonged to the region of the merely probable. To his heart, kindly as he was, everything in the outer world seemed foreign, except that which for the time engrossed it. His nature was Epicurean at one side, Platonist at the other—and both by irresistible instinct. The Aristotelian definition, the Stoical dogma, the Academical disputation, were to him all alike unmeaning. His poetic gift was not a separate faculty which he could exercise or restrain as he pleased, and direct to whatever object he chose. It was when 'by predominance of thought oppressed' that there fell on him that still, poetic vision of truth and beauty which only thus truly comes. The 'burden' of his inspiration came to him 'in leni aurâ,' like the visits of the gods; yet his fragile nature bent before it like a reed; it was not shaken or disturbed, but wielded by it wholly.

To the sluggish temperaments of ordinary men excitement is pleasure. The fervour of Keats preyed upon him with a pain from which Shelley was protected by a mercurial mobility; and it was with the languor of rest that Keats associated the idea of enjoyment. How much is implied in this description of exhaustion! 'Pleasure has no show of enticement, and Pain no unbearable frown; neither Poetry, nor Ambition, nor Love have any alertness of countenance; as they pass me by they seem rather like three figures on a Greek vase—two men and a woman, whom no one but myself could distinguish in their disguisement. This is the *only happiness*; and is a rare instance of advantage in the body overcoming the mind.' (P. 264. vol. i.) A nobler relief was afforded to him by that versatility which made him live in the objects around him. It is thus that he writes:—'I scarcely remember counting on any happiness. I look not for it, if it be not in the present hour. Nothing startles me beyond the moment. The setting sun will always set me to rights; or if a sparrow were before my window, I take part in its existence, and pick with it, about the gravel.' (P. 67. vol. i.) Elsewhere he speaks thus of that form of poetic genius which belonged to him, and which he contradistinguishes from the 'egotistical sublime.' 'It has no self. It is every thing and nothing—it has no character—it enjoys light and shade—it lives in gusts, be it foul or fair, high or low, rich or poor, mean or elevated—it has as much delight in conceiving an Iago as an Imogen.' (P. 221. vol. i.) In this passage, as elsewhere, he seems to confound versatility with the absence of personal character. That versatility of imagination is however by no means incompatible with depth of nature and tenacity of purpose we have already observed; and our opinion is confirmed by a remark of Mr Milnes, whose life of Keats, from which we have so largely quoted, is enriched with many pieces of admirable criticism. Keats's versatility showed itself, like Mr Tennyson's, not only in the dramatic skill with which he realised various and alien forms of existence, but also, though to a lesser degree, in the fact that the character of his poetry varied according to the model he had been studying. In *Endymion* he reminds us of Chaucer and Spenser; in *Hyperion* of Milton; in his 'Cap and Bells' of Ariosto; and in his drama, the last act of which is very fine, of Ford. Mr Milnes remarks, with reference to the last two works, that Keats's occasional resemblance to other poets, though it proves that his genius was still in a growing state, in no degree detracts from his originality. He did not imitate others, Mr Milnes observes, so much as emulate them; and no matter whom he may resemble, he is still always himself.

The character of Keats's intellect corresponded well with his large imagination and versatile temperament. He had not Mr Shelley's various and sleepless faculties, but he had the larger mind. Keats could neither form systems nor dispute about them; though germs of deep and original thought are to be found scattered in his most careless letters. The two friends used sometimes to contend as to the relative worth of truth and of beauty. Beauty is the visible embodiment of a certain species of truth; and it was with that species that the mind of Keats, which always worked in and through the sensibilities, held *conscious* relations. He fancied that he had no access to philosophy, because he was averse to definitions and dogmas, and sometimes saw glimpses of truth in adverse systems. His mind had itself much of that 'negative capability' which he remarked on as a large part of Shakspeare's greatness, and which he described as a power 'of being in uncertainties, mysteries, doubts, without any irritable reaching after fact and reason.' (P. 93. vol. i.) There is assuredly such a thing as philosophical doubt, as well as of philosophical belief: it is the doubt which belongs to the mind, not to the will; to which we are not drawn by love of singularity, and from which we are not scared by nervous tremours; the doubt which is not the denial of any thing, so much as the proving of all things; the doubt of one who would rather walk in mystery than in false lights, who waits that he may win, and who prefers the broken fragments of truth to the imposing completeness of a delusion. Such is that uncertainty of a large mind, which a small mind cannot understand; and such no doubt was, in part, that of Keats, who was fond of saying that 'every point of thought is the centre of an intellectual world.' The passive part of intellect, the powers of susceptibility and appreciation, Keats possessed to an almost infinite degree: but in this respect his mind appears to have been cast in a feminine mould; and that masculine energy which Shakspeare combined with a susceptive temperament unfathomably deep, in him either existed deficiently, or had not had time for its development.

If we turn from the poet to the man, from the works to the life, the retrospect is less painful in the case of Keats than of Shelley. He also suffered from ill-health, and from a temperament which, when its fine edge had to encounter the jars of life, was subject to a morbid despondency: but he had many sources of enjoyment, and his power of enjoyment was extraordinary. His disposition, which was not only sweet and simple, but tolerant and kindly, procured and preserved for him many friends. It has been commonly supposed that adverse criticism had wounded him deeply: but the charge receives a complete refutation from a letter written on the occasion referred to. In it he says, 'Praise or blame has but a momentary effect on the man whose love of beauty in the abstract makes him a severe critic on his own works. . . . I will write independently. I have written independently *without judgment*. I may write independently, and *with judgment*, hereafter. The Genius of Poetry must work out its own salvation in a man. . . . I was never afraid of failure.'

There are, however, trials in the world from which the most imaginative cannot escape; and which are more real than those which self-love alone can make important to us. Keats's sensibility amounted to disease. 'I would reject,' he writes, 'a Petrarchal coronation—on account of my dying day—and because women have cancers!' A few months later, after visiting the house of Burns, he wrote thus,—'His misery is a dead weight on the nimbleness of one's quill: I tried to forget it . . . it won't do. . . . We can see, horribly clear, in the works of such a man, his whole life, as if we were God's spies.' (P. 171.) It was this extreme sensibility, not less than his ideal tendencies, which made him shrink with prescient fear from the world of actual things. Reality frowned above him like a cliff seen by a man in a nightmare dream. It fell on him at last! The most interesting of all his letters is that to his brother (P. 224. vol. i.), in which he, with little anticipation of results, describes his first meeting with the Oriental beauty who soon after became the object of his passion. In love he had always been, in one sense: and personal love was but the devotion to that in a concentrated form which he had previously and more safely loved as a thing scattered and diffused. He loved and he won; but death cheated him of the prize. Tragical indeed were his sufferings during the months of his decline. In leaving life he lost what can never be known by the multitudes who but half live: and poetry at least could assuredly have presented him but in scant measure with the consolations which the Epicurean can dispense with most easily, but which are needed most by those whose natures are most spiritual, and whose thirst after immortality is strongest. Let us not, however, intrude into what we know not. In many things we are allowed to rejoice with him. His life had been one long revel. 'The open sky,' he writes to a friend, 'sits upon our senses like a sapphire crown: the air is our robe of state; the earth is our throne; and the sea a mighty minstrel playing before it!' Less a human being than an Imagination embodied, he passed, 'like a new-born spirit,' over a world that for him ever retained the dew of the morning; and bathing in all its freshest joys he partook but little of its stain.

Shelley and Keats remained with us only long enough to let us know how much we have lost—

> We have beheld these lights but not possessed them.

The genius of the poet whose latest work we have discussed at the beginning of this paper has been more justly appreciated than that of either of them: But it will now probably be asked to which of the two great schools of English poetry illustrated by us *he* is to be referred? The answer to that question is not easy, for in truth he has much in common with both. His earlier poems might sometimes be classed in the same category with those of Shelley and Keats: For, the three have in common an ardent temperament, a versatile imagination, and an admirable power of embodying the classical; but in other respects they differ widely. Tennyson has indeed, like Keats, with whom he has most in common, a profound sense of the beautiful, a calm and often soft intensity, a certain voluptuousness in style, that reminds us of the Venetian school of painting, and a marvellous depth and affluence of diction—but here the resemblance ends. We do not yet observe in his works, to the same degree, that union of strength with lightness and freedom of touch, which, like the unerring but unlaboured handling of a great master, characterised Keats's latest works. On the other hand, Tennyson has greater variety. Wide indeed is his domain—extending as it does from that of Keats, whose chief characteristic was ideal beauty, to that of Burns, whose songs, native to the soil, gush out as spontaneously as the warbling of the bird or the murmuring of the brook. Even in their delineation of beauty, how different are the two poets. In Keats that beauty is chiefly beauty of form; in Tennyson that of colour has at least an equal place: one consequence of which is, that while Keats, in his descriptions of nature, contents himself with embodying separate objects with a luxurious vividness, Tennyson's gallery abounds with cool far-stretching landscapes, in which the fair green plain and winding river, and violet mountain ridge and peaks of remotest snow, are harmonised through all the gradations of aerial distance. Yet his is not to be classed with that recent poetry which has been noted for a devotion, almost religious, to mere outward nature. His landscapes, like those of Titian, are for the most part but a beautiful background to the figures. Men and manners are more his theme than nature. His genius seems to tend as naturally to the idyllic as that of Shelley did to the lyrical, or that of Keats to the epic.

The moral range of Mr Tennyson's poetry, too, is as wide as the imaginative. It is remarkable how little place, notwithstanding the ardour of Shelley and of Keats, is given in their works, to the affections properly so called. They abound in emotion and passion: in which respect Mr Tennyson resembles them; but he is not less happy in the delineation of those human affections which depend not on instinct or imagination alone, but which, growing out of the heart, are modified by circumstance and association, and constitute the varied texture of social existence.

63. The language of actual life

1851

Extract from D. M. Moir's *Sketches of the Poetical Literature of the Past Half-Century* (1851), 215–21.

David Macbeth Moir (1798–1851) had written for *Blackwood's* over the signature 'Delta'. His *Sketches of the Poetical Literature* contains a series of lectures given in the year of his death. In earlier lectures he has argued that before Keats there were three 'schools' of English poetry: 1. Chaucer to Shirley; 2. Dryden and Pope; 3. Wordsworth, Coleridge, and others. Finally 'a fourth school began to exhibit itself about thirty years ago, and since then has been gradually gaining an ascendancy. . . . The source of this new composite school was at first very distinctly Italian. . . . I do not think we can trace an origin to this school,—which soon comprehended among its disciples Keats, Shelley, and Barry Cornwall . . . farther back than 1816, when it showed itself in full-blown perfection in the *Story of Rimini*, by Leigh Hunt.' Moir's lecture on Keats is given unabridged except for the quotations.

It is very evident that John Keats, the greatest of all our poets who have died in early youth—not excepting Michael Bruce, Kirke White, or Chatterton—imbibed in boyhood a sincere admiration for the poetry of Leigh Hunt, and primarily adopted him as his model in style and diction; although, ere he ventured before the public, he had considerably altered and modified, or rather extended his views on these matters, by a reverential study of the antique English pastoral poets, Drayton, Spenser, and William Browne—the last of whom he especially followed in the selection of his imagery, and the varied harmony of his numbers. Crude, unsustained, and extravagant as these juvenile attempts in most part are, we have ever and anon indications of a fine original genius. His garden, though unweeded, is full of freshness and fragrance; the bindweed strangles the mignionette; and docks and dandelions half conceal the yellow cowslip and the purple violet; but we are wooed to this corner by the bud of the moss-rose, and to that by the double wall-flower. We feel it to be a wilderness; but it is a wilderness of many sweets. I allude here more particularly to his first little volume, published in 1817, with a head of Spenser on the title-page, and dedicated to Leigh Hunt.

Images of majesty and beauty continued to crowd on the imagination of the young poet; but either his taste in selection was deficient, or he shrank from the requisite labour; and in the following year appeared his *Endymion*, a poetic romance. It would be difficult to point out anywhere a work more remarkable for its amount of beauties and blemishes, inextricably entertwined. Its mythology is Greek, and its imagery the sylvan-pastoral—reminding us now of the pine-flavoured Idyllia of Theocritus, and now of the 'bosky bournes and bushy dells' of Milton's *Comus*. Preparatory to its composition, he had saturated his mind with the 'leafy luxury' of our early dramatists; and we have many reflections of the rural beauty and repose pervading *The Faithful Shepherdess* of Fletcher, and *The Sad Shepherd* of Ben Jonson; as well as of the early Milton of the 'Arcades' and 'Lycidas.' We are entranced with the prodigal profusion of imagery, and the exquisite variety of metres sweeping along with an Æolian harmony, at once so refined and yet seemingly so inartificial. All is, however, a wild luxurious revel merely, where Imagination laughs at Taste, and bids defiance to Judgment and Reason. There is no discrimination, no selection—even the very rhymes seem sometimes to have suggested the thoughts that follow; and whatever comes uppermost comes out, provided it be florid, gorgeous, or glittering. The work is a perfect mosaic of bright tints and graceful forms, despotically commingled, almost without regard to plan or congruity; so that we often lose the thin thread of story altogether in the fantastic exuberance of ornament and decoration. Ever and anon, however, we come to bits of exquisite beauty—patches of deep, serene blue sky, amid the rolling clouds, which compel us to pause in admiration—glimpses of nature full of tenderness and truth—touches of sentiment deep as they are delicate. His opening line, 'A thing of beauty is a joy for ever,' conveys a fine philosophic sentiment, and is the key-note to the whole body of his poetry. Crude, unequal, extravagant, nay, absurd as he sometimes is—for there is scarcely an isolated page in *Endymion* to which one or more of these harsh epithets may not in some degree be justly applied—yet, on the other hand, it would be difficult to point out any twenty lines in sequence unredeemed by some happy turn of thought, some bright image, or some eloquent expression.

That all this was the result of imaginative wealth and youthful inexperience, is demonstrated by the last poems John Keats was permitted to give the world, and which are as rich, but much more select, in imagery, purer in taste, and more fastidious in diction, as well as more felicitous and artistic. He had found out that, to keep interest alive, it was necessary to deal less with the shadowy, the remote, and the abstract; and that, without losing in dignity, he might descend more to the thoughts and feelings—nay, even to the ways, and habits, and language of actual life. From the pure mythological of *Endymion* he attempted a blending of the real with the supernatural in 'Lamia', and exactly with the degree of success which might, in the management of such elements, have been expected from him. 'Isabella, or the Pot of Basil,' his version of Boccaccio's exquisite little story, is much less questionable. We have therein character and incident as well as description; and to these the last is made subordinate. We there also see, for the first time, that instead of playing with his theme, he has set himself in earnest to grapple with it. The composition is more elaborate and we have a selection of thoughts and images instead of the indiscriminate pouring forth of all. The faults of affectation and quaintness, although not entirely got rid of, are there less glaring and offensive; and along with the mere garniture of fancy, we have a story of human interest, of love and revenge and suffering, well though peculiarly told. In this poem he wonderfully triumphed over his earlier besetting frailties—want of precision and carelessness of style—and exhibited such rapid strides of improvement, as enable us to form some probable estimate of what his genius might have achieved, had he been destined to reach maturer years.

His two latest were also his two most perfect compositions, yet completely opposite in their character—'The Eve of St Agnes,' of the most florid Gothic, remarkable for its sensuous beauty; and *Hyperion*, a fragment equally remarkable for its Greek severity and antique solemnity of outline. To the same latest period of his strangely fevered and brief career—for he died at twenty-four—are referable the four exquisite odes,—'To a Nightingale,' 'To a Grecian Urn,' 'To Melancholy,' and 'To Autumn,'—all so pregnant with deep thought, so picturesque in their limning, and so suggestive.

Let us take three stanzas from 'The Eve of St Agnes.' They describe Madeline at her devotions before lying down to sleep on that charmed night. She has just entered her chamber, when—

> Out went the taper as she hurried in;

[Quotes 'The Eve of St Agnes', stanzas 23–5.]

We have here a specimen of descriptive power luxuriously rich and original; but the following lines, from the 'Ode to a Nightingale,' flow from a far more profound fountain of inspiration. After addressing the bird as a

> light-winged Dryad of the trees,
> In some melodious plot
> Of beechen green and shadows numberless,
> Singing of summer in full-throated ease,

he adds, somewhat fantastically, it must be owned, at first—

> Oh, for a beaker full of the warm south,

[Quotes 'Ode to a Nightingale', lines 15–30, and 61 to the end.]

In his earlier pieces Keats was too extramundane—too fond of the visionary. His fancy and feelings rioted in a sort of sun-coloured cloud-land, where all was gorgeous and glowing, rose-tinctured or thunderous; but ever most indistinct, and often incomprehensible, save when regarded as dream-like imaginings—the morning reveries of a young enthusiast. His genius, however, was gradually coming under the control of judgment; his powers of conception and of expression were alike maturing; and his heart was day by day expanding to the genial influences of healthy simple nature. A large portion of what he has left behind is crude, unconcocted, and unsatisfactory, exhibiting rather poetical materials than poetical superstructure; but his happier strains vindicate the presence of a great poet in something more than embryo. Which of our acknowledged magnates, if cut off at the same age, would have left so much really excellent? Altogether, whether we regard his short fevered life, or the quality of his genius, John Keats was assuredly one of the most remarkable men in the range of our poetical literature; nor, while taste and sensibility remain in the world, can ever his prediction of his own fate be verified, when he dictated his epitaph as that of one 'whose name was written in water.'

As an example of Keats' severer manner, I give the magnificent portrait of Saturn, with which *Hyperion* opens. In the same fragment we find several other passages equally grand and solemn.

[Quotes *Hyperion*, lines 1–21.]

64. Bagehot on Keats

1853, 1856, 1859

Walter Bagehot (1826–77), economist, financier, and journalist. In Extract (a), Bagehot has been arguing that the mind of Shakespeare contains the mind of Keats, because Shakespeare has three poetic subjects, human life, Nature, and 'fancies', whereas Keats (in *Endymion*) has only the last.

(a) Extracts from unsigned article 'Shakespeare': 'The fanciful class of poems differ from others in being laid, so far as their scene goes, in a perfectly unseen world. The type of such productions is Keats's *Endymion*. We mean that it is the type, not as giving the abstract perfection of this sort of art, but because it shows and embodies both its excellencies and defects in a very marked and prominent manner. In that poem there are no passions and no actions, there is no heart and no life, but there is beauty, and that is meant to be enough, and to a reader of one-and-twenty it is enough and more. . . . What is . . . a real view of human life in any kind whatever, to people who do not know and do not care what human life is? . . . And the literature of this period of human life runs naturally away from the real world; away from the less ideal portion of it, from stocks and stones, and aunts and uncles, and rests on mere half-embodied sentiments, which in the hands of great poets assume a kind of semi-personality, and are, to the distinction between things and persons, "as moonlight unto sunlight, and as water unto wine." ' (*Prospective Review* (July 1853), ix, 430–1.)

(b) Extracts from unsigned article 'Percy Bysshe Shelley': 'One of the most essentially modern of recent poets has an "Ode to a Grecian Urn:" it begins—

> Thou still unravish'd bride of quietness!
> Thou foster-child of Silence and slow Time,
> Sylvan historian! who canst thus express
> A flowery tale more sweetly than our rhyme:
> What leaf-fringed legend haunts about thy shape
> Of deities or mortals, or of both,
> In Tempe or the dales of Arcady?
> What men or gods are these? What maidens loth?
> What mad pursuit? What struggle to escape?
> What pipes and timbrels? What wild ecstasy?

No ancient poet would have dreamed of writing thus. There would have been no indistinct shadowy warmth, no breath of surrounding beauty: his delineation would have been cold, distinct, chiselled like the urn itself. The use which such a poet as Keats makes of ancient mythology is exactly similar. He owes his fame to the inexplicable art with which he has breathed a soft tint over the marble forms of gods and goddesses, enhancing their beauty without impairing their chasteness. . . .

It is only necessary to open Shelley, to show how essentially classical in its highest efforts his art is. . . . The exact opposite, however, to Shelley, in the nature of his sensibility, is Keats. That great poet used to pepper his tongue, "to enjoy in all its grandeur the cool flavour of delicious claret." When you know it, you seem to read it in his poetry. There is the same luxurious sentiment; the same poise on fine sensation. Shelley was the reverse of this; he was a waterdrinker; his verse runs quick and chill, like a pure crystal stream. The sensibility of Keats was attracted too by the spectacle of the universe; he could not keep his eye from seeing, or his ears from hearing, the glories of it. All the beautiful objects of nature reappear by name in his poetry. The abstract idea of beauty is for ever celebrated in Shelley; it haunted his soul. But it was independent of special things; it was the general surface of beauty which lies upon all things. It was the smile of the universe and the expression of the world; it was not the vision of a land of corn and wine.' *National Review* (October 1856), iii, 374–9.)

(c) Extracts from unsigned article, probably by Bagehot, 'Tennyson's Idylls': 'The early poetry of Mr Tennyson—and the same may be said of nearly all the poetry of Shelley and Keats—labours under the defect that it is written, almost professedly, for young people—especially young men—of rather heated imaginations. . . . Almost all poetry . . . is addressed more to young men than to others. But the early poetry of Tennyson, and of the other poets we have named, is addressed to that class even more peculiarly. In the greatest poets, in Shakespeare and in Homer, there is a great deal besides poetry. There are broad descriptions of character, dramatic scenes, eloquence, argument, a deep knowledge of manly and busy life. . . . Shelley and Keats, on the other hand, have presented their poetry to the world in its pure essence; they have not added—we scarcely know whether they would have been able to add—the more worldly and terrestrial elements; . . . they have been content to rely on imaginatively expressed sentiment, and sentiment-exciting imagery; in short, on that which in its more subtle sense we call poetry, exclusively and wholly. In consequence, their works have had a great influence on young men; they retain a hold on many mature men only because they are associated with their youth. . . . Mr Tennyson is deficient in the most marked peculiarity which Shelley and Keats have in common. Both of these poets are singularly gifted with a sustained faculty of lyrical expression . . . [Shelley] is ever soaring; and whilst soaring, ever singing. Keats . . . did not ascend to so extreme an elevation. He did not belong to the upper air. He had no abstract labour, no haunting speculations, no attenuated thoughts. He was the poet of the obvious beauty of the world. His genius was of the earth—of the autumn earth—rich and mellow; and it was lavish. He did not carry his art high or deep; he neither enlightens our eyes much, nor expands our ears much; but pleases our fancies with a prolonged strain of simple rich melody. He does not pause, or stay, or hesitate. His genius is continuous; the flow of it is as obvious at the best moments as the excellence, and at inferior moments is more so. . . .

Over Keats, however, Mr Tennyson may perhaps claim a general superiority. . . . Out of the infinite thoughts, discoveries, and speculations which are scattered, more or less perfectly, through society, certain minds have a knack of taking up and making their own that which is true, and healthy, and valuable; and they reject the rest. . . . They are continually thinking the subjects in question over: they have the details of them in their minds: they have a floating picture of endless particulars about them in their imaginations. . . . This kind of meditative tact and slow selective judgment Mr Tennyson possesses in a very great measure; and there is nothing of which Keats was so entirely destitute. It does not, perhaps, occur to you while reading him that he is deficient in it. It belongs to an order of merit completely out of his way. It is the reflective gift of a mature man: Keats's best gifts are those of an impulsive, original, and refined boy.' (*National Review* (October 1859), ix, 370–90.)

65. Ideas made concrete

1853

Extract from signed review of E. S. Dallas's *Poetics: An Essay on Poetry* (1852), *North British Review* (August 1853), xix, 316–27.

David Masson (1822–1907) had been appointed Professor of English Literature at University College, London, in 1852, and was to spend thirty years as Professor of Rhetoric and English Literature at Edinburgh. This is the first comment on Keats's poetry by a professional academic, and the first scrap of 'close analysis' since Leigh Hunt's exposition of 'The Eve of St Agnes' in 1835 (No. 49). See also No. 69.

To clothe his feelings with *circumstance*; to weave forth whatever arises in his mind into an objective tissue of imagery and incident that shall substantiate it and make it visible; such is the constant aim and art of the poet. Take an example. The idea of life occurs to the poet Keats, and how does he express it?

> Stop and consider! life is but a day;
> A fragile dew-drop on its perilous way
> From a tree's summit; a poor Indian's sleep
> While his boat hastens to the monstrous steep
> Of Montmorenci. Why so sad a moan?
> Life is the rose's hope while yet unblown;

The reading of an ever-changing tale;
The light uplifting of a maiden's veil;
A pigeon tumbling in clear summer air;
A laughing school-boy, without grief or care,
Riding the springy branches of an elm.[1]

This is true *ποίησις*.[2] What with the power of innate analogy, what with the occult suasion of the rhyme, there arose first in the poet's mind, contemporaneous with the idea of life, nay, as incorporate with that idea, the imaginary object or vision of the dew-drop falling through foliage—that imagined circumstance is, therefore, flung forth as representative of the idea. But even this does not exhaust the creative force; the idea bodies itself again in the new imaginary circumstance of the Indian in his boat; and that, too, is flung forth. Then there is a rest; but the idea still buds, still seeks to express itself in new circumstance, and five other translations of it follow. And these seven pictures, these seven morsels of imagined concrete, supposing them all to be intellectually genuine, are as truly the poet's *thoughts* about life as any seven scientific definitions would be the thoughts of the physiologist or the metaphysician. . . .

A Keats, though always poetical, may often be poetical with so small a stimulus, that only lovers of poetry for its own sake feel themselves sufficiently interested. . . . It has been usual, of late, to give the palm to imagery. Thus, it was a remark of Lord Jeffrey—and the remark has almost passed into a proverb—that a want of relish for such rich sensuous poetry as that of Keats would argue a want of true poetical taste. . . . Some poets, as Keats, Shakespeare, and Milton in much of his poetry, so teem with accumulated concrete circumstance, or generate it so fast, as their imagination works, that every imagined circumstance as it is put forth from them takes with it an accompaniment of parasitic fancies. . . . As regards the question *when* imagery is excessive, *when* the richness of a poet's language is to be called extravagance, no general principle can be laid down. . . . A useful distinction, under this head, might possibly be drawn between the liberty of the poet and the duty of the artist. Keats's *Endymion*, one might safely, in reference to such a distinction, pronounce to be too rich; for in that poem there is no proportion between the imagery, or accessory concrete, and the main stem of the imagined circumstance from which the poem derives its name. In the 'Eve of St Agnes', on the other hand, there is no such fault.

[1] 'Sleep and Poetry', lines 85–95.

[2] 'making', poetry.

66. Lowell on Keats

1854

Extract from 'The Life of Keats', signed 'J.R.L.', prefixed to *The Poetical Works of John Keats*, Boston, 1854, xv–xxxvi.

James Russell Lowell's essay, reprinted in successive editions of Keats's *Works* from 1854 onwards, reached a wide public in America, and was eventually enlarged into the essay in *Among My Books*, second series, Boston, 1876.

It is curious that men should resent more fiercely what they suspect to be good verses, than what they know to be bad morals. Is it because they feel themselves incapable of the one, and not of the other? However it be, the best poetry has been the most savagely attacked, and men who scrupulously practised the Ten Commandments as if there were never a *not* in any of them, felt every sentiment of their better nature outraged by the *Lyrical Ballads*. It is idle to attempt to show that Keats did not suffer keenly from the vulgarities of *Blackwood* and the *Quarterly*. He suffered in proportion as his ideal was high, and he was conscious of falling below it. In England, especially, it is not pleasant to be ridiculous, even if you are a lord; but to be ridiculous and an apothecary at the same time, is almost as bad as it was formerly to be excommunicated. *A priori*, there was something absurd in poetry written by the son of an assistant in the livery-stables of Mr Jennings, even though they were an establishment, and a large establishment, and nearly opposite Finsbury Circus. Mr Gifford, the ex-cobbler, thought so in the *Quarterly*, and Mr Terry, the actor,* thought so even more distinctly in *Blackwood*, bidding the young apothecary 'back to his gallipots!' It is not pleasant to be talked down upon by your inferiors who happen to have the advantage of position, nor to be drenched with ditch-water, though you know it to be thrown by a scullion in a garret.

Keats, as his was a temperament in which sensibility was excessive,

* Haydon (*Autobiography*, vol. i. p. 379,) says that he 'strongly suspects' Terry to have written the articles in *Blackwood*.

could not but be galled by this treatment. He was galled the more that he was also a man of strong sense, and capable of understanding clearly how hard it is to make men acknowledge solid value in a person whom they have once heartily laughed at. Reputation is in itself only a farthing-candle, of wavering and uncertain flame, and easily blown out, but it is the light by which the world looks for and finds merit. Keats longed for fame, but longed above all to deserve it. Thrilling with the electric touch of sacred leaves, he saw in vision, like Dante, that small procession of the elder poets to which only elect centuries can add another laurelled head. Might he, too, deserve from posterity the love and reverence which he paid to those antique glories? It was no unworthy ambition, but every thing was against him,—birth, health, even friends, since it was partly on their account that he was sneered at. His very name stood in his way, for Fame loves best such syllables as are sweet and sonorous on the tongue like Spenserian, Shaksperian. In spite of Juliet, there is a great deal in names, and when the fairies come with their gifts to the cradle of the selected child, let one, wiser than the rest, choose a name for him from which well-sounding derivatives can be made, and best of all with a termination in *on*. Men judge the current coin of opinion by the ring, and are readier to take without question whatever is Platonic, Baconian, Newtonian, Johnsonian, Washingtonian, Jeffersonian, Napoleonic, and all the rest. You cannot make a good adjective out of Keats,—the more pity,—and to say a thing is *Keatsy* is to contemn it. Fate likes fine names.

Haydon tells us that Keats was very much depressed by the fortunes of his book. This was natural enough, but he took it all in a manly way, and determined to revenge himself by writing better poetry. He knew that activity, and not despondency, is the true counterpoise to misfortune. Haydon is sure of the change in his spirits, because he would come to the painting-room and sit silent for hours. But we rather think that the conversation, where Mr Haydon was, resembled that in a young author's first play, where the other interlocutors are only brought in as convenient points for the hero to hitch the interminable web of his monologue on. Besides, Keats had been continuing his education this year, by a course of Elgin marbles and pictures by the great Italians, and might very naturally have found little to say about Mr Haydon's extensive works, which he would have cared to hear. Mr Milnes, on the other hand, in his eagerness to prove that Keats was not killed by the article in the *Quarterly*, is carried too far toward the opposite extreme, and more than hints that he was not even hurt by it.

This would have been true of Wordsworth, who, by a constant companionship with mountains, had acquired something of their manners, but was simply impossible to a man of Keats's temperament.

On the whole, perhaps, we need not respect Keats the less for having been gifted with sensibility, and may even say what we believe to be true, that his health was injured by the failure of his book. A man cannot have a sensuous nature and be pachydermatous at the same time, and if he be imaginative as well as sensuous, he suffers just in proportion to the amount of his imagination. It is perfectly true that what we call the world, in these affairs, is nothing more than a mere Brocken spectre, the projected shadow of ourselves; but as long as we do not know it, it is a very passable giant. We are not without experience of natures so purely intellectual that their bodies had no more concern in their mental doings and sufferings, than a house has with the good or ill fortune of its occupant. But poets are not built on this plan, and especially poets like Keats, in whom the moral seems to have so perfectly interfused the physical man, that you might almost say he could feel sorrow with his hands, so truly did his body, like that of Donne's mistress, think and remember and forebode. The healthiest poet of whom our civilization has been capable says that when he beholds

> —— desert a beggar born,
> And strength by limping sway disableed,
> And art made tongue-tied by authority,

(alluding, plainly enough, to the Giffords of his day,)

> And simple truth miscalled simplicity,

(as it was long afterward in Wordsworth's case,)

> And Captive Good attending Captain Ill,

that then even he, the poet to whom of all others, life seems to have been dearest, as it was also the fullest of enjoyment, 'tired of all these,' had nothing for it but to cry for 'restful Death.' . . .

One cannot help contrasting Keats with Wordsworth; the one altogether poet, the other essentially a Wordsworth with the poetic faculty added; the one shifting from form to form, and from style to style, and pouring his hot throbbing life into every mould; the other remaining always the individual, producing works, and not so much living in his poems, as memorially recording his life in them. When Wordsworth alludes to the foolish criticisms on his writings, he speaks serenely and generously of Wordsworth the poet, as if he were an unbiased third person, who takes up the argument merely in the interest of literature. He towers into a bald egotism which is quite above and beyond selfishness. Poesy was his employment; it was Keats's very existence, and he felt the rough treatment of his verses as if it had been the wounding of a limb. To Wordsworth, composing was a healthy exercise; his slow pulse and unimpressible nature gave him assurance of a life so long that he could wait; and when we read his poems we should never suspect the existence in him of any sense but that of observation, as if Wordsworth the poet were only a great sleepless eye, accompanied by Mr Wordsworth, the distributer of stamps, as a reverential scribe and Baruch. But every one of Keats's poems was a sacrifice of vitality; a virtue went away from him into every one of them; even yet, as we turn the leaves, they seem to warm and thrill our fingers with the flush of his fine senses, and the flutter of his electrical nerves, and we do not wonder he felt that what he did was to be done swiftly. . . .

The faults of Keats's poetry are obvious enough, but it should be remembered that he died at twenty-four, and that he offends by superabundance and not poverty. That he was overlanguaged at first there can be no doubt, and in this was implied the possibility of falling back to the perfect mean of diction. It is only by the rich that the costly plainness, which at once satisfies the taste and the imagination, is attainable.

Whether Keats was original or not we do not think it useful to discuss until it has been settled what originality is. Mr Milnes tells us that this merit (whatever it is) has been denied to Keats because his poems take the color of the authors he happened to be reading at the time he wrote them. But men have their intellectual ancestry, and the likeness of some one of them is forever unexpectedly flashing out in the features of a descendant, it may be after a gap of several generations. In the parliament of the present, every man represents a constituency of the past. It is true that Keats has the accent of the men from whom he learned to speak, but this is to make originality a mere question of externals, and in this sense the author of a dictionary might bring an action of trover against every author who used his words. It is the man behind the words that gives them value, and if Shakspeare help himself to a verse or a phrase, it is with ears that have learned of him to listen that we feel the harmony of the one, and it is the mass of his intellect that makes the other weighty with meaning. Enough that we recognize in Keats that undefinable newness and unexpectedness that we call genius. The sunset is original every evening, though for thousands of years it has built out of the same light and vapor its visionary cities with domes and pinnacles, and its delectable mountains which night shall utterly abase and destroy.

Three men, almost contemporaneous with each other, Wordsworth, Keats, and Byron, were the great means of bringing back English poetry from the sandy deserts of rhetoric, and recovering for her her triple inheritance of simplicity, sensuousness and passion. Of these, Wordsworth was the only conscious reformer, and his hostility to the existing formalism injured his earlier poems by tinging them with something of iconoclastic extravagance. He was the deepest thinker, Keats the most essentially a poet, and Byron the most keenly intellectual of the three. Keats had the broadest mind, or at least his mind was open in more sides, and he was able to understand Wordsworth and judge Byron, equally conscious, through his artistic sense, of the greatnesses of the one, and the many littlenesses of the other, while Wordsworth was isolated in a feeling of his prophetic character, and Byron had only an uneasy and jealous instinct of contemporary merit. The poems of Wordsworth, as he was the most individual, accordingly reflect the moods of his own nature; those of Keats, from sensitiveness of organization, the moods of his own taste and feeling; and those of Byron, who was impressible chiefly through the understanding, the intellectual and moral wants of the times in which he lived. Wordsworth has influenced most the ideas of succeeding poets; Keats their forms; and Byron, interesting to men of imagination less for his writings than for what his writings indicate, reappears no more in poetry, but presents an ideal to youth made restless with vague desires not yet regulated by experience nor supplied with motives by the duties of life.

As every young person goes through all the world-old experiences, fancying them something peculiar and personal to himself, so it is with every new generation, whose youth always finds its representatives in its poets. Keats rediscovered the delight and wonder that lay enchanted in the dictionary. Wordsworth revolted at the poetic diction which he found in vogue, but his own language rarely rises above it except when it is upborne by the thought. Keats had an instinct for fine words, which are in themselves pictures and ideas, and had more of the power of poetic expression than any modern English poet. And by poetic expression we do not mean merely a vividness in particulars, but the right feeling which heightens or subdues a passage or a whole poem to the proper tone, and gives entireness to the effect. There is a great deal more than is commonly supposed in this choice of words. Men's thoughts and opinions are in a great degree vassals of him who invents a new phrase or reapplies an old epithet. The thought or feeling a thousand times repeated, becomes his at last who utters it best. This power of language is veiled in the old legends which make the invisible powers the servants of some word. As soon as we have discovered the word for our joy or sorrow we are no longer its serfs, but its lords. We reward the discoverer of an anæsthetic for the body and make him member of all the societies, but him who finds a nepenthe for the soul we elect into the small academy of the immortals.

The poems of Keats mark an epoch in English poetry; for, however often we may find traces of it in others, in them found its strongest expression, that reaction against the barrel-organ style which had been reigning by a kind of sleepy divine right for half a century. The lowest point was indicated when there was such an utter confounding of the common and the uncommon sense that Dr Johnson wrote verse and Burke prose. The most profound gospel of criticism was, that nothing was good poetry that could not be translated into good prose, as if one should say that the test of sufficient moonlight was that tallow-candles could be made of it. We find Keats at first going to the other extreme, and endeavoring to extract green cucumbers from the rays of tallow; but we see also incontestable proof of the greatness and purity of his poetic gift in the constant return toward equilibrium and repose in his later poems. And it is a repose always lofty and clear-aired, like that of the eagle balanced in incommunicable sunshine. In him a vigorous understanding developed itself in equal measure with the divine faculty; thought emancipated itself from expression without becoming its tyrant; and music and meaning floated together, accordant as swan and shadow, on the smooth element of his verse. Without losing its sensuousness, his poetry refined itself and grew more inward, and the sensational was elevated into the typical by the control of that finer sense which underlies the senses and is the spirit of them.

67. Cardinal Wiseman on Keats

1855

Extract from lecture, 1855, *On the Perception of Natural Beauty by the Ancients and the Moderns*, 1856, 13–14.

Nicholas Wiseman (1802–65) was created Cardinal and head of the Catholic Church in England in 1850. His appointment, at the climax of a series of conversions to Rome, caused a wave of anti-Catholic feeling. He was the original of Browning's poem 'Bishop Blougram's Apology'. Wiseman's strictures on Keats ('No moral glow, no virtuous emotion', 'cheerless affections') provoked Leigh Hunt to defend him in *Fraser's Magazine* (December 1859). See Introduction, p. 6.

We must dwell a few moments, by way of illustration of this subject, on two modern, but both departed, poets. The first is one who, cut off yet young, had developed so enthusiastic a love of nature, and so vigorous a power of expressing it, that had his moral faculties been equal to his perceptive organisation, he would have stood without a rival in this class of poetry.—The other lived to mature age, only to ripen and perfect his early affection for nature in its most noble form.

In Keats, the love of nature is a wild and almost frenzied passion, which pours itself out with a voluminous richness of imagery and diction, that carries you forward in rapture for a time. But by degrees you begin to feel the chillness of the torrent that bears you; even when rolling on through a sunny sky and genial atmosphere, its waters are icy cold. No moral glow, no virtuous emotion, no sight of that real Sun, the 'intellectual Light' of Dante, without whom nature is dull, cheers the most dainty landscape: and you disengage yourself with a sigh from the voluptuous stream, lamenting that such a bright spirit should have walked so entirely upon earth; but not wondering that 'Endymion,' the enamoured of the cold moon, should be the type of his cheerless affections.

Not so with Wordsworth, in whom the love of nature. and of her simplest forms, was sound, noble, and moral.

68. Keats in the *Encyclopedia Britannica*

1857

Extract from signed article by Alexander Smith, *Encyclopedia Britannica*, eighth edition (1857), xiii. 56–7.

Alexander Smith (1830–67), Scottish poet, was Secretary and Registrar to Edinburgh University. In 1853 A. H. Clough had called him 'the latest disciple of the school of Keats', and in the following year he was himself pilloried by *Blackwood's* as member of a 'spasmodic' school of poetry. Keats's entry in the *Britannica* occupies four columns.

Although nothing could be calmer and nobler than the temper of Keats' mind, or more resolute than his purpose to cultivate himself to the utmost, he did not altogether escape the taint of weak sentiment. His first volume, although it contains one of the grandest sonnets in the language, and although the reader is every now and again delighted with fresh and unexpected beauties, is exceedingly crude and immature. The poet maunders about flowers and streams; he weeps for the mere delight he has in weeping, and disports himself in the strangest and uncouthest phraseology. *Endymion*, perhaps the richest poem in colour and music given to the world since the *Comus* of Milton, is far from being perfect. The reader is smothered in roses. The story is lost in ornament. You cannot see the string for the beads. The charm lies in single lines—seldom in linked and sustained passages. It is full of the same barbarous and dissonant diction, the same lax and nerveless versification, which disfigured his earlier productions. He still wrote in a style of babyish effeminacy about

> Plums
> Ready to melt between an infant's gums.

These and lines of a similar nauseous sweetness are of the most frequent occurrence. . . .

After Chatterton, Keats is the most extraordinary phenomenon in our poetic literature; and, had life been granted him, there is reason to believe he would have taken his place in the very first rank of English poets. Misunderstood at the time, and supposed by many to be a sentimental weakling, oppressed by adverse circumstances, and bowed down by a mortal disease, his mind was of the noblest strain. His ambition was lofty, but he duly estimated his own powers and the difficulties he had to encounter; he shrank from no labour, and gathered ardour from defeat. Those who are accustomed to consider him a poetic visionary,—who turned from the realities of life to shed melodious tears over morning roses, and to fall into unnatural extasies at the sight of beautiful women, will be surprised to find in his letters warm human sympathies, practical sense, clear judgment, a considerable knowledge of mankind, and a healthy contempt of everything mean and degrading; they will see the sun of a strong intellect, rising out of the coloured mists of fancy and sentiment, consuming them in its path, and will be led to form the highest anticipations of the day which would have followed, had not the luminary been arrested by the hand of death just when it emerged full-orbed above them all.

The advance from *Endymion* to *Hyperion*, taking into consideration the shortness of the time in which it was accomplished,—about three years,—is without a parallel in our literary history. The glorious and uncultured profusion of the earlier poem is displeasing to a pure taste, from its very flush of colour and excess of sweetness. All form and outline are lost in the exuberance of ornament. In his latter poems, *Hyperion* especially, he had learned to husband his strength, and had acquired that last gift of the artist, to know where to stop. There is no excess, nothing extraneous, everything is clear and well-defined, as the naked limbs of an Apollo. He had overcome, too, the fopperies of style, the taste for conceits and fantastical diction so characteristic of the poets amongst whom he lived, and which so often marred the beauty of his earlier performances, and had gained a noble simplicity, and a pomp and depth of music which seems caught from the 'far-foamed sea sands.' One could hardly have expected that the florid and luscious fancies of *Endymion* should have ripened into the terrible power which gave us the picture of the fallen gods, stretched here and there on the flinty rocks, and veiled with everlasting twilight,—

Their clenched teeth still clenched, and all their limbs
Locked up like veins of metal cramped and screwed.

The same wonderful artistic sense is exhibited in the 'Eve of St Agnes'. It is rich in colour as the stained windows of a Gothic cathedral, and every verse bursts into picturesque and graceful fancies; yet all this abundance is so subdued and harmonized in such wonderful keeping with the story and the mediaeval period, as to render it a perfect chrysolite—a precious gem of art. Perhaps the most exquisite specimen of Keats' poetry is the 'Ode to the Grecian Urn'; it breathes the very spirit of antiquity,—eternal beauty and eternal repose.

In one of his letters, Keats gives utterance to the hope, that 'after his death he would be among the English poets.' This anticipation has been abundantly verified. Even in his lifetime the tide had turned in his favour. The late Lord Jeffrey, in 1820, after regretting that his attention had not been earlier turned to the book, remarks, that '*Endymion* is, in truth, at least as full of genius as absurdity;' and concludes, 'We are very much inclined, indeed, to add, that we do not know any book which we would sooner employ as a test to ascertain whether any one had in him a native relish for poetry, and a genuine sensibility to its intrinsic charm.' With but one or two exceptions, no poet of the last generation stands at this moment higher in the popular estimation, and certainly no one has in a greater degree influenced the poetic development of the last thirty years.

69. A rich intellectual foundation

1860

Extracts from signed article, 'The Life and Poetry of Keats', *Macmillan's Magazine* (November 1860), iii, 1–16.

David Masson was the editor of *Macmillan's Magazine* when this article was published. In pointing to Keats's objectivity, to the mental energy shown in his 'remarkable letters', to the 'universality of his sensuousness' in which all five senses nevertheless work 'in harmony at the bidding of a higher intellectual power', and to other qualities, Masson anticipates some of the directions in which later criticism will move, and his study shows greater maturity of understanding than anything else written on Keats up to 1860. The essay is, however, extremely long, and has had to be considerably abridged, especially in its illustrations.

From Edmonton, Keats was continually walking over to Enfield to see his young friend, Cowden Clarke, and to borrow books. It was some time in 1812 that he borrowed Spenser's *Faery Queene*. The effect was immediate and extraordinary. 'He ramped' says Mr Clarke, 'through the scenes of the romance;' he would talk of nothing but Spenser; he had whole passages by heart, which he would repeat; and he would dwell with an ecstacy of delight on fine particular phrases, such as that of the 'sea-shouldering whale.' His first known poetical composition (he was then seventeen), was a piece expressly entitled 'In Imitation of Spenser.'

Now Morning from her orient chamber came,
And her first footsteps touch'd a verdant hill,
Crowning its lawny crest with amber flame,
Silvering the untainted gushes of its rill;
Which, pure from mossy beds, &c.

From that moment it seemed as if Keats lived only to read poetry and to write it. From Spenser he went to Chaucer, from Chaucer to

Milton, and so on and on, with ever-widening range, through all our sweeter and greater poets. He luxuriated in them by himself; he talked about them, and read parts of them aloud to his friends; he became a critic of their thoughts, their words, their rhymes, their cadences. His chief partner in these tastes was Mr Cowden Clarke, with whom he would take walks, or sit up whole evenings, discoursing of poets and poetry; and he acknowledges, in one of his metrical epistles, the influence which Mr Clarke had in forming his literary likings. Above all it was Mr Clarke that first introduced him to any knowledge of ancient Greek poetry. This was effected by lending him Chapman's Homer, his first acquaintance with which, and its effects on him, are celebrated in one of the finest and best-known of his sonnets. Thenceforward Greek poetry, so far as it was accessible to him in translation, had peculiar fascinations for him. By similar means he became fondly familiar with some of the softer Italian poets, and with the stories of Boccaccio. It was noted by one of his friends that his preferences at this time, whether in English or in other poetry, were still for passages of sweet, sensuous description, or of sensuous-ideal beauty, such as are to be found in the minor poems of Milton, Shakespeare and Chaucer, and in Spenser throughout, and that he rarely seemed to dwell with the same enthusiasm on passages of fervid feeling, of severe reference to life, or of powerful human interest. At this time, in fact, his feeling for poetry was very much that of an artist in language, observing effects which particularly delighted him, and studying them with a professional admiration of the exquisite. He brooded over fine phrases like a lover; and often, when he met a quaint or delicious word in the course of his reading, he would take pains to make it his own by using it, as speedily as possible, in some poem he was writing....

Poetry was his ceaseless thought, and to be a Poet his one ambition.

> O for ten years, that I may overwhelm
> Myself in Poesy! So I may do the deed
> That my own soul has to itself decreed!

Of what *kind* this intended deed was we have also some indication. Like all the fresher young poets of his time, Keats had imbibed, partly from constitutional predisposition, partly from conscious reasoning, that theory of Poetry which, for more than twenty years, Wordsworth had been disseminating by precept and by example through the literary mind of England. This theory, in its historical aspect, I will venture to call *Pre-Drydenism*. Its doctrine, historically, was that the age of true English Poetry was the period anterior to Dryden—the period of Chaucer, Spenser, Shakespeare, Fletcher, and Milton; and that, with a few exceptions, the subsequent period, from Dryden inclusively down to the time of Wordsworth's own appearance as a poet, had been a prosaic interregnum, during which what passed for poetry was either an inflated style of diction which custom had rendered pleasing, or, at best, shrewd sense and wit, or miscellaneous cogitation more or less weighty, put into metre. . . .

Keats, then, was a Pre-Drydenist in his notions of poetry, and in his own intentions as a poetic artist. But I will say more. Wordsworth had then so far conquered the opposition through which he had been struggling that a modified Pre-Drydenism was universally diffused through English literary society; and the so-called Cockney, or Hampstead-Heath, School, with which accident had associated Keats, were largely tinged with it. They did not, indeed, go all the length with Wordsworth in depreciating Dryden and Pope (as who could?); but a superior relish for the older poets was one of their avowed characteristics. But in this, I believe, Keats went beyond the rest of them. It may be perceived, I think, that, with all his esteem for Hunt and Shelley, both as kind personal friends and as poets, he had notions respecting himself which led him, even while in their society and accounted one of them, to fix his gaze with steadier reverence than they did on the distant veteran of Rydal Mount. To Wordsworth alone does he seem to have looked as, all in all, a sublimity among contemporary poets.

So far, however, as Keats had yet been publicly heard of, it was only as one fledgling more in the brood of poets whose verses were praised in the *Examiner*. What he had yet published were but little studies in language and versification preparatory to something that could be called a poem. Such a poem he now resolved to write. Always drawn by a kind of mental affinity to the sensuous Mythology of the Greeks, he had chosen for his subject the legend of Endymion, the youthful lover of the moon-goddess Artemis. 'A long poem,' he said, 'is the test of invention; and it will be a test of my invention if I can make 4,000 lines out of this one bare circumstance, and fill them with poetry.' To accomplish his task, he left London in the spring of 1817, and took up his abode first in the Isle of Wight, then at Margate (at both of which places he revelled in the views of the sea as a newly-found pleasure), and then, successively, at Canterbury, Oxford, and other places inland. In the winter of 1817–18 he returned to Hampstead with the four books of his *Endymion* completed. The absence of seven or eight months, during which this poem was written, was also the period during which many of those letters to his friends were written which have been edited by Mr Monckton Milnes, in his Memoir of the poet. These letters have hardly received the attention they deserve. They are very remarkable letters. One can see, indeed, that they are the letters of an intellectual invalid, of a poor youth too conscious of 'the endeavour of this present breath,' watching incessantly his own morbid symptoms, and communicating them to his friends. There is also in them a somewhat unnatural straining after quaint and facetious conceits, as if he would not write common-place, but would force himself by the mere brief rumination of the moment into some minute originality or whim of fancy. On the whole, however, with the proper allowance, the letters may be read without any injury to the highest notion of him that may be formed from his compositions that were meant for publication; and there have not been many young poets of whose casual letters as much could be said. They abound in shrewd observations, in delicate and subtle criticisms, in fine touches of description, and in thoughts of a philosophical kind that are at once comprehensive and deep.

Endymion: A Poetic Romance, appeared in the beginning of 1818. Its reception was not wholly satisfactory. It made Keats's name more widely known; it procured him visits and invitations; and, when he attended Hazlitt's lectures, ladies to whom he was pointed out looked at him instead of listening to the lecturer. But Hunt, Shelley, and the rest, though they admired the poem, and thought some passages in it very wonderful, had many faults to find. The language in many parts was juvenile, not to say untasteful; such phrases as 'honey-feel of bliss' were too frequent; it was impossible for any understanding of a rational sort to reconcile itself to such a bewildering plentitude of luxuriant invention raised on such a mere nothing of a basis; and, on the whole, there was too evident a waywardness in the sequence of the thoughts, arising from a passive dependence of the matter at every point on the mere suggestion of the rhyme! These and other such objections were heard on all hands. . . .

Keats, there is no doubt, was prepared to wait and work on. The story of his having been killed by the savage article in the *Quarterly* is proved to have been wholly untrue. He had sense enough and pluck enough to get over that chagrin within the usual period of twenty-four hours, which, if there is any use for human spirits in the earth's rotation, ought to bring them as well as other things round again to the *status quo*. But other causes were at work, some of which are but dimly revealed by his biographer, but the chief of which was his hereditary malady of consumption. In the winter of 1819–20 he was seized with the fatal blood-spitting, which he had long dreaded; after a few months of lingering, during which he seemed partly to fight with Death as one to whom life was precious, partly to long to die as one who had nothing to live for, he was removed to Italy; and there, having suffered much, he breathed his last at Rome on the 23rd of February, 1821, at the age of twenty-five years and four months. He had wished for 'ten years' of poetic life, but not half that term had been allowed him. The sole literary event of his life, after the publication of his *Endymion* in 1818, had been the publication of his *Lamia, The Eve of St Agnes, and Other Poems*, in 1820; and the sole variation of his manner of life had consisted in his leaving Hampstead for a ramble or a residence in the country, and returning again from the country to Hampstead or London.

After all, whether a man is a poet, a philosopher, or a man of action, there *is* a common standard by which he may be tried, so as to measure his relative intellectual importance. The determination of this standard is difficult; but ultimately, I believe, the truest measure of every man, in intellectual respects, is the measure of his speculative or purely philosophical faculty. So far as this may be demurred to, the objection will arise, I fancy, from the practical difficulty of applying the test. It is only certain poets that give us the opportunity of judging of the strength of their rational or purely *noetic* organ—that faculty by which men speculate, or frame what are called 'thoughts' or 'propositions.' Whenever this is done, however, then, *cæteris paribus*, the deeper thinker is the greater poet. Hence it is an excellent thing for the critic to catch his poet writing prose. He has him then at his mercy; he can keep him in the trap, and study him through the bars at his leisure. If he is a poor creature, he will be found out; if he has genuine vigour, then, with all allowance for any ungainliness arising from his being out of his proper element, there will be evidences of it. Now, tried by any test of this kind, Keats will be found to have been no weakling. . . .

[Quotes widely and fully from the prose letters to display 'thoughts of some pith and substance'.]

As the aphorisms and casual spurts of speculation of a youth of twenty-two (and all the passages I have quoted are from letters of his written before his twenty-third year) these, I think, are sufficient proof that Keats had an intellect from which his superiority in some literary walk or other might have been surely anticipated.

What we independently know enables us to say that it was pre-eminently as a poet that he was fitted to be distinguished. He was constitutionally a poet—one of those minds in whom, to speak generally, Imagination or Ideality is the sovereign faculty. But, as we had occasion to explain in a previous paper on Shelley, there are two recognized orders of poets, each of which has its representatives in our literature (and we must beg pardon for boring the reader again with so pedantic and well-thumbed a distinction)—that order, called 'subjective,' to which Shelley himself belonged, and whose peculiarity it is that their poems are vehicles for certain fixed ideas lying in the minds of their authors, outbursts of their personal character, impersonations under shifting guises of their wishes, feelings and beliefs; and that order, on the other hand, distinguished as 'objective,' who simply fashion their creations by a kind of inventive craft working amid materials supplied by sense, memory, and reading, without the distinct infusion of any element of personal opinion. To this latter order, as I said, belong Chaucer, Shakespeare, and Scott. Now, indubitably, Keats, by the bulk of his poetry, belongs to this order too. The contrast between him and Shelley, in this respect, is complete. Contemporaries and friends, they were poets of quite opposite schools and tendencies; and, so far as they were repelled by each other's poetry (which they were to a certain extent, despite their friendship) it arose from this circumstance. Unlike the feminine and ethereal Shelley, whose whole life was a shrill supernatural shriek in behalf of certain principles, Keats was a slack, slouching youth, with a thick torso, a deep grave voice, and no fixed principles. He had, as we have seen, his passing spurts of speculation, but he had no system of philosophy. So far as religious belief was concerned, he had no wish to disturb existing opinions and institutions—partly because he had really no such quarrel with them as Shelley had, partly because he had no confidence in his ability to dogmatise on such points. In politics, away from his personal connexions, he was rather conservative than otherwise. He thought the Liverpool-and-Castlereagh policy very bad and oppressive; but he did not expect that his friends, the Liberals, would bring things very much nearer to the millennium; and he distinctly avows that he was not, like some of his friends, a Godwin-perfectibility man, or an admirer of America as an advance beyond Europe. In short, he kept aloof from opinion, doctrine, controversy, as by a natural instinct; he was most at home in the world of sense and imagery, where it was his pleasure to weave forth phantasies; and, if his intelligence did now and then indulge in a discursive flight, it was but by way of exercise, or because opinions, doctrines, and controversies may be considered as facts, and therefore as materials to be worked into poetic language.

In quoting from Keats's letters I have purposely selected passages showing that such was not only his practice, but also his theory. His very principle of poetry, it will be observed, almost amounts to this, that the poet should have no principles. The distinction he makes between men of genius and men of power is that the action of the former is like that of an ethereal chemical, a subtle imponderable, passing forth on diverse materials and rousing their affinities, whereas the latter impress by their solid individuality. So, again, when he speaks of the quality that forms men for great literary achievement as being what he calls a 'negative capability'—a power of remaining, and, as it were, luxuriously lolling, in doubts, mysteries, and half-solutions, toying with them, and tossing them, in all their complexity, into forms of beauty, instead of piercing on narrowly and in pain after Truth absolute and inaccessible. A Wordsworth, he admits, might have a genius of the explorative or mystery-piercing kind, and might come back from his excursions into the region of the metaphysical with handfuls of new truth to be worked up into his phantasies; but even *he* might be too dogmatic; and, as for himself, though he might fancy that occasionally he reached the bourne of the mysterious and caught glimpses beyond, it would be presumption to put his half-seeings into speech for others! . . .

Only on one subject does he profess to have any fixed opinions—namely, on his own art or craft. 'I have not one opinion,' he says, 'upon anything except matters of taste.' This is one of the most startling and significant sayings ever uttered by a man respecting himself.

If I am not mistaken, the definition which Keats here gives of the poetical character corresponds with the notion which is most popular. Though critics distinguish between 'subjective' and 'objective' poets, and enumerate men in the one class as famous as men in the other, yet, in our more vague talk, we are in the habit of leaving out of view those who are called 'subjective' poets, and seeking the typical poet among their 'objective' brethren, such as Homer and Shakespeare. How this habit is to be explained—whether it proceeds from a perception that the men of the second order are more truly and purely *poets*, and that the others, though often glorious in poetry, might, in strict science, be referred in half to another genus—I will not inquire. It may be remarked, however, that, be this as it may, it is by no means necessary to go all the length with Keats in the interpretation of his theory, and to fancy that the poet approaching most nearly to the perfect type must be a man having no strong individuality, no permanent moral gesture. Scott, for example, was a man of very distinct character, with a mode of thinking and acting in the society in which he lived as proper to himself as his physiognomy or corporeal figure. So, no doubt, it was with Chaucer and Shakespeare; and Milton, who may, by much of his poetry, be referred to the same order, was a man with a personality to shake a nation. What is meant is that, when they betook themselves from miscellaneous action among their fellows to the exercise of their art, they all, more or less, allowed their personality to melt and fold itself in the imagination—all, more or less, as it were, sat within themselves, as within a chamber in which their own hopes, convictions, anxieties, and principles lay about neglected, while they plied their mighty craft, like the swing of some gigantic arm, with reference to all without. Keats did the same; only, in his case, the chamber wherein he sat had, by his own confession, very few fixtures or other proper furniture. It was a painter's studio, with very little in it besides the easel.

Still, as cannot be too often repeated, there *are* subtle laws connecting the creations of the most purely artistic poet with his personal character and experience. . . . So also with the poetry of Keats. Impersonal as it is in comparison with such poetry as Shelley's, it has yet a certain assemblage of characteristics, which the reader learns to recognise as distinctive; and these it owes to the character of its author.

At the foundation of the character of Keats lay an extraordinary keenness of all the bodily sensibilities and the mental sensibilities which depend upon them. He led, in great part, a life of passive sensation, of pleasure and pain through the senses. Take a book of Physiology and go over the so-called classes of sensations one by one—the sensations of the mere muscular states; the sensations connected with such vital processes as circulation, alimentation, respiration, and electrical intercommunication with surrounding bodies; the sensations of taste; those of odour; those of touch; those of hearing; and those of sight—and Keats will be found to have been unusually endowed in them all. He had, for example, an extreme sensibility to the pleasures of the palate. The painter Haydon tells a story of his once seeing him cover his tongue with cayenne pepper, in order, as he said, that he might enjoy the delicious sensation of a draught of cold claret after it. 'Talking of pleasure,' he says himself in one of his letters, 'this moment I was writing with one hand, and with the other holding to my mouth a nectarine;' and he goes on to describe the nectarine in language that would reawaken gustativeness in the oldest fruiterer. This of one of the more ignoble senses—if it is right to call those senses ignoble that minister the least visibly to the intellect. But it was the same with the nobler or more intellectual senses of hearing and sight. He was passionately fond of music; and his sensitiveness to colour, light, and other kinds of visual impression was preternaturally acute. He possessed, in short, simply in virtue of his organization, a rich intellectual foundation of that kind which consists of notions furnished directly by sensations, and of a corresponding stock of names and terms. Even had he remained without education, his natural vocabulary of words for all the varieties of thrills, tastes, odours, sounds, colours, and tactual perceptions, would have been unusually precise and extensive. As it was, this native capacity for keen and abundant sensation was developed, educated and harmonised by the influences of reading, intellectual conversation, and more or less laborious thought, into that richer and more cultivated sensuousness, which, under the name of sensibility to natural beauty, is an accepted requisite in the constitution of painters and poets.

It is a fact on which physiologists have recently been dwelling much, that the imagination of any bodily state or action calls into play exactly those nervous, muscular, and vascular processes, though in weaker degree, which are called into play by the real bodily state or action so simulated—that the imagination of sugar in the mouth causes the same exact flow of physical incidents within the lips which would be caused by sugar really tasted; that the imagination of firing a rifle does actually compel to the entire gesture of shooting, down even to the bending of the forefinger round the ideal trigger, though the mimic attitude may be baulked of completion; that the imagination of a pain in any part may be persevered in till a pain is actually induced in that part. Whether or not this fact shall ever serve much towards the elucidation of the connexion between the imagination and the personal character—whether or not it may ever be developed into a wholesale doctrine that the habits of a man's own real being mark, by an *à priori* necessity, the directions in which his imagination will work most naturally and strongly—one can hardly avoid thinking of it in studying the genius of

Keats. The most obvious characteristic of Keats's poetry, that which strikes most instantaneously and palpably, is certainly its abundant *sensuousness*. Some of his finest little poems are all but literally lyrics of the sensuous—embodiments of the feelings of ennui, fatigue, physical languor, and the like, in tissues of fancied circumstance and sensation, the imagination of which soothes and refreshes. . . .

It is the same in those longer pieces of narrative phantasy which form the larger portion of his writings. Selecting, as in *Endymion*, a legend of the sensuous Grecian mythology, or, as in 'Isabella, or the Pot of Basil,' a story from Boccaccio, or, as in 'St Agnes's Eve,' the hint of a middle-age superstition, or, as in 'Lamia', a story of Greek witchcraft, he sets himself to weave out the little text of substance so given into a linked succession of imaginary movements and incidents taking place in the dim depths of ideal scenery, whether of forest, grotto, sea-shore, the interior of a gothic castle, or the marble vestibule of a Corinthian palace. In following him in these luxurious excursions into a world of ideal nature and life, we see his imagination winging about, as it were his disembodied senses, hovering insect-like in one humming group, all keeping together in harmony at the bidding of a higher intellectual power, and yet each catering for itself in that species of circumstance and sensation which is its peculiar food. Thus, the disembodied sense of Taste—

Here is wine
Alive with sparkles—never, I aver,
Since Ariadne was a vintager,
So cool a purple: taste these juicy pears
Sent me by sad Vertumnus, when his fears
Were high about Pomona: here is cream
Deepening to richness from a snowy gleam—
Sweeter than that nurse Amalthea skimm'd
For the boy Jupiter; and here, undimm'd
By any touch, a bunch of blooming plums
Ready to melt between an infant's gums.

Or, again, in the description of the dainties in the chapel in the 'Eve of St Agnes'—

And still she slept an azure-lidded sleep
In blanchèd linen, smooth and lavender'd,
While he from forth the closet brought a heap
Of candied apple, quince, and plum, and gourd,
With jellies soother than the creamy curd,

And lucent syrups tinct with cinnamon,
Manna and dates, in argosy transferr'd
From Fez, and spicèd dainties every one
From silken Samarcand to cedar'd Lebanon.

As an instance of the disembodied delight in sweet odour, take the lines in 'Isabella'—

Then in a silken scarf, sweet with the dews
Of precious flowers pluck'd in Araby,
And divine liquids with odorous ooze
Through the cold serpent-pipe refreshfully,
She wrapp'd it up.

Delicacy and richness in ideal sensations of touch and sound are found throughout. Thus, even the sensation of cold water on the hands:—

When in an antechamber every guest
Had felt the cold full sponge to pleasure press'd
By ministering slaves upon his hands and feet.

or the ideal tremulation of a string:—

Be thou in the van
Of circumstance; yea, seize the arrow's barb
Before the tense string murmur.

But let us pass to the sense of sight, with its various perceptions of colour, light, and lustre. Here Keats is, in some respects, *facile princeps* even among our most sensuous poets. Here is the description of Lamia while she was still a serpent:—

She was a gordian shape of dazzling hue,
Vermilion-spotted, golden, green, and blue,
Striped like a zebra, freckled like a pard,
Eyed like a peacock, and all crimson-barr'd,
And full of silver moons that, as she breathed,
Dissolved, or brighter shone, or interwreathed
Their lustres with the gloomier tapestries.

Here is a passage somewhat more various—the description of the bower in which Adonis was sleeping—

Above his head
Four lily-stalks did their white honours wed
To make a coronal; and round him grew
All tendrils green, of every bloom and hue,

Together intertwined and tramell'd fresh—
The vine of glossy sprout, the ivy mesh
Shading the Ethiop berries, and woodbine
Of velvet leaves and bugle-blooms divine,
Convolvulus in streakèd vases flush,
The creeper mellowing for an autumn blush,
And virgin's bower trailing airily,
With others of the sisterhood.

These last quotations suggest a remark which does not seem unimportant. When critics or poets themselves speak of the love of nature or the perception of natural beauty as essential in the constitution of the poet, it will often be found that what they chiefly mean is an unusual sensibility to the pleasures of one of the senses—the sense of sight. What they mean is chiefly a fine sense of form, colour, lustre and the like. Now, though it may be admitted that, in so far as ministration of material for the intellect is concerned, sight is the most important of the senses, yet this all but absolute identification of love of nature with sensibility to visual pleasures seems erroneous. It is a kind of treason to the other senses—all of which are avenues of communication between nature and the mind, though sight may be the main avenue. In this respect I believe that one of the most remarkable characteristics of Keats is the universality of his sensuousness. But farther:—not only, in popular language, does the love of nature seem to be identified with a sensibility to the pleasures of the one sense of sight; but, by a more injurious restriction still, this love of nature or perception of natural beauty seems to have been identified, especially of late, with one class of the pleasures of this one sense of sight—to wit, the pleasures derived from the contemplation of vegetation. Roses, lilies, grass, trees, cornfields, ferns, heaths and poppies—this is what passes for 'nature' with not a few modern poets and critics of poetry. It seems as if, since Wordsworth refulminated the advice to poets to go back to nature and to study nature, it had been the impression of many that the proper way to comply with the advice was to walk out in the fields to some spot where the grass was thick and the weeds and wild-flowers plentiful, and there lie flat upon the turf, chins downwards, peering into grasses and flowers and inhaling their breath. Now, it ought to be distinctly represented, in correction of this, that ever so minute and loving a study of vegetation, though laudable and delightful in itself, does not amount to a study of nature—that, in fact, vegetation, though a very respectable part of visible nature, is not the whole of it. When night comes, for example, where or how much is your vegetation then? Vegetation is *not* nature—I know no proposition that should be more frequently dinned in the ears of our young poets than this. The peculiar notion of natural beauty involved in the habit spoken of may be said to have come in with the microscope. In the ancient Greek poets we have very little of it. They give us trees and grass and flowers, but they give them more by mere suggestion; and, so far as they introduce physical nature at all (which is chiefly by way of a platform for human action) it is with the larger forms and aspects of nature that they deal—the wide and simple modifications of the great natural elements. Shakespeare, when he chooses, is minutely and lusciously rich in his scenes of vegetation (and, indeed, in comparing modern and romantic with ancient and classical poets generally, it is clear that, in this respect, there has been a gradual development of literary tendency which might be historically and scientifically accounted for); but no man more signally than Shakespeare keeps the just proportion. Wordsworth himself, when he called out for the study of nature, and set the example in his own case by retiring to the Lakes, did not commit the error of confounding nature with vegetation. In that district, indeed, where there were mountains and tarns, incessant cloud-variations, and other forms of nature on the great scale to employ the eye, it was not likely that it would disproportionately exercise itself on particular banks and gardens or individual herbs and flowers. Such an affection for the minutiæ of vegetation was reserved perhaps for the so-called Cockney poets; and one can see that, if it were once supposed that they introduced the taste, the fact might be humorously explained by recollecting that nature to most of them was nature as seen from Hampstead Heath.

Now, undoubtedly, Keats is great in botanical circumstance. . . .

But, though Keats did 'joy in all that is bloomy,' I do not know that he joyed 'too much;' though luscious vegetation was one of his delights, I do not think that in him there is such a disproportion between this and other kinds of imagery as there has been in other and inferior poets. There is sea and cloud in his poetry, as well as herbage and turf; he is as rich in mineralogical and zoological circumstance as in that of botany. His most obvious characteristic, I repeat, is the universality of his sensuousness. And this it is, added to his exquisite mastery in language and verse, that makes it such a luxury to read him. In reading Shelley, even when we admire him most, there is always a sense of pain; the influence of Keats is uniformly soothing. In part, as I have said, this arises from his exquisite mastery in language and verse—which, in itself, is one form or result of his sensuousness. There is hardly any recent poet in connexion with whom the mechanism of verse in relation to thought may be studied more delightfully. Occasionally, it is true, there is the shock of a horrible Cockney rhyme. Thus:—

> I shall again see Phœbus in the morning,
> Or flushed Aurora in the roseate dawning.

Or worse still:—

> Couldst thou wish for lineage higher
> Than twin-sister of Thalia?

Throughout, too, there are ungainly traces of the dependence of the matter upon the rhyme. But where, on the whole, shall we find language softer and richer, verse more harmonious and sweetly-linked, and, though usually after the model of some older poet, more thoroughly novel and original; or where shall we see more beautifully exemplified the power of that high artifice of rhyme by which, as by little coloured lamps of light thrown out in advance of the prow of their thoughts from moment to moment, poets steer their way so windingly through the fantastic gloom?

In virtue of that magnificent and universal sensuousness which all must discern in Keats (and which, as being perhaps his most distinctive characteristic, I have chosen chiefly to illustrate in the quotations I have made), he would certainly—even had there been less in him than there was of that power of reflective and constructive intellect by which alone so abundant a wealth of the sensuous element could have been ruled and shaped into artistic literary forms—have been very memorable among English poets. The earlier poems of Shakespeare were, in the main, such tissues of sensuous phantasy; and I believe that, compared even with these, the poems that Keats has left us would not seem inferior, if the comparison could be impartially made. The same might be said of certain portions of Spenser's poetry, the resemblance of which to much of Keats's would strike any reader acquainted with both poets, even if he did not know that Keats was a student of Spenser. Perhaps the likest poet to Keats in the whole list of preceding English poets is William Browne, the author of *Britannia's Pastorals*; but, rich and delicious as the poetry of Browne is, beyond much that capricious chance has preserved in greater repute, that of Keats is, in Browne's own qualities of richness and deliciousness, immeasurably superior.

But sensuousness alone, will not, nor will sensuousness governed by a reflective and fanciful intellect, constitute a great poet; and, however highly endowed a youthful poet may be in these, his only chance of real greatness is in passing on, by due transition and gradation, to that more matured state of mind in which, though the sensuous may remain and the cool fancy may weave its tissues as before, human interest and sympathy with the human heart and grand human action shall predominate in all. Now, in the case of Keats, there is evidence of the fact of this gradation—of a progress both intellectually and morally; of a disposition, already consciously known to himself, to move forward out of the sensuous or merely sensuous-ideal mood, into the mood of the truly epic poet, the poet of life, sublimity and action. There is evidence of this in his prose-letters. Thus, in one, he says 'Although I take Poetry to be the chief, yet there is something else wanting to one who passes his life among books and thoughts of books.' And again, 'I find earlier days are gone by; I find that I can have no enjoyment in the world but continual drinking of knowledge. I find there is no worthy pursuit but the idea of doing some good to the world. Some do it with their society; some with their art; some with their benevolence; some with a sort of power of conferring pleasure and good humour on all they meet—and, in a thousand ways, all dutiful to the command of nature. There is but one way for me. The road lies through application, study and thought. I will pursue it. I have been hovering for some time between an exquisite sense of the luxurious and a love for philosophy. Were I calculated for the former, I should be glad; but, as I am not, I shall turn all my soul to the latter.' In his poetry we have similar evidence. Even in his earlier poems, one is struck not only by the steady presence of a keen and subtle intellect, but by frequent flashes of permanently deep meaning, frequent lines of lyric thoughtfulness and occasional maxims of weighty historic generality. What we have quoted for our special purpose would fail utterly to convey the proper impression of the merits of Keats in these respects, or indeed of his poetic genius generally, unless the memory of the reader were to suggest the necessary supplement. From *Endymion* itself, sensuous to very wildness as that poem is considered, scores of passages might be quoted proving that, already, while it was being written, intellect, feeling and experience were doing their work with Keats—that, in fact, to use his own figure, he had then already advanced for some time out of the Infant Chamber, or Chamber of mere Sensation, into the Chamber of Maiden Thought, and had even there begun to distinguish the openings of the dark passages beyond and around, and to be seized with the longing to explore them. Seeing this, looking then at such of his later poems as 'Lamia' and the 'Eve of St Agnes', and contemplating last of all that wonderful fragment of *Hyperion* which he hurled, as it were, into the world as he was leaving it, and of which Byron but expressed the common opinion when he said 'It seems actually inspired by the Titans, and is as sublime as Æschylus,' we can hardly be wrong in believing that, had Keats lived to the ordinary age of man, he would have been one of the greatest of all our poets. As it is, though he died at the age of twenty-five and left only what in all does not amount to much more than a day's leisurely reading, I believe we shall all be disposed to place him very near indeed to our very best.

70. Cowden Clarke on Keats

1861

Article signed 'By an Old School-Fellow', entitled 'Recollections of Keats', *Atlantic Monthly* (January 1861), vii, 86–100.

Charles Cowden Clarke (1787–1877) was the son of Keats's headmaster at Enfield School, and Keats's most influential early friend. He introduced Keats to Hunt; but had little contact with him after the publication of *Endymion.*

This important account, first published in America, demonstrates the new status of Keats as a major poet on both sides of the Atlantic, and although sometimes biographical and digressive it is here given entire. Fourteen years later, Cowden Clarke published an 'augmented summary' in the *Gentleman's Magazine* (February 1874, n.s. xii, 177–204), though the additions are either quotations or anecdotes from later sources; and after his death his widow reprinted that version in *Recollections of Writers* (1878), which is the best-known text.

In the village of Enfield, in Middlesex, ten miles on the north road from London, was my father, John Clarke's school. The house had been built by a West India merchant, in the latter end of the seventeenth or beginning of the eighteenth century. It was of the better character of the domestic architecture of that period,—the whole front being of the purest red brick, wrought, by means of moulds, into rich designs of flowers and pomegranates, with heads of cherubim over two niches in the centre of the building. The elegance of the design and the perfect finish of the structure were such as to secure its protection, when a branch railway was brought from the Ware and Cambridge line to Enfield. The old school-house was converted into the station-house, and the railway company had the good taste to leave intact one of the few remaining specimens of the graceful English domestic architecture of long-gone days. Any of my readers who may happen to have a file of the London *Illustrated News*, may find in No. 360, March 3, 1849, a not prodigiously enchanting wood-cut of the edifice.

Here it was that John Keats all but commenced and did complete his school-education. He was born on the 29th of October, 1795; and I think he was one of the little fellows who had not wholly emerged from the child's costume upon being placed under my father's care. It will be readily conceived difficult to recall from the 'dark backward and abysm' of nearly sixty years the general acts of perhaps the youngest individual in a corporation of between seventy and eighty youngsters; and very little more of Keats's child-life can I remember than that he had a brisk, winning face, and was a favorite with all, particularly with my mother.

His maternal grandfather, Jennings, was proprietor of a large livery-stable, called 'The Swan and Hoop,' on the pavement in Moorfields, opposite the entrance into Finsbury Circus. He had two sons at my father's school. The elder was an officer in Duncan's ship in the fight off Camperdown. After the battle, the Dutch Admiral, De Winter, pointing to young Jennings, told Duncan that he had fired several shots at that young man, and always missed his mark;—no credit to his steadiness of aim; for Jennings, like his own admiral, was considerably above the ordinary dimensions of stature.

Keats's father was the principal servant at the Swan and Hoop Stables,—a man of so remarkably fine a commonsense and native respectability, that I perfectly remember the warm terms in which his demeanor used to be canvassed by my parents after he had been to visit his boys. He was short of stature and well-knit in person, (John resembling him both in make and feature,) with brown hair and dark hazel eyes. He was killed by a fall from his horse, in returning from a visit to the school. John's two brothers, George, older, and Thomas, younger than himself, were like the mother,—who was tall, of good figure, with large, oval face, sombre features, and grave in behavior. The last of the family was a sister,—Fanny, I think, much younger than all,—of whom I remember my mother once speaking with much fondness, for her pretty, simple manners, while she was walking in the garden with her brothers. She married Mr Llanos, a Spanish refugee, the author of *Don Estéban*, and *Sandoval, the Free-Mason*. He was a man of liberal principles, attractive manners, and more than ordinary accomplishments.—This is the amount of my knowledge and recollection of the family.

In the early part of his school-life, John gave no extraordinary indications of intellectual character; but it was remembered of him afterwards, that there was ever present a determined and steady spirit in all his undertakings; and, although of a strong and impulsive will, I never knew it misdirected in his required pursuit of study. He was a most orderly scholar. The future ramifications of that noble genius were then closely shut in the seed, and greedily drinking in the moisture which made it afterwards burst forth so kindly into luxuriance and beauty.

My father was in the habit, at each half-year's vacation, of bestowing prizes upon those pupils who had performed the greatest quantity of voluntary extra work; and such was Keats's indefatigable energy for the last two or three successive half-years of his remaining at school, that, upon each occasion, he took the first prize by a considerable distance. He was at work before the first school-hour began, and that was at seven o'clock; almost all the intervening times of recreation were so devoted; and during the afternoon-holidays, when all were at play, I have seen him in the school,—almost the only one,—at his Latin or French translation; and so unconscious and regardless was he of the consequences of this close and persevering application, that he never would have taken the necessary exercise, had he not been sometimes driven out by one of us for the purpose.

I have said that he was a favorite with all. Not the less beloved was he for having a highly pugnacious spirit, which, when roused, was one of the most picturesque exhibitions—off the stage—I ever saw. One of the transports of that marvellous actor, Edmund Kean—whom, by the way, he idolized—was its nearest resemblance; and the two were not very dissimilar in face and figure. I remember, upon one occasion, when an usher, on account of some impertinent behavior, had boxed his brother Tom's ears, John rushed up, put himself in the received posture of offence, and, I believe, struck the usher,—who could have put him into his pocket. His passions at times were almost ungovernable; his brother George, being considerably the taller and stronger, used frequently to hold him down by main force, when he was in 'one of his moods' and was endeavoring to beat him. It was all, however, a wisp-of-straw conflagration; for he had an intensely tender affection for his brothers, and proved it upon the most trying occasions. He was not merely the 'favorite of all,' like a pet prize-fighter, for his terrier courage; but his high-mindedness, his utter unconsciousness of a mean motive, his placability, his generosity, wrought so general a feeling in his behalf, that I never heard a word of disapproval from any one who had known him, superior or equal.

The latter part of the time—perhaps eighteen months—that he

remained at school, he occupied the hours during meals in reading. Thus his *whole* time was engrossed. He had a tolerably retentive memory, and the quantity that he read was surprising. He must in those last months have exhausted the school-library, which consisted principally of abridgments of all the voyages and travels of any note; Mavor's Collection; also his Universal History; Robertson's Histories of Scotland, America, and Charles the Fifth; all Miss Edgeworth's productions; together with many other works, equally well calculated for youth, not necessary to be enumerated. The books, however, that were his constantly recurrent sources of attraction were Tooke's *Pantheon*, Lemprière's *Classical Dictionary*, which he appeared to *learn*, and Spence's *Polymetis*. This was the store whence he acquired his perfect intimacy with the Greek mythology; here was he 'suckled in that creed outworn'; for his amount of classical attainment extended no farther than the *Æneid*; with which epic, indeed, he was so fascinated, that before leaving school he had *voluntarily* translated in writing a considerable portion. And yet I remember that at that early age,—mayhap under fourteen,—notwithstanding and through all its incidental attractiveness, he hazarded the opinion to me that there was feebleness in the structure of the work. He must have gone through all the better publications in the school-library, for he asked me to lend him some of my own books; and I think I now see him at supper, (we had all our meals in the school-room,) sitting back on the form, and holding the folio volume of Burnet's *History of his own Time* between himself and the table, eating his meal from beyond it. This work, and Leigh Hunt's *Examiner* newspaper,—which my father took in, and I used to lend to Keats,—I make no doubt laid the foundation of his love of civil and religious liberty. He once told me, smiling, that one of his guardians, being informed what books I had lent him to read, declared, that, if he had fifty children, he would not send one of them to my father's school.

When he left us,—I think at fourteen years of age,—he was apprenticed to Mr Thomas Hammond, a medical man, residing in Church Street, Edmonton, and exactly two miles from Enfield. This arrangement appeared to give him satisfaction; and I fear that it was the most placid period of his painful life; for now, with the exception of the duty he had to perform in the surgery, and which was by no means an onerous one, his whole leisure hours were employed in indulging his passion for reading and translating. It was during his apprenticeship that he finished the latter portion of the *Æneid*.

The distance between our residences being so short, I encouraged his inclination to come over, when he could be spared; and in consequence, I saw him about five or six times a month, commonly on Wednesdays and Saturdays, those afternoons being my own most leisure times. He rarely came empty-handed; either he had a book to read, or brought one with him to be exchanged. When the weather permitted, we always sat in an arbor at the end of a spacious garden, and, in Boswellian phrase, 'we had good talk.'

I cannot at this time remember what was the spark that fired the train of his poetical tendencies,—I do not remember what was the first signalized poetry he read; but he must have given me unmistakable tokens of his bent of taste; otherwise, at that early stage of his career, I never could have read to him the 'Epithalamion' of Spenser; and this I perfectly remember having done, and in that (to me) hallowed old arbor, the scene of many bland and graceful associations,—all the substances having passed away. He was at that time, I should suppose, fifteen or sixteen years old; and at that period of life he certainly appreciated the general beauty of the composition, and felt the more passionate passages; for his features and exclamations were ecstatic. How often have I in after-times heard him quote these lines:—

Behold, whiles she before the altar stands,
Hearing the holy priest that to her speaks,
And blesses her with his two happy hands,
How the red roses flush up in her cheeks!
And the pure snow, with goodly vermil stain,
Like crimson dyed in grain,
That even the angels, which continually
About the sacred altar do remain,
Forget their service, and about her fly,
Oft peeping in her face, that seems more fair,
The more they on it stare;
But her sad eyes, still fastened on the ground,
Are governèd with goodly modesty,
That suffers not one look to glance awry,
Which may let in a little thought unsound.

That night he took away with him the first volume of the *Faery Queen*, and went through it, as I told his biographer, Mr Monckton Milnes, 'as a young horse would through a spring meadow,—ramping!' Like a true poet, too,—a poet 'born, not manufactured,'—a poet in grain,—he especially singled out the epithets, for that felicity and power in which Spenser is so eminent. He hoisted himself up, and looked burly and dominant, as he said,—'What an image that is,—"*Sea-shouldering whales*"!'

It was a treat to see as well as hear him read a pathetic passage. Once, when reading the *Cymbeline* aloud, I saw his eyes fill with tears, and for some moments he was unable to proceed, when he came to the departure of Posthumus, and Imogen's saying she would have watched him

> till the diminution
> Of space had pointed him sharp as my needle;
> Nay, followed him till he had *melted from*
> *The smallness of a gnat to air;* and then
> Have *turned mine eye and wept.*

I cannot quite reconcile the time of our separating at this stage of his career,—which of us first went to London; but it was upon an occasion when I was walking thither, and, I think, to see Leigh Hunt, who had just fulfilled his penalty of confinement in Horsemonger-Lane Prison for the trivial libel upon the Prince Regent, that Keats, who was coming over to Enfield, met me, and, turning, accompanied me back part of the way to Edmonton. At the last field-gate, when taking leave, he gave me the sonnet entitled, 'Written on the Day that Mr Leigh Hunt left Prison.' Unless I am utterly mistaken, this was the first proof I had received of his having committed himself in verse; and how clearly can I recall the conscious look with which he hesitatingly offered it! There are some momentary glances of beloved friends that fade only with life. I am not in a position to contradict the statement of his biographer, that 'the lines in imitation of Spenser,

> Now Morning from her orient chamber came,
> And her first footsteps touched a verdant hill, etc.,

are the earliest known verses of his composition'; from the subject being the inspiration of his first love—and such a love!—in poetry, it is most probable; but certainly his first published poem was the sonnet commencing,

> O Solitude! if I must with thee dwell;

and that will be found in the *Examiner*, some time, as I conjecture, in 1816,—for I have not the paper to refer to, and, indeed, at this distance, both of time and removal from the means of verification, I would not be dogmatical.

When we both had come to London,—he to enter as a student of St

Thomas's Hospital,—he was not long in discovering that my abode was with my brother-in-law, in Little Warner Street, Clerkenwell; and just at that time I was installed housekeeper, and was solitary. He, therefore, would come and revive his loved gossip, till, as the author of the *Urn Burial* says, 'we were acting our antipodes,—the huntsmen were up in America, and they already were past their first sleep in Persia.' At this time he lived in his first lodging upon coming to London, near to St Thomas's Hospital. I find his address in a letter which must have preceded my appointing him to come and lighten my darkness in Clerkenwell. At the close of the letter, he says,—'Although the Borough is a beastly place in dirt, turnings, and windings, yet No. 8, Dean Street, is not difficult to find; and if you would run the gauntlet over London Bridge, take the first turning to the left, and then the first to the right, and, moreover, knock at my door, which is nearly opposite a meeting, you would do me a charity, which, as St Paul saith, is the father of all the virtues. At all events, let me hear from you soon: I say, at all events, not excepting the gout in your fingers.' I have little doubt that this letter (which has no other date than the day of the week, and no post-mark) preceded our first symposium; and a memorable night it was in my life's career.

A copy, and a beautiful one, of the folio edition of Chapman's Homer had been lent me. It was the property of Mr Alsager, the gentleman who for years had contributed no small share of celebrity to the great reputation of the *Times* newspaper, by the masterly manner in which he conducted the money-market department of that journal. At the time when I was first introduced to Mr Alsager, he was living opposite Horsemonger-Lane Prison; and upon Mr Leigh Hunt's being sentenced for the libel, his first day's dinner was sent over by Mr Alsager. He was a man of the most studiously correct demeanor, with a highly cultivated taste and judgment in the fine arts and music. He succeeded Hazlitt, (which was no insignificant honor,) and for some time contributed the critiques upon the theatres, but ended by being the reporter of the state of the money-market. He had long been accustomed to have the first trial at his own house of the best-reputed new foreign instrumental music, which he used to import from Germany.

Well, then, we were put in possession of the Homer of Chapman, and to work we went, turning to some of the 'famousest' passages, as we had scrappily known them in Pope's version. There was, for instance, that perfect scene of the conversation on Troy wall of the old

Senators with Helen, who is pointing out to them the several Greek captains, with that wonderfully vivid portrait of an orator, in Ulysses, in the Third Book, beginning at the 237th line,—

> But when the prudent Ithacus did to his counsels rise;

the helmet and shield of Diomed, in the opening of the Fifth Book; the prodigious description of Neptune's passage in his chariot to the Achive ships, in the opening of the Thirteenth Book,—

> The woods, and all the great hills near, trembled beneath
> the weight
> Of his immortal moving feet.

The last was the whole of the shipwreck of Ulysses in the Fifth Book of the *Odyssey*. I think his expression of delight, during the reading of those dozen lines, was never surpassed:—

> Then forth he came, his both knees faltering, both
> His strong hands hanging down, and all with froth
> His cheeks and nostrils flowing, voice and breath
> Spent to all use, and down he sunk to death.
> *The sea had soaked his heart through;* all his veins
> His toils had racked t' a laboring woman's pains.
> Dead weary was he.

On an after-occasion I showed him the couplet of Pope's upon the same passage:—

> From mouth and nose the briny torrent ran,
> *And lost in lassitude lay all the man.*

Chapman supplied us with many an after-feast; but it was in the teeming wonderment of this, his first introduction, that, when I came down to breakfast the next morning, I found upon my table a letter with no other inclosure than his famous sonnet, 'On first looking into Chapman's Homer.' We had parted, as I have already said, at day-spring; yet he contrived that I should receive the poem, from a distance of nearly two miles, before 10, A.M. In the published copy of this sonnet he made an alteration in the seventh line:—

> Yet did I never breathe its pure serene.

The original, which he sent me, had the phrase,

> Yet could I never tell what men could mean;

which he said was bald, and too simply wondering. No one could more earnestly chastise his thoughts than Keats. His favorite among

Chapman's Hymns of Homer was the one to Pan, and which he himself rivalled in the *Endymion.*

In one of our conversations about this period, I alluded to his position at St Thomas's Hospital,—coasting and reconnoitring, as it were, that I might discover how he got on, and, with the total absorption that had evidently taken place of every other mood of his mind than that of imaginative composition, what was his bias for the future, and what his feeling with regard to the profession that had been *chosen for him,*—a circumstance I did not know at that time. He made no secret, however, that he could not sympathize with the science of anatomy, as a main pursuit in life; for one of the expressions that he used, in describing his unfitness for its mastery, was perfectly characteristic. He said, in illustration of his argument,—'The other day, for instance, during the lecture, there came a sunbeam into the room, and with it a whole troop of creatures floating in the ray; and I was off with them to Oberon and Fairy-land.' And yet, with all this self-styled unfitness for the pursuit, I was afterwards informed, that at his subsequent examination he displayed an amount of acquirement which surprised his fellow-students, who had scarcely any other association with him than that of a cheerful, crochety rhymester.

It was about this period, that, going to call upon Mr Leigh Hunt, who then occupied a pretty little cottage in the 'Vale of Health,' on Hampstead Heath, I took with me two or three of the poems I had received from Keats. I did expect that Hunt would speak encouragingly, and indeed approvingly, of the compositions,—written, too, by a youth under age; but my partial spirit was not prepared for the unhesitating and prompt admiration which broke forth before he had read twenty lines of the first poem. Mr Horace Smith happened to be there, on the occasion, and was not less demonstrative in his praise of their merits. The piece which he read out, I remember, was the sonnet,—

> How many bards gild the lapses of time!

marking with particular emphasis and approbation the last six lines:—

> So the unnumbered sounds that evening store,—
> The songs of birds, the whispering of the leaves,
> The voice of waters, the great bell that heaves
> With solemn sound, and thousand others more,
> *That distance of recognizance bereaves,*—
> Make pleasing music, and not wild uproar.

Smith repeated, with applause, the line in Italics, saying, 'What a well-condensed expression!' After making numerous and eager inquiries about him, personally, and with reference to any peculiarities of mind and manner, the visit ended in my being requested to bring him over to the Vale of Health. That was a red-letter day in the young poet's life,—and one which will never fade with me, as long as memory lasts. The character and expression of Keats's features would unfailingly arrest even the casual passenger in the street; and now they were wrought to a tone of animation that I could not but watch with intense interest, knowing what was in store for him from the bland encouragement, and Spartan deference in attention, with fascinating conversational eloquence, that he was to receive and encounter. When we reached the Heath, I have present the rising and accelerated step, with the gradual subsidence of all talk, as we drew towards the cottage. The interview, which stretched into three 'morning calls,' was the prelude to many after-scenes and saunterings about Caen Wood and its neighborhood; for Keats was suddenly made a familiar of the household, and was always welcomed.

It was in the library at Hunt's cottage, where an extemporary bed had been made up for him on the sofa, that he composed the framework and many lines of the poem on 'Sleep and Poetry,'—the last sixty or seventy being an inventory of the art-garniture of the room. The sonnet,

> Keen, fitful gusts are whispering here and there,

he gave me the day after one of our visits, and very shortly after his installation at the cottage.

> Give me a golden pen, and let me lean,

was another, upon being compelled to leave 'at an early hour.' But the occasion that recurs to me with the liveliest interest was the evening when, some observations having been made upon the character, habits, and pleasant associations of that reverenced denizen of the hearth, the cheerful little fireside grasshopper, Hunt proposed to Keats the challenge of writing, then, there, and to time, a sonnet 'On the Grasshopper and the Cricket.' No one was present but myself, and they accordingly set to. I, absent with a book at the end of the sofa, could not avoid furtive glances, every now and then, at the emulants. I cannot say how long the trial lasted; I was not proposed umpire, and had no stop-watch for the occasion: the time, however, was short, for such a performance; and Keats won, as to time. But the event of the after-scrutiny was one of many such occurrences which have riveted the memory of Leigh Hunt in my affectionate regard and admiration, for unaffected generosity and perfectly unpretentious encouragement: his sincere look of pleasure at the first line,—

> The poetry of earth is never dead;

'Such a prosperous opening!' he said; and when he came to the tenth and eleventh lines,—

> On a lone winter evening, *when the frost*
> *Has wrought a silence*;

'Ah! that's perfect! bravo, Keats!'—and then he went on in a dilation upon the dumbness of all Nature during the season's suspension and torpidity. With all the kind and gratifying things that were said to him, Keats protested to me, as we were afterwards walking home, that he preferred Hunt's treatment of the subject to his own.

He had left the neighborhood of the Borough, and was now living with his brothers in apartments on the second floor of a house in the Poultry, over the passage leading to the Queen's Head Tavern, and opposite one of the City Companies' Halls,—the Ironmongers', if I mistake not. I have the associating reminiscence of many happy hours spent in this lodging. Here was determined upon, in great part written, and sent forth to the world, the first little, but vigorous, offspring of his brain:—

POEMS

BY

JOHN KEATS.

> What more felicity can fall to creature
> Than to enjoy delight with liberty?
> *Fate of the Butterfly.*—SPENSER.

LONDON:

PRINTED FOR

C. AND J. OLLIER, 3, WELBECK STREET,

CAVENDISH SQUARE.

1817.

Here, on the evening that the last proof-sheet was brought from the printer, and, as his biographer has recorded, upon being informed, if he purposed having a Dedication to the book, that it must be sent forthwith, he went to a side-table, and, in the midst of mixed conversation, (for there were several friends in the room,) he brought to Charles Ollier, the publisher, the Dedication-Sonnet to Leigh Hunt. If the original manuscript of that poem—a legitimate sonnet, with every restriction of rhyme and metre—could now be produced, and the time recorded in which it was written, it would be pronounced an extraordinary performance; added to which, the non-alteration of a single word in the poem (a circumstance noted at the time) claims for it, I should suppose, a merit without a parallel.

'The poem which commences the volume,' says Mr Monckton Milnes, 'was suggested to Keats by a delightful summer's day, as he stood beside the gate that leads from the battery on Hampstead Heath into a field by Caen Wood'; and the lovely passage beginning,

Linger awhile upon some bending planks,

and which contains the description of the 'swarms of minnows that show their little heads,' Keats told me was the recollection of our having frequently loitered over the rail of a foot-bridge that spanned a little brook in the last field upon entering Edmonton. He himself thought the picture was correct, and liked it; and I do not know who could improve it.

Another example of his promptly suggestive imagination, and uncommon facility in giving it utterance, occurred one day upon his returning home and finding me asleep upon the sofa, with my volume of Chaucer open at the 'Flower and the Leaf.' After expressing his admiration of the poem, which he had been reading, he gave me the fine testimony of that opinion, in pointing to the sonnet he had written at the close of it, which was an extempore effusion, and it has not the alteration of a single word. It lies before me now, signed, 'J. K., Feb., 1817.' If my memory does not betray me, this charming out-door fancy-scene was Keats's first introduction to Chaucer. Certain I am that the *Troilus and Cresseide* was an after-acquaintance; and clearly do I remember his approbation of the favorite passages that I had marked. I desired him to retrace the poem, and with his pen confirm and denote those which were congenial with his own feeling and judgment. These two circumstances, connected with the literary career of this cherished object of his friend's esteem and love, have stamped a priceless value upon that friend's miniature 18mo copy of Chaucer.

The little first volume of Keats's Muse was launched amid the cheers and fond anticipations of all his circle. Every one of us expected that it would create a sensation in the literary world; and we calculated upon, at least, a succession of reprints. Alas! it might have emerged in Timbuctoo with stronger chance of fame and favor. It never passed to a second edition; the first was but a small one, and that was never sold off. The whole community, as if by compact, determined to know nothing about it. The word had been passed that its author was a Radical; and in those blessed days of 'Bible-Crown-and-Constitution' supremacy, he might with better chance of success have been a robber, —there were many prosperous public ones,—if he had also been an Anti-Jacobin. Keats had made no demonstration of political opinion; but he had dedicated his book to Leigh Hunt, a Radical news-writer, and a dubbed partisan of the French ruler, because he did not call him the 'Corsican monster,' and other disgusting names. Verily, 'the former times were *not* better than these.' Men can now write the word 'Liberty' without being chalked on the back and hounded out.

Poor Keats! he little anticipated, and as little deserved, the cowardly and scoundrel treatment that was in store for him upon the publication of his second composition, the *Endymion*. It was in the interval of the two productions that he had moved from the Poultry, and had taken a lodging in Well Walk, Hampstead,—in the first or second house, on the right hand, going up to the Heath. I have an impression that he had been some weeks absent at the sea-side before settling in this domicile; for the *Endymion* had been begun, and he had made considerable advances in his plan. He came to me one Sunday, and I walked with him, spending the whole day in Well Walk. His constant and enviable friend Severn, I remember, was present on the occasion, by the circumstance of our exchanging looks upon Keats's reading to us portions of his new work that had pleased himself. One of these, I think, was the 'Hymn to Pan'; and another, I am sure, was the 'Bower of Adonis,' because his own expression of face will never pass from me (if I were a Reynolds or a Gainsborough, I could now stamp it forever) as he read the description of the latter, with the descent and ascent of the car of Venus. The 'Hymn to Pan' occurs early in the First Book:—

> O thou, whose mighty palace-roof doth hang
> From jagged trunks, etc.

And the 'Bower of Adonis,' in the Second Book, commences,—

> After a thousand mazes overgone.

Keats was indebted for his introduction to Mr Severn to his school-fellow Edward Holmes, who also had been one of the child-scholars at Enfield; for he came to us in the frock-dress. They were sworn companions at school, and remained friends through life. Mr Holmes ought to have been an educated musician from his first childhood; for the passion was in him. I used to amuse myself with the piano-forte after supper, when all had gone to bed. Upon some sudden occasion, leaving the parlor, I heard a scuffle on the stairs, and discovered that my young gentleman had left his bed to hear the music. At other times, during the day, and in the intervals of school-hours, he would stand under the window, listening. He at length intrusted to me his heart's secret, that he should like to learn music. So I taught him his notes; and he soon knew and could do as much as his tutor. Upon leaving Enfield, he was apprenticed to the elder Seeley, a bookseller in Fleet Street; but, hating his occupation, left it, I believe, before he was of age. He had not lost sight of me; and I introduced him to Mr Vincent Novello, who had made himself a friend to me, and who not merely, with rare profusion of bounty, gave Holmes instruction, but received him into his house, and made him one of his family. With them he resided some years. I was also the fortunate means of recommending him to the chief proprietor of the *Atlas* newspaper; and to that journal, during a long period, he contributed a series of essays and critiques upon the science and practice of music, which raised the journal into a reference and an authority in the art. He wrote for the proprietors of the *Atlas* that elegant little book of dilettante criticism, *A Ramble among the Musicians in Germany*. He latterly contributed to the *Musical Times* a whole series of masterly essays and analyses upon the Masses of Haydn, Mozart, and Beethoven. But the work upon which his reputation will rest was a *Life of Mozart*, which was purchased by Chapman and Hall.

I have said that Holmes used to listen on the stairs. In after-years, when Keats was reading to me his 'Eve of St Agnes,' (and what a happy day was that! I had come up to see him from Ramsgate, where I then lived,) at the passage where Porphyro in Madeleine's chamber is fearfully listening to the hubbub of the dancing and the music in the hall below, and the verse says,—

> The boisterous midnight festive clarion,
> The kettle-drum and far-heard clarionet,
> Affray his ears, though but in dying tone:
> *The hall-door shuts again, and all the noise is gone,*—

'That line,' said he, 'came into my head when I remembered how I used to listen, in bed, to your music at school.' Interesting would be a record of the germs and first causes of all the greatest poets' conceptions! The elder Brunel's first hint for his 'shield,' in constructing the tunnel under the Thames, was taken from watching the labor of a sea-insect, which, having a projecting hood, could bore into the ship's timber, unmolested by the waves.

I fancy it was about this time that Keats gave that signal example of his courage and stamina, in the recorded instance of his pugilistic contest with a butcher-boy. He told me—and in his characteristic manner—of their 'passage of *arms*.' The brute, he said, was tormenting a kitten, and he interfered, when a threat offered was enough for his mettle, and they set to. He thought he should be beaten; for the fellow was the taller and stronger; but, like an authentic pugilist, my young poet found that he had planted a blow which 'told' upon his antagonist. In every succeeding round, therefore, (for they fought nearly an hour,) he never failed of returning to the weak point; and the contest ended in the hulk being led or carried home. In all my knowledge of my fellow-beings, I never knew one who so thoroughly combined the sweetness with the power of gentleness and the irresistible sway of anger as Keats. His indignation would have made the boldest grave; and those who have seen him under the influence of tyranny, injustice, and meanness of soul will never forget the expression of his features,—'the form of his visage was changed.'

He had a strong sense of humor; yet, so to speak, he was not, in the strict sense of the term, a humorist. His comic fancy lurked in the outermost and most unlooked-for images of association,—which, indeed, may be said to be the components of humor; nevertheless, I think they did not extend beyond the *quaint*, in fulfilment and success. But his perception of humor, with the power of transmitting it by imitation, was both vivid and irresistibly amusing. He once described to me his having gone to see a bear-baiting,—the animal, the property of a Mr Tom Oliver. The performance not having begun, Keats was near to and watched a young aspirant, who had brought a younger under his wing to witness the solemnity, and whom he oppressively patronized, instructing him in the names and qualities of all the magnates present. Now and then, in his zeal to manifest and impart his knowledge, he would forget himself, and stray beyond the prescribed bounds, into the ring,—to the lashing resentment of its comptroller, Mr William Soames; who, after some hints of a practical nature, to 'keep back,' began laying about him with indiscriminate and unmitigable vivacity, —the Peripatetic signifying to his pupil,—'My eyes! Bill Soames giv' me sich a licker!'—evidently grateful, and considering himself complimented, upon being included in the general dispensation. Keats's entertainment with this minor scene of low life has often recurred to me. But his subsequent description of the baiting, with his position, of his legs and arms bent and shortened, till he looked like Bruin on his hind-legs, dabbing his fore-paws hither and thither, as the dogs snapped at him, and now and then acting the gasp of one that had been suddenly caught and hugged, his own capacious mouth adding force to the personation, was a memorable display. I am never reminded of this amusing relation, but it is associated with that forcible picture in Shakspeare, (and what subject can we not associate with him?) in the *Henry VI.*:—

> as a bear encompassed round with dogs,
> Who having *pinched* a few and *made them cry*,
> The rest stand all aloof and bark at him.

Keats also attended a prize-fight between two of the most skilful and enduring 'light-weights,'—Randal and Turner. It was, I believe, at that remarkable wager, when, the men being so equally matched and accomplished, they had been sparring for three-quarters of an hour before a blow had been struck. In describing the rapidity of Randal's blows while the other was falling, Keats tapped his fingers on the window-pane.

I make no apology for recording these events in his life; they are characteristics of the natural man,—and prove, moreover, that the indulgence in such exhibitions did not for one moment blunt the gentler emotions of his heart, or vulgarize his inborn love of all that was beautiful and true. His own line was the axiom of his moral existence, his political creed:—'A thing of beauty is a joy forever'; and I can fancy no coarser consociation able to win him from this faith. Had he been born in squalor, he would have emerged a gentleman. Keats was not an easily swayable man; in differing with those he loved, his firmness kept equal pace with the sweetness of his persuasion; but with the rough and the unlovable he kept no terms,—within the conventional precincts, I mean, of social order.

From Well Walk he moved to another quarter of the Heath,—Wentworth Place the name, if I recollect. Here he became a sharing inmate with Mr Charles Armitage Brown, a gentleman who had been a Russia merchant, and had retired to a literary leisure upon an independence. I do not know how they became acquainted; but Keats never had a more zealous, a firmer, or more practical friend and adviser than Brown. His robust eagerness and zeal, with a headstrong determination of will, led him into an undue prejudice against the brother, George, respecting some money-transactions with John, which, however, the former redeemed to the perfect satisfaction of all the friends of the family. After the death of Keats, Armitage Brown went to reside in Florence, where he remained some few years; then he settled at Plymouth, and there brought out a work entitled, *Shakespeare's Autobiographical Poems. Being his Sonnets clearly developed; with his Character, drawn chiefly from his Works.* It cannot be said that in this work the author has clearly educed his theory; but, in the face of his failure upon that main point, the book is interesting, for the heart-whole zeal and homage with which he has gone into his subject. Brown was no half-measure man; 'whatsoever his hand found to do, he did it with his might.' His last stage-scene in life was passed in New Zealand, whither he emigrated with his son, having purchased some land,—or, as his own letter stated, having been thoroughly defrauded in the transaction. Brown accompanied Keats in his tour in the Hebrides, a worthy event in the poet's career, seeing that it led to the production of that magnificent sonnet to 'Ailsa Rock.' As a passing observation, and to show how the minutest circumstance did not escape him, he told me, that, when he first came upon the view of Loch Lomond, the sun was setting; the lake was in shade, and of a deep blue; and at the farther end was '*a slash across it,* of deep orange.' The description of the traceried window in the 'Eve of St Agnes' gives proof of the intensity of his feeling for color.

It was during his abode in Wentworth Place that the savage and vulgar attacks upon the *Endymion* appeared in the *Quarterly Review*, and in *Blackwood's Magazine.* There was, indeed, ruffian, low-lived work,—especially in the latter publication, which had reached a pitch of blackguardism, (it used to be called 'Blackguard's Magazine,') with *personal abuse,*—ABUSE,—the only word,—that would damage the sale of any review at this day. The very reverse of its present management. There would not now be the *inclination* for such rascal bush-fighting; and even then, or indeed at any period of the Magazine's career, the stalwart and noble mind of John Wilson would never have made itself editorially responsible for such trash. As to him of the *Quarterly*, a thimble would have been 'a mansion, a court,' for his whole soul. The style of the articles directed against the Radical writers, and those especially whom the party had nicknamed the 'Cockney school' of poetry, may be conceived by its provoking the following observation from Hazlitt to me:—'To pay those fellows, Sir, *in their own coin*, the way would be, to begin with Walter Scott, and *have at his clump-foot*.' 'Verily, the former times were not better than these.'

To say that these disgusting misrepresentations did not affect the consciousness and self-respect of Keats would be to underrate the sensitiveness of his nature. He felt the insult, but more the injustice of the treatment he had received; he told me so, as we lay awake one night, when I slept in his brother's bed. They had injured him in the most wanton manner; but if they, or my Lord Byron, ever for one moment supposed that he was crushed or even cowed in spirit by the treatment he had received, never were they more deluded. 'Snuffed out by an article,' indeed! He had infinitely more magnanimity, in its fullest sense, than that very spoiled, self-willed, and mean-souled man,—and I have authority for the last term. To say nothing of personal and private transactions, pages 204–207 in the first volume of Mr Monckton Milnes's life of our poet will be full authority for my estimate of his Lordship. 'Johnny Keats' had, indeed, 'a little body with a mighty heart,' and he showed it in the best way: not by fighting the ruffians,—though he could have done that,—but by the resolve that he would produce brain-work which not one of their party could approach; and he did.

In the year 1820 appeared the 'Lamia', 'Isabella,' 'Eve of St Agnes,' and *Hyperion*, etc. But, alas! the insidious disease which carried him off had made its approach, and he was going to, or had already departed for, Italy, attended by his constant and self-sacrificing friend, Severn. Keats's mother died of consumption; and he nursed his younger brother in the same disease, to the last,—and, by so doing, in all probability, hastened his own summons. Upon the publication of the last volume of poems, Charles Lamb wrote one of his own finely appreciative and cordial critiques in the *Morning Chronicle*. This was sent to me in the country, where I had for some time resided. I had not heard of the dangerous state of Keats's health,—only that he and Severn were going to Italy; it was, therefore, an unprepared shock which brought me the news that he had died in Rome.

Mr Monckton Milnes has related the anecdote of Keats's introduction to Wordsworth, with the latter's appreciation of the 'Hymn to Pan,' which its author had been desired to repeat, and the Rydal

Mount poet's snow-capped comment upon it,—'Uhm! a pretty piece of Paganism!' Mr Milnes, with his genial and placable nature, has made an amiable defence for the apparent coldness of Wordsworth's appreciation,—'That it was probably intended for some slight rebuke to his youthful compeer, whom he saw absorbed in an order of ideas that to him appeared merely sensuous, and would have desired that the bright traits of Greek mythology should be sobered down by a graver faith.' Keats, like Shakspeare, and every other true poet, put his whole soul into what he imagined, portrayed, or embodied; and hence he appeared the young Greek, 'suckled in that creed outworn.' The wonder is, that Mr Wordsworth forgot to quote himself. From Keats's description of his Mentor's manner, as well as behavior, that evening, I cannot but believe it to have been one of the usual ebullitions of the egoism, not to say of the uneasiness, known to those who were accustomed to hear the great moral philosopher discourse upon his own productions and descant upon those of a contemporary. During this same visit, he was dilating upon some question in poetry, when, upon Keats's insinuating a confirmatory suggestion to his argument, Mrs Wordsworth put her hand upon his arm, saying,—'Mr Wordsworth is never interrupted.' Again, during the same interview, some one had said that the next Waverley novel was to be *Rob Roy*; when Mr Wordsworth took down his volume of Ballads, and read to the company 'Rob Roy's Grave,'—then, returning it to the shelf, observed, 'I do not know what more Mr Scott can have to say upon the subject.' When Leigh Hunt had his first interview with Wordsworth, the latter lectured to him—finely, indeed—upon his own writings; and repeated the entire sonnet,

Great men have been among us,—

which Hunt said he did 'in a grand and earnest tone.' Some one in a company quoting the passage from *Henry V.*,—

So work the honey-bees,

and each 'picking out his pet plum' from that perfect piece of natural history, Wordsworth objected to the line,

The singing masons building roofs of gold,

because, he said, of the unpleasant repetition of the '*ing*' in it! Where were his ears and judgment on that occasion? But I have more than once heard it said that Wordsworth had not a genuine love of Shakspeare,—that, when he could, he always accompanied a '*pro*' with his '*con*,' and, Atticus-like, would 'just hint a fault and hesitate dislike.' Truly, indeed, we are all of 'a mingled yarn, good and ill together.'

I can scarcely conceive of anything more unjust than the account which that ill-ordered being, Haydon, left behind him in his *Diary*, respecting the idolized object of his former intimacy, John Keats. At his own eager request, after reading the manuscript specimens I had left with Leigh Hunt, I had introduced their author to him; and for some time subsequently I had frequent opportunities of seeing them together, and can testify to the laudations that Haydon trowelled on to the young poet. Before I left London, however, it had been said that things and opinions had changed,—and, in short, that Haydon had abjured all acquaintance with, and had even ignored, such a person as the author of the sonnet to him, and those 'On the Elgin Marbles.' I say nothing of the grounds of their separation; but, knowing the two men, and knowing, I believe, to the core, the humane principle of the poet, I have such faith in his steadfastness of friendship, that I am sure he would never have left behind him an unfavorable *truth*, while nothing could have induced him to utter a *calumny* of one who had received pledges of his former regard and esteem. Haydon's detraction was the more odious because its object could not contradict the charge, and because it supplied his old critical antagonists (if any remained) with an authority for their charge against him of Cockney ostentation and display. The most mean-spirited and trumpery twaddle in the paragraph was, that Keats was so far gone in sensual excitement as to put Cayenne pepper upon his tongue, when taking his claret! Poor fellow! he never purchased a bottle of claret, within my knowledge of him; and, from such observation as could not escape me, I am bound to assert that his domestic expenses never could have occasioned him a regret or a self-reproof.

When Shelley left England for Italy, Keats told me that he had received from him an invitation to become his guest,—and, in short, to make one of his household. It was upon the purest principle that Keats declined the noble proffer; for he entertained an exalted opinion of Shelley's genius, in itself an inducement; he also knew of his deeds of bounty; and lastly, from their frequent intercourse, he had full faith in the sincerity of his proposal; for a more crystalline heart than Shelley's never beat in human bosom. He was incapable of an untruth or of a deceit in any ill form. Keats told me, that, in declining the invitation, his sole motive was the consciousness, which would be ever prevalent with him, of his not being, in its utter extent, a free agent,—even within such a circle as Shelley's,—himself, nevertheless, the most unrestricted of beings. Mr Trelawney, a familiar of the family, has confirmed the unwavering testimony to Shelley's bounty of nature, where he says, 'Shelley was a being absolutely without selfishness.' The poorest cottagers knew and benefited by the thoroughly *practical* and unselfish character of his Christianity, during his residence at Marlow, when he would visit them, and, having gone through a course of study in medicine, in order that he might assist them with his advice, would commonly administer the tonic which such systems usually require,—a good basin of broth, or pea-soup. And I believe I am infringing on no private domestic delicacy, when I repeat, that he has been known, upon a sudden and immediate emergency, to purloin ('*convey* the wise it call') a portion of the warmest of Mrs Shelley's wardrobe, to protect some poor starving sister. One of the richer residents of Marlow told me that '*they all* considered him a madman.' I wish he had bitten the whole squad.

> No settled senses of the world can match
> The 'wisdom' of that madness.

Shelley's figure was a little above the middle height, slender, and of delicate construction, which appeared the rather from a lounging or waving manner in his gait, as though his frame was compounded merely of muscle and tendon, and that the power of walking was an achievement with him, and not a natural habit. Yet I should suppose that he was not a valetudinarian, although that has been said of him, on account of his spare and vegetable diet: for I have the remembrance of his scampering and bounding over the gorse-bushes on Hampstead Heath, late one night,—now close upon us, and now shouting from the height, like a wild school-boy. He was both an active and an enduring walker,—feats which do not accompany an ailing and feeble constitution. His face was round, flat, pale, with small features; mouth beautifully shaped; hair, bright-brown and wavy; and such a pair of eyes as are rarely seen in the human or any other head,—intensely blue, with a gentle and lambent expression, yet wonderfully alert and engrossing: nothing appeared to escape his knowledge.

Whatever peculiarity there might have been in Shelley's religious faith, I have the best authority for believing that it was confined to the early period of his life. The *practical* result of its course of *action*, I am sure, had its source from the 'Sermon on the Mount.' There is not one clause in that divine code which his conduct towards his fellow-mortals did not confirm, and substantiate him to be a follower of Christ. Yet, when the news arrived in London of the death of Shelley and Captain Williams by drowning, the *Courier* newspaper—an evening journal of that day—capped the intelligence with the following remark:—'He will now know whether there is a hell or not!'—I believe that there are still one or two public fanatics who would *think* that surmise, but not one would dare to utter it in his journal. So much for the progress of liberality, and the power of opinion.

At page 100 of the *Life of Keats*, Vol. I., Mr Monckton Milnes has quoted a literary portrait of him, which he received from a lady who used to see him at Hazlitt's lectures at the Surrey Institution. The building was on the south or right-hand side, and close to Blackfriars' Bridge. I believe that the whole of Hazlitt's lectures, on the British Poets, the Writers of the Time of Elizabeth, and the Comic Writers, were delivered in that Institution, during the years 1817 and 1818; shortly after which time the establishment appears to have been broken up. The lady's remark upon the character and expression of Keats's features is both happy and true. She says,—'His countenance lives in my mind as one of singular beauty and brightness; it had an expression *as if he had been looking on some glorious sight.*' That's excellent.—'His mouth was full, and less intellectual than his other features.' True again. But when our artist pronounces that 'his eyes were large and *blue*,' and that 'his hair was *auburn*,' I am naturally reminded of the fable of the 'Chameleon':—'They're *brown*, Ma'am,—*brown*, I assure you!' The fact is, the lady was enchanted—and I cannot wonder at it—with the whole character of that beaming face; and 'blue' and 'auburn' being the favorite tints of the human front divine, in the lords of the creation, the poet's eyes consequently became 'blue,' and his hair 'auburn.' Colors, however, vary with the prejudice or partiality of the spectator; and, moreover, people do not agree even upon the most palpable prismatic tint. A writing-master whom we had at Enfield was an artist of more than ordinary merit; but he had one dominant defect: he could not distinguish between true blue and true green. So that, upon one occasion, when he was exhibiting to us a landscape he had just completed, I hazarded the critical question, why he painted his trees so *blue*? 'Blue!' he replied,—'what do you call green?'—Reader, alter in your copy of Monckton Milnes's *Life of Keats*, Vol. I., page 103, 'eyes' *light hazel*, 'hair' *lightish-brown and wavy*.

The most perfect, and withal the favorite portrait of him, was the one by Severn, published in Leigh Hunt's *Lord Byron and his Contemporaries*, and which I remember the artist's sketching in a few minutes, one evening, when several of Keats's friends were at his apartments in the Poultry. The portrait prefixed to the *Life*, also by Severn, is a most excellent one-look-and-expression likeness,—an every-day, and of 'the earth, earthy' one;—and the last, which the same artist painted, and which is now in the possession of Mr John Hunter, of Craig Crook, Edinburgh, may be an equally felicitous rendering of one look and manner; but I do not intimately recognize it. There is another, and a *curiously unconscious* likeness of him, in the charming Dulwich Gallery of Pictures. It is in the portrait of Wouvermans, by Rembrandt. It is just so much of a resemblance as to remind the friends of the poet,—though not such a one as the immortal Dutchman would have made, had the poet been his sitter. It has a plaintive and melancholy expression, which, I rejoice to say, I do not associate with him.

There is one of his attitudes, during familiar conversation, which, at times, (with the whole earnest manner and sweet expression of the man) presents itself to me, as though I had seen him only last week. The attitude I speak of was that of cherishing one leg over the knee of the other, smoothing the instep with the palm of his hand. In this action I mostly associate him in an eager parley with Leigh Hunt, in his little cottage in the 'Vale of Health.' This position, if I mistake not, is in the last portrait of him at Craig Crook; if not, it is in a reminiscent one, painted after his death.

His stature could have been very little more than five feet; but he was, withal, compactly made and well-proportioned; and before the hereditary disorder which carried him off began to show itself, he was active, athletic, and enduringly strong,—as the fight with the butcher gave full attestation.

The critical world,—by which term I mean the censorious portion of it; for many have no other idea of criticism than that of censure and objection,—the critical world have so gloated over the feebler, or, if they will, the defective side of Keats's genius, and his friends, his gloryingly partial friends, have so amply justified him, that I feel inclined to add no more to the category of opinions than to say, that the only fault in his poetry I could discover was a redundancy of imagery,—that exuberance, by-the-by, being a quality of the greatest promise, seeing that it is the constant accompaniment of a young and teeming genius. But his steady friend, Leigh Hunt, has rendered the amplest and truest record of his mental accomplishment in the Preface to the *Foliage*, quoted at page 150 of the first volume of the *Life of Keats*; and his biographer has so zealously, and, I would say, so amiably, summed up his character and intellectual qualities, that I can add no more than my assent.

Keats's whole course of life, to the very last act of it, was one routine of unselfishness and of consideration for others' feelings. The approaches of death having come on, he said to his untiring nurse-friend,—'Severn, —I,—lift me up,—I am dying:—*I shall die easy; don't be frightened;*—be firm, and thank God it has come.'

There are constant indications through the memoirs, and in the letters of Keats, of his profound reverence for Shakspeare. His own intensity of thought and expression visibly strengthened with the study of his idol; and he knew but little of him till he himself had become an author. A marginal note by him in a folio copy of the Plays is an example of the complete absorption his mind had undergone during the process of his matriculation;—and, through life, however long with any of us, we are all in progress of matriculation, as we study the 'myriad-minded's' system of philosophy. The note that Keats made was this:—'The genius of Shakspeare was an *innate universality*; wherefore he laid the achievements of human intellect prostrate beneath his indolent and kingly gaze: *he could do easily men's utmost;* his plan of tasks to come was not of this world. If what he proposed to do hereafter would not in the idea answer the aim, how tremendous must have been his conception of ultimates!'

71. Joseph Severn looks back

1863

Signed article 'On the Vicissitudes of Keats's Fame', *Atlantic Monthly* (April 1863), xi, 401–7.

Joseph Severn (1793–1879), the most revered of Keats's friends, owed much of his minor success as a painter, and of his great success as British Consul in Rome, to his devotion. Special permission was obtained for him to be buried beside Keats in the disused part of the Protestant Cemetery.

Although the interval of forty years, and Severn's own piety, caused some amiable wanderings of memory, this triumphant retrospect by 'the friend of Keats' is an essential document in the history of Keats's critical reception.

I well remember being struck with the clear and independent manner in which Washington Allston, in the year 1818, expressed his opinion of John Keats's verse, when the young poet's writings first appeared, amid the ridicule of most English readers. Mr Allston was at that time the only discriminating judge among the strangers to Keats who were residing abroad, and he took occasion to emphasize in my hearing his opinion of the early effusions of the young poet in words like these:—'They are crude materials of real poetry, and Keats is sure to become a great poet.'

It is a singular pleasure to the few personal friends of Keats in England (who may still have to defend him against the old and worn-out slanders) that in America he has always had a solid fame, independent of the old English prejudices.

Here in Rome, as I write, I look back through forty years of worldly changes to behold Keats's dear image again in memory. It seems as if he should be living with me now, inasmuch as I never could understand his strange and contradictory death, his falling away so suddenly from health and strength. He had that fine compactness of person which we regard as the promise of longevity, and no mind was ever more exultant in youthful feeling. I cannot summon a sufficient reason why in one short year he should have been thus cut off, 'with all his imperfections on his head.' Was it that he lived too soon,—that the world he sought was not ready for him?

For more than the year I am now dwelling on, he had fostered a tender and enduring love for a young girl nearly of his own age, and this love was reciprocal, not only in itself, but in all the worldly advantages arising from it of fortune on her part and fame on his. It was encouraged by the sole parent of the lady; and the fond mother was happy in seeing her daughter so betrothed, and pleased that her inheritance would fall to so worthy an object as Keats. This was all well settled in the minds and hearts of the mutual friends of both parties, when poor Keats, soon after the death of his younger brother, unaccountably showed signs of consumption: at least, he himself thought so, though the doctors were widely undecided about it. By degrees it began to be deemed needful that the young poet should go to Italy, even to preserve his life. This was at last accomplished, but too late; and now that I am reviewing all the progress of his illness from his first symptoms, I cannot but think his life might have been preserved by an Italian sojourn, if it had been adopted in time, and if circumstances had been improved as they presented themselves. And, further, if he had had the good fortune to go to America, which he partly contemplated before the death of his younger brother, not only would his life and health have been preserved, but his early fame would have been insured. He would have lived independent of the London world, which was striving to drag him down in his poetic career, and adding to the sufferings which I consider the immediate cause of his early death.

In Italy he always shrank from speaking in direct terms of the actual things which were killing him. Certainly the *Blackwood* attack was one of the least of his miseries, for he never even mentioned it to me. The greater trouble which was ingulfing him he signified in a hundred ways. Was it to be wondered at, that at the time when the happiest life was presented to his view, when it was arranged that he was to marry a young person of beauty and fortune, when the little knot of friends who valued him saw such a future for the beloved poet, and he himself, with generous, unselfish feelings, looked forward to it more delighted on their account,—was it to be wondered at, that, on the appearance of consumption, his ardent mind should have sunk into despair? He seemed struck down from the highest happiness to the lowest misery. He felt crushed at the prospect of being cut off at the early age of twenty-four, when the cup was at his lips, and he was beginning to drink that draught of delight which was to last his mortal life through, which would have insured to him the happiness of home, (happiness he had never felt, for he was an orphan,) and which was to be a barrier for him against a cold and (to him) a malignant world.

He kept continually in his hand a polished, oval, white carnelian, the gift of his widowing love, and at times it seemed his only consolation, the only thing left him in this world clearly tangible. Many letters which he was unable to read came for him. Some he allowed me to read to him; others were too worldly,—for, as he said, he had 'already journeyed far beyond them.' There were two letters, I remember, for which he had no words, but he made me understand that I was to place them on his heart within his winding-sheet.

Those bright falcon eyes, which I had known only in joyous intercourse, while revelling in books and Nature, or while he was reciting his own poetry, now beamed an unearthly brightness and a penetrating steadfastness that could not be looked at. It was not the fear of death,—on the contrary, he earnestly wished to die,—but it was the fear of lingering on and on, that now distressed him; and this was wholly on my account. Amidst the world of emotions that were crowding and increasing as his end approached, I could always see that his generous concern for me in my isolated position at Rome was one of his greatest cares. In a little basket of medicines I had bought at Gravesend at his request there was a bottle of laudanum, and this I afterwards found was destined by him 'to close his mortal career,' when no hope was left, and to prevent a long, lingering death, for my poor sake. When the dismal time came, and Sir James Clark was unable to encounter Keats's penetrating look and eager demand, he insisted on having the bottle, which I had already put away. Then came the most touching scenes. He now explained to me the exact procedure of his gradual dissolution, enumerated my deprivations and toils, and dwelt upon the danger to my life, and certainly to my fortunes, from my continued attendance upon him. One whole day was spent in earnest representations of this sort, to which, at the same time that they wrung my heart to hear and his to utter, I was obliged to oppose a firm resistance. On the second day, his tender appeal turned to despair, in all the power of his ardent imagination and bursting heart.

From day to day, after this time, he would always demand of Sir James Clark, 'How long is this *posthumous* life of mine to last?' On finding me inflexible in my purpose of remaining with him, he became calm, and tranquilly said that he was sure why I held up so patiently was owing to my Christian faith, and that he was disgusted with himself for ever appearing before me in such savage guise; that he now felt convinced how much every human being required the support of religion, that he might die decently. 'Here am I,' said he, 'with desperation in death that would disgrace the commonest fellow. Now, my dear Severn, I am sure, if you could get some of the works of Jeremy Taylor to read to me, I might become *really* a Christian, and leave this world in peace.' Most fortunately, I was able to procure the *Holy Living and Dying*. I read some passages to him, and prayed with him, and I could tell by the grasp of his dear hand that his mind was reviving. He was a great lover of Jeremy Taylor, and it did not seem to require much effort in him to embrace the Holy Spirit in these comforting works.

Thus he gained strength of mind from day to day just in proportion as his poor body grew weaker and weaker. At last I had the consolation of finding him calm, trusting, and more prepared for his end than I was. He tranquilly rehearsed to me what would be the process of his dying, what I was to do, and how I was to *bear it*. He was even minute in his details, evidently rejoicing that his death was at hand. In all he then uttered he breathed a simple, Christian spirit; indeed, I always think that he died a Christian, that 'Mercy' was trembling on his dying lips, and that his tortured soul was received by those Blessed Hands which could alone welcome it.*

After the death of Keats, my countrymen in Rome seemed to vie with one another in evincing the greatest kindness towards me. I found myself in the midst of persons who admired and encouraged my beautiful pursuit of painting, in which I was then indeed but a very poor student, but with my eyes opening and my soul awakening to a new region of Art, and beginning to feel the wings growing for artistic flights I had always been dreaming about.

In all this, however, there was a solitary drawback: there were few

* Whilst this was passing at Rome, another scene of the tragedy was enacting in London. The violence of the Tory party in attacking Keats had increased after his leaving England, but he had found able defenders, and amongst them Mr John Scott, the editor of the *Champion*, who published a powerful vindication of Keats, with a denunciation of the party-spirit of his critics. This led to a challenge from Mr Scott to Mr Lockhart, who was then one of the editors of *Blackwood*. The challenge was shifted over to a Mr Christie, and he and Mr Scott fought at Chalk Farm, with the tragic result of the death of Keats's defender,—and this within a few days of the poet's death at Rome. The deplorable catastrophe was not without its compensations, for ever after there was a more chastened feeling in both parties.

Englishmen at Rome who knew Keats's works, and I could scarcely persuade any one to make the effort to read them, such was the prejudice against him as a poet; but when his gravestone was placed, with his own expressive line, 'Here lies one whose name was writ in water,' then a host started up, not of admirers, but of scoffers, and a silly jest was often repeated in my hearing, 'Here lies one whose name was writ in water, and *his works in milk and water*'; and this I was condemned to hear for years repeated, as though it had been a pasquinade; but I should explain that it was from those who were not aware that I was the friend of Keats.

At the first Easter after his death I had a singular encounter with the late venerable poet, Samuel Rogers, at the table of Sir George Beaumont, the distinguished amateur artist. Perhaps in compliment to my friendship for Keats, the subject of his death was mentioned by Sir George, and he asked Mr Rogers if he had been acquainted with the young poet in England. Mr Rogers replied, that he had had more acquaintance than he liked, for the poems were tedious enough, and the author had come upon him several times for money. This was an intolerable falsehood, and I could not restrain myself until I had corrected him, which I did with my utmost forbearance,—explaining that Mr Rogers must have mistaken some other person for Keats,—that I was positive my friend had never done such a thing in any shape, or even had occasion to do it,—that he possessed a small independence in money, and *a large one in mind.*

The old poet received the correction with much kindness, and thanked me for so effectually setting him right. Indeed, this encounter was the groundwork of a long and to me advantageous friendship between us. I soon discovered that it was the principle of his sarcastic wit not only to sacrifice all truth to it, but even all his friends, and that he did not care to know any who would not allow themselves to be abused for the purpose of lighting up his breakfast with sparkling wit, though not quite, indeed, at the expense of the persons then present. I well remember, on one occasion afterwards, Mr Rogers was entertaining us with a volley of sarcasms upon a disagreeable lawyer, who made pretensions to knowledge and standing not to be borne; on this occasion the old poet went on, not only to the end of the breakfast, but to the announcement of the very man himself on an accidental visit, and then, with a bland smile and a cordial shake of the hand, he said to him, 'My dear fellow, we have all been talking about you up to this very minute,'—and looking at his company still at table, and with a significant wink, he, with extraordinary adroitness and experienced tact, repeated many of the good things, reversing the meaning of them, and giving us the enjoyment of the *double-entendre*. The visitor was charmed, nor even dreamed of the ugliness of his position. This incident gave me a painful and repugnant impression of Mr Rogers, yet no doubt it was after the manner of his time, and such as had been the fashion in Walpole's and Johnson's days.

I should be unjust to the venerable poet not to add, that notwithstanding what is here related of him, he often-times showed himself the generous and noble-hearted man. I think that in all my long acquaintance with him he evinced a kind of indirect regret that he had commenced with me in such an ugly attack on dear Keats, whose fame, when I went to England in 1838, was not only well established, but was increasing from day to day, and Mr Rogers was often at the pains to tell me so, and to relate the many histories of poets who had been less fortunate than Keats.

It was in the year of the Reform Bill, 1830, that I first heard of the Paris edition (Galignani's) of Keats's works, and I confess that I was quite taken by surprise, nor could I really believe the report until I saw the book with the engraved portrait from my own drawing; for, after all the vicissitudes of Keats's fame which I had witnessed, I could not easily understand his becoming the poet of 'the million.' I had now the continued gratification in Rome of receiving frequent visits from the admirers of Keats and Shelley, who sought every way of showing kindness to me. One great cause of this change, no doubt, was the rise of all kinds of mysticism in religious opinions, which often associated themselves with Shelley's poetry, and I then for the first time heard him named as the only really religious poet of the age. To the growing fame of Keats I can attribute some of the pleasantest and most valuable associations of my after-life, as it included almost the whole society of gifted young men at that time called 'Young England.' Here I may allude to the extraordinary change I now observed in the manners and morals of Englishmen generally: the foppish love of dress was in a great measure abandoned, and all intellectual pursuits were caught up with avidity, and even made fashionable.

The most remarkable example of the strange capriciousness of Keats's fame which fell under my personal observation occurred in my later Roman years, during the painful visit of Sir Walter Scott to Rome in the winding-up days of his eventful life, when he was broken down not only by incurable illness and premature old age, but also by the accumulated misfortunes of fatal speculations and the heavy responsibility of making up all with the pen then trembling in his failing hand.

I had been indirectly made known to him by his favorite ward and *protégée*, the late Lady Northampton, who, accustomed to write to him monthly, often made mention of me; for I was on terms of friendship with all her family, an intimacy which in great part arose from the delight she always had in Keats's poetry, being herself a poetess, and a most enlightened and liberal critic.

When Sir Walter arrived, he received me like an old and attached friend; indeed, he involuntarily tried to make me fill up the terrible void then recently created by the death of Lady Northampton at the age of thirty-seven years. I went at his request to breakfast with him every morning, when he invariably commenced talking of his lost friend, of her beauty, her singularly varied accomplishments, of his growing delight in watching her from a child in the Island of Mull, and of his making her so often the model of his most successful female characters, the Lady of the Lake and Flora MacIvor particularly. Then he would stop short to lament her unlooked-for death with tears and groans of bitterness such as I had never before witnessed in any one,—his head sinking down on his heaving breast. When he revived, (and this agonizing scene took place every morning,) he implored me to pity him, and not heed his weakness,—that in his great misfortunes, in all their complications, he had looked forward to Rome and his dear Lady Northampton as his last and certain hope of repose; she was to be his comfort in the winding-up of life's pilgrimage: now, on his arrival, his life and fortune almost exhausted, she was gone! *gone*! After these pathetic outpourings, he would gradually recover his old cheerfulness, his expressive gray eye would sparkle even in tears, and soon that wonderful power he had for description would show itself, when he would often stand up to enact the incident of which he spoke, so ardent was he, and so earnest in the recital.

Each morning, at his request, I took for his examination some little picture or sketch that might interest him, and amongst the rest a picture of Keats, (now in the National Portrait Gallery of London,) but this I was surprised to find was the only production of mine that seemed not to interest him; he remained silent about it, but on all the others he was ready with interesting comments and speculations. Observing this, and wondering within myself at his apathy with regard to the young lost poet, as I had reason to be proud of Keats's growing fame, I ventured to talk about him, and of the extraordinary caprices of that fame, which at last had found it resting-place in the hearts of *all real lovers of poetry*.

I soon perceived that I was touching on an embarrassing theme, and I became quite bewildered on seeing Miss Scott turn away her face, already crimsoned with emotion. Sir Walter then falteringly remarked, 'Yes, yes, the world finds out these things *for itself at last*,' and taking my hand, closed the interview,—our last, for the following night he was taken seriously ill, and I never saw him again, as his physician immediately hurried him away from Rome.

The incomprehensibleness of this scene induced me to mention it on the same day to Mr Woodhouse, the active and discriminating friend of Keats, who had collected every written record of the poet, and to whom we owe the preservation of many of the finest of his productions. He was astonished at my recital, and at my being ignorant of the fact that *Sir Walter Scott was a prominent contributor to the Review which through its false and malicious criticisms had always been considered to have caused the death of Keats*.

My surprise was as great as his at my having lived all those seventeen years in Rome and been so removed from the great world, that this, a fact so interesting to me to know, had never reached me. I had been unconsciously the painful means of disturbing poor old Sir Walter with a subject so sore and unwelcome that I could only conclude it must have been the immediate cause of his sudden illness. Nothing could be farther from my nature than to have been guilty of such seemingly wanton inhumanity; but I had no opportunity afterwards of explaining the truth, or of justifying my conduct in any way.

This was the last striking incident connected with Keats's fame which fell within my own experience, and perhaps may have been the last, or one of the last, symptoms of that party-spirit which in the artificial times of George IV. was so common even among poets in their treatment of one another,—they assuming to be mere politicians, and striving to be oblivious of their heart-ennobling pursuit.

It only remains for me to speak of my return to Rome in 1861, after an absence of twenty years, and of the favorable change and the enlargement during that time of Keats's fame,—not as manifested by new editions of his works, or by the contests of publishers about him, or by the way in which most new works are illustrated with quotations from him, or by the fact that some favorite lines of his have passed into proverbs, but by the touching evidence of his *silent grave*. That grave, which I can remember as once the object of ridicule, has now become the poetic shrine of the world's pilgrims who care and strive to live in the happy and imaginative region of poetry. The head-stone, having twice sunk, owing to its faulty foundation, has been twice renewed by loving strangers, and each time, as I am informed, these strangers were Americans. Here they do not strew flowers, as was the wont of olden times, but they pluck everything that is green and living on the grave of the poet. The *Custode* tells me, that, notwithstanding all his pains in sowing and planting, he cannot 'meet the great consumption.' Latterly an English lady, alarmed at the rapid disappearance of the verdure on and around the grave, actually left an annual sum to renew it. When the *Custode* complained to me of the continued thefts, and asked what he was to do, I replied, 'Sow and plant twice as much; extend the poet's domain; for, as it was so scanty during his short life, surely it ought to be afforded to him twofold in his grave.'

Here on my return to Rome, all kinds of happy associations with the poet surround me, but none so touching as my recent meeting with his sister. I had known her in her childhood, during my first acquaintance with Keats, but had never seen her since. I knew of her marriage to a distinguished Spanish patriot, Señor Llanos, and of her permanent residence in Spain; but it was reserved for me to have the felicity of thus accidentally meeting her, like a new-found sister, in Rome. This city has an additional sacredness for both of us as the closing scene of her illustrious brother's life, and I am held by her and her charming family in loving regard as the last faithful friend of the poet. That I may indulge the pleasures of memory and unite them with the sympathy of present incidents, I am now engaged on a picture of the poet's grave, and am treating it with all the picturesque advantages which the antique locality gives me, as well as the elevated associations which this poetic shrine inspires. The classic story of Endymion being the subject of Keats's principal poem, I have introduced a young Roman shepherd sleeping against the head-stone with his flock about him, whilst the moon from behind the pyramid illuminates his figure and serves to realize the poet's favorite theme in the presence of his grave. This interesting incident is not fanciful, but is what I actually saw on an autumn evening at Monte Tertanio the year following the poet's death.

APPENDIX: THE PRINCIPAL EARLY EDITIONS OF KEATS'S POETRY

Separate publications

Poems: published 3 March 1817.

Endymion: a Poetic Romance: published at the end of April 1818.

Lamia, Isabella, the Eve of St Agnes, and Other Poems: published at the end of June 1820.

[*The Fall of Hyperion—a Dream*], edited by R. M. Milnes, *Miscellanie of the Philobiblon Society*, iii (1856–7).

None of Keats's volumes reached a second edition in the half-century following his death. For a list of his poems first published in periodicals, see the *New Cambridge Bibliography of English Literature* (1969), iii. 346–7.

Collected poems

The Poetical Works of Coleridge, Shelley and Keats: Paris 1829, Philadelphia 1831 (the first American edition), 1832, Buffalo 1834, Philadelphia 1835, 1836, 1838, 1839, 1844, 1847, 1849, 1853. Galignani's edition, the first 'collected poems', with a memoir by Cyrus Redding (see No. 45).

The Poetical Works of Howitt, Milman and Keats: Philadelphia 1840, 1846, 1847, 1849, 1852. An American edition of the Galignani Keats text, with Howitt and Milman substituted for Coleridge and Shelley.

The Poetical Works of John Keats: 1840, 1844. The first London edition (a paperback at 2*s*.) in 'Smith's Standard Library'.

The Poetical Works of John Keats: 1846, 1847, 1850, 1851, 1853.

The Poetical Works of John Keats. New York 1846, 1848, 1850, 1855, 1857.

The Poetical Works (with memoir by R. M. Milnes): 1854, Philadelphia 1855, London 1856, 1858, 1861, 1862, 1866, 1868, 1869, 1871, 1876 (with a brief new Life).

The Poetical Works (with Life by J. R. Lowell): Boston 1854, 1859, 1863, 1864, 1866, 1871, 1878.

Other works

Life, Letters and Literary Remains of John Keats, edited by R. M. Milnes, 2 vols. 1848, New York 1848, 1 vol. London 1867 (revised).

Letters of John Keats to Fanny Brawne, edited by H. B. Forman, 1878, New York 1878, London 1889 (revised edition).

BIBLIOGRAPHY

A selection of books and articles dealing with the critical reception of Keats during the nineteenth century.

Bibliographies of critical articles

ANDERSON, J. P., Bibliography, appended to W. M. Rossetti's *Life of John Keats*, 1887: still very useful, especially for criticism of the period 1847–87.

MACGILLIVRAY, J. R., *Keats: A Bibliography and Reference Guide with an Essay on Keats' Reputation*, Toronto, 1949: the standard bibliography, but very selective, especially in the period after 1821.

MARSH, G. L., and WHITE, N. I., 'Keats and the Periodicals of his Time', *Modern Philology*, xxxii (August 1934), 37–53.

Reviews and publishers

BLUNDEN, E., *Leigh Hunt's 'Examiner' Examined*, 1928: reprints the reviews and notices of Keats in the *Examiner*.

BLUNDEN, E., *Keats's Publisher: a Memoir of John Taylor*, 1936: explores the publishing history of Keats's volumes.

COX, R. G., 'The Great Reviews', *Scrutiny*, vi (June 1937), 1–20, a reappraisal of the principles and practice of the major reviews, only incidentally concerned with Keats.

HAYDEN, J. O., *The Romantic Reviewers*, 1968.

HEWLETT, D., *Adonais: a Life of Keats*, 1937, revised (1949, 1970) as *A Life of John Keats*. Contains a useful account of the early reviews.

WAIN, J., *Contemporary Reviews of Romantic Poetry*, 1953: contains severely abridged reprints of the reviews of Keats in *Blackwood's*, the *Quarterly Review*, and the *Edinburgh Review*, with an interesting introduction and a bibliography.

Keats's readers

BLUNDEN, E. (editor), *Shelley and Keats as They Struck Their Contemporaries*, 1925: various notices and recollections, but mainly about Shelley.

FORD, G. H., *Keats and the Victorians. A Study of His Influence and Rise to Fame 1821–1895*, New Haven, 1944.

FORMAN, M. B., and BLUNDEN, E., 'Tributes and Allusions in Verse to Keats, During the Years 1816–1920', M. B. Forman and Edmund Blunden, *Notes and Queries*, Vol. cxcii No. 12 (14 June), 248–251; No. 15 (26 July), 318–319; No. 17 (23 August), 364–5; No. 20 (4 October), 432–4; No. 22 (1 November), 476–7; No. 24 (29 November 1947), 522–3; Vol. cxciii No. 9 (1 May 1948), 189–191 (by M. B. Perry).

ROLLINS, H. E., *Keats' Reputation in America to 1848*, Cambridge, Mass., 1946.

VILLARD, L., *The Influence of Keats on Tennyson and Rossetti*, St. Étienne, 1914.

SELECT INDEX

I. KEATS'S WORKS

2. TOPICS

3. NAMES AND TITLES

THE CRITICAL HERITAGE SERIES

GENERAL EDITOR: B. C. SOUTHAM

Volumes published and forthcoming

JANE AUSTEN	B. C. Southam
BROWNING	Boyd Litzinger and Donald Smalley
BYRON	Andrew Rutherford
THOMAS CARLYLE	Jules Paul Seigel
CLOUGH	Michael Thorpe
COLERIDGE	J. R. de J. Jackson
DICKENS	Philip Collins
DRYDEN	James and Helen Kinsley
GEORGE ELIOT	David Carroll
HENRY FIELDING	Ronald Paulson and Thomas Lockwood
FORD MADOX FORD	Frank MacShane
THOMAS HARDY	R. G. Cox
HAWTHORNE	J. Donald Crowley
HENRY JAMES	Roger Gard
JOHNSON	James T. Boulton
JAMES JOYCE (in 2 vols)	Robert H. Deming
KEATS	G. M. Matthews
KIPLING	Roger Lancelyn Green
D. H. LAWRENCE	R. P. Draper
MEREDITH	Ioan Williams
MILTON	John T. Shawcross
EZRA POUND	Eric Homberger
ROCHESTER	David Farley-Hills
SCOTT	John O. Hayden
SPENSER	R. M. Cummings
SWIFT	Kathleen Williams
SWINBURNE	Clyde K. Hyder
TENNYSON	John D. Jump
THACKERAY	Geoffrey Tillotson and Donald Hawes
ANTHONY TROLLOPE	Donald Smalley
MARK TWAIN	Frederick Anderson
WALT WHITMAN	Milton Hindus
OSCAR WILDE	Karl Beckson